What Price Utopia?

What Price Utopia?

Essays on Ideological Policing, Feminism, and Academic Affairs

Daphne Patai

ROWMAN & LITTLEFIELD PUBLISHERS, INC.
Lanham • Boulder • New York • Toronto • Plymouth, UK

ROWMAN & LITTLEFIELD PUBLISHERS, INC.

Published in the United States of America
by Rowman & Littlefield Publishers, Inc.
A wholly owned subsidary of The Rowman & Littlefield Publishing Group, Inc.
4501 Forbes Boulevard, Suite 200, Lanham, Maryland 20706
www.rowmanlittlefield.com

Estover Road
Plymouth PL6 7PY
United Kingdom

British Library Cataloguing in Publication Information Available

Library of Congress Cataloging-in-Publication Data

Patai, Daphne, 1943–
    What price utopia? : essays on ideological policing, feminism, and academic
affairs / Daphne Patai.
        p. cm.
    Includes bibliographical references and index.
    ISBN-13: 978-0-7425-2226-8 (cloth : alk. paper)
    ISBN-10: 0-7425-2226-1 (cloth : alk. paper)
    ISBN-13: 978-0-7425-2227-5 (pbk. : alk. paper)
    ISBN-10: 0-7425-2227-X (pbk. : alk. paper)
    1. Feminism and higher education—United States. 2. Feminism—United
States. 3. Feminist theory—United States. 4. Women's studies—United States.
I. Title.
LC197.P37 2008
378.0082—dc22   2007047912

Printed in the United States of America

∞™ The paper used in this publication meets the minimum requirements of
American National Standard for Information Sciences—Permanence of Paper
for Printed Library Materials, ANSI/NISO Z39.48-1992.

This book is dedicated in loving memory to my husband, Gerald Strauss, who died with courage and serenity in March 2006.

DP

Contents

Preface   ix

Introduction: The Fading Face of Humanism   1

Part I: Utopia for Whom?

1   The Struggle for Feminist Purity Threatens the
    Goals of Feminism   15

2   What Price Utopia?   21

3   There Ought to Be a Law   25

4   Justice Comes to U. Mass.   43

5   Third Thoughts about Orwell?   47

6   Letter to a Friend: On Islamic Fundamentalism   61

Part II: Women's Words

7   Who's Calling Whom "Subaltern"?   71

8   Sick and Tired of Scholars' Nouveau Solipsism   79

9   Feminism and the Future   83

10 Domesticating Tranquility   97

11 Will the Real Feminists in Academe Please Stand Up?   105

12 Whose Truth? Iconicity and Accuracy in the
    World of Testimonial Literature   113

Part III: Heterophobia

13 Heterophobia: The Feminist Turn Against Men   133

14 Casting The First Stone   147

15 Politicizing the Personal   153

16 Do They Have to Be Wrong? On Writing about Rape   157

17 Women on Top   167

18 MacKinnon as Bully   181

Part IV: Academic Affairs

19 Why Not a Feminist Overhaul of Higher Education?   207

20 Speak Freely, Professor—Within the Speech Code   211

21 The Great Tattling Scare on Campus   217

22 Academic Affairs   223

23 You Say Social Justice, I Say Political Censorship   251

24 Feminist Pedagogy Reconsidered   253

25 On Writing *Theory's Empire* (with Will H. Corral)   277

Index   289

About the Author   309

Preface

For more than three decades, I have studied, taught, and written about utopian projections and possibilities—not as abstract and unrealizable fantasies but as food for the imagination and as speculative explorations of alternative worlds, inviting us to contemplate the principles and practices that might bring about those better worlds. My many years of engagement with feminism—one of the most utopian of late twentieth-century political movements—were a vital aspect of my interest in such matters. But over the years I, like others before me, came to realize that an enormous gap separates utopian aspirations from their realization and that the means by which we attempt to bridge that gap come to be the defining characteristics of a given historical epoch—and therefore need to be examined with great care.

Thus it was that, after years of doing feminist research (and being considered a feminist in good standing), I was led by my experiences in women's studies, and in the world of academic activism more broadly speaking, to a critical reconsideration of the wisdom and appropriateness of using the academy as a staging ground for political action. This shift is described in the opening essay of part I, dating from 1992. But my growing skepticism about what passed for feminist pedagogy and scholarship preceded that essay by several years. My work on Brazilian literature and culture (my "official" field) had acquainted me with a phrase used by a leading Brazilian filmmaker, Carlos Diegues, in the late 1970s, as military rule in Brazil began to crumble. Tired of the incessant demands of his colleagues that creative work meet leftist expectations, Diegues coined the phrase *patrulhas ideológicas*—ideological patrols—for the practice he found rampant on the left of keeping tabs on one another. First used partly as an inside joke, the phrase caught on, just as "political correctness" did a decade later in the United States. I admired Diegues's stance and his refusal to allow the existence of the military dictatorship to excuse the policing actions of his own side. His phrase stuck in my mind, and I often thought of it as I contemplated the academic practices and attitudes I saw (and still see) unfolding around me, which seemed mired in a delusional politics that was more rhetoric and posturing than substance.

When, about two decades ago, I first considered writing a book critical of feminism in the academy, the title I had in mind for the project was "Ideological Policing in Contemporary Feminism." At that time, however, I couldn't quite reconcile myself to the idea of publicly criticizing feminism. I accepted the standard rejoinder (repeated to this day) that criticisms should not be aired in public because doing so would only aid our "enemies." Fortunately, I got over it—and the result was the book I coauthored with Noretta Koertge, *Professing Feminism* (1994; expanded edition, 2003). Less fortunately, what allowed me to do so was the increasingly overt and shameless propagandizing that characterized women's studies, where the ceaseless pressures of identity politics and competition for most-oppressed status seemed to govern more and more aspects of academic life. Though women's studies originally had to defend its existence on intellectual grounds (as shown by internal memos at many universities documenting the creation and development of women's studies programs), over time few faculty members even bothered to pretend that our mission was above all education, not indoctrination. Instead, political grandstanding became rampant in women's studies and other programs rooted in identity politics, and from there spread to other parts of the university. In his book *The Twilight of Common Dreams*, Todd Gitlin has referred to these developments in the academy with the scathing phrase "marching on the English Department." Precisely.

But the erosion of the intellectual bases on which a university education should rest was no laughing matter. It has created a generation of unquestioning ideologues whose sense of self-righteousness knows no bounds. Eventually, I realized that the rhetoric—ever more extreme—of academic feminists and other self-defined political activists on campus expressed a belief I could neither support nor disregard. And one day it came to me in crystal-clear form: I had not become a university teacher in order to do political agitation on behalf of my particular views, though many of my colleagues proudly embraced this as their raison d'être. In addition, I couldn't help but note that there was plenty of time left in the day for people to act on their political commitments, without, in the first instance, making them the focus of their teaching. This conviction put me increasingly at odds with the fundamental tenets of many colleagues, who were determined to make intellectual values subservient to political goals in the one arena—the academy—in which intellectual independence above all should be sought and protected. Such subservience by now is routine on college campuses and defended explicitly by many academics and even administrators. What this means in practice—in a variety of academic and intellectual arenas—emerges throughout this book.

When I began this journey, I did not foresee that it would bring me to a renewed appreciation of the liberal and humanistic values on which American education has long rested. Where those values had been found to be weak, they needed—and were achieving—better implementation, not wholesale destruction. Yet in recent decades, core Western values of reason, objectivity, commitment to the search for truth (however hard to achieve), and dispassionate appraisal of knowledge claims have increasingly come under attack—predominantly and even routinely from people who consider themselves to be on the left. Will it take the loss of long-established rights to stir from complacency those who can't be bothered to defend those values, who even speak of them disdainfully as ideals their own brand of politics has superseded? Perhaps so, for today those who once upon a time laid claim to tolerance, openness, and universal human rights in order to get their foot in the door are now seeking to shut the door of free speech and academic integrity behind them.

Though my own involvement with these issues developed slowly, it brought me to the position I now hold, which is explored and explained in this volume's introductory essay, "The Fading Face of Humanism." The subsequent essays were written in a number of different contexts. Some began as brief opinion pieces written for *The Chronicle of Higher Education*, others as talks I gave at conferences and universities or as essays published in books or journals; still others formed the kernel of a number of my books written over the past fifteen years. Many of the essays have been edited slightly from their original versions. Two of the pieces have not been published before. Chapter 6, "Letter to a Friend: On Islamic Fundamentalism," indeed began life as a letter written to one of the many friends and acquaintances who, these days, strain to argue that Muslim fundamentalism is no more serious a threat than Christian fundamentalism. Finally, chapter 18 was written specifically for this volume. It deals with Catharine MacKinnon's threat, in 2003, to sue me and my coauthor Noretta Koertge over our characterization, in our book *Professing Feminism*, of her views on heterosexual intercourse. The story of that legal effort to browbeat us into submission is here told for the first time.

Amherst, Massachusetts
August 2007

Introduction: The Fading Face of Humanism

We are born through separation and live and die alone. Defining our selves in relation to a world full of other selves, each inescapably aware of its insularity, is a never-ending task No matter how much we claim to be part of a group, no matter how often we participate in mass demonstrations, parades, boycotts, or petitions, our unique organisms persist, encapsulated by our separate bodies and minds. Whether a million of us are lined up and shot sequentially or vaporized at the same instant, each of us still experiences only our own individual death, even if that death is multiplied one million times. This is the sad and glorious fact of our existence—that we are numerous yet unique, each alone, each an individual self, however profound the links we forge with others through empathy and imagination, made all the more necessary given our fundamental condition. We cannot escape this individuality as long as we still have brains, bodies, and minds.

Why, then, do we see such a resurgence of the phenomenon of identity politics? Why this eagerness to categorize individuals first and foremost as members and defenders of this and that group, embodiments of one or another collective identity, always set in opposition to some other group identity?

Certainly numerous historical examples exist that should have cured us of any enthusiasm for such habits: Whites played identity politics when they deprived blacks of their civil rights, and men when they bestowed on women a second-class status. Identity politics can be just as lethal when the identity in question is not an immediately obvious, visible identity. So we find Hitler defining Jews as a virus on the body politic, even if precisely who counted as a Jew was something to be worked out by law. Turks played identity politics when they slaughtered Armenians. Mao did too when he launched an attack on intellectuals. And so did Pakistanis when they massacred Bengalis. Contemporary Islamists are hardly shy about their view of Jews these days. The examples—and the body count—go on and on. Yes, these injuries were done to groups, but they were experienced by individuals, each one encountering as a self-conscious entity the fate that was imposed on the group.

With such a tradition, it's hard to imagine that, today, identity politics could be considered acceptable. Yet it is the most common game found in our universities and has spread from there both up (to the workplace and the society at large) and down (to primary and secondary education). "Just desserts," some might say, but there has been no increase in the moral and political health of the world. Indeed, identity politics is today considered not only acceptable but desirable and even obligatory. As if the only progress that has been made were that of reversal: The first shall be the last, and the least among you shall have the best claim to. . . .

To what? An interesting question. Minority identity, once a stigma, is now often considered a badge. A graduate student mocks the few professors at an elite school who dare express dissatisfaction with his work: "They can't touch me because I'm Chicano!" he explains to fellow students. An applicant for an academic position begins a letter with a statement of identity: "I am one-eighth Navajo." A committee searching for a "Chinese scholar" in a languages and literatures department has to clarify whether they are naming a racial identity or a subject matter—and opts for both. A local writer tries to get speaking gigs by pitching her work in terms of identity: "I am a Jewish lesbian. . . ." A student says in a college literature class, "As whites, we shouldn't criticize a black writer's metaphors."

Perhaps it's time to lend Samuel Johnson's famous observation new life by varying just one element: "Identity politics is the last refuge of a scoundrel." Given the general public agreement that self-esteem is crucial for healthy development, and in light of our species' sorry history of persecution based on differences among human groups, how can I hold this view? Because (as that sorry history impresses upon us) only a recognition of our common humanity—rooted in an inescapable individuality, to which, however, we can bring our uniquely human qualities of empathy, imagination, and mutual recognition—provides a lasting basis for building a just society. By contrast, identity politics today is always an invitation to extortion or to exculpation, familiar manifestations of what Noretta Koertge and I have called "the oppression sweepstakes."[1]

Where, in this all-too-familiar scene (played out repeatedly in schools and workplaces as well as in the political arena), is the human being? Fading from sight as identity-group membership asserts itself. The individual self extolled by humanism and by the Enlightenment tradition, possessed of qualities and rights by virtue of a common humanity, imbued with an ability to reason—that beleaguered individual these days rushes to hide behind the group, evading responsibility for what he or she is and does. Or, rather, evading responsibility as long as a claim can be made to belong to one or another oppressed identity, however far back in the family history. Alleged oppressors, of course, get a parallel treatment, each group member being held equally responsible for past sins and expected to engage in ceaseless self-abasement. Praise and blame, pride and shame. Categories, not individual selves, appear everywhere that we look.

Thus we now have, in higher education, fields such as "whiteness studies"— which, of course, are indictments of the behavior of whites, something rather different than what we get in celebratory fields such as "black studies" or "women's studies." And because in cultural matters, what begins in the universities trickles down, I wasn't surprised when a friend recently told me that his son, a junior high school student, came home from a class that had dealt with race and announced to his father "I hate whites!" Does it matter whether or not the boy saying this is white?

Accompanying the new grievance studies is the decline of free speech as schools have devised "harassment policies" that treat speech as verbal action and name those identity groups that are to be protected from unpleasantness. Details of which groups are to be protected vary slightly from school to school, but the parameters are the familiar ones. Recently, for example, Harvard University added "gender identity" to its anti-harassment policies, in view of complaints by transgendered students. This move (made also by dozens of other universities) attracted the attention of civil liberties attorney Harvey Silverglate, cofounder of FIRE, the Foundation for Individual Rights in Education. Silverglate sent a letter to Harvard's General Counsel:

> I read in yesterday's *Harvard Crimson* that the university has finally taken the giant step of making Harvard "safe" for trans-gendered students, much as it has in the past made it so "safe" for so many sub-groups of humanity that it is no longer safe even to speak one's mind on the campus lest an errant thought offend a member of a protected group. Ah, progress! This alum suggests that the university get rid of all of its ridiculous "civil rights" policies, which are very harmful in that they keep dividing and sub-dividing humanity into ever smaller and ever-more-contentious sub-groups and then restore "rights" to these groups by punishing the speech of all.

Silverglate suggested that Harvard supplant all its current "civil rights" codes with one simple statement, as follows:

> Harvard being a meritocracy, it is hereby declared a violation of university policy to deprive any student of any benefits offered by the university, or to punish or disadvantage any student, on the basis of any factor or condition that is not rationally related to the student's abilities and demonstrated character.[2]

Although he does not use the term "humanism," Silverglate's criticism obviously rests on precisely such a concept, in opposition to the identity politics that currently prevail. In the absence of a broad commitment to humanism, instead of defending the inalienable rights we possess as human beings, we are explained, and explained away, by our supposed identities, even as these constantly shift in response to newly emerging identity categories and the credit or blame that can be attributed to them.

Two important ingredients in the rise of identity groups—both of them inimical to humanism—are the dogma of social constructionism and the rhetoric of postmodernism. Social constructionism insists on the manmade status of all significant aspects of our being, while postmodernism provides a fashionable lexicon that sounds sophisticated as it undermines any and all claims about humans as a collectivity. Both are used opportunistically, forcing biology (and with it a common humanity) to disappear from view, forcing reason as a characteristic of the species to be undermined, and appealing to have logic and empirical evidence cast aside as mere verbal tropes. A currently popular example is the insistence by many feminists in the academy that heterosexuality is a social construct, not rooted in biology, and that even sexual dimorphism is a social rather than biological fact.[3]

What is gained by such a stance? The need to combat prejudice resting on pseudo-scientific views understandably has led to challenges to those views, but somehow over the years those challenges, having outlived their political usefulness, have had to rest on broader and broader rejections of biology altogether. And this incurs a significant cost. It bores away at our common heritage, at what we all share, and at the same time provides a delusion of control over all aspects of our world—thus seeming to justify any particular group's political demands while giving them grounds for permanent gripes against others. All sorts of inconvenient facts can be challenged (or, better yet, "interrogated") by such strategies. To insist that biology plays a role in human affairs, for example, these days is to leave oneself open to charges of being in thrall to notions of scientific objectivity rendered obsolete by postmodernism and by progressive politics.

If one wishes to criticize some ideas using minimal energy, and those ideas happen to belong to your opponents, what better weapon is there than to insist that all ideas are equally vulnerable and reflect group interests (a self-refuting claim as soon as it is uttered)? Or that truth is nothing more than one person's (or group's) narrative? Of course, such claims are typically applied to others' views, not one's own. Mere assertion replaces argumentation, and, however well-based the ideas of one's opponents, they can be readily dismissed as an expression of their political interests.

So we see feminist legal theorists argue that the First Amendment protects the interests of privileged white men, whose speech is damaging to women. And scholars in the field of critical legal studies now make the same argument about "white" law generally. Though no one can adhere to such claims with any consistency, the rhetoric goes on. To admit that reason, empirical evidence, and knowledge are not just the opinions of a group is dangerous. For one's own favored views might be subjected to as severe a scrutiny as anyone else's. Unless, of course, their moral superiority is considered sufficient grounds for holding them. Today, even lawyers can be found parroting postmodern notions about truth (usually "truth") as they defend a particular client.[4]

It is far more convenient, of course, to dismiss an idea because of the identity of its proponents (the "genetic fallacy") and to suggest that challenges to this procedure are evidence of racism, sexism, heterosexism, or one of the many other isms floating around ready to replace reflection. One result of this habit is an atmosphere in which "who says what" comes to have extraordinary weight as people on all sides abdicate a commitment to reasoned discourse and investigation of facts. "Facts," I ought to write. For they too can these days be dismissed as nothing more than the expression of the notions of an opposing identity group. In the absence of a commitment to the pursuit of knowledge not made subservient to politics, identity politics steps in, hastening to adjudicate among competing knowledge claims. This leads to the blossoming of "standpoint epistemology"—that old feminist favorite—by which who is doing the knowing is of more significance than careful appraisal of the validity of the knowledge itself. Although this is mostly warmed-over Marxism (the ideas of the ruling class become the ruling ideas), Marx never imagined how handy a tool his view would become.[5]

Humanism, by contrast, would impose a far higher standard on us all—the standard of rationality, evidence, and fairness. As John Searle writes, in his defense of rules of investigation (against the mere assertions favored by punsters such as Derrida): "It is not enough to say 'I call that distinction into question.' You actually have to have an argument."[6] And the problem with arguments, alas, is that they need to be judged according to norms of argumentation—norms that do not and should not include who said what, how fervently someone holds to an idea, or whether that idea reinforces his or her own interests. But to grant this is to adhere to a standard by which mere identity would not be a decisive factor—and this would disempower people hoping to pressure others into going along with them on the basis of supposed past guilt and blame.

Contemporary writers attempting to defend humanism argue—as does Frank Furedi, for example—that humanism stresses "subjectivity," which may at first glance appear to undermine identity politics by stressing respect for individuality. But subjectivity too is vulnerable to all the abuses derived from claims about group suffering. Feelings untempered by reason, impervious to investigation, and refusing to be moderated by contrary evidence are a danger all too common at the present time. Sincere feelings are no doubt even worse than just plain feelings, since the latter may be held more lightly and hence be more amenable to alteration in the face of convincing arguments.

Unlike scholars worried about the way ideas about nature can strengthen determinism and undermine human intervention, I, coming from feminist debates and academic orthodoxies, see quite a different danger: that of promoting the determinism of social constructionism, with its corollary that nothing escapes our political designs. Most universities in the United States today are secular institutions, and the recent demand of fundamentalists to impose creationism in the classroom will never take hold as long as academic freedom and a commitment to reason prevail. But many academics today are not in a good position to mount such a defense, for they have themselves engaged in attacks on science and on the very notion of objectivity.

A. C. Grayling, another British scholar, like Furedi embraces humanism because of its challenge to religious ideas. And yet a third British writer, the polymath physician and philosopher Raymond Tallis, warns that the advance of science may lead to the reduction of human beings to mere organisms—all brain and no mind. All these scholars worry that human subjectivity is in danger of being pushed aside as emphasis falls on impersonal forces (the typical criticism of evolutionary psychology, for example).[7] But from what I have observed in the academic world, I would respond that the danger is equally great from those who would stress subjectivity and altogether deny the role of biology in human affairs.

Why one would want to engage in such a denial is a complex question: Some scholars have stressed the assault on our egos that occurs when we are forced to see ourselves as animals, akin to other animals. And so, to counter this assault, we insist on a different kind of determinism: social constructionism, which sees not nature but nurture as the key ingredient in making us what we are. Although more sophisticated scholars today claim to see nature and nurture as inextricably melded, often in practice they make these arguments in order to continue to dethrone the authority of science. Such views today are commonplace in women's studies programs as well as in other politically motivated identity programs in colleges and universities.

The danger, it seems to me, for students coming out of humanities and social science programs these days is not so much that these students are likely to see humans as irretrievably linked to nature (and thus deprived of agency), but the contrary: seeing human beings as having no links to nature, no underlying conditions of existence. For into that vacuum drive those with the most ruthless political will. While this may seem like an absurdity, it makes sense for soi-disant progressives to denounce views that treat human beings as in some sense rooted in nature, for it is obvious that arguments from nature can be used to undermine programs for change or at the very least limit the parameters of that change.

It is therefore easy to demonstrate that skepticism toward received ideas is a good thing and that, for example, a commitment to cultural relativism may lead to efforts to understand cultural differences, to criticisms of one's own culture, to a flexibility in one's mental style, and a drawing away from absolute judgments. But these qualities can, with surprising ease, also turn into defects. When all knowledge claims are seen as situational and interested, what will prevent fundamentalists of various types from imposing their views? All those who have played identity politics now will be in a poor position to challenge on rational grounds views damaging to them—regardless of how ill- or well-founded those views are.

It is a mistake to think that, these days, humanism is challenged only by religious fundamentalists who wish to attack science (though these certainly exist). In the past few decades, some of the core tenets of humanism—a commitment to reason and the evaluation of evidence, to promoting human autonomy and individuality, to the pursuit of knowledge and truth (which depends upon free inquiry and free expression), to the rejection of metaphysical explanations in favor of naturalistic ones—oddly enough, have come under attack from people one would not have expected to do so. Among these are feminists and other political activists of the left. Perhaps contaminated by the excesses of postmodernism, they have failed to defend core values of humanism on which their own views nonetheless depend. Just as religious belief provides a framework within which many disparate phenomena make (or seem to make) sense, so feminist ideology aims at a coherent worldview that provides answers to many questions.

Those answers reside in some of the favored tenets of Western feminism: a belief in the patriarchy whose existence explains much, if not all, that is wrong with the world; a rejection of pre- and non-feminist knowledge as defective due to its roots in patriarchy; a critique of law as the special province of white male elites (again, the patriarchy); a view at times bordering on mystical of the special qualities inhering in women; and, more recently, a complex sounding but in fact simplistic educational approach found in hundreds of women's studies mission statements. This approach is what has come to be known as "the integrated analysis" supposedly offered by feminism, that is, a neat package of good versus bad identities: race, class, sexuality, ethnicity, and other such elements that arise as the discussion proceeds. This "integrated analysis" is by now a staple of women's studies programs. Such a neatly packaged approach to what is a multifaceted and confusing reality must be a great source of comfort to its adherents. But what are they giving up in exchange for the word-magic of their feminist analysis?

Above all, they are giving up adherence to reason, logic, and standards of evidence. All of these can be cavalierly swept aside by the special "epistemology" now attributed to formerly oppressed groups and resting on group perceptions.

Thus, I want to stress not the secular underpinnings of humanism—as important as I recognize these to be—but rather the universal aspiration of humanism. I cannot imagine a humanist saying: "Slavery is bad in the Western world, but who are we to criticize it in Africa or Asia?" And yet views analogous to this are frequently held these days. Western societies, we are told, are still deeply in thrall to the patriarchy, inherently racist and homophobic, and a danger to the world, while say, Muslim societies—well, we mustn't criticize them because to do so is Eurocentric and Orientalist. Or, as an outraged feminist wrote into the country's leading women's studies listserve: It is "racist" to criticize honor killings in the Muslim world. Clearly identity politics relating to race, religion, and culture overrode this feminist's commitment to women. And by doing so, she turned her back on humanism.[8]

If humanism is based on reason, then it stands in stark contradiction to any system of thought that deplores reason, dismisses it as a Western imposition, and opts instead for respecting "local knowledges" regardless of their content. But from my point of view, whatever the motivation, it is no better to dismiss reason as a creature of "patriarchy" than to dismiss it as contravening the will of God or Allah. Identity politics demands special status not by virtue of fundamental human rights (which necessarily must be based on something other than distinct national, racial, sexual, or other identities) but of grievances. And it constricts its ethical claims by refusing to make harsh criticism of certain behaviors no matter who originates them.

But perhaps the greatest irony is that people who play identity politics count on others to respond in a humanistic way—with concern for individual welfare based on a shared humanity. Without such an underlying ethos, identity politics could not function in a democratic and liberal society, for it would be reduced to nothing more than a violent struggle between and among groups. That such physical battles do not constantly break out, for example, in the United States in recent decades is because of the assent given by non-group members to the claims of oppressed or formerly oppressed groups. In other words, human beings can be relied on to see beyond their group interests, to exercise empathy and imagination, and thus to be led to support actions based on general humanistic commitments rather than narrow identity politics.

But such assent is always provisional, depending on particular historical conditions. And a tacit awareness of this short-lived largesse explains why identity groups invariably pursue a the-worse-the-better strategy: It's the only way they can continue to gain a semblance of legitimacy for their claims on others' attention. Still, such claims are always contradictory. Advocates for women, blacks, or gay rights begin by demanding that attention be paid to their claims and grievances and soon enough (as I have seen repeatedly in academic settings) move on to complaints about having to educate others. "Why should we," they say, "be obliged to spend our time educating others? We're tired of doing this; they should take responsibility for educating themselves about our issues. Failure to do so is merely another way of oppressing us and excluding us."

These demands, in turn, contribute to an atmosphere of hypervigilance, in which everyone is on the lookout for what state of consciousness raising and commitment everyone else has achieved. And so we find ourselves back to praise and blame, abject apologies and hidden resentments, distortions and hyperbole, as individuals sort themselves into the specific identity categories that carry the most weight at the moment and play out the oppression sweepstakes as if it leads to a better world rather than merely to more group conflict.

In the end, it seems to me that those of us who have most enjoyed the benefits of the Western humanist tradition must be the ones to speak up, for it is in our own consciousness that we have encountered its strengths: Humanism is universal in scope, founded on respect for the individual, reasoned discourse rather than violence, evidence instead of dogma, and self-correction in place of doctrinaire rigidity. All this is worth defending.

NOTES

A version of this essay first appeared in shortened form in *The Liberal # 6* (September/October 2005), and then in *Debating Humanism*, edited by Dolan Cummings (Exeter, UK: Societas Imprint Academic, 2006), pp. 65–74.

1. See Daphne Patai and Noretta Koertge, *Professing Feminism: Education and Indoctrination in Women's Studies* (Lanham, Md.: Lexington Books, 2003). (Expanded edition of our 1994 book, *Professing Feminism: Cautionary Tales from the Strange World of Women's Studies* [New York: Basic Books, 1994]).

2. Harvey A. Silverglate, e-mail to Robert Iuliano, April 13, 2006; used by permission. Disclosure: I am on the Board of Directors of FIRE, which is a nonpartisan defender of First Amendment rights in higher education. See the website www .thefire.org—on which cases from all over the United States are described.

3. I have amply documented these claims. See, for example, chapters 10 and 11 in the 2003 edition of *Professing Feminism*. For more recent examples, see the women's studies e-mail list discussion on July 2, 2006 ff., archived at www.umbc .edu/wmst/simplesearch.html.

4. See, for example, the comments by David Lane, attorney for Ward Churchill, the University of Colorado professor whose plagiarism and false claims to a Native

American identity won him fame and an academic position. Regarding the recent university committee's recommendation that Churchill be fired, Lane said, "Everybody has their truth. In this 125-page document put together by this committee, they have arrived at their versions of the truth." On *The O'Reilly Factor*, June 30, 2006, available at www.foxnews.com/story/0,2933,196047,00.html.

5. Many of the "ruling ideas" in particular settings seem to challenge Marx's view. To take an obvious example, academic feminists still maintain that universities are patriarchal institutions, yet it is feminist rather than patriarchal ideas that are embodied in speech codes and harassment policies, which are by now the norm in higher education. And consider as well how Lawrence H. Summers was forced first to grovel and then to resign as president of Harvard University for suggesting that innate differences might play a role in explaining why fewer women than men pursue careers in science and mathematics. Though other factors no doubt also contributed to Summers's downfall, it appears that the ruling ideas at Harvard are those of feminists wishing to impede free discussion.

6. John R. Searle, "Literary Theory and Its Discontents," in *Theory's Empire: An Anthology of Dissent*, edited by Daphne Patai and Will H. Corral (New York: Columbia University Press, 2005), 149.

7. I mention these three scholars because it was on a panel with them that I first made the arguments in the present essay. The occasion was the October 2005 Battle of Ideas event in London, sponsored by the Institute of Ideas.

8. In October 2006 a typical exchange took place on the women's studies e-mail list (WMST-L) (which has more than five thousand subscribers) about white male violence. Great anger was displayed at the few women who wrote in suggesting there are worse problems among other groups—for example, violence in Muslim countries, or the rates of murder and rape among blacks versus whites in this country. The discussion provided yet another indication of how identity politics is being pursued at this time. In academe, in particular, people object to generalizations about blacks or about Muslims or any other group that is nonwhite and non-Anglo. They rush to defend these groups because, as presumably oppressed or formerly oppressed groups, they have identities that nowadays exempt them from criticism. But the same reticent people are free with their generalizations about America being a "rape culture," or confidently assert that white male violence is the primary problem we all have to deal with.

These discussions have nothing to do with identity formation in a positive sense; instead they are instances of identity politics: plus or minus signs being associated with a particular identity in advance of any serious investigation. Thus, many feminists on the WMST-L "know" that white male violence is a constant threat to all women, but somehow they manage to think that worrying about Islamist fundamentalism is just a sign of racism and xenophobia. They have no patience, however, for any sort of defense of evangelicals or Christian fundamentalists at home. What seems to drive such a stance, in my view, is a compulsion to view the United States in a negative light, thus demonstrating one's proper "internationalist" credentials.

This is so much the case that one rarely finds on the WMST-L support for or even positive mention of any Muslim dissidents, not even feminist ones. Thus, a couple of years ago, people on the list criticized Ayaan Hirsi Ali, the Somalian-born feminist politician and writer whose life had been threatened by radical Muslims in Holland (who had already murdered her friend and colleague, filmmaker Theo Van Gogh). Why was she unpopular among these feminist academicians? For being a critic of Islam and—more nefarious still, apparently—for having accepted a position at the American Enterprise Institute in Washington, D.C. I posted a message to the list asking how many women's centers in the United States had offered Hirsi Ali a place when they heard she needed to leave Holland. No one responded.

More recently, the journalist Katha Pollitt, a relative newcomer to the WMST-L, has found herself at odds with other list members over basic values. She disagreed, for example, with list members who were irate at the collapsing charges against the Duke University lacrosse players. Taking a line familiar from the Tawana Brawley debacle, the most vocal list members insisted that the actual guilt or innocence of the specific athletes charged was not significant, only the race and privilege of the accuser and accused. Pollitt also felt that criticism, even ridicule, of publicly made statements was to be expected and that feminists should cease being thin-skinned and crying foul whenever they were subjected to it. Instead, she argued, feminists needed to learn to fight fair. But worst of all, Pollitt criticized honor killings in Muslim societies, a position for which she was quickly admonished by other subscribers who argued that these are no different from acts of domestic violence in the United States. When a few (very few, I among them) wrote in that there were indeed significant differences, a message on the list simply declared such a viewpoint "racist." As usual, that effectively closed down the discussion.

In just a short time, then, Pollitt went from being treated as a valued presence on the list to being on the receiving end of the usual feminist name-calling. After one of these exchanges, Pollitt wrote in that the list made her feel she had to watch her every word—a view I have expressed many times. Such observations are usually denied by women's studies people, who both try to shut down opposing views and refuse to admit that they are doing so.

I

UTOPIA FOR WHOM?

1

The Struggle for Feminist Purity Threatens the Goals of Feminism

A number of years ago, I got the idea of putting together a volume with the title "Ideological Policing in Contemporary Feminism." The episodes leading to this intention are by now a bit vague in my mind, but they included stories told to me by feminist colleagues about, for example, being criticized by other feminists for wearing make-up, being heterosexual, or wanting a door put on an office and thus gaining some unsisterly privacy from the feminist staff members in the adjoining office.

In my own courses in women's studies, I have seen similar examples of intolerance among my students: eyes rolled to the ceiling in exaggerated disapproval of a classmate's reference to her boyfriend; heated criticisms by young women in sturdy boots and pants of the "conventional" apparel of other women in the class; an urgent need to ferret out examples of latent unfeminist tendencies; a certain aggressiveness in displaying one's ideological credentials. Of course, there was surely just as much intolerance elsewhere in the university—antagonism, say, to lesbian students—but at least in my own women's studies courses, I did not see that kind of hostility emerge. It was obvious that women's studies classrooms provided a safe arena in which interesting reversals of prevailing reality could take place. It didn't surprise me that, among young students at least, this might lead to excessive zeal.

All this, of course, was before the burning intellectual question of the day revolved around political correctness.

I never wrote that book—and a major reason I didn't was that I couldn't decide how to write a critique of feminism that would not in some way hurt feminism and that would not automatically place me in the enemy camp. Despite opponents' assertions, feminist concerns had not had such resounding success in the world that I wanted to hazard a public critique. And the ease with which the charges of PC have been catching on shows that I was right to be wary of writing something that could be taken to support such charges.

But everything one tolerates that one shouldn't inevitably returns.

So, today, I am once again exercised over ideological policing within feminism. I am still worried about the best way to write about this subject without making my views useful to the opposition—the very real opposition that exists to feminism and to women's studies programs. Indeed, the difficulty in making up my mind about this dilemma is part of what motivates this essay. But its context is provided by the following concatenation of events:

On October 30, 1991, I published a commentary in *The Chronicle of Higher Education* on "surplus visibility" and the stigma of minority status. In November, as responses to the article came in, I discovered that my argument apparently had led some people to assume that I must be black. Thus, I received a letter requesting that I contribute a brief life story to a book on blacks who had "made it" in academe. At the same time, in my own women's studies program at the University of Massachusetts, I found myself called a racist because, as acting director, I had been unable to come up with extra money for an elective course on indigenous women proposed by two Native American graduate students. Simultaneously, I had used the last bit of money in our budget to finance a required course on the intellectual foundations of feminism, to be taught by a teaching assistant who happened to be white.

The same error was being made in both cases: identity politics—the assumption that a person's racial or ethnic identity and views are one and the same. If people found what I said sympathetic or useful to blacks, I must be black. If minority women were frustrated or disappointed by an administrative decision I made, I, in my white skin, must be racist.

The consequences of these two cases of mistaken identity were, however, vastly different. In the first case, I merely wrote to explain that I was white and hence not an appropriate candidate for a book on black academics. In the latter case, I tried to explain that racism had nothing to do with the events in question. This simple denial brought a storm down upon my head. I was told by a young black colleague that when a woman of color says she has experienced racism, she is the authority on that experience and cannot be challenged. More protests on my part—that this made any kind of discussion impossible—only made the situation worse, as memos and charges came from every direction. Every direction but one: Not one of my colleagues who clearly believed that the charges were absurd (and told me so privately) was willing to say so publicly.

I began to realize that we were confronting a new dogma sanctifying a reversal of privilege: Instead of the old privileges accompanying the status of "white," truth, righteousness, and automatic justification in the world of women's studies now reside with "women of color." As if in compensation for past oppression, no one now can challenge or gainsay their version of reality. What can be said for such a turnabout, of course, is that it spreads racial misery around, and this may serve some larger plan of justice, sub specie aeternitatis.

But this is hardly adequate for those who believe earthly justice must be pursued case by case and cannot be won by means that are themselves unjust. In this instance, however, the facts of the case were of no importance: only identity counted. This, let me emphasize, was no misinterpretation on my part, for some memos actually did state that it was absurd for a white, tenured professor to claim she was being unjustly accused. By virtue of having a certain identity (white) and occupying a certain position (tenured), an individual would necessarily be guilty of whatever accusations a woman of color (or an untenured individual) might make against her.

Among my other offenses was an expression of concern at the way some of our students were using the term "Eurocentric" as a new slur: By dismissing an entire culture as racist, they relieved themselves of the burden of learning anything about it. An administrator at my university told me of a student activist who heatedly said: "Do you know who's teaching Spanish in the Spanish Department? Spaniards!" Nor do I take this merely as a joke; I have often wondered how soon it will be before someone suggests that my "identity" (North American) should cause me to cease teaching classes in one of my areas of research, Brazilian women.

The situation that I describe is, alas, hardly unique. What adds to my distress is that it is not usually discussed. For another dogma of women's studies seems to be that our problems must not be aired. There are some good reasons for this reluctance, of course, given the eagerness with which opponents of women's studies might seize on any disagreements. But the consequences are nonetheless dreadful: a kind of siege mentality, in which demands for loyalty thrive and very little fresh air gets in. What does flourish in this confined atmosphere is a flaunting of correct postures, which everyone rushes to embrace, perhaps in an effort to compensate for sexual, racial, or other identities that have been called into question.

Thus, students in my course on utopian fiction by women wrote papers this past semester displaying attitudes that they apparently had learned were the appropriate ones in their women's studies classes. A young white woman too shy to speak in class wrote repeatedly of having to come to terms with her status as a "white oppressor." A young man wrote that a novel we had read taught him that his relationship with Mother Earth was one of rape and pillage; he now saw his rock collection in a new light. I wondered whether he had intended this as parody—which would have been a more original response.

An extremely articulate student wrote eloquently (and without any apparent irony) about how, as a woman, she was silenced and lacked a language. And a white student who criticized a black writer's metaphorical use of the word "slavery" to describe a casual labor exchange was coldly told by another white student that it was not appropriate for a white person to criticize a black writer's metaphors. It is true, of course, that white society has historically oppressed black people, men have damaged the environment, and women indeed have been silenced, but these facts do not mean that everyone today inherits a simple identity or is personally guilty of everything her or his predecessors did.

Identity politics is a dead end. We are neither right nor wrong because of who we are, but only, as the feminist scholar Jenny Bourne wrote in an essay several years ago, because of what we do.

But why should identity politics not serve as another weapon for faculty members in a scarce job market and poor economy? Why not use this, too, in the scramble for the goodies of our profession—jobs, tenure, legitimacy? What is distressing is that this tactic is no feminist departure from the bad old ways of "white patriarchal hegemony," but a replication of those ways, pure and simple. Old forms, new contents. What feminism adds to it, however, is its own tone of moral superiority. Part of what makes conflicts within feminist groups so unpleasant is surely the sense of fraud that accompanies familiar old ambitions dressed up in appropriate ideology.

Feminism has played a major role in questioning canonical knowledge and standards. Should we be surprised then, when, on a women's studies search committee, one group's view that a particular candidate is poorly qualified is met by attacks on the very concepts of "qualifications," "standards," and "knowledge"? Feminism itself has provided the weapons to unleash this sort of self-destructive attack, which can be pursued ad infinitum. While particular criteria have been used in academe in the past to exclude certain groups, you cannot have a university without making judgments about people's expertise. The intellectual and political questions posed by feminism were developed to challenge unfair stereotyping and exclusion of women, not to exempt them from evaluation.

Perhaps "identity" must fill all the gaps left if such attacks prevail, however. For, as I have written previously, feminists today often engage in rhetorical maneuvers that are rapidly acquiring the status of incantations: "as a white working-class heterosexual" or "as a black feminist activist." Such tropes, which do nothing to change the world, carry their own aura of self-righteousness, whether offered as an apology or (as is more often the case) deployed as a badge. In their worst form, they lead to a veritable oppression sweepstakes. And it is not uncommon, in women's studies programs, to hear someone's claim to identity in one category negated by a slur in another—

as when a colleague commented to me disparagingly that a student in our program, although she was Latin American, was "upper class."

Where will it end? My fear is that the search—and demand —for feminist purity (of both attitudes and identity) will eventually result in a massive rejection of the very important things that feminism, broadly speaking, aims to achieve. Today, feminists who have the temerity to criticize negative tendencies within feminism risk being automatically placed in the enemy camp, thus seeming to swell the ranks of opponents of progressive scholarship, a conservative group that may actually represent only a small number of people. Marginalizing friendly critics will not advance the credibility of women's studies or other revisionist scholarship.

Unfortunately, the situation I've described is not the first time that rigid factionalism has splintered leftist politics. The entire history of the left is replete with purges and divisions. What is more banal than that the powerless should turn against one another? Who else can they effectively trounce?

Feminism is hurting itself with identity politics. Those of us who are feminists but who do not accept this simplistic stereotyping and ideological policing must speak up—in defense of feminism.

NOTE

First published in *The Chronicle of Higher Education*, February 5, 1992, B1.

2

What Price Utopia?

When the academic year began in September, I once again felt a familiar dread: that I might inadvertently commit some offense against a student or colleague or, worse, fall victim myself (if only I were smart enough to realize it!) to someone else's aggression. I had long since become convinced that the unregulated life was not worth living, and I was eager to learn what new rules and guidelines the guardians of collegial comfort—wiser and more thoughtful than I—had mandated. Therefore it was with keen anticipation that I awaited the speaker from my university's ombuds office, who was to address my department's first meeting of the year. Sexual harassment policy, I was happy to learn, has ripened over the years. Besides obviously egregious instances (such as giving good grades in return for sex—which by now even a Neanderthal understands as "quid pro quo harassment"), other offenses have been identified, and these have multiplied the categories of protection afforded to vulnerable folks. An example, the ombuds officer explained, is "third party harassment," such as when two officemates tell each other dirty jokes in the presence of a third, who would rather not hear them. A still broader category—the most common type, according to our speaker—is "hostile environment harassment," which includes "leering, explicit jokes, offensive remarks, and posters."

As I listened to this expose of what she called "a whole wide range of behavior," about whose nastiness no reasonable person could quibble, the benefits of a policy designed to insure the highest possible level of comfort for everyone began to be apparent to me. But a distressing thought intervened: Isn't it true that my own most painful experiences in academe have had nothing to do with dirty jokes or leers? What of the hostile slights and dismissive glances to which I have been exposed? The harsh criticisms and demoralizing comments? Are there any of us, I asked myself, who have not spent hours recuperating from such affronts, much to the detriment of our productivity?

Almost as if she were reading my mind, the speaker announced that a new category of harassment has been identified, for which a policy was being developed. I waited breathlessly. It is called "general environmental harassment," she said. Typical instances might include a professor's demeaning remarks and mean-spirited comments, she said, so it would cover speech not specifically related to race or gender.

I pinched myself. Had I heard correctly? I had indeed, for our speaker elaborated. Insensitive criticisms in the classroom fall into this category, she said. So does excessive harshness on the part of supervisors.

At once, incidents from the past came back to me. My cheeks burning, I recalled the indignities to which I had been subjected since my early undergraduate days: professors curtly telling me that they were disappointed in my work, or showing markedly greater enthusiasm for another student's contribution, or suggesting improvements on my grammar and even syntax, made in tones of utter certitude and non-negotiability. But was there not more, much more, in my general environment that had caused me to feel harassed?

Thrilled, I realized that our ombuds office was standing on the threshold of a major breakthrough. Armed with the new concept of general environmental harassment, we could now venture beyond the small-scale struggles to which our preoccupation with sex has confined us. At long last, the nastiness of one-upmanship—a standard feature of academic life—could be seen as the debilitating problem it is for everyone up and down, and even across, the academic hierarchy.

Could we not find a more descriptive label for general environmental harassment, I wondered? Then it came to me: "competitive harassment." That, in a nutshell, is the problem of life in academe. How could anyone ever have thought that consideration and graciousness could be left in that murky area of social relations known as tact and good manners? They cannot be. We must have rules!

Relishing the prospect of universal well-being and happiness—these being the birthright of every American—I realized that had this concept been identified in the past, I would have been spared the scores of slights that now flashed before my eyes, all of which, far more than the occasional sexual taunt, had made my life in academe so disagreeable.

In graduate school, I had had to tolerate a colleague coyly informing me that she was taking her Ph.D. examinations a semester later than I was, because "the department expects great things" of her. Surely this was a case of competitive harassment. What about the faculty member who had sat filing her nails while I gave a lecture during my on-campus job interview? Such a devastating attack on my self-confidence should not have gone unpunished.

Then I remembered the colleagues who, on first seeing me after a long summer break, hardly had bothered to say hello before informing me that they were just back from Bellagio, had attended a major international conference in Budapest, or were rushing off to a meeting in Buenos Aires. Senior colleagues, oblivious to the harm they were doing me, feigned near exhaustion as they complained of the strain of correcting the proofs of their latest book. I thought of all the people who for decades had monopolized my attention, talking about their work without ever asking about mine, never pausing to wonder whether the role of Big Ear suited me. They would now find their behavior subject to official censure.

I also recalled female colleagues' looking me over, as if to suggest that my appearance left something, perhaps a great deal, to be desired. Of course, it was not only women who injured me in this way. Once, in response to my query about his wife's health, a male colleague answered: "She's fine, she looks great. She's maintained the same weight, 105 pounds, since we were married twenty years ago!" This pointed comment depressed me for half a day, making me realize how indirect might be the slings and arrows cast in the competitive, anything-goes world of academic "collegiality," and how vigilant I needed to be to catch every slight.

All these abuses, all these barbs, could now be actionable as harassment. Never again need be heard a discouraging word. Goodbye negative nuance, hidden hostility. What a blissful prospect! True, we might all have to watch our every word, gesture, and even thought. But who would not be willing to pay this price in exchange for an untroubled work environment?

My mind wandered further, back to some nineteenth-century utopian stories that I had read years earlier. In particular, two tales by British writers lighted the path to the delightful social structure that now seemed within reach.

In 1873, Bertha Thomas published a story about a futuristic society committed to rectifying the "Iniquitous Original Division of Personal Stock." The remedy included such measures as keeping athletes of above-average strength or agility from participating in sports; reducing the over–healthy to the standard set by the weak; making beautiful people wear ugly clothes; granting titles to people with physical defects (the greater the defect, the grander the title); actively preventing good-looking girls from "appropriating the affections of the whole youth of the Commune"; and carefully neglecting the education of the handsome and the witty.

In 1891, Jerome K. Jerome described a similar society, in which absolute harmony and equality would be achieved by allowing no one to engage in "wrong" or "silly" behavior. All would now be equal, and, to avoid demoralization, all must look equal: Men and women would have the same hair color and wear the same clothes. Improving on Thomas's vision, Jerome's "new utopia" was a country in which the tallest would have an arm or a leg lopped off, and surgery would be performed to reduce brains to average capacity. Beauty, of course, would be abolished, because of its long and ignoble history of interfering with full equality.

So far ahead of their time were these two writers that no one had given their ideas serious consideration, which, listening to our speaker, I now saw they merited. More recently, Kurt Vonnegut wrote a similar story, in which the United States "Handicapper General" and her team of agents mete out disabilities and impediments, guaranteeing equality by doing away with all competitive advantage and its attendant demoralization for the not so advantaged.

With their finely tuned moral sense and their visionary politics, all of these writers understood perfectly that regulating mental and physical attributes, as well as behavior, is an inevitable and necessary step in the larger struggle against inequality and discomfort. Obviously, in our own day, serious commitment to a benign and equitable social order, of which the university must surely serve as exemplar, requires nothing less than the drastic remedies they proposed. How else can we eliminate the power differentials and comfort imbalances that plague us?

As I came out of my reverie, the speaker from the ombuds office was wrapping up her presentation by urging us all to send for our copies of the complete harassment guidelines. Then she offered to answer any questions. I looked around. My colleagues sat silently, perhaps as caught up as I was in the glorious vision of a permanently unharassed future, within our grasp at last.

NOTE

First published in *The Chronicle of Higher Education*, October 27, 1995, B7.

3

There Ought to Be a Law

Ah love! could you and I with Fate conspire
To grasp this sorry Scheme of Things entire,
Would not we shatter it to bits—and then
Re-mould it nearer to the Heart's Desire!

> Edward Fitzgerald, trans., *The Rubaiyat of Omar Khayyam*,
> 2nd version, 1868.

Nothing is more likely to be abused than the power of officials who think
they are doing the right thing.

> Anthony Lewis, *The Firing Line*, PBS, August 25, 1995.

I have called this talk "There Ought to Be a Law," because I remember this
as a frequently heard phrase from years ago, giving voice to the wish that
one's desire should become the law of the land, allowing or prohibiting
precisely those things that one wished to see or wished not to see in the
world. But it is one thing to express such a desire casually and quite another
to try to implement it. And it is the latter that is going on at the moment,
in ways that should alarm all of us.

I have been studying utopian and anti-utopian literature for over twenty
years and teaching it for more than fifteen. In the past, I assumed that anti-
utopian fiction—texts that, like *Brave New World*, were intended to warn us
about the dangers of attempting to construct perfect futures—were expressions of their authors' conservative politics, and this supposition affected
my entire perspective on the warnings they were sounding. Thus when, in
the early 1980s, I read several nineteenth-century antisocialist satires depicting societies in which the demand for equality has run wild, I took them

to be nothing more than mean-spirited attacks on the idea of equality and gave them little further thought.

But as the years went by I discovered that life was beginning to imitate art. Colleagues I had considered on my side politically were now supporting speech codes, demanding conformity, embracing vastly exaggerated definitions of "harassment," and arguing for administrative control of personal relationships between professors and students. Out of the depths of my memory, those long-forgotten anti-utopian stories came rushing back to my mind. And now I find them hovering over me as I watch universities struggling with (it often looks more like capitulating to) demands for intervention in all areas of campus life—the very thing that, back in the sixties, students had been trying to persuade university administrations to stop doing.

In such a state of mind, I attended my department's first meeting in early September. What I heard there struck me as more worthy of satire than of denunciation, and so I went home and wrote a short piece, which was later published in *The Chronicle of Higher Education* under the title "What Price Utopia?" (see preceding chapter).

But even before my essay appeared in print, reality overtook satire as the chancellor's office at my university circulated a proposal for a new harassment policy. Negotiated over an eighteen-month period by the administration and the Graduate Employee Organization, without consultation with either lawyers or faculty, the proposed policy itself seemed perilously close to satire. Aiming to prohibit harassment, the policy defines it as:

> Verbal or physical conduct that a reasonable person, with the same characteristics as the targeted individual or group of individuals, would find discriminatorily alters the conditions under which the targeted individual or group of individuals participate(s) in the activities of the university, on the basis of race, color, national or ethnic origin, gender, sexual orientation, age, religion, marital status, veteran status, or disability.[3]

The Graduate Employee Organization, dissatisfied with the list of protected categories, wished to expand it further, so as to include "citizenship, culture, HIV status, language, parental status, political affiliation or belief, and pregnancy status." The administration's response to this list was to declare, in the proposed policy, that it "believes such categories are already protected under those previously listed."

Undeterred both by judicial decisions that had struck down comparable policies at public and private universities (such as Wisconsin, Michigan, and Stanford) and by negative publicity in the press, Chancellor David K. Scott made it perfectly clear when four critics of the policy—I among them—met with him, that his aspiration was for the University of Massachusetts to succeed where other schools had failed, namely in carving out an exception to the First Amendment by crafting a rule that would stand with existing restrictions on free speech such as libel and "fighting words." As the chancellor also indicated, the policy would require a "double standard" of application: Historically oppressed groups would be protected from offensive speech, while historically powerful groups would not be.[4]

Of course, the University of Massachusetts is not alone in attempting to make language do the work of social engineering. In 1995, the women's studies e-mail list (WMST-L) featured a message posted by a feminist philosophy professor who asserted that she could no longer in good conscience use the word *intellectual*; to do so, she wrote, would imply that some women are better than others. And, quite predictably, later in the year, when a professor shared with the list her interest in starting a women's studies honor society, her idea aroused strong opposition from some respondents, all of them alarmed at the "hierarchical" values present in any designation of honors for some students and not for others.

I have also watched in dismay as professors and students who consider themselves progressive increasingly advocate censorship of language and the monitoring of behavior and attitudes and call for rules and regulations to govern virtually every aspect of academic life. To my ears, their demands sound ominously like a foreshadowing of all-too-familiar dystopian visions, which, alas, I can no longer dismiss as old-fashioned conservative ranting. To be sure, many past dystopian fantasies are plainly antisocialist. But this fact no longer tells me all I need to know about them. Instead, I now view them as dire warnings or—worse—as crazy analogues to equally zany but very real events that are indeed going on before my eyes.

By now, even Hollywood has noticed the trend and gotten in on the act. The 1993 film *Demolition Man*, one of my students pointed out to me after we read *Brave New World* in class, was clearly based on Huxley's novel. Most of the film is set in the year 2032, precisely one hundred years after Huxley's book was published, and its heroine is named Lenina Huxley. But, as befitting a film made sixty years after *Brave New World*, it extends Huxley's satire of a perfectly managed future to the point where total and constant monitoring of individuals touches every aspect of life. Nothing so crude as the telescreens in Orwell's *Nineteen Eighty-Four* appears in the film. Rather, organically bioengineered microchips are sewn into everyone's skin, and these devices "code" people so that they can be tracked wherever they are. Police have become almost entirely unnecessary because "things don't happen any more," as the warden of a cryogenic prison says with satisfaction. Everyone can go to "compu-chat" machines on the street for instant therapy and encouragement. Using offensive language causes the omnipresent computers automatically to fine the individual one or more credits and announce it publicly in a monotonous computer voice.

In this future California, no one has died from unnatural causes in sixteen years, and the police don't have the vaguest notion of how to deal with a Code 187—a "Murder Death Kill," as they call it—when, following the demands of the plot, a murder occurs for the first time in more than twenty years. Attempting to deal with a killer from our time who escapes from his fast-frozen imprisonment, the computer provides the police with such pieces of advice as: "With a firm tone of voice, demand maniac to lie down, with hands behind back." This is, of course, ineffective, which is where Sylvester Stallone comes in. Using a defamiliarization technique typical of utopian novels, in which a person from our own time reacts with amazement to the newly encountered future, the film makes our hero inadvertently contravene all the norms of the perfect society.

In *Brave New World*, Aldous Huxley had written: "There isn't any need for a civilized man to bear anything that's seriously unpleasant."[5] *Demolition Man* extends that principle as we learn that whatever is not good for people is considered bad, and, for this reason, has been made illegal; the list includes alcohol, caffeine, contact sports, meat, offensive language, chocolate, anything spicy, gasoline, un-educational toys, abortion—but also pregnancy if you don't have a license. Not only is reproduction state-controlled and managed hygienically in laboratories, but, as a result of AIDS and other epidemics, body contact has been proscribed. Sexual pleasure is achieved through direct brain stimulation via matching headsets. At one point, Lenina exclaims with disgust at Stallone's idea of sex: "Don't you know what the exchange of bodily fluids leads to?!" He replies, "Yeah, I do: kids, smoking, a desire to raid the fridge." So successfully does the film convey the sense of life in a completely regulated society—at least to a utopias junkie like me—that, on hearing this line, I actually felt a touch of nostalgia.

The beauty of literary or cinematic utopias, in contrast to the political treatise or essay, is precisely this: If successful, they set in motion before the mind's eye how life might actually be lived in another kind of society. Moreover, they make us see our own society in a different light. So, when I first came across some very nasty novels depicting women's rule—books such as Edmund Cooper's novel *Who Needs Men?* (1972),[6] which was renamed *Gender Genocide* when it was published in the United States—I took them for misogynistic works, inspired by contempt for women and fear of their domination in the future. To be sure, some of them do deserve such a reading. But I was puzzled that women, too, had written such books. For example, a writer named Pamela Kettle published, in 1969, a novel called *The Day of the Women*, which describes how a female political party comes to power in England and develops into an anti-male tyrannical oligarchy, complete with spying, selective breeding, and killing of male babies.[7]

Over time, of course, my views underwent modification. What I initially took as exaggeration—hyperbolic depictions of venomous women in power who hate men, hunt them down, and are contemptuous of heterosexuals—all came to have an oddly familiar ring. I was shocked to eventually realize

I had been encountering ideas for some years, written not by such men fearfully imagining women in authority, but by women themselves, especially by women calling themselves radical feminists.

By now I have become so dismayed with the unrelenting male-bashing common in feminism (though many feminists disingenuously insist this image is a media invention to discredit feminism, merely another example of "backlash") that I am writing a book on the subject called *Heterophobia* [published in 1998]. It is true that radical feminists (whom I prefer to call "feminist extremists," since I do not believe they go to the root of anything) are small in number. However, through such spokeswomen as Catharine MacKinnon, Andrea Dworkin, and Mary Daly, they are highly visible and audible, as well as widely read, certainly in women's studies courses. Their influence has been inordinate and should not readily be dismissed merely because it represents an extremist position.

Sensitized as I now am to this subject, it seems to me that much of the zealotry we are seeing in the university today on the issue of sexual harassment should be construed as an attack, quite specifically, not only on men, but also on heterosexuality itself. It is of course true that women too are occasionally caught in the web spun by zealots. But this does not alter the fact that men are the main target and that the suppression of heterosexual interest seems to be the chief agenda in the sanitized world demanded by many feminists. What is perhaps more surprising is that many heterosexual women who identify themselves as feminists have sat quietly by as their own preferences and ways of life have become the subject of grotesque and demeaning caricatures set forth in the name of feminism.

Nowadays I can observe the new heterophobia almost on a daily basis as I read of one or another effort meant to make the world a comfortable place for women, regardless of the cost at which such comfort shall be obtained. A recent example—which I have absolutely no doubt would win the support of many of my feminist sisters—was the recommendation that construction crews in Minneapolis should cease engaging in "visual harassment" of women passing their construction sites.[8] Perhaps all men should be told that they must keep their eyes on the ground, as black men in the South once did to avoid being accused of giving offense to white women. I do not think we should assuage our outrage over such infringements of people's rights with the assurance that the most egregious cases will be dismissed by the courts.[9] Before that happens, they will certainly have contributed to a climate in which men have become—as one lesbian friend of mine noted in disgust—"the universal scapegoat."

To take another example, consider a much-publicized recent incident at the University of British Columbia. At that institution a report costing a quarter of a million dollars was produced that indicted the Department of Political Science for sexism and racism. It includes an appendix of several pages listing allegations of misconduct so astonishingly trivial that it's hard to believe any of it was meant seriously.[10] Professors are charged with making criticisms of their students' work, or bestowing more praise on one student than on another; of being aloof, or not being aloof enough; of failing to engage students in discussion of new ideas; of being dismissive of students' Marxist perspectives. They were also accused of making the kind of personal comments that one might well argue professors should not make. But these charges too turned out to be so trivial, so far from any dereliction that a society that had not lost its balance would ever consider actionable, that the only conclusion a reasonable person can draw from them is that professors must watch their every word and every gesture, that silence is no less dangerous than speaking, that attention and lack of attention are equally suspect, and that students are weak and pitiful children, the fragility of whose egos must at all times be foremost in professors' minds.

Since this incident occurred in Canada, shall we in the United States pay no attention to it? I don't think so, for we all know of comparable home-grown cases. Who has not heard of professors being driven from jobs on the basis of flimsy and unsubstantiated allegations? Most of us know professors who are afraid to appear too friendly with their students because charges of sexual harassment are now given more or less automatic credence, often in astonishing disregard of due process. If, in the bad old days, women's accusations against men were routinely met with skepticism, today a general reversal has occurred. This reversal of course makes it far more likely, as Noretta Koertge and I point out in our book *Professing Feminism: Cautionary Tales from the Strange World of Women's Studies*,[11] that accusations with little or no foundation will indeed be directed against professors, whether out of pique, envy, irritation, or genuine displeasure with something they have said or done. I have also heard of many cases in which feminist faculty have automatically supported a female student's allegations against a male professor, prior to any investigation of the facts or, worse yet, even in disregard of evidence of the professor's innocence. And why should this surprise us? In the brave new world in which heterophobia reigns, men are all equally suspect.

Is it therefore out of panic that regulations are now called for even by professors and not merely by zealous young students? Has life in academe become so hazardous that for their own safety, professors want explicit rules governing their every word and gesture? Have they, and the students demanding regulatory action, given any serious thought to precisely what life would be like under such a regime?

Several things strike me about the present call for intervention on the part of people who used to be considered liberals, even civil libertarians. First, when comparing today's activists with some of their distinguished socialist forerunners, I find it hard to ignore their utter lack of concern for genuine economic and political reforms. Today, the changes we talk about—in language and pictures used in the classroom, in permissible relations between professors and students, between men and women in the workplace—relate primarily to the realm of culture and, one might well say, to a particularly narrow segment of culture at that.

It's above all *manners* that wishful thinkers aim to reform. The fundamental inequality of incomes is seldom mentioned. I am not saying that I would be more optimistic about the outcome of reformist impulses rooted in economic egalitarianism. But if they were rooted there, I might credit these impulses with being something more than opportunist chiming in with this year's cultural pieties. There is also a puzzling aspect to the exaggerated attention being devoted to the leveling of "power differentials" without even the pretense of a concern with economic equality. Perhaps it is precisely the lack of material substance that gives such spurious egalitarian moves their hysterical and intolerant edge. I may not really want to share my computer, but I will certainly clean up my language (and thereby establish my politically correct credentials) so no one need be offended. Especially in higher education, the political rhetoric seems to be only that: rhetoric. It has no real political impact.

To take an obvious example: All the feminist and "Marxist" polemic about doing away with hierarchy and authority in the classroom—what I call the "leveling" impulse in feminism—has never, to my knowledge, resulted in proposals for salary sharing. At one university, I was told about the existence of a teaching collective involving graduate students, undergraduates, staff, and faculty—all in women's studies. But my interview with a staff member who had participated in this collective brought out the fact that no discussion of salary sharing had ever taken place. Obviously, she said, no faculty member would have been willing to be involved if such a demand were voiced.

It is one thing to argue that women and blacks rightly resent language that is demeaning to them and that may even injure them (though the tensions between free speech and prescribed niceness persist). But it's quite another to argue that the injuries suffered by the poor reside in the word *poor* when it is used in a phrase such as "poor workmanship" or "you poor thing!"—or that it is "ableist" to use the phrase "ill-fated." These particular examples come from a pamphlet published at my university, entitled "Overcoming Oppression within Groups," which warned against ableism, anti-Semitism, racism, classism, sexism, and heterosexism.[12] Reducing real social problems to the level of language and attitudes, this publication epitomizes the "activism" that has characterized the academy since about the mid-1980s. It also illustrates the foolish belief that the solution to these problems lies in purifying our every word and thought. Never mentioned in such proposals are the costs inevitably incurred in the pursuit of these policies: the ensuing vigilante atmosphere, the "gotcha" alertness as disgruntled individuals try to catch one another in an offense, the chilling of free and easy interactions.

Nor have years of concern with language led to deeper understanding of problems of discrimination. A paper written for a women's studies class at my university recently was still cast as moral exhortation, ending with the plea that we all be allowed to be "who we are" without bearing any stigma. The writer's exemplary categories of "who we are" included working class, feminist, and lesbian—as if these were all on a par and "identity" were the real glue in maintaining social cohesion.

Lest skeptics think I am inventing anecdotes for one of those compendia of politically correct jokes, let me state that I personally was present at a women's studies event several years ago at which a lesbian feminist speaker used the metaphor of vision—as in "I now see"—to refer to her increasing understanding of a problem. A student in the audience interrupted her to point out that she'd used an ableist metaphor. The speaker at once acknowledged this error and apologized for it.

It is my belief that many of the individuals displaying this kind of zeal today do so out of a lack of experience with totalitarian systems. They have become so accustomed to individual liberties that these rights have grown tedious to them. Only young women who have grown up with relative sexual freedom (in a world in which every second word in many films is an obscenity that is then graphically simulated on the screen) would be so ready to believe that "all intercourse is rape" and that men, in general, are the enemy. If they had been brought up by repressive parents, who kept them away from their boyfriends or washed their mouths out with soap, they would, I have no doubt, today be hippies reenacting the Berkeley free speech movement.

I taught English in Brazil in 1968–1969, during the worst phase of the military dictatorship. The classroom in which I was teaching was bugged. No discussion of politics could take place. In the Brazilian public school system at that time, teachers feared denunciation by their students—and this did in fact occur, resulting in arrests. Academic freedom came under attack as whole departments (for example, sociology at the prestigious University of São Paulo) were shut down and their faculty driven into exile. Indeed, one of the exiles was Fernando Henrique Cardoso, a well-known leftist sociologist who became president of Brazil in 1995 (demonstrating, of course, that things can and do change for the better, and one should not despair). I remember the atmosphere in Brazil even outside the classroom: One day I said apologetically to a Brazilian acquaintance, "I'm sorry, my Portuguese isn't good enough, I can't talk about politics." My acquaintance smiled and said sadly, "Neither can we."

It dismays me, then, to meet students today who take their right to utter any opinion and say any word so much for granted that they actually support censoring speech—always assuming, of course, that this will be *other* people's speech, for supporters of speech codes seem invariably to see themselves as sensitive individuals, in no need of correction. Again, I believe only lack of any actual experience with censorship can explain their facile embrace of the censor's mentality and their naïve belief that censorship can lead to a better world.

But all this has happened before. To my mind it is one of the most astonishing things about the present climate that today's zealots live in utter disregard of cautionary examples from the history of our own twentieth century of what happens when speech and thought are monitored in the name of cultural politics. There is no shortage of books describing Mao's Cultural Revolution (to take just one notorious example of special pertinence to the realm of education).[13] I have just finished reading an autobiography by Anchee Min, a Chinese woman who came to America in 1984, having been a member of the Little Red Guards when she was fifteen. After a local party leader convinced her that she was being "mentally poisoned" by a beloved and dedicated teacher (whose father was a Chinese American still living in America), Anchee Min witnessed this teacher being humiliated in front of two thousand people but refusing to confess her guilt. Anchee Min recounts how she, identified as a "victim" of this teacher, stood up and read a speech she had prepared, accusing her teacher of attempting to turn her students into running dogs of imperialism. How had the teacher done this? By giving her students readings from Hans Christian Andersen, stories about princes and princesses and other enemies of the people. The teacher tried to talk to her pupil before the crowd, urging her to tell the truth, but Anchee Min stuck to her denunciation. The episode ends thus: "I was never forgiven. Even after twenty-some years. After the Revolution was over. It was after my begging for forgiveness, I heard the familiar hoarse voice say, I am very sorry, I don't remember you. I don't think I ever had you as my student."[14]

Anchee Min's book also describes the endless sloganeering and pious appeals to the thought of Chairman Mao. Perhaps most interesting to me about this memoir is the sense it conveys (postmodernism notwithstanding) that certain aspirations are indeed universal: the right to a private life, to personal happiness, to an intimate sphere not invaded by the state and organized according to political demands; the desire for love; the discovery of an inner self at odds with the "official" society; the small, everyday transgressions sprouting under the posture of outward conformity.

Anchee Min also writes of the conflict between desire and politics—the former controlled and outlawed in the name of the latter but springing to life anyway, despite enormous dangers. She describes a collective farm on which she lived for a time, where all sexual relations were suppressed. When one young woman is found making love in the fields, she is "saved" by the farm commander who urges her to claim that she was raped. She complies. The young man involved is executed, and the woman goes mad. The book is filled with telling examples and illustrations of what happens when a culture is in thrall to politics, when those much-maligned "liberal" values that teach respect for the rights of the individual are treated with disdain.

And this brings us back to the ingenious solution offered in *Brave New World*, summed up by Huxley's Director of Hatcheries, who says: "That is the secret of happiness and virtue—liking what you've *got* to do."[15] Huxley's fictional world, with its ectogenesis, neo-Pavlovian conditioning, and hypnopaedia, makes this shift possible. In fact, it makes any other attitude impossible.

Since unpleasant emotions frequently occur in connection with personal relations and the arena of sexuality, most fictional utopias (especially the ones written as dystopian satires) regulate personal life in order to achieve the maximum social harmony. In Zamiatin's *We*, the brilliant Russian novel that served as a model for Huxley and most subsequent twentieth-century dystopias, people have numbers, not names, and virtually all aspects of life have been brought under state control.[16] Sexual conflicts, competitiveness, and personal attachments have all been done away with by the great, historic "Lex Sexualis," which states: "A Number may obtain a license to use any other Number as a sexual product."[17] One need merely sign up for such use during the personal hours, the only hours when curtains can be lowered on the glass walls of the huge dormitories in which everyone dwells. Zamiatin's narrator initially looks forward to the time when even these personal hours will be abolished, as all life comes under the control of the perfectly regulated world state.

Huxley uses a similar approach. In his novel promiscuity is encouraged, and orgies are a routine part of orchestrated pseudo-religious rites. Orwell, whose future England makes no pretense to be organized for the happiness of its citizens, opts for suppressing sex altogether, though not very successfully, as it turns out. What is important to recognize is that it matters little whether sex is prohibited or promiscuity encouraged. Either way, the management of sexuality is a key element in these dystopias, which through such manipulation attempt to erase the private sphere (either by turning it into a commodity, as does Huxley, or by prohibiting it altogether, as does Orwell) and refocus their citizens' attentions on the collectivity and its leader.

We, living in the United States today, are of course relative beginners in the use of such controls, which is perhaps a saving grace. One could even argue that stretching the definition of sexual harassment, so that everyone has to watch every word and gesture, and prohibiting personal relations between those in "asymmetrical" positions relative to one another (such as professors

and students, and employers and employees) will actually increase the sexualization of campus and workplace. It is, in fact, hard to see how any learning can go on in an academy constantly on the lookout for sexual or other
offensive innuendo. And, as in the old jokes about censors spending their
days looking at pornography, opponents of professor-student relationships
do seem to have an intense and perhaps bizarre preoccupation with sex. It
cannot genuinely be "power differentials" that concern them, since these are
manifest in many forms quite unrelated to sex, and most of these forms are
not objects of concern to the social engineers proliferating in academic offices. Is anyone (yet?) claiming that it should be prohibited, say, for a professor to give time and attention to a particularly promising student? That it
should be illegal to coauthor a paper with a talented student, as happens in
many fields, and not with all students in the cohort? And yet any such prefer-
ment not only subjects the student to the professor, but also increases the
risks of a painful rejection later. Clearly, the work of regulating academic life
is far from over.

Still it does appear to be the fear of sexual involvement specifically that
elicits concern over the power differentials supposedly making these relationships illegitimate. No one seems willing to let common sense guide
professors in their contact with students. But if the would-be regulators of
all such associations have their way, I foresee a paradoxical resurgence of romance. For, in a post-banning society, a professor will be genuinely heroic
if he (or, less often, she) acts on an attraction to a student or responds to a
student's initiative—a little-recognized occurrence that is, I believe, far more
common than actual sexual harassment initiated by professors. What student would remain unmoved by a professor willing to take such risks?

Instead of protecting the concept and practice of academic freedom,
which to my mind includes not only freedom of speech but also freedom
of association between consenting adults, many academics today appear to
view this freedom with alarm. They seem to see it as "academic license"—
license, presumably, to exploit and abuse and hence in need of curtailment.
Once again, since professors are perfectly able to decide, individually, *not* to
engage in personal relationships with students, it appears that the censors'
concern is above all with regulating the behavior of *others*, not of themselves. But supporting the regulation of private and voluntary relationships
presupposes a massive distortion on the banners' part of the supposed
"power" of professors, as well as of the "powerlessness" of students who are,
by this attribution, infantilized or suspected of a dependency that would
make them into replicas of psychiatric patients in need of both therapy and
protection from unscrupulous therapists.

Where does it all come from, this lack of confidence in ourselves and our
fellows and this desire to *force* adults to "do the right thing?" Perhaps here
too we have literary and historical precedents to guide us.

Many of the famous dystopias written in the twentieth century feature what can be called a "Grand Inquisitor" scene—in which the leader of the fictional society explains to the rebellious protagonist that people are happier now that they have been relieved of the burden of freedom and have been told what to do, what to think, how to behave, and, of course, what to read. What they are allowed to read, in many cases, turns out to be nothing, for these societies all strive for conformity, and books and ideas tend to make people dissatisfied with their condition.

This danger of reading is a major theme in Ray Bradbury's 1953 novel *Fahrenheit 451* (the temperature at which books burn). Books lead to reflection and even conflict: This is what Montag, the novel's protagonist, hears from Faber, a former English professor thrown out of work when the last liberal arts college closed its doors decades earlier due to lack of students and patronage. Books have to be destroyed because they convey the "texture" of life, Faber says. They "show the pores in the face of life. The comfortable people want only wax moon faces, poreless, hairless, expressionless."[18] But by now, Faber explains, the firemen are rarely necessary: "So few want to be rebels any more."[19]

Writing more than forty years ago, Bradbury creates a Grand Inquisitor scene that springs to life because it sounds uncannily familiar to readers today. Captain Beatty, the fire chief, explains to Montag:

> Bigger the population, the more minorities. Don't step on the toes of the dog lovers, the cat lovers, doctors, lawyers, merchants, chiefs, Mormons, Baptists, Unitarians, second-generation Chinese, Swedes, Italians, Germans, Texans, Brooklynites, Irishmen, people from Oregon or Mexico. . . . It didn't come from the Government down. There was no dictum, no declaration, no censorship to start with, no! Technology, mass exploitation, and minority pressure carried the trick, thank God. Today, thanks to them, you can stay happy all the time, . . .
>
> You must understand that our civilization is so vast that we can't have our minorities upset and stirred. Ask yourself, What do we want in this country, above all? People want to be happy, isn't that right? Haven't you heard it all your life? . . .
>
> Colored people don't like *Little Black Sambo*. Burn it. White people don't feel good about *Uncle Tom's Cabin*. Burn it. . . .
>
> If you don't want a man unhappy politically, don't give him two sides to a question to worry him; give him one. Better yet, give him none. . . .
>
> We [the firemen] stand against the small tide of those who want to make everyone unhappy with conflicting theory and thought. We have our fingers in the dike.[20]

Bradbury's Grand Inquisitor scene, like others in dystopian fiction from Zamiatin on, is based on Dostoyevsky's prototype in *The Brothers Karamazov*, in which Ivan Karamazov relates a parable of Christ's return to sixteenth-century Seville, where he is imprisoned by the Grand Inquisitor. In a long monologue, the Grand Inquisitor explains to Christ why he will be burned as a heretic. It has taken the Roman Catholic Church centuries to vanquish the freedom that Christ bequeathed to men. Freedom of conscience is a burden of which people beg to be relieved, the Grand Inquisitor says. The Church has accepted this burden on their behalf, giving them instead what they crave: miracle, mystery, and authority.[21]

We, today, are witnessing a latter-day version of the Grand Inquisitor's vision as ordinary people—and in the academy, these are, of course, intellectuals—demand social salvation by turning power and control over to some force beyond themselves. Hence the call for rules and regulations, or the quasi-legal codes instituted on college campuses—anything to save us from the messiness and possible unpleasantness of everyday human interactions; from disappointment and bitterness in love; from unsuccessful sexual encounters; from work environments filled with the tensions of human beings still capable of having private selves, still free to make unkind comments on our foibles or criticisms of our efforts.

Do our students really want the safety and security promised by a Grand Inquisitor? Some certainly do—or, in the absence of such a sense of security, imagine that they do. In my women's studies course on women's utopian fiction, for example, I was surprised to discover that many of the young women in my class found the safety of women as depicted in Margaret Atwood's *The Handmaid's Tale* a very appealing prospect. True, the novel, which envisions a takeover by religious fundamentalists, also institutionalizes rape (for the sake of reproduction) in a carefully orchestrated monthly performance that involves the handmaid (who is fertile), the commander (her master), and the commander's infertile wife. If only the role of handmaid were abolished, some of my students argued, the scenario wouldn't be so bad. Atwood's vision of hysterical women tearing a man limb from limb for the (alleged) crime of rape did not seem to bother many of them. In the same class, these students expressed approval of the flogging of an American youth in Singapore for defacing walls with graffiti: a really safe and clean society, they said, may be worth such brutality.

I was struck by their fears and anxieties, caused, I believe, not only by the real problems of American life, but also by the inflamed statistics promoted by feminists. On one of the stalls in the bathroom right outside the classroom in which I was teaching, I read that one out of every two women will be raped in her lifetime. The young women in my course do not seem to question such statistics and are willing to give away much in exchange for the security they feel they lack. Far from appreciating freedom (academic or other), they act as if they are living in a society in which others' words and actions are a constant threat. Having no personal experience with situations where speech is prohibited, where speech codes similar to those these students endorse are the norm, where personal behavior is highly regulated, and where there is no freedom of association, they have no trouble thinking they might like such a society if only it made them feel safe. An atmosphere of panic, bolstered by scare statistics, is clearly a prerequisite if zealous solutions are to win support. And, in my experience, a great deal of the teaching that goes on in lower-level women's studies courses in particular is designed to induce precisely such feelings of panic.

To be effective, education should promote the play of the imagination. But I see few signs of such imagination at work as students and colleagues not only fail to defend the academic freedom they take for granted, but actively assail it. I am not sure there is enough imagination around at the present time to let them even learn from the experiences related by others. Consider, for example, the views of a Chinese political scientist now working in the United States, as set forth in a discussion on FEMISA (an e-mail list devoted to gender and international relations). I was in a distinctly minority position when I argued on that list for the importance of free speech, which—in that particular context—meant tolerating the messages of male contributors who were making themselves unpopular. I contended that even obnoxious males should not be struck from the list, and that intolerance of ideas we don't like can quickly move into the prohibitory mode, as if the people with whom we disagree had no right to speak freely. Pursuing such a course, I said, we will soon find ourselves instituting censorship, public humiliation, shunning, ganging-up-on, and so on, so as to protect the orthodoxy of a few.

Kate Zhou posted the following response:

Dear Sisters:
We should pay attention to Daphne's concern. I am a feminist from China. For many years, sexist language was banned by the Chinese state (at least in the urban public sphere). Urban Chinese women were very much "free" from sexist verbal attacks. Many women including myself were willing to give up freedom for some degree of protection and security. When everyone lost the freedom to speak, women's independent voice was also gone. When women's voices were silenced, women suffered.

Yes, we did not have to be bothered by sexist language and pornography. But we could not complain that we had to line up two or three hours for basic food. We had to take less interesting work because we had to take care of the family. It was not politically correct to complain about the double burden.

Is it clear to feminists that there has been no feminist movement in those countries that practice state censorship?

My experience in China seems to suggest that women are often victims of any kind of censorship. As a feminist, I believe that women have the ability and power to defend their interests if given a chance. We should welcome complex and diversified debates. Difficult and complex debates help to train us. If we try to shut someone up because we dislike what he has to say, we just confirm our weakness and sexism.[22]

FEMISA did not take this sound advice. Recently, after more postings from argumentative men (who sometimes were merely pointing out that hateful language about men was routinely posted on the list by women while men's objections and criticisms were being treated as intolerable flames), the listowners proved their point by barring various men from the list and moving the entire list onto "moderated" status, the better, it appears, to control its discussions.

I believe that we must heed the experiences of people in societies where individual freedom has been construed as inimical to the greater social good and hence restricted by the state and its institutions. We often seem to gravitate toward what is absent from our own historical situation. When there is censorship of reading material, we get protests such as those that arose around the obscenity trial of Radclyffe Hall's book *The Well of Loneliness* in England in 1928, or around D. H. Lawrence's *Lady Chatterley's Lover* in this country in 1959. When girls (but not boys) must be in their dormitories by a certain hour, and a couple is required to have three feet on the floor (common dormitory rules when I was an undergraduate in the early sixties), these regulations cause resentment and rebellion. And when all such rules are lacking, as they are today, why should it surprise us that people cry out to be saved from themselves and from one another?

But for adults who have enjoyed freedom of expression and association to throw it away so cavalierly certainly suggests they have not taken a look at either the abundant literary models or the actual societies in which such restrictions have been in force. Does it make a difference whether the rules and constraints (which no supporter has been able to demonstrate are actually likely to lead to a better society) are demanded by feminists or by—say—fundamentalists? I don't believe so. Once set in motion, where will such social engineering stop? Whom should we trust to define the good society for us?

NOTES

This article is based on a speech given at the Academic Freedom Symposium organized by Neil W. Hamilton at the William Mitchell Law School. First published in the *William Mitchell Law Review* 22:2 (1996), 491-516. Some endnotes have been eliminated.

3. University of Massachusetts at Amherst, "Proposed Harassment Policy," distributed on October 20, 1995. The cover letter, dated September 20, 1995, states that the University and the GEO (Graduate Employee Organization), which together worked out the policy, "are unanimous in our support of the basic elements of the policy proposal." It invites discussion of the policy by the entire university community, to help "in the resolution of our remaining differences" and affirms the administration's desire "to have a policy in place early in the spring 1996 semester."

Because of both the content of the proposed policy and the summary way in which it was presented to the university, a process apparently designed to discourage genuine discussion, about half a dozen faculty members, including myself, publicly protested the policy. This led to the appearance of articles in the *Boston Globe, New York Times, The Chronicle of Higher Education,* and elsewhere, in most instances opposed to the proposed policy. As of the time of writing (January 1996), the status of the proposed policy is unclear, but UMass Chancellor David K. Scott has expressed his determination to pursue what he prefers to characterize as a "harassment" policy rather than a "speech" code.

Grateful thanks to Harvey A. Silverglate, of the Boston law firm Silverglate & Good, for his memorandum to me, dated November 24, 1995, with a detailed critique of the proposed UMass policy, and to Jonathan Knight, Associate Secretary of the AAUP, for his letter of November 28, 1995 (addressed to Professor Robert Costrell), explaining why the UMass policy, "if enacted as currently written, would pose a serious threat to the freedom to teach and the freedom to learn at the University of Massachusetts, Amherst"; and to both Harvey Silverglate and Professor Eugene Volokh, of the UCLA Law School, for consultations via e-mail.

4. This "double standard" approach was explicitly articulated by University of Massachusetts at Amherst's Associate Chancellor Susan Pearson, on a Boston radio talk show (*Connections* on WBUR) hosted by Christopher Leyden, December 5, 1995. It is based on the work of critical race theorists Mari Matsuda, Charles R. Lawrence III, and Richard Delgado, whose articles Ms. Pearson distributed to us at the December 21, 1995, meeting. In response to my direct question at that meeting as to whether he endorsed such a double standard, the chancellor, with some circumlocution, affirmed that this is what he had in mind. After all, he said, minority students are suffering as a result of the unpleasant things said to them. For an illuminating discussion of these issues, see Lawrence Douglas, "The Force of Words: Fish, Matsuda, MacKinnon, and the Theory of Discursive Violence," *Law and Society Review* 29:1 (1995), 169–191.

5. Aldous Huxley, *Brave New World* (1932; New York: Harper & Row, Perennial Library, 1969), 243.

6. Edmund Cooper, *Who Needs Men?* (London: Hodder and Stoughton, 1972).

7. Pamela Kettle, *The Day of the Women* (London: Leslie Frewin, 1969).

8. See, for example, Wayne Washington, "No Eyeful, so City Gets an Earful," *Minneapolis Star-Tribune,* August 5, 1995, 1A.

9. See, e.g., Harvey Silverglate, "Harvard Law Caves in to the Censors," *Wall Street Journal,* January 8, 1996, A18 (discussing a recently adopted sexual harassment policy at Harvard Law School).

10. See Joan I. McEwen, "Report in Respect of the Political Science Department of the University of British Columbia" (June 15, 1995; on file with author). This report was prepared for the deans of the Faculty of Arts and Graduate studies, University of British Columbia, Vancouver, Canada.

11. Daphne Patai and Noretta Koertge, *Professing Feminism: Cautionary Tales from the Strange World of Women's Studies* (New York: Basic Books, 1994).

12. Student Center for Educational Research and Advocacy (SCERA), "Overcoming Oppression within Groups" (pamphlet, University of Massachusetts at Amherst, 1987). I do not know if this pamphlet is still being circulated.

13. Equally pertinent is the detail that the burning of books in Germany in May 1933 was not, as hitherto believed, orchestrated by Goebbels, Hitler's propaganda minister, but in fact was initiated by the German Students' Association (GSA), a non-Nazi organization founded in 1919 to act as German university students' representative at the national level. The GSA in April 1933 organized the propaganda campaign entitled "Against the un-German Spirit." This campaign, which included an anti-Semitic poster and a script for ceremonial book burning, indeed culminated, in early May 1933, in book burnings in German universities. See Ehrhard Bahr, "Nazi Cultural Politics: Intentionalism vs. Functionalism," in *National Socialist Cultural Policy*, ed. Glenn R. Cuomo (New York: St. Martin's Press, 1995), 5–22. Bahr, drawing on the work of Geoffrey J. Giles, *Students and National Socialism in Germany* (Princeton, N.J.: Princeton University Press, 1985), notes that "non-Nazi organizations, such as the German Students' Association, were eager to preempt the policies of rival Nazi organizations" (12).

14. Anchee Min, *Red Azalea* (New York: Pantheon, 1994), 38.

15. Huxley, *Brave New World*, 15; emphasis in original.

16. Eugene Zamiatin [Yevgeny Zamyatin], *We*, trans. Gregory Zilboorg (New York: E. P. Dutton, 1924).

17. Zamiatin, *We*, 22.

18. Ray Bradbury, *Fahrenheit 451* (1953; New York: Ballantine Books, 1991), 83.

19. Bradbury, *Fahrenheit 451*, 87. On the failure to speak out while one still can, see the foreword to Yang Jaing, *A Cadre School Life: Six Chapters*, trans. Geremie Barmé with the assistance of Bennett Lee (Hong Kong: Joint Publishing Co., 1982). The author was a professor emeritus of English who, in 1969 at the age of sixty, was sent to a "cadre school"—one of the reform camps set up in 1966 for intellectuals during Mao's Cultural Revolution. The author's husband Qian Zhongshu (Mocun), himself a writer and scholar, notes in the foreword that his wife has left out a chapter, "one that might be called "Politics—Chapter on Shame" (11). Three different types of people could be discerned in the Cultural Revolution, as in the preceding political movements, he writes. These are:

> First, the hapless victims, the comrades who were falsely accused of crimes, then criticised and struggled. If they wrote memoirs, they would probably include a "Chapter on Being Wronged," or a "Chapter on Indignation."
>
> The second consists of the broad masses of China. In their recollections of that period there might be a "Chapter on Remorse," recording their gullibility and readiness to believe all of the trumped up charges made against others, and their thoughtless complicity in the persecution of innocents. Some, myself included, would record our remorse for our lack of courage. For it was people like me who, although aware of the injustices being perpetrated on those around us, were too cowardly to take a stand and speak out against what was happening. Our only boldness was a lack of enthusiasm for the endless movements and struggles in which we participated.
>
> The third group is made up of those who knew all too well that things had gone wrong, and that basic questions of principle had long ago been buried under mountains of confusion and deception. In spite of this, however, they continued to play the role of the revolutionary, instigating witch-hunts and acts of violence, and setting themselves up as the sole arbiters of truth. These people have the most reason to write a "Chapter on Shame." But they have the shortest memory of all; to them remorse is an unwelcome emotion. Of

course, they may have unconsciously suppressed their sense of guilt. Or, what is more probable, they honestly believe they have done nothing to be ashamed of.

20. Bradbury, *Fahrenheit 451*, 59–62.

21. Fyodor Dostoyevsky, *The Brothers Karamazov*, trans. David Magarshack (Harmondsworth, Middlesex: Penguin Books, 1958), 289–311.

22. Kate Zhou, May 5, 1995. My thanks to Professor Zhou for allowing me to cite her words. I have made a few slight corrections to her English.

4

Justice Comes to U. Mass.

At the University of Massachusetts at Amherst, spring training in the politics of protest went off without a hitch. For six days last month, more than 150 minority students and their supporters occupied the controller's office in a campus building named Goodell Hall. The students were demanding increased enrollment of minority students, a voice in hiring faculty and staff members, and more. Friends, local merchants, and the university (the latter in blissful disregard of its own rules and regulations) tended to the protesters' needs during this stressful time, and the occupation concluded happily for all sides.

The hallowed U. Mass. tradition of civil disobedience at no cost to the disobedient was reaffirmed when the administration signed off on a "living document" accepting almost all of the students' demands. This included the reaffirmation of a promise, made after a previous student takeover in 1992, to recruit an undergraduate enrollment of 20 percent minority students. (This is not, the university claims, to be confused with a quota.) The protesters were unimpressed that U. Mass. had already attained the 20 percent mark in the freshman class and 16 percent among all undergraduates. Apparently stricken by its failure to live up fully to the letter of its earlier promise, the university this time agreed to both "recruit and retain" a minority student enrollment of 20 percent.

In addition, the students demanded and the administration agreed (no doubt as a guarantee of fairness and justice) that no minority student would be denied admission without a review of his or her application by a minority staff member.

Interim Provost Patricia Crosson, in the absence of Chancellor David K. Scott, sent an e-mail message to all faculty members defending the administration's decision not to take any punitive action against the protesters. In a matchless spirit of cooperation, she offered an invaluable new definition of education: "University education is about freedom of expression and the balance between civil disobedience and the enforcement of laws." She went on to congratulate the protesters for having provided "learning opportunities for our students."

Hitherto, I must acknowledge, I have been a curmudgeonly critic of the university for its untiring efforts to impose its political agenda of the moment on the campus. More than a year ago, I objected to the administration's attempt to inflict a highly restrictive speech code on students and faculty and staff members; more recently, I questioned the use of a new annual form asking faculty members to describe their "significant contributions to multiculturalism" in the areas of service, teaching, and research. At the time of the March takeover of Goodell, I happened to be teaching B. F. Skinner's *Walden Two* in my course on utopian fiction. The administration's response to the student protesters, I realized, perfectly modeled Skinner's notions of operant conditioning through positive reinforcement.

At first, I was skeptical of entrusting the university with the role of behavioral engineer, but then I finally saw the light and realized the important implications of the decision to insist that a staff member from a minority group review applications from any minority students slated for rejection. That being the case, I composed the following memo to the chancellor, offered here for the edification of colleagues everywhere:

Dear Chancellor:

I am writing to you because the recent resolution of the Goodell takeover, so enthusiastically confirmed by you upon your return to campus, has caused me to reconsider my position. When I realized that the university is agreeing to place members of racial and ethnic minority groups in key positions within the university (such as on admissions committees), the better to block the inevitable racist predilections of white staffers, I suddenly understood the scope of the problems you are facing in your struggle to bring fairness and justice to the university.

Surely you would not be taking such a step if you were not convinced of the bankruptcy of the old ways of doing things, which, though pretending color-blindness, merely served as a cover-up for prejudice and discrimination.

In particular, I have begun to understand that I, as a white faculty member, am no different from white staff members in the admissions office who cannot be trusted to treat all applicants equitably. It would be reprehensible of me to claim otherwise.

I am, therefore, anxious to assure you that I eagerly look forward to working with representatives of identity groups whom you will, I trust, soon be placing in my classroom to assist me. I would not dream of grading the papers of minority students on my own, lest I, too, find myself unable to treat them with the evenhandedness and integrity they deserve.

In fact, now that you have forced me to confront this admittedly painful issue, I rather doubt that even my non-grading contacts with students different from myself are to be trusted. I am embarrassed by the memory of my years of teaching without proper oversight by designated minority representatives. Please fulfill your promises to the protesting students as rapidly as possible so that those of us who, regrettably, possess identities of privilege are prevented from wreaking our usual harm in the classroom.

I leave it to your wisdom to sort out precisely how this is to be accomplished. Perhaps you will want to consider options similar to those you have endorsed for the admissions office, such as assigning racially appropriate staff members to oversee the design of courses and to vet reading lists, or to revise assignments and examinations to make sure that they are "inclusive." You might even appoint "interaction coordinators" to monitor exchanges in the classroom.

Let me assure you that I understand that it is indispensable for the university to devote an ever-greater share of its budget to non-teaching functions. While I have deplored this trend in the past, I now see that it is necessary to meet the demands of a truly enlightened, properly administered university.

I congratulate you and your staff on the efforts that you have made to ensure that identity issues are treated with the vigilance they warrant. If we can convince our students that justice and equitable treatment are available only within one's own identity group, we will have successfully grasped another of those splendid "learning opportunities" cited by your administration during the recent takeover.

Respectfully yours,
A Loyal Convert

P.S. I gladly volunteer my services to act as white associate in the classroom or laboratory of any colleague of color eager to apply the university's admirable new standards across the board.

NOTE

First published in *The Chronicle of Higher Education*, April 25, 1997, B8.

5

Third Thoughts about Orwell?

Years ago, I was an Orwell fan— a purely conventional one, admiring him for what I took to be his honesty, fair-mindedness, and passion for justice. Then, careful reading and re-reading of his work, over many semesters during which I was teaching courses on utopian fiction, gave me second thoughts. These were set out in my book *The Orwell Mystique: A Study in Male Ideology*, published in 1984. The feminist reading of Orwell's work I undertook in that book produced an appraisal that found Orwell a most peculiar kind of moral exemplar and political hero.

My basic argument at the time was twofold: First, Orwell's famed decency, honesty, and political rectitude stopped well short of including questions of gender justice, though this was an important theme of his time, evident in the writings of well-known contemporaries such as Virginia Woolf and Vera Brittain; and second, Orwell's overt political commitments were being constantly undermined by his anxiety about eroding masculinity, which made him fear that socialism would lead to the sort of soft, feminized world that he distinctly despised. I supported these contentions with a very close reading of everything I could get my hands on written by Orwell, published and unpublished.[1]

Since then, two things have happened to make me reconsider Orwell's importance and to alter my opinion of his contributions and their worth. One is general and the other personal. The first is the spread of postmodernist rhetoric, with its pretended skepticism about everything, its attempt to reduce all reality to a "text," and its wild claims about the instability and self-referentiality of language. These uncannily recall Orwell's description of Ingsoc, with its denial of objective reality and embrace of an eternally mutable past. By contrast, Orwell's plain-spoken assertions, in his essays, about language and his conviction that it could adequately describe reality, seem more important to me now than they appeared to be a few decades ago, when I had not yet been exposed to the vacuity of many academic intellectuals' pronouncements on this subject. I lack the space here to dwell on these ludicrous assertions (noting only that even postmodernists get penicillin shots rather than disinfecting their discourse) but will merely refer to the hoax perpetrated in 1996 by Alan Sokal, which beautifully exposed the grandiosity and sheer stupidity of humanities' professors who somehow manage to reconcile their "correct" politics with a sweeping disavowal of reality. The dishonesty, pretentiousness, and viscosity of their positions naturally brought Orwell—the writer who celebrated lucidity and commonsense—to mind.[2]

The second event that caused me to reconsider Orwell's work, although it was largely personal, also relates to a general phenomenon in academe, and that is my own disillusionment with the role of feminism in teaching and research. The dismay I experienced in the course of spending ten years in a women's studies program is, of course, similar to the disillusionment that many other former loyalists have gone through as they have seen movements for which they once held great hopes succumb to orthodoxy, intolerance, and petty policing. In particular, it seems to me now that I had neglected to grasp the depth of the disappointment and irascibility that accompany such awakenings. Not surprisingly perhaps, this experience too made me think differently, and more sympathetically, about Orwell's trajectory.

Of course, Orwell is not the only dystopian writer or political essayist who has frequently come to my mind in recent years as I contemplated and participated in the academic scene. Oftentimes it was Zamyatin, especially his 1923 essay "On Literature, Revolution, Entropy, and Other Matters"[3] and his novel *We* (first published in English translation in 1924), without which neither *Brave New World* nor *Nineteen Eighty-Four* would in all likelihood have been written. Zamyatin tirelessly warns against the entropy that invariably leads to rigidity and ossification of once vibrant social movements and ideas. He argues for the necessity of perpetual heresy if the tendency for new thought to become calcified is to be avoided, and he writes compellingly of the horrors of a panoptical world in which private space has been eliminated. The case he makes is for passion and imagination against the domination of mathematical reasoning. And to these appeals, writing in a different (ideologically stultifying and Stalinist) context, Orwell, in *Nineteen Eighty-Four*, added the case for reason, logic, and the ability to think for oneself as the foundations of a free society.

Actually, the two trends I found so disturbing—feminism and postmodernism—have joined forces in recent feminist attacks on logic, reason, and the primacy of facts. Let me give some examples of this collusion.

Not long ago I found myself defending the claim that sexual dimorphism in humans is a biological fact. The majority of contributors to a discussion of this subject on the women's studies e-mail list (WMST-L), which has 4,500 contributors—mostly academics in women's studies—challenged this view on the basis of the catch-all notion of "social constructionism." Sexual dimorphism, they argued, is a "social construct." Evidently, what these discussants were doing was simply defending a current orthodoxy of feminist teaching, which sees not only gender roles but sexual difference itself (and, not least, heterosexuality) as a "social construct."[4]

Redefining terms has, to be sure, played a major role within feminism in recent decades. I have been present at departmental meetings at which a feminist colleague asked in all earnestness: "Who's to say what 'scholarship' really means?" This was, of course, an effort to promote the hiring of a poorly qualified candidate who was, however, a political activist of the right stripe. And I have heard feminists (and other political activists) defend Rigoberta Menchú's distortions—detailed by David Stoll in his now notorious exposé[5]— as insignificant, since (so they claim) "larger truths" (as long as they are the preferred ones) justify specific falsehoods.[6] I have observed too many feminists parrot Catharine MacKinnon's assertions that words *are* deeds—thus making sexual slurs tantamount to rape—and that women in our society are not really empowered to give meaningful consent to heterosexual relations. And I have seen terms like truth and logic set in sneer quotes, the better to discredit them as a masculinist ruse, and incoherence celebrated as a daring challenge to narrow linear (male) thinking that women are supposedly superior to—at least if they are the right kind of feminists. At some point, moreover, it became clear to me that these feminists were attacking science and reason opportunistically, their chief objective being to leave themselves free to make whatever claims they wished, without being held to any standard—all standards having been conveniently exposed as masculine contrivances.

And then there have been the blatant power grabs: At my university, a philosophy professor and former head of women's studies, appealing to "equity for women," attempted to defend a large-scale plan to turn feminists into the supreme arbiters of curricular and personnel matters. When other faculty members objected to the proposed intrusion on their academic freedom, she stated—this was at a meeting of the faculty senate— "We can't lose track of the wider goal in order to defend some narrow definition of academic freedom, which might amount to a right not to have to respond to new knowledges that are relevant to someone's own field of expertise."[7] Similarly, campus activists have attacked free speech as nothing more than a form of white male privilege: On many campuses feminists are among those faculty members who have supported restrictive speech codes that would institutionalize clear double standards—this in accordance with the claims of critical race theorists that members of "historically oppressed" groups must be protected from verbal slights, while they themselves could say whatever they want to representatives of "historically powerful" groups. Thus, group identity and the ostensible needs of a given "community" are elevated above individual rights and freedoms, as if the twentieth century had never provided clear examples of the horrors that result from such commitments to political expediency.

I have also witnessed the spread throughout the country of sexual harassment policies, which (since they target "verbal or physical conduct") are in effect speech codes. Such policies are unable to distinguish between a look and rape, allow offense to be in the eyes of the complainant (recast in feminist literature as a "survivor"), and routinely include bans even on "third party harassment," which may occur when someone has overheard a perhaps offensive joke or feels personally aggrieved by someone else's "asymmetrical relationship." In this climate of vigilantism, I have seen due process given short shrift, so that some of the accused have a hard time even learning what the charges are against them or who has accused them.[8] Sometimes it has seemed to me that these feminist triumphs of the late twentieth century closely resemble Junior Anti-Sex League propaganda.

Many of these abuses have been perpetrated in the interest of advancing the feminist claim that "the personal is political." In utter disregard of the totalitarian potential of the principle behind such a slogan (exposed amply in both dystopian literature and in real-life fascist and communist regimes around the world), feminists have proudly embraced it as a means by which to efface the boundaries between the public and the private and have attempted to micromanage everyday life—all in the name of ushering in what they seem to see as a utopian future in which women would be safe from the depredations of the Patriarchy.

In the face of such assaults—and I'm speaking only of the privileged setting of the academy, not even of similar attacks occurring outside it—I have learned that clinging to reason, evidence, and clearly defined laws is a crucial counterstrategy. And indeed it was Orwell who, whatever his shortcomings, defended these claims over and over again.

Here, then, is my brief reassessment, in light of my experiences since 1984, of the key points of my earlier critique of Orwell.

1. A man deemed to be the "conscience of his generation" and considered a moral exemplar should *not* have been hostile to basic feminist aspirations and to women in general, as his work clearly shows him to have been. In particular, his run-of-the-mill misogyny strikes me as unworthy of him. Of the many examples one could cite, I mention only one, a smug aside in a review Orwell wrote of a novel by Joseph Conrad: "One of the surest signs of his genius is that women dislike

his books."[9] This is still, I believe, a significant and accurate charge against him, and it calls into question the hyperbole surrounding Orwell's reputation, which by now is far removed from the man himself.

2. Where my argument rested on a close reading of Orwell's work, it still has merit. For example, it is worth thinking about Orwell's incontrovertible ambivalence toward socialism because of his fear that it would make men "soft."

3. Where I went wrong in my book was whenever I deviated too much from Orwell's texts and made inferences and general statements conforming to the feminist framework to which I held at the time. Thus, for example, I argued that had Orwell been less mired in androcentrism, he would have seen that women, with their different, noncompetitive, more cooperative, and less violent ways of doing things, represent hope. This image of women I can, alas, no longer believe. To have written such a thing in the 1980s seems to me today to have indulged in a dogmatic or quasireligious statement rather than one based on evidence.

   Thus, my conclusion that Orwell's despair was the result of his androcentrism seems to me all wrong now. Or, at least, the prevailing mood in his works is matched these days by my own dismay over what feminism has brought us. My best guess today is that Orwell's pessimism was largely a matter of temperament and personal and historical circumstances, and that it had little to do with his distaste for feminist causes. Here was a clear case where I let my feminist politics dictate the results of my analysis. Experience has taught me better.

4. On the other hand, my application of game theory to *Nineteen Eighty-Four*, which helped me focus on the details of the interaction between O'Brien and Winston Smith, and my argument that this is the most important relationship in the book, still, I think, have merit.

5. My detailed analyses of Orwell's language, which revealed his attraction to war and its noises, his idealization of working-class men, and his denigration of women, are still, I think, of interest—in the way that all careful analysis that illuminates a literary work or figure can be. Again, however, I see a discrepancy between the close readings and my larger claims—and it's the latter I would no longer want to defend now, since I myself have come to question so many of them.

Having attempted this reappraisal of my own arguments, I also think it important to note how Orwell continues to be used for the sake of political slam dunks (or efforts at these), regardless of the inappropriateness of the particular cause in which his name is being invoked. Toward the end of the preface to my 1984 book, I wrote: "In the future, I think, interest in Orwell will focus not on his work but on the phenomenon of his fame and what it reveals about our own civilization."[10] Certainly, Orwell's reputation has been the subject of interesting work since then (most notably by John Rodden); however, there has been little letup in the tendency to idealize him and to borrow his moral authority in support of one's own positions, whatever these happen to be. The extent to which this is still true can be seen in the extraordinary use made of him in relation to the war in Iraq. A Google search (on April 23, 2003) simply with the terms "Orwell + Saddam" turned up nearly 15,000 hits; a search under "Newspeak + Bush" turned up about 5,000, including some references to "Bushspeak." It appears that Orwell has been particularly useful for those wishing to attack the Bush administration[11]—though most everyone can and does borrow from Orwell as the occasion arises.

I am as convinced as I was twenty years ago that the habit of citing Orwell in defense or promotion of one's own causes is a way of asserting one's moral superiority—and clearly this is a game all sides can play. What is of greater interest to me in the present context is the disregarded Orwell, the one who can and did make the most outlandish statements without, somehow, having them threaten his moral authority or undermine his reputation for straight talk and honesty. Perhaps this is because he liked to adopt a "voice in the wilderness" persona and was in the habit of presenting his often idiosyncratic views as self-evident or prophetic truths that only he himself was courageous enough to proclaim or detect.

Here are a few examples, drawn from my book: In a letter dated December 28, 1938, Orwell wrote, remarkably: "I think it's really time someone began looking into Fascism seriously."[12] That so late in the thirties Orwell should come to this realization is one of many indications, I think, of a peculiar habit of his: a tendency to believe that until something captured his own attention, it could not really be considered important. Contrast this with a 1933 essay by Joseph Roth, a well-known journalist and novelist who published, in the Parisian journal *Cahiers Juifs* in September/November 1933, an essay titled "The Auto-da-Fé of the Mind." Responding to the book burning and persecution that were occurring in Germany within a few months of Hitler's rise to power, Roth wrote these astonishing lines:

> Let me say it loud and clear: The European mind is capitulating. It is capitulating out of weakness, out of sloth, out of apathy, out of lack of imagination (it will be the task of some future generation to establish the reasons for this disgraceful capitulation).[13]

But it wasn't only journalists such as Roth, or the *Manchester Guardian* reporter Frederick Voigt, who persistently took "seriously" the advent of fascism. Many novelists too, including Storm Jameson, Naomi Mitchison, and Katharine Burdekin (from whom, I have argued, Orwell borrowed major elements for *Nineteen Eighty-Four*), were definitely looking seriously into fascism long before Orwell declared that it was about time for "someone" to do so.[14]

In a similar tone, Orwell announced in a 1947 column that anti-Semitism "has never been looked into, or only in a very sketchy way."[15] Perhaps, in making such a strange claim, Orwell had in mind statements such as his own in an entry in his wartime diary dated October 25, 1940:

> What is bad about Jews is that they are not only conspicuous, but go out of their way to make themselves so. . . . What I do feel is that any Jew, i.e. Euro-pean Jew, would prefer Hitler's kind of social system to ours, if it were not that he happens to persecute them. Ditto with almost any Central European, e.g. the refugees. They make use of England as a sanctuary, but they cannot help feeling the profoundest contempt for it. You can see this in their eyes, even when they don't say it outright.[16]

Even in 1943, Orwell still attributes this viewpoint about Jews to "many thoughtful people," in a discussion of anti-Semitism filled with caricatures of pushy "Jewesses."[17] That in 1945—1945!—Orwell wrote an essay critical of anti-Semitism does not undo the damage, for his admirers do not generally qualify their approbation by restricting it to particular moments or positions.

My point here is not to vilify Orwell but to suggest that we should think again about using him as a touchstone for decent opinions and good judg-ment. True, he was not alone in holding to such ideas (Virginia Woolf's anti-Semitic comments about her mother-in-law, for example, are a distinct blemish on her reputation, though they appear in her diaries, not in her published writings). But Orwell is unmatched in the moral authority he has been granted throughout the past half century, despite his often ordinary perceptions and prejudices. His writings are replete with dismissive pro-nouncements, and it is fascinating to see the convolutions undertaken by writers today as they attempt to deal with this reality. Christopher Hitchens, for example, in his recent book *Why Orwell Matters*, after quite rightly ob-jecting to the cloying veneration of Orwell evident in many quarters,[18] nonetheless in the end attempts to redeem him. Hitchens distinguishes Or-well from "most intellectuals" of his time, who, says Hitchens, "were fatally compromised by accommodation to one or another" of the three great causes of the twentieth century—imperialism, fascism, and Stalinism.

But as Hitchens wll knows, Orwell's thought was marred by his many prejudices—against feminists (and against birth control), against women in general, against homosexuals ("pansies" in particular), against militarists and against pacifists (at different times, of course), against vegetarians, against teetotalers. Except for homosexuality (toward which Hitchens ad-mits that Orwell maintained an "unexamined and philistine prejudice"),[19] Hitchens seems satisfied that Orwell overcame his prejudices through con-scious self-mastery.[20] Yet, typically, it is the whole man who is apotheosized, as when Hitchens writes: "It has lately proved possible to reprint [in the twenty volumes of the *Complete Works* edited by Peter Davison and published in 1998] every single letter, book review and essay composed by Orwell without exposing him to any embarrassment."[21]

Contra Hitchens, what seems to me to matter most is not how Orwell came around to this or that correct position, but to be aware of the unvarying rhetoric Orwell maintained as he changed positions. This is something I analyzed in great detail in my book, for it allowed me to see the constancy in the turn of mind (and of phrase) that persisted through shifts in political and other views. An important example, perhaps pertinent to the war in Iraq in relation to which Orwell has been so often cited, is apparent in Orwell's change of attitude regarding conflict with Germany.

In 1937 Orwell argued that British rule in India was just as bad as German fascism and went on to write: "I do not see how one can oppose Fascism except by working for the overthrow of capitalism, starting, of course, in one's own country. If one collaborates with a capitalist-imperialist government in a struggle 'against Fascism,' i.e. against a rival imperialism, one is simply letting Fascism in by the back door."[22]

Compare this with Orwell's statement a few years later, in 1940: "Already it is common among the more soft-boiled intellectuals of the Left to declare that if we fight against the Nazis we shall 'go Nazi' ourselves. They might almost equally well say that if we fight against Negroes we shall turn black."[23]

The image of "soft-boiled intellectuals of the Left" is further clarified in another of Orwell's shifts of position that, again, failed to result in any change in his rhetoric. He opposed militarism as sarcastically in 1938–1939 as he did pacifism thereafter (which explains why people today can use his words to defend both sides in the arguments over the war in Iraq). Thus, in 1938 we find Orwell blaming "the pansy left" and "hack-journalists" for stirring up war fever and contrasting them with "ordinary decent people"—who, according to Orwell, opposed war.[24] By 1940, however, when Orwell himself had abandoned his anti-war stance, it wasn't ordinary decent people who opposed the war, but rather, once again, the "pansy left," and now also the "Fascifists" (Orwell's term for "pro-fascist" pacifists), who were, Orwell claimed, trying to hush up "the fact" that the working class is almost always antifascist.[25] As I argued when I first discussed these examples two decades ago, the values inherent in Orwell's assaults remain the same; only the targets change.

To follow the implications of this example further, consider that in 1938 and 1939, still in his brief antimilitarist phase, Orwell accused men who argued for war against Germany of not being real men. They promoted war, he said, because of the softness and security of their life in England. They thirsted for blood out of lack of experience of it. But a few years later he was claiming the very opposite: "To abjure violence it is necessary to have no experience of it," he wrote, and this explains why the "real working class" is "never really pacifist"—because they do have experience of violence.[26] Orwell's sense of the proper manly virtues has evidently remained unchanged, allowing him at each point to portray his opponents as unmanly. So, in the 1940s, we find Orwell writing of "the spiritual need for patriotism and the military virtues, for which, however little the boiled rabbits of the Left may like them, no substitute has yet been found."[27] At this stage of his thinking, Orwell managed to make patriotism the crux upon which revolutionary socialism would be built, while also arguing that the war against Hitler could not be won "without introducing Socialism [into England]."[28]

Far from being a subtle thinker, Orwell often held simplistic and extreme views of complex questions. It is also significant, I think, that his most famous single line was lifted from another writer (he was an inveterate borrower, in fact). As Richard Mayne pointed out in 1982,[29] in Philip Guedalla's brief anti-communist satire "A Russian Fairy Tale," published in 1930, there appears a Good Fairy "who believed that all fairies were equal before the law, but held strongly that some fairies were more equal than others."[30]

Orwell's tone in his writing was self-righteous and judgmental. He had a marked preference for coercive discourse— that is to say, sweeping assertions and generalizations that tended to ward off criticisms by the sheer certainty with which they were declared, as when he attributes his current view (whatever it is at a given moment) to "all decent people," and to "everyone." An example of this technique can be seen in the following comment, from a notebook Orwell kept near the end of his life: "Who has not felt when talking to a Czech, a Pole—to any Central European, but above all to a German or a German Jew—'How superior their minds are to ours, after all?' And who has not followed this up a few minutes later with the complementary thought: 'But unfortunately they are all mad?'"[31]

Still, familiar though I was with Orwell's judgmentalism and coercive rhetoric, I remember clearly my dismay when, in May 1983, I sat in the Orwell Archives at University College, London, and held in my hands the list—or, as I called it in my notes at the time, the Notebook of Names—that Orwell kept toward the end of his life, in which he recorded the names and his appraisal of individuals he considered politically unreliable. When the archivist accidentally delivered to me this notebook, on the cover of which was clearly marked "Closed except with Mrs. Orwell's permission," in a box with other materials, I naturally read it quickly and quietly. Uncertain how to deal with this find at the time, I mentioned it briefly in my book on Orwell, but otherwise did not draw attention to it.

I do not want to dredge up the recent debate this notebook elicited when it came to light in the late 1990s,[32] except to comment that I think Alexander Cockburn—with whom I rarely agree—was right when, in his December 7, 1998, column for *The Nation*, he objected to the "forgiving" attitude of most Orwell admirers toward Orwell's "mini-diatribes," as he labeled them, against blacks, homosexuals and Jews, and toward the very fact that Orwell compiled such a list.[33]

That day in the archive, twenty years ago, I was shocked by what I was reading. Despite having become a critic of Orwell in the several years during which I'd been working on him in the early eighties, I still did not expect such a thing from someone who claimed to so abhor the vigilante mentality. After all, I knew Orwell's 1939 essay "Inside the Whale," in which he had written that what most frightened him about the war in Spain was the "immediate reappearance in left-wing circles of the mental atmosphere of the Great War," as people "rushed straight back into the mental slum of 1915. All the familiar war-time idiocies, spy-hunting, orthodoxy-sniffing (Sniff, sniff. Are you a good anti-Fascist?)."[34]

Yet ten years later here was Orwell, indulging in precisely such vigilantism. As I read his Notebook of Names, what most distressed me, beyond the mere existence of it— which would have been easy to explain innocently since I knew Orwell loved to make lists—was the smug tone, the sanctimonious manner of one enjoying total confidence in his own judgments and opinions, one ready to label scores of people according to the pettiest criteria: not just presumed political reliability in what might become critical circumstances, but labels such as Jew, Zionist, "probably venal," "tendency toward homosexuality," and "crippled hand."

This last comment was made of Alex Comfort, with whom Orwell had carried on a verse polemic in 1943. Comfort's name, like those of Naomi Mitchison, Max Lerner, and several dozen others, was omitted in Davison's 1998 version of Orwell's *Complete Works* (only recently the Orwell Estate has finally granted permission to divulge the complete list). Of Comfort, Orwell wrote in his Notebook of Names: "Potential only. Is pacifist-anarchist. Main emphasis anti-British. Subjectively pro-German during war, appears temperamentally pro-totalitarianism. Not morally courageous. Has crippled hand." And then one additional (mitigating?) comment: "Very talented."

Especially interesting in this entry is the wording of Orwell's claim that Comfort was "subjectively pro-German" during the war, for in a review some years earlier, Orwell had called Comfort "objectively" pro-German. Perhaps late in his life Orwell backed away from the Leninist habit of labeling people "objectively" this or that, a habit which in the early forties had led him to classify pacifists as "objectively pro-Fascist."

As for Naomi Mitchison—who, by the way, in 1935, several years before Orwell thought someone should "seriously" look into fascism, published an anti-fascist novel called *We Have Been Warned*—Orwell wrote in his Notebook of Names, "Sentimental sympathiser only. Sister of J. B. S. Haldane (C.P.). Unreliable." Also interesting in Orwell's list is the frequency with which he labeled people "silly" or "stupid"—as if these, like Comfort's "crippled hand," had some political significance.

Peter Davison's exhaustive editing of Orwell's complete works has made virtually every facet of Orwell's writing available to us. Now all can see the warts, the contradictions, as well as the strengths of this restless character. Yet Davison's volumes also have something of the fetishistic about them, as if the minutiae of everyday life could provide us finally with that sense, so elusive, of another person's reality. But do we really think we can better grasp a life once we have been allowed to read every last trivial notation made by its subject? In Doris Lessing's novel *The Golden Notebook*, the author's alterego, Anna, attempts to capture the sense of everyday life by recording everything that takes place on a particular day, including changing her sanitary napkins; but she soon realizes the futility of all this as a means of registering a human life. There's more than a touch of absurdity, I think, in treating Orwell as if every passing remark reveals something significant. It seems to me that the texture of everyday life *is* its ordinariness, and we all are experts in that regard. Does knowing that on a certain day Orwell's cylinder of gas ran out really matter?[35]

But, like reality TV, the voyeurism implicit in wanting to read every last scrap that Orwell wrote suggests that somehow the reality of life always escapes us; hence we struggle to grasp it and think we can do so by observing other people's lives, as if they had a denser existence than our own. No; clearly Orwell's importance lies not in the minutiae of his life but in the constant appeal to his words and slogans made by people today, and this is much more an appeal to a symbol than to a person, as can be seen in the overuse of the term "Orwellian." For example, Morris Dickstein in a recent article praises the *Partisan Review* in the post-war years for its "Orwellian hatred of totalitarianism."[36] Evidently the adjective conveys a more compelling emotion than just a plain hatred of totalitarianism.

What is disturbingly new in our time is not the terror envisioned by Orwell at the end of *Nineteen Eighty-Four*—which always struck me as a bit ludicrous and incompatible with the rest of his understanding of power politics. It is not any such terror that endangers us today, but the apparently voluntary abdication of reason and freedom by many intellectuals on the left. It is the ordinary activism of supposedly well-intentioned people who, while enjoying the freedoms of our society, appear ready to renounce these very freedoms in the name of the "better" society they believe they are constructing. And although Orwell coined some excellent slogans and tags and gave us a compelling explanation of Newspeak as a language designed eventually to make "thoughtcrime" literally impossible, he can't really do much for us in the battle against this renunciation.

Many literary scholars these days pretend that, as the *Norton Anthology of Theory and Criticism* (which covers 2,500 years) tells us on the very first page of its preface, to do theory is "to engage in resistance."[37] Other professors claim that teaching is their form of "activism." In thrall to the notion that all education is political, contemporary academic vigilantes cultivate an ersatz politics from the safety of their tenured positions, while being unwilling, it appears, to defend art and imagination except when they serve particular political concerns. And in support of student censors, too many faculty members pretend that an unkind word or offending idea inflicts terrible damage on members of certain identity groups. As Harvey Silverglate and Greg Lukianoff recently wrote in *The Chronicle of Higher Education*: "The Foundation for Individual Rights in Education defines a speech code as any campus regulation that punishes, forbids, heavily regulates, or restricts a substantial amount of protected speech. Thus defined, speech codes are the rule rather than the exception in higher education."[38]

All this has forced me to see with a sharper eye the crucial distinction between politics and teaching, politics and art, and politics and scholarship. The point is to be able to distinguish one from the other, not to conflate them all into some simplistic and self-righteous bottom line of the sort students often indulge in as they engage in blame or praise of the authors they read and the historical figures they study.

We shouldn't fight these battles (those of us who want to) by appealing to figures who have acquired mythical status. We have to argue for free speech, truth telling, reason, logic, and the force of evidence on their own merits, defending them by reference not to authority but rather to historical alternatives, of which, lamentably, we have many examples. Orwell needs to be seen in the context of other British writers of the thirties and forties, not as a uniquely heroic figure. Invoking him doesn't help us in our struggles. There is enough in his work to be useful to almost any side of most of the issues he addresses. To build one's case by citing Orwell, at this late date, is simply and ironically to abdicate the very habit of independent thinking for which he is being celebrated.

NOTES

An abbreviated version of this essay was first presented at the Orwell Centennial Conference at Wellesley College in May 2003. This essay previously appeared in Thomas Cushman and John Rodden, eds., *George Orwell: Into the Twenty-First Century* (Boulder, Colo.: Paradigm Publishers, 2004), 200–211.

1. See Daphne Patai, *The Orwell Mystique: A Study in Male Ideology* (Amherst, Mass.: University of Massachusetts Press, 1984).

2. See Alan Sokal and Jean Bricmont, *Fashionable Nonsense: Postmodern Intellectuals' Abuse of Science* (New York: Picador, 1998).

3. In Yevgeny Zamyatin, *A Soviet Heretic: Essays,* trans. Mirra Ginzburg (Chicago and London: University of Chicago Press, 1970), 107-111.

4. See the discussion of this episode in Daphne Patai and Noretta Koertge, *Professing Feminism: Education and Indoctrination in Women's Studies,* revised edition (Lanham, Md.: Lexington Books, 2003), 307–316, 356–363, 359, 399–400.

5. David Stoll, *Rigoberta Menchú and the Story of All Poor Guatemalans* (Boulder, Colo.: Westview Press, 1999). Included as chapter 12 in the present volume.

6. See, for example, many of the essays in Arturo Arias, ed., *The Rigoberta Menchú Controversy* (Minneapolis: University of Minnesota Press, 2001).

7. See Daphne Patai, "Why Not a Feminist Overhaul of Higher Education?" *The Chronicle of Higher Education,* January 23, 1998, A56. Included as chapter 19 in this volume.

8. For examples of the above, see Daphne Patai, *Heterophobia: Sexual Harassment and the Future of Feminism* (Lanham, Md.: Rowman & Littlefield 1998).

9. Sonia Orwell and Ian Angus, eds., *Collected Essays, Journalism, and Letters of George Orwell,* vol. 1 of 4 (New York: Harcourt Brace Jovanovich, 1968), 227. This edition is now superseded by Peter Davison's edition of *The Complete Works of George Orwell* (London: Secker and Warburg, 1998).

10. Patai, *The Orwell Mystique,* x.

11. See, for example, the comment by Paul Foot headed "Triumph of Doublethink in 2003: Orwell Warned Against the Kind of Lies We Are Being Fed about Iraq," in *The Guardian,* January 1, 2003.

12. Orwell and Angus, *CEJL,* vol. 1, 370.

13. In Joseph Roth, *What I Saw: Reports from Berlin 1920-1933,* trans. Michael Hofmann (New York: Norton, 2003; published in German in 1996), 207.

14. On this subject, see also Andy Croft's *Red Letter Days: British Fiction in the 1930s* (London: Lawrence and Wishart, 1990).

15. Orwell and Angus, *CEJL,* vol. 4, 311.

16. Orwell and Angus, *CEJL,* vol. 3, 377–378

17. Orwell and Angus, *CEJL,* vol. 2, 290.

18. Christopher Hitchens, *Why Orwell Matters* (New York: Basic Books, 2002), 3. Philip French's review of Hitchens' book (published in England under the title *Orwell's Victory*) is titled, significantly, "A Saint Carved in Stone, Very Weathered." See *The Times Literary Supplement,* June 7, 2002, 23.

19. Hitchens, *Why Orwell Matters,* 206.

20. Hitchens, *Why Orwell Matters,* 9.

21. Hitchens, *Why Orwell Matters,* 4; the other exception—Orwell's notebook of names—Hitchens discusses in a separate chapter called "The List," in which he goes to considerable lengths to defend Orwell.

22. Orwell and Angus, *CEJL,* vol. 1, 284.

23. Orwell and Angus, *CEJL,* vol. 2, 102.

24. Orwell and Angus, *CEJL,* vol. 1, 332.

25. Orwell and Angus, *CEJL,* vol. 2, 226–228.

26. Orwell and Angus, *CEJL,* vol 2, 167.

27. Orwell and Angus, *CEJL*, vol. 1, 540.

28. Orwell and Angus, *CEJL*, vol. 2, 94.

29. Richard Mayne, *Times Literary Supplement*, November 26, 1982. I discuss this in *The Orwell Mystique*, 309, n. 18.

30. Philip Guedalla, "A Russian Fairy Tale," *The Missing Muse* (New York: Harper and Brothers, 1930), 206. Let me clarify that I would not consider this borrowing significant were it not for the fact that many critics refer to this line as a particularly felicitous example of Orwell's concision and clarity as a prose writer. See, for example, Raymond Williams, *Orwell* (Glasgow: Fontana/Collins, 1971), 4, which cites [Orwell's version of] this line as an example of the "exceptionally strong and pure prose" Orwell was "able to release" in *Animal Farm*. My own view is that Orwell had an excellent ear for slogans and catch phrases (his own and others'), and hence also understood the significance of propaganda.

31. Quoted in *The Orwell Mystique*, 10.

32. See, for example, the exchange of letters between Christopher Hitchens and Perry Anderson, in the *London Review of Books*, January and February 2000 (in response to Anderson's article on 25 November 1999).

33. Alexander Cockburn, "St. George's List," *The Nation*, December 7, 1998, 9.

34. Orwell and Angus, *CEJL*, vol. 1, 517–518.

35. See Orwell's domestic diary for July 19, 1947, in Davison, *Complete Works*, vol. 19, "It is what I think."

36. Morris Dickstein, "Waving Not Drowning," *Times Literary Supplement*, October 25, 2002, 14.

37. Vincent B. Leitch, ed., *The Norton Anthology of Theory and Criticism* (New York: Norton, 2001), xxxiii.

38. Harvey A. Silverglate and Greg Lukianoff, "Speech Codes: Alive and Well at Colleges," *The Chronicle of Higher Education*, August 1, 2003. See also Alan Charles Kors and Harvey A. Silverglate, *The Shadow University: The Betrayal of Liberty on America's Campuses* (New York: The Free Press, 1998). Silverglate and Kors went on to found FIRE—the Foundation for Individual Rights in Education—to defend civil rights on campus. [Disclosure statement: I am on the Board of Advisors of this organization.]

6

Letter to a Friend: On Islamic Fundamentalism

September 11, 2006, 8 p.m.

Today is September 11th, and I suppose everyone in this country knows what they were doing on this date five years ago. I recall the feeling of unreality I had as I watched a small TV screen here at home repeatedly play tiny images of two towers collapsing. And then, in the immediate aftermath, do you remember how many in this country—especially among intellectuals and academics—wanted to discuss what "we" had done to "deserve" this? Those were hard days, and in many respects the years since then have been harder still, for although I had by then already spent decades in the strange ideological climate of American academic life, I never expected to see such an orgy of "blame America first" unleashed in this country. Nor did I have any way of anticipating how serious the real consequences would be when those attitudes, nurtured in the idle confines of academia, spilled over into the very dangerous world outside.

I would hate it if our old friendship were to dissolve over politics, mere politics. But I can't not respond to your last letter, in which you stated that you were just as worried by Christian as by Muslim fundamentalists. Repeatedly in the past few years I've heard acquaintances, even relatives, express the same view. To my mind, however, this is a preposterous comment, for it evades the crucial recognition that something new has been unfolding before our eyes. Not that 9/11 inaugurated that new stage. I think, rather, it marked the end of the beginning, and the subsequent stage, the middle part, is still underway. How it will play out is unclear, but I believe that failure to recognize the significance of Muslim terrorism is extremely dangerous and may well haunt us in the future. Equally myopic, I think, are parallels between Christianity in premodern times, or violence in the Hebrew Bible, and

Islamism today. The fact is that Judaism and Christianity have undergone re-forms that took hundreds of years, and Islam, despite some attempts at re-form, has not done so, as many Muslim scholars note. So invoking the Cru-sades and the Inquisition as counters to Islamism today is a misguided thing to do. Yes, possibly Islam might eventually evolve in a more liberal direction, but right now it is fighting any such changes tooth and nail and taking that fight global.

Perhaps you don't realize that the popularity of radical Islam is rapidly increasing all over the world, to the point that some terrorists in the west are, these days, recent converts to Islam or immigrants who are unwilling to adapt to the values of the societies in which they sought refuge. But I don't see how it's possible to ignore not only the real violence but also the mere threat of violence, which, in conjunction with the spread of radical Islam, is having a profound effect. Who would have expected the most liberal so-cieties (e.g., the Scandinavian countries) to fail to defend their own values against the demands of Muslim immigrants? Consider the episode of the cartoons of Mohammed. With the sole exception of Denmark, where the cartoons were first published last year, the Scandinavian countries didn't even dare defend free speech and a free press—at least not if Muslims ob-jected. But these same countries do defend the rights of Muslims, probably out of fear of them, to engage in the most open hate-speech. In fact, these still-liberal countries are often financing the very Islamist communities that aim to dismantle them, communities that are insisting on their own sepa-rate laws, and courts, and customs. And such demands, backed by threats, seem to be spreading to other countries as well.

It's true I share your distaste for all types of religious fundamentalism. But that doesn't prevent me from noting the different demands and agen-das of each type, as well as their numbers and influence in the real world today. Where are the Christian fundamentalist leaders whose intent is to de-stroy another country? Yet many Muslim leaders publicly state that their aim is to destroy Israel: Jews first, then Israel, then Western culture. As Nas-rallah, head of Hezbollah, said about Jews: "If they all gather in Israel, it will save us the trouble of going after them worldwide." And Ahmadinejad, the president of Iran, states plainly his aspiration to get rid of both America and Israel. There's no dispute about the statements made by these and other Muslim leaders, merely about whether or not they should be taken seri-ously. Given the Islamist attacks that have been occurring around the world in recent decades (leaving aside for now the centuries-old matter of Islamic imperialism), the answer appears self-evident.

. . . I'm pausing here, because I see that in the preceding paragraph I jumped from the general subject of radical Islam to its not-so-hidden agenda, and that has to do with Jews and the state of Israel. This is without doubt at the heart of so much of the debate about the place of Islamism in the contemporary world. It's worth looking at a map of the Middle East in order to grasp the significance of the rise of radical Islam. There are twenty-two Arab countries. Look at the space they occupy. By contrast, note how small Israel is—in both area and population. Does anyone think or claim that Israel is trying to take over any Arab country? Or that Israel aspires to destroy Arabs, Muslims, or any non-Jews generally? That's a laughable suggestion, isn't it? Did you know that Israel has about seven million people (of whom one million are not Jews), and that the whole world today has only about fourteen million Jews? But there are two hundred million Arabs just surrounding Israel. (This is worth remembering when one reads death rates from the latest military conflicts, which show Israel is more effective militarily than its enemies (thus far at least, no doubt because it has had to be to survive). And there are perhaps 1.5 billion Muslims in the world today. Not all of them of the same type, of course, but there's simply no comparison between the numbers of Muslim fundamentalists and Christian ones, much less Jewish ones, of whom there are very few. Nor, if one tracks their actions, which is far more important than their rhetoric, does it appear that each type of fundamentalism is equally harmful, equally destructive in its influence around the world.

And then there is the matter of the forgotten or ignored history of the Middle East. Few people who weigh in on these subjects seem aware that in 1948 about the same number of Jews—800,000—left Arab countries as Arabs left Israel. Those Jews were all welcomed into the small new nation of Israel, while the Arabs who left or were expelled from Israel (the narratives vary) were for the most part not accepted into the surrounding Arab countries. Instead, they were set up in refugee camps to fester as a group that could be used against the new state. My guess is you didn't know this detail, because the view even (or especially) of educated people is so one-sided on the conflict between Jews and Arabs. For some years it's been clear to me that Arabs are winning the propaganda war against Israel, and the displaced Palestinians have had an enormous role in this success. The plan, in other words, has succeeded marvelously and has distracted the entire Arab world for generations now from dealing with its own tyrannies, its critical social and health problems, its populations' lack of political representation, its brutality toward non-Muslims, its gross inequalities of every kind—all of which dwarf any problems Israel might have in forging a just society. Sure, it's easy enough to criticize one or another Israeli policy, but that does not alter the fact that Arab and Muslim hostility to Israel (both physical and ideological) goes back to before 1973, before 1967, before 1948. Have you heard about the forced conversion of Jews to Islam as late as the nineteenth century? About the Arab riots in Jerusalem that began in 1920 and the effort to force Jews out of Palestine decades before the creation of the state of Israel? About the anti-western Muslim Brotherhood, ancestor of Hamas, and other radical

Muslim groups, which came into being in the 1920s in Egypt and spread from there?

Did you know that until 1967 there wasn't even a "Palestinian" identity among those Arabs that had left Israel? There was only a general undifferentiated Arab identity, riven by internecine conflicts and with shifting borders as political and doctrinal quarrels unfolded. Though you're acquainted a bit with my family history, it probably never occurred to you that I am actually a Palestinian, born in Palestine, where my mother's family went (When do you think? Do you believe we were all refugees from Nazi Europe?) at the beginning of the 20th century. But of course no Jew today is considered Palestinian, a term that has acquired a specific political connotation. The radical Muslim view (which flies in the face of thousands of years of history) that Jews have no historical ties in that part of the world has gained considerable ground of late, as I was reminded by an "innocent" comment made to me recently by a historian colleague, a decent person no doubt, who wondered aloud whether it really was a good idea to have established the state of Israel in the first place. About what other country in the world is such a question ever raised?

Though I was born in Jerusalem, you and I have rarely discussed the Middle East. Every other political issue in the world, yes, but not that one. Perhaps we avoided it; or perhaps I did so—out of a desire not to engage in any special pleading. Certainly, I was never a defender of Israel. For years I followed the line that the conflict between Israelis and Palestinians (using the now-conventional terms) was one of two competing nationalisms, a view that makes it unnecessary to actually learn any history! I even used to defend the one-state solution, Palestinians and Israelis living in harmony together. In the radical circles that I frequented at the time, no one pointed out that simple demographics would mean Israel would soon enough turn into a non-Jewish state; nor did I know anything about the long history of *dhimmitude*—the subjection of non-Muslim peoples to Islam, or what it meant.

I think it was only about eight or ten years ago that I became increasingly impatient with the standard anti-Israeli and pro-Palestinian views in my academic milieu. No doubt this was part of my growing disillusionment with so much academic discourse. The more I saw particular views (on the left) take on the status of unquestioned truths, the more skeptical I grew. And it became impossible for me not to notice what seemed to be an unwritten code among us academics: Israel was not to be defended, nor were Jews. Our Vietnam-era politics seem to have automatically assigned us to the pro-Palestinian side, befitting all our other third world sympathies, often unencumbered by real information.

But even once I did start to wake up, you and I still never discussed the Middle East. I knew it was not a subject that interested you much, and it was easy for me to ignore it as well. No more. I wonder, now, at the "postmod-ernist" equanimity that refuses to register the reality of different societies, their histories, their values. For the reality is that Israel is virtually the only country in the Middle East where there exists a free press and free elections (and real opposition in politics), where women have full political and civil rights, and where there is open homosexuality—just to mention a few things that are sine qua non for campus activists. And all these too are un-der attack by radical Muslims who want to spread *Sharia* throughout the world, who openly talk about reestablishing the caliphate, the high point of Muslim domination of the world. Meanwhile, in Arab and Muslim coun-tries, anti-Semitic propaganda is now routine, with the *Protocols of the Elders of Zion* once again widely circulated and believed and with TV shows that are blatantly anti-Semitic (and of course anti-Zionist) targeting children in the Middle East. In Europe too anti-Semitism is spreading at an alarming rate and is evidently once again becoming respectable. True, it's mostly in Africa and the Middle East that the standard view, not the extremist view, is that no Jews were killed in the World Trade Center because they'd all been warned and therefore hadn't gone to work that day; but even in Europe and the United States, one hears this claim made in all seriousness from time to time.

Have you seen footage in the last few years of the major anti-war groups in the United States? The anti-war movement is mired in anti-Israel and pro-Palestinian sentiment—which suggests that anti-Bush anti-war passions aren't really about whether or not Bush was justified in invading Iraq. I sus-pect that a great many people on the left have had their brains permanently addled by their hatred of Bush, to the point that they'd be satisfied if Iraq turned into a total disaster—just so that Bush could be blamed for it.

And then there is the incontrovertible reality that Israel is criticized for things no other country in the world is criticized for (including the right to defend itself). This detail ought to make any rational person wonder about the energy driving these criticisms. Actually, Israel's actions are constantly debated by its own population, where no one is afraid of voicing dissent. But when one contemplates the very different standards to which Israel is held, it's hard to avoid the implication that no one expects Muslims to be-have in a civilized way, so they don't get subjected to criticism even when their actions are far more savage than anything Israel has ever done. What do you suppose the reaction would be if Israelis beheaded a kidnapped journalist and sent those photos around the world? And, by the way, Daniel Pearl was far from the only person beheaded in recent years by Islamists. Where is the outrage about such barbarism? Instead one finds apologetics and cautions to not generalize about Islam from "isolated incidents."

The recent war between Israel and Lebanon has provided another handy occasion for the closet anti-Semites to come out, by claiming they're not at all anti-Semitic, merely anti-Israeli. This would be a legitimate distinction if there weren't a complete identity between these two in the minds of many Muslims and their sympathizers. Just read what Muslims say about Jews— not that they're much kinder to Christians. Do you know about the centuries-old Muslim attacks on Christian communities in the Middle East? Have you noticed that the moderate Muslims we hope actually exist in the Middle East and elsewhere rarely speak up and thus have virtually no representation anywhere? It's probably because they know better than most how their co-religionists traditionally deal with dissenters (as with apostates).

Did you notice how little attention was given to the fact—plainly reported but rarely discussed—that the two Fox news journalists kidnapped in Gaza (in August 2006) were forced to convert to Islam in order to save their own lives? As if this were an insignificant detail instead of a major indicator of what Muslim radicals have in mind. (Are Christian fundamentalists forcing conversions on anyone?) Equally interesting was that no one bothered to consider the significance of the detail that the journalists themselves and everyone concerned about them breathed a sigh of relief when they were back in Israel, that supposedly iniquitous country! Apparently everyone knows, despite all the bad press about Israel being just like Nazi Germany, that Israel is in fact a liberal democracy and that these men would be safe there, as are the gay Muslims who take refuge in Israel. Yet it's Israel, not any Arab or Muslim country, that is the object of attacks in the media (where staged events are reported as outrages committed by Israel), and it's Israel alone that is the target of divestment campaigns and boycotts by Westerners.

I am astonished that so many academics on the supposedly progressive side simply do not admit that everything they value (including cultural diversity, gay rights, women's empowerment, the freedom to express their own ideas) is literally intolerable to radical Islam, and that millions of people today adhere to this view of Islam and loudly proclaim their hatred of the west and all it stands for. The silence of most American feminists is particularly appalling, and I can only imagine that they are caught in their own ideological schemata, which somehow blind them to the necessity of protesting oppression when it is perpetrated by non-Anglo, nonwhite people.

Despite all the charges of racism, I don't see much anti-Arab or anti-Muslim sentiment in this country. Certainly not on college campuses where criticism of Israel and the United States is constantly voiced and seldom challenged. It's striking that even our conservative president feels obliged to echo standard liberal pro-multicultural ideas—for example, to carefully distinguish between the "few" bad guys and all the other Muslims in the United States. But he's right that there is an Islamic fascism, if one understands fascism as a totalitarian control over all aspects of life. Read what Islamist leaders say quite openly about their agenda; it absolutely does not include tolerance of opposing or dissenting ideas, free speech, freedom of religion or conscience, or women's rights. Why shouldn't Islamic fundamentalists be ever more blatant about their beliefs? They are growing in popularity and their numbers are increasing. The history of Islamic terrorism over the past few decades (even leaving aside the long historical record) reveals that it's not because of what Bush or his predecessors have done, but because of the whole complex of modernization, liberalization, and secularization that these fundamentalists cannot abide, for these will indeed challenge and assail their beliefs and perhaps change them.

If you are still tempted to worry *as much*, as you wrote, about Christian fundamentalists as about Muslim ones, just ask yourself about the agenda of each group, their numbers, their geographical presence, their past and present violent actions, the political responses to them, and the sort of press they each get in the west. So, the problem of phony parallels (between Muslim and other fundamentalists; between Israel and South Africa or—as is openly said these days—between Israel and Nazi Germany) really does need to be cleared up. True, not all terrorists are Muslims. But in fact global terrorism these days is almost entirely an expression of radical Islam—with a political-theological program and a clearly articulated agenda. Do Basque terrorists attack North America? Did the IRA? Nor should anyone think these Islamists are just isolated fanatics; Nasrallah has become a hero in much of the Muslim world, as is Bin Laden.

Few of our colleagues seem to understand that Islam is not merely a religion. It is a religious *and* a political movement, and in these intertwined aspects it does represent a threat to western, modernizing, and liberal values everywhere. Yet on campus (and far too often in the media) we are busily treating the Islamic world as a third world underdog that has to be defended, excused, and protected from criticism. At least that's the most generous explanation I can think of for so many colleagues' gross ignorance and lethal politics. Or is it that they don't really believe there's any danger? Do they have so little respect for Muslims today that they assume they could never succeed in imposing their views on the non-Muslim world? If not, why are they so unconcerned about their own future? Have they truly no clue as to what an Islamist regime would mean for *everything*—every single value, belief, principle, and everyday matter—these academics hold dear? And these are the very academics who constantly assert that all education is political, which gives them a pretext for not even trying to keep their politics out of the classroom. What, then, do you suppose they're conveying to their students?

But what most distresses me is that our generation of professors has contributed in a major way to the current atmosphere, one in which many academics are reticent about criticism of Islamism while also being unable or unwilling to see our own society as worth defending. It's as if those of us who have had the best that this country has to offer have, through some twisted logic, become unable to see what it is about this society that, whatever its defects, makes people from all over the world wish to live here. After all, it's our generation that caricatured the western tradition as the work merely of "dead white men"; it's people like you and me who led the charge against "ethnocentrism" and "Eurocentrism," who popularized ceaseless talk of "white privilege," and who promoted attacks on science and reason as uniquely western prejudices.

For years we echoed the standard nonsense about the bankruptcy of the Enlightenment project and repeated Marcuse's views on "repressive tolerance," as if these were a real response to the tyranny and censorship found in so many other societies. No wonder so few of our colleagues and students are able, let alone willing, to defend those western values. And why should I even be surprised at anything that goes on in academic and intellectual circles? I'm sure I've told you that, merely for describing the intolerance and dogmatism so rampant in women's studies programs, I've been labeled an "anti-feminist supporter of white male supremacists" (I kid you not), and a reactionary, and . . . the labels go on and on. But the personal annoyances of such things matter not at all in this sorry story compared to the possibility that we are watching our society commit suicide, with "the best and the brightest" lighting the way.

There is a passage from the famous Jewish sage Hillel that I often think of these days. More than two thousand years ago he wrote: "If I am not for myself, who will be for me? But if I am only for myself, what am I? And if not now, when?"

Daphne
September 2006–September 2007

NOTE

Previously published in *Butterflies and Wheels*. www.butterfliesandwheels.com, September 7, 2007.

II

WOMEN'S WORDS

7

Who's Calling Whom "Subaltern"?

My title refers to Gayatri Chakravorty Spivak's essay "Can the Subaltern Speak?"[1] Spivak's argument—which proceeds through more than thirty-five turgid pages—culminates in her assertion that no, the subaltern cannot speak.[2] My concern here is with the practical implications, for researchers such as myself, of Spivak's argument. Since I recently published a book entitled *Brazilian Women Speak: Contemporary Life Stories*, which includes twenty accounts by Brazilian women of different races, ages, and socioeconomic statuses, it's a good bet that my answer to the question "Can the subaltern speak?" is likely to be rather different from Spivak's.[3]

Let me open a parenthesis here and state that I met Gayatri Spivak only once, several years ago, when I attended a faculty seminar at which she was the featured speaker, sponsored by Five Colleges, Inc., a consortium that unites Amherst, Hampshire, Mount Holyoke, and Smith Colleges and the University of Massachusetts in Amherst, where I teach. In the context of a discussion of third world feminism, I—a white, North American woman—mentioned that I had been interviewing women in Brazil. Spivak, in an aggressive and censorious tone noted by several colleagues as well as by myself, asked me why I was doing those interviews. I replied that I was writing an oral history of Brazilian women. Spivak sharply asked "Why?" I said: "Because I'm interested in what they have to say" (or words to that effect). Now that I have read her essay, I can better understand her suspicions of my project.

Spivak is right to call into question a model that assumes first world scholars "allow" third world people to speak. Among researchers (especially feminists) working with living sources, this is not a new concern. Nor is it a concern only when race, class, and economic status divide the researchers from the researched, though certainly such divisions exacerbate the issue. The broader ethical and political problems of using living sources as research subjects are apparent, for example, in an essay by Calvin Pryluck on the ethics of documentary film making. Pryluck comments: "Ultimately, we are all outsiders in the lives of others. We can take our gear and go home; they have to continue their lives where they are."[4] And my own concern, which arose in the context of interviews I conducted with poor women in Brazil, is about developing possible strategies for dealing with the very real material inequalities separating the researcher and the researched. These problems of inequality are, I believe, crucial to feminists or people otherwise committed to changing the distribution of privilege which, among its many other implications, makes "other people" always serve as the subjects of "our" research projects.

But it is quite possible that these research problems can best be approached on a local, individual basis, rather than through global denunciation that, paradoxically, is heard by almost no one. My initial criticism of Spivak's work, then, is not due to disagreement about the important question it raises—which could be extended in the oral history situation and reformulated as: "Whose voice is heard in the resulting texts?" Rather, it is to the label "subaltern" and to the project Spivak undertakes to adduce proof that this "subaltern" indeed cannot speak.

It seems to me that scholars often write from noisy and aggressive senses of "self"—not remotely amenable to the types of assumptions they make about others' words and lives. But, one may ask, do the "subalterns"—a label that, according to the Oxford English Dictionary, means "of inferior status, quality, or importance"—see themselves as nothing but the negative pole of a hierarchy? While I do not doubt that those situated at the other extreme of that hierarchy—the superalterns, let us call them—see those they label "subaltern" in such terms, I wonder how the label comes to be used by intellectuals who claim to seek to change the reality to which it refers. This is not to question the existence of inequality and exploitation in the real world, or of the domination needed to maintain them; it is merely to rephrase in yet another way Spivak's question and ask: Does the subaltern truly exist? And in whose mind? Who uses this label? (Who is in a position to use it?) Who believes the label is "full" of significance and accuracy?

Such terminology—summing up entire lives as nothing but a position in a hierarchy—makes me wonder whether those who use the label believe real human beings (other than "we" intellectuals, of course) exist in the world. Does not the recourse to such hypostatized categories finally and simply set "them" apart from "us" in a way our articles do nothing whatsoever to alter? Why is it so hard for "us" to recognize that other people have lives as meaningful to them, and as narratable, as ours are to us? It strikes me as grotesque to imagine otherwise: It is one more illustration of intellectuals' tendency to empty other people's lives of meaning or content, often in the name of an endless self-examination, a self-examination ennobled by being called "critical" while, as usual, it hogs center stage.

Spivak writes: "If, in the context of colonial production, the subaltern has no history and cannot speak, the subaltern as female is even more deeply in shadow."[5] Does Spivak's second formulation not require that the first statement be true, and the second therefore doubly true? Does this notion of the subaltern's insuperable silence not give intellectuals a stake in believing in the permanent loss of this constituted object (an object of romantic longing and scholarly self-flagellation), the "subaltern," especially the "female subaltern"? Where "subalterns" dare to speak, or are sought out, must their speech be delegitimized by intellectuals committed to the analysis of its nonexistence?

In her article, Spivak criticizes the subaltern studies group for sharing with Western Marxist intellectuals the assumption "that there *is* a pure form of consciousness"[6] (which can then be sought out). Certainly there is a danger, even or especially for feminist researchers, of in effect offering up the people we study (and note how impossible it is to even discuss this subject without replicating an us-versus-them terminology) as Perfect Others. But is there no alternative except either silence or foolish claims that we ("we" intellectuals or researchers working on or with the "subaltern") have touched "their" pure consciousness? Spivak objects to the "privileging of the intellectual" that is concealed, in her view, by Foucault's concern for the politics of the oppressed; she thinks this is what accounts for much of Foucault's appeal,[7] even as she demonstrates this same privileging in her own work. Against Foucault, she sets up (and defends) Derrida, who, though difficult—and here she clearly bashes almost all "first world intellectuals"—"is less dangerous when understood than the first world intellectual masquerading as the absent nonrepresenter who lets the oppressed speak for themselves."[8]

One question Spivak's essay raises, of special concern to feminist researchers, is whether any research posture is possible besides that of dupe or exploiter. Spivak spells out her view in a way that should strike fear and trembling into the heart of any privileged researcher foolish enough to attempt to hear what "subaltern women" have to say: "On the other side of the international division of labor, the subject of exploitation cannot know and speak the text of female exploitation, even if the absurdity of the nonrepresenting intellectual making space for her to speak is achieved. The woman is doubly in shadow."[9] Here Spivak indicates what an authentic content for the shadowy woman's speech would and should be—"the text of female exploitation." Whatever else she might say (and there might be much) is not relevant. Yet Spivak does not call attention to the problem inherent in this very formulation, the problem she is purportedly addressing: of intellectuals and their representation (and demands) of the subaltern.

My concern is that by the very designation of a given group as "subaltern," intellectuals, as usual, decide what kind of speech counts as authentic speech. When Spivak argues that the subaltern cannot speak, she does not move away from the entire scenario she has created to ask about her own role as an intellectual declaring that someone else (an other, an abstraction of third world subalternity) cannot speak. She does not question who, in this picture, has the power to validate or invalidate speech. And what is new about this situation? For to call attention to it (and this Spivak certainly is doing) is not necessarily to question its terms. Are we talking about individuals or groups? People or abstractions? Decisions about research priorities and consequences vary greatly depending upon how we situate ourselves in relation to this question. Furthermore, do "groups" ever speak, or do only individuals speak? If the latter, then the very question with which Spivak titles her article is misconceived. It makes no more sense than asking "does history speak?"

For individuals to speak, someone must be listening, and this complicates the situation considerably, as many of those engaged in oral history and life history work are well aware. Spivak's subaltern who cannot speak is in no sense a living, breathing person, and Spivak herself seems to be speaking entirely on the level of abstraction. But the Brazilian women I interviewed were very much living, breathing, and speaking persons, and their speech is, I believe, much more their own than a creation of mine (I discuss this problem in the introduction to my book), just as Spivak's is her own even as it represents a certain kind of discourse produced in the context of particular intellectual debates in particular parts of the world in our time. To assert that it is indeed some Brazilian women who "speak" in my book is not, however, to deny that their speech emerges through my mediation, and in another language, and even that it is constrained in many ways, or that the very conditions of production of this type of research are problematic.

But, after all that, I must ask: Why would a leftist intellectual seek to prove that any group of people—especially the historically silenced: women—cannot speak? In the name of what sort of knowledge? What program? And what are we to make of the garrulousness of these intellectuals as they go about arguing the impossibility of other people's speech? To refuse to grant that other people can and do speak, that they are not merely researchers' puppets or ideological creations is, I believe, to overvalue the role of the researcher and to undervalue that of the people who make the research possible. Anthropology, as a field, has gone through much the same sorts of shifts over the years, from the assumption of the transparency of the anthropologist (related, indeed, to the development of the "discipline" at the height of nineteenth-century imperialism), to the current overemphasis on the anthropologist as narrator, as intervenor, even as hero, which often threatens to totally efface the purported subjects of the research.

But there are other problems as well. Spivak's analysis "speaks" to a minute number of people, least among these the "subalterns" who are her apparent concern. What does it mean to write in a mode that is inaccessible to virtually everyone (even assuming both literacy and a specific knowledge of English), while appearing to do so as an "internal" critic of left discourses? What does it mean to write in a way that the "subalterns"—whoever they are—could never understand, a way they could not possibly "read"? This mode of writing would tell "them" (if there were genuine people behind this designation) not only that they cannot speak, but also that they cannot read or think.

Feminist research, with its basic tenet of "returning" the research to the people who make it possible, attempts—even if only formally—to start to deal with this problem.

Certainly it is necessary to point out, perhaps especially to feminist researchers, the potential fraudulence of an easy assumption of identity. In her essay "Can There Be a Feminist Ethnography?" Judith Stacey writes of the dangers of feminist researchers' seductiveness toward their research subjects.[10] And Nicole-Claude Mathieu, in her article "'Woman' in Ethnography: The Other of the Other, and the Other of the Self," speaks of the importance of a critical distancing if one is to make visible the routinely invisible constitution of woman as Other.[11] As researchers we do "use" others in our work. And it is important to recognize the real divisions that exist between researchers and researched, especially in cross-cultural situations, and not attempt to gloss over them by, for example, succumbing or resorting to the appeal of "sisterhood," a supposed mystical communion of women as women.

The failure to recognize distance leads to mystification. A clear instance of this, in the North American context, occurs in a recent article by Carole J. Spitzack, "Body Talk: The Politics of Weight Loss and Female Identity." Spitzack's posture toward the subjects of her research can well be called seductive. Using Ann Oakley's work on the importance of nonhierarchical conversations as the proper model for interviewing women, Spitzack explains that she spent considerable time talking with each woman prior to the actual interview: "Before proceeding with the taping, I wanted each woman to understand that she was not simply an exploitable information source, but someone I wished to talk *with* about body experience, a person with whom I would choose to spend some time outside the context of academic research."[12] The obvious problem with this statement is its disingenuousness. Can—and ought—we do research only when we like and "would choose to spend time with" the people we're interviewing? Is it even honest to suggest that all research subjects are potential friends? Or is it a particularly egregious form of manipulation? Spitzack's comment, in its odd parodying of women's traditional nurturing roles, reveals the tyranny of sentiment as a political tool, a very real danger as feminists attempt to devise alternative research practices.

Is there no choice, then, except insuperable distance on the one hand and excesses of identity on the other? In relation to my book on Brazilian women, for example, must I inevitably be charged with minimizing (covering up) the role of first world intellectuals (myself) by insisting, by implication at least, that some of the Brazilian women I interviewed could indeed speak, and that the stories they told me were in the end determined far more by themselves—and these are individual selves, with different stories to tell—than by me? Or must I instead be taken to task for any generalizing statements I might make about the women, which could seem to imply that I view them as an undifferentiated group, the hypostatized third world women of a first world feminist's dominating imagination? Either way I act in bad faith; either way I am vulnerable to charges of mystification, lack of self-awareness, or disingenuousness. Are we, as researchers, doomed to act out of a conviction, stupid or venal, either in our own transparency or in the existence of that Perfect Other known as third world Woman? Or are we doomed, instead, to effacing the very real and specific voices of the women who are willing to speak to us by assenting to Spivak's general argument that the subaltern cannot speak? Is no other situation possible?

Can we not, for example, recognize the limits and imperfections of our research; recognize and attempt to combat our own complicity and privilege, where these in fact exist; recognize (as many oral historians and ethnographers have done for some time now) the complex interactions of research situations involving other human beings, which should always keep us both from taking the stories we gather as simple windows onto the world and also from judging our own role to be that of mere facilitators? And yet, can we not, simultaneously, respect the autonomy, however constrained, of the people who talk with us, respect their interest in their own lives, their belief in their own "selves"—just as we believe in ours, not least those intellectuals who analyze the concept while never for a moment doubting in practice (regardless of their high theoretical pronouncements on the issue) the coherent subject position from which they themselves speak and speak and speak?

My experience in Brazil is that doing research with women is not one thing. It was clear, for example, that the economic position of the women I interviewed had much to do with their access or lack of access even to the time needed to talk with me. But I think they would be astounded by our worries over whether we have heard their voices or our own, and even more astounded at the entire discussion of whether "the subaltern can speak." What strikes me is the gross egocentrism of such a question. In an obvious and clear sense, the women with whom I talked—who would surely have been less inclined to talk with me if they suspected I was approaching them with labels such as "subaltern" in my head—would recognize themselves in the stories that appear in my book (and some of them have indeed commented to me on this). By no means does this imply, to use conventional and suspect terminology, that I have captured the "essence" of their lives (as if there were such a thing) or that they would necessarily agree today with the version of their lives they presented to me several years ago. It means only that each would be able to pick out "her" story from among the twenty in the book. Where they might substantially disagree is in regard to the researcher's interpretation or framing of those stories.

There is no purity or safety in this kind of work, no perfect way to do this sort of research. Oral histories are texts gathered in highly varying conditions at particular points in time and in particular settings, with enormous variation too in the amount of interference on the part of the interviewer and the nature of the interaction. We all know the pitfalls of tightly structured and controlled interviews, and we've become aware, as well, of the problems of even the most conscientiously conducted interview. What I am suggesting is that we recognize, without complacency, the extraordinary imperfections in the work we do and the world in which we do it. If we have feminist commitments, this means especially being attuned to the contradictions between our research practices—which are not only sustained by but too often in turn sustain the world we claim to want to change—and our purported political objectives. But it is a mistake, I believe, to let ourselves by absorbed by these problems.

The current emphasis on the researcher—on the endless question: What are we *really* doing as we do X?—strikes me as part of a new preoccupation with an old subject: ourselves. Just as literary critics today often usurp the pride of place formerly held by creative writers, so researchers, in their rush toward political correctness (which Spivak would call "piety," one of her favorite expressions of opprobrium), are in danger of making their research yet another pretext for their favorite trendy activity: learning about themselves.

The messiness of doing cross-cultural research is no reason to contemplate only ourselves. Ultimately we have to decide whether our research is worth doing or not. Scholarly solipsism is a dead end.

NOTES

This essay originally appeared in *Women and Language* 11:2 (Winter 1988), 23–26.

1. Gayatri Chakravorty Spivak, "Can the Subaltern Speak?" in *Marxism and the Interpretation of Culture*, ed. Cary Nelson and Lawrence Grossberg (Urbana: University of Illinois Press, 1988), 271–313.

2. Spivak, "Can the Subaltern Speak?", 308. Curiously, the story of Bhuvaneswari Bhaduri with which Spivak ends her essay contradicts in a very practical way the conclusion that "the subaltern cannot speak." It may have taken years, but the "speech"

of Bhuvaneswari's suicidal gesture seems to have been heard by Spivak, and, through her discussion of it, is now communicated far beyond its original setting.

3. Daphne Patai, *Brazilian Women Speak: Contemporary Life Stories* (New Brunswick: N.J.: Rutgers University Press, 1988).

4. Calvin Pryluck, "Ultimately We Are All Outsiders: The Ethics of Documentary Filmmaking," *Journal of the University Film Association* 28:1 (Winter 1976), 22. I cite this essay in my article "Ethical Problems of Personal Narratives, or, Who Should Eat the Last Piece of Cake?" *International Journal of Oral History* 8:1 (February 1987), 5–27.

5. Spivak, "Can the Subaltern Speak?", 287.

6. Spivak, "Can the Subaltern Speak?", 286.

7. Spivak, "Can the Subaltern Speak?", 292.

8. Spivak, "Can the Subaltern Speak?", 292.

9. Spivak, "Can the Subaltern Speak?", 288.

10. Judith Stacey, "Can There Be a Feminist Ethnography?" *Women's Studies International Forum* 11:1 (1988), 21–27.

11. Nicole-Claude Mathieu, "'Woman' in Ethnology: The Other of the Other, and the Other of the Self," *Feminist Issues* 8:1 (Spring 1988), 3–14.

12. Carole J. Spitzack, "Body Talk: The Politics of Weight Loss and Female Identity," in *Women Communicating: Studies of Women's Talk*, ed. Barbara Bate and Anita Taylor (Norwood, N.J.: Ablex Publishing Corp., 1988), 54–55. Ann Oakley's essay is "Interviewing Women: A Contradiction in Terms," in *Doing Feminist Research*, ed. Helen Roberts (London: Routledge & Kegan Paul, 1981), 30–61.

8

Sick and Tired of Scholars' Nouveau Solipsism

Astonishing deference is paid these days to the varied gestures of postmodernist self-reflexivity that many scholars include in their work: identifying themselves in terms of immutable traits such as race, ethnicity, or sex; reflecting on what some scholars call their personal "positioning" in politics or culture; discussing the dilemmas they face as researchers; or merely making personal disclosures. Taking account of our own positions and circumstances is a healthy corrective to the old, now much-maligned "positivist" model of a neutral and unbiased researcher reporting on the world. But why is it that we never seem able to correct one extreme without veering to another?

At present, in my view, we are spending too much effort wading in the morass of our own positionings. It's nice to recognize that we ought not hide behind a spurious objectivity, but just how much space should we devote to self-analysis and to the methodological discourse that has sprouted, mushroom-like, around it? When is enough enough?

It wasn't that long ago that the self-critical stance was unpopular in feminist academic circles, where it is now so much the rage. At a conference less than ten years ago, I presented some reflections on the ethical problems that I had faced while interviewing Brazilian women for an oral-history project. At the time, I gained the distinct impression that I was regarded as something of a killjoy for raising uncomfortable and ultimately ambiguous questions concerning the appropriateness of white feminist academics like myself doing research on women of other races, classes, or nationalities: How can one do this kind of cross-cultural research without exploiting others?

As I continued to speak about this subject over the next few years, I kept encountering impatience from some listeners. Most people who came to hear me were interested in learning about my research, not about the problems I had encountered doing it or the anguish those problems had caused me. They could not understand why I was plaguing myself with moral questions.

Over time, I myself got bored with questions that were so much easier to propound than to answer. It is important to keep these ethical questions in mind, but it does no good to let ourselves be paralyzed by them or to turn them into empty rhetorical gestures. I was struck particularly by a comment made by Michael Frisch, a historian at the State University of New York at Buffalo, at a conference a few years ago. Frisch, who has done much to demystify the methodology of oral history, asked whether all our methodological angst was not somehow beside the point.

Urging us to put our own roles in perspective, he recounted his own experience going over tapes of interviews that he had conducted. He noted that often, despite all the roadblocks he inadvertently created, speakers returned to their own themes. They seemed determined to tell him what was important to them and patiently worked their way around the obstacles he set in their path. They typically would answer politely when he derailed them, and then get back to what was really on their minds. Thus, he argued, it is not necessary to flagellate ourselves quite so much over our own roles as interviewers.

I have come to believe he was right: We just aren't *that* important. Yet academics have reached new heights in the self-important pretense that the world's ills can be set right merely by making personal disclosures. They seem to believe that, whenever they write an article in which they sincerely declare their own positions, they are "doing politics." But self-reflexivity does not change reality. It does not redistribute income, gain political rights for the powerless, create housing for the homeless, or improve health.

Feminist scholars, in particular, have jumped with great zeal on the bandwagon of "getting personal." It's as though the centuries in which women were silenced and invisible had produced a drive for self-disclosure that has led, at its best, to new heights of sensitivity and awareness but, at its worst, to new depths of "me, me, me!" Is wearing one's identity and experience on one's sleeve a token of shame and repentance? A badge of pride? A display of admirable forthrightness? It is all these, and more.

Are we really expected to take seriously—and read "generously"—the anthropologist Ruth Behar's claim that her struggles to get tenure at an American university should be seen as parallel to the struggles of Esperanza, a Mexican street peddler?[1] Or, to take a different type of example of telling or claiming too much, do readers really benefit from the feminist scholar Nancy K. Miller's description of her father's penis, to which she devotes the closing chapter of her book *Getting Personal*?[2] While I admire much in the work of these scholars, such personal reflections add little to it.

Doris Lessing addressed the issue of the futile attempt to capture reality through minute, and usually suppressed, detail years ago in *The Golden Notebook*. What Lessing's character discovered, of course, was that a precise account of her day in no sense helped her get closer to her goal of reproducing on paper the sense of a life, or even just one day in a life. Many feminists might reply by citing the favored slogan "the personal is political." They argue that making public the long-neglected personal stories of women disrupts the traditional version of masculine culture and challenges the conventional boundaries between public and private life. But this phrase has been reduced to near meaninglessness through sheer overextension.

Feminists have been in the vanguard in the battle against the notion that anyone can "speak for" another, arguing that, just as men cannot speak for women, one group of women cannot speak for another. But the other side of this constructive awareness has been a tendency toward a cacophony of competing particularisms. You now have to display that you are a member of Group X in order to write about the group. As a result, self-reflexivity is constantly contaminated by identity politics. Too often, what might have been a serious and informative reflection on oneself turns into a weapon of aggression: The verbal gesture of speaking as a member of a group establishes a scholar as an authority on the group in question and discredits others who are not members.

Such rhetorical weapons have been used particularly against white feminists. On the one hand, white feminists are portrayed by critics as the epitome of privilege (never mind that many white women too have struggled to get an education and to gain entry into professions). On the other hand, a few turns of the screw later, because many white academic feminists have accepted the fact that they cannot speak for non-white women, other scholars now complain that white feminists ignore the problems and oppression that women of color experience. In other words, damned if you do concern yourself with issues and groups beyond your immediate ken, damned if you don't.

The new vogue for autobiographical writing may appeal to many scholars as a way to perform the balancing act required to avoid academic sniping. Such writing is relatively safe, at a time when precious few things are. Writing about yourself insures that no one can dispute your authority, even if it means an enormous reduction in the scope of issues about which you can do research and write.

But the logical extension of the current academic fascination with self-reflexivity is, unfortunately, that you can never tell *enough*, never take full enough account of your position and identity in a work otherwise devoted to issues beyond your personal experience. A few prefatory words of self-identification (naturally touching the key bases of race, gender, ethnicity, class, sexual orientation) can be seen as skimpy.

Will longer passages of identification, then, do the trick? Perhaps, in the end, an entire preliminary autobiography will become *de rigueur*, so that all one's biases and predilections and positionings are made clear to the unwary reader who picks up someone's scholarly work. And of course, that reader will need to remember that all this personal honesty may itself be a ruse, an instance of the famous "inoculation" technique, as Roland Barthes called it, in which a small dose of truth inoculates against a larger lie.

Or should we insist on a truth-in-scholarship bill and print warnings on every book, even find a way to prevent people from reading the scholarly work unless they have first read the autobiography—and, of course, its accompanying disclaimers? But what will be the point of trying to reveal our personal truths when literary critics tell us these days that every autobiography is also a work of fiction?

I doubt that I am the only one who is weary of the nouveau solipsism—all this individual and collective breast-beating, grandstanding, and plain old egocentricity. Where does it all leave us? With nothing more than a shared awareness that scholarly works do not descend from heaven but are written by human beings—and that every human being's arguments and evidence must be carefully evaluated using some agreed-upon procedures that distinguish facts from interpretations, sound arguments from hollow claims, hyperbole from straight talk.

Funny, I seem to recall that this is what scholarship was supposed to be about. Never mind. Let us adopt the admirable dictum "begin where you are." Thus, if we are scholars, let us acknowledge that we have learned a little something from the sensitivity training, guilt tripping, and self-reflexivity of the past few decades—and get on with our work. The last time I looked, there still *was* a world out there.

NOTES

First published in *The Chronicle of Higher Education*, February 23, 1994, A52.

   1. Ruth Behar, *Translated Woman: Crossing the Border with Esperanza's Story* (Boston: Beacon Press, 1993).
   2. Nancy K. Miller, *Getting Personal* (New York and London: Routledge, 1991).

9

Feminism and the Future

Every time I publicly make criticisms of feminism—especially its academic wing, which is women's studies—the very first rejoinder from feminists in the audience is that I've grossly misrepresented a complex situation, that there is no such thing as "feminism," only "feminisms," in the plural, representing many different positions, all of these positions testifying to the diversity and health of the umbrella concept, feminism. I am also accused of mean-spiritedly focusing on problems—as if it were possible for a social movement that hopes to succeed (at least, through democratic means) to avoid internal criticism. And that—my representation of myself as an "internal" critic of feminism—is also typically challenged as I am recast, instead, as an enemy. So, I want first of all to clarify why and how I've become a critic of what is being done in the name of feminism today, above all in academic circles. And let me begin with an affirmation:

No person with the slightest regard for historical accuracy would argue that feminism has not helped women in important ways. It was feminist impulses—however loosely defined as the desire to extend women's rights and participation in the public sphere—that energized the first-wave suffrage movement. It was feminism that encouraged a reconsideration of women's domestic and professional roles. It is feminism that urges women to take their lives seriously, to not look to men for personal salvation, to become active agents in what Charlotte Perkins Gilman called "the world's work," and to cease, again in Gilman's terms, to be "sexual specialists."

Why, then, do I take issue with what feminism in our time has become? My answer is this: I take issue with feminism because almost everywhere that one sees positive efforts, one also hears the language of hate, recrimination, gross generalization, and attacks upon other human groups—in

other words, attacks upon persons rather than principles or practices. I did
not always pay much attention to this. Like other feminists, for a long time
I was absorbed by what I saw to be the positive project of social transformation that feminism had tackled. Let me quote from an essay of mine
published nearly fifteen years ago.

I wrote, "Feminism, today, is the most utopian project around. That is, it
demands the most radical and truly revolutionary transformation of society, and it is going on in an extraordinary variety of ways."[1] I wrote that line
in the early 1980s, full of hope, energized by the rapid growth of women's
studies programs in the United States (one of the great success stories—so
it would seem—of second-wave feminism). My words expressed the belief
I then held that feminism's enormous reach made it the proper fulfillment
of generations of utopian aspirations.

At the time I had had no experience with women's studies programs, but
I had been writing about utopian fiction from a feminist perspective since
my graduate school days in the early 1970s. As a teacher, I initially saw no
problem with the ubiquitous slogan "women's studies is the academic arm
of feminism." In fact, I found it exhilarating and inspiring. But that was before I spent a dozen years involved with women's studies, nearly ten of
those years with a joint appointment in women's studies and Spanish and
Portuguese, at the University of Massachusetts at Amherst. Now that I am
once again out of women's studies and can look back upon the experiences
that made me want to sever my connections with it, I am shocked that I, a
student of utopian literature, could have ever forgotten how routinely
utopian dreams turn into dystopian nightmares and could have failed to
foresee the enormous cost of attempting to institutionalize a politicized
form of education in American universities. Sadly, I now realize, feminism
is no different from other grand totalizing schemes that are far more problematic in the implementation than in the imagining.

In late 1994, together with Noretta Koertge, a philosopher of science at Indiana University in Bloomington, I published a book entitled *Professing Feminism: Cautionary Tales from the Strange World of Women's Studies.* This book
details our critique of how badly awry feminism has gone in the academy. It
was a painful book for us to contemplate, and we put off the writing of it for
a long time. We first talked about such a project in the mid-1980s. In other
words, even in my early years in women's studies, I saw grave problems with
it. But for years the project remained just that: talk. Neither Noretta nor I initially had the stomach to face up to the full consequences of the critique we
found ourselves making in private and to one another as we discovered that,
coming from very different parts of the country and of academe, we had observed strikingly similar practices among feminists. But as we became increasingly sensitive to—and incensed by—proliferating instances of intoler-

ance, orthodoxy-sniffing, and general bad-mouthing of other women as not-good-enough feminists, not-the-right-kind-of-feminists, or lacking the right credentials of race or class or sexual orientation—we realized that it was feminists themselves, not opponents of feminism, who needed to speak out about all this and to do it without further delay.

We knew, of course, that the book was likely to cause us to be viewed as "enemies," especially by feminists in the academy—the very people we were hoping to reach. Susan Faludi's best-seller *Backlash* was providing a handy tag for dismissing any and every criticism of feminism, no matter how justified. But even before the vocabulary of *Backlash* became current, we had observed feminist double standards at work, such as proclaiming the authority of my experience, while denouncing the authority of yours; or asserting that my personal is political, while yours is delusional. The belligerent and intolerant self-promotion within contemporary feminism, allied to its anti-intellectualism, struck us as depressingly similar to traits we disliked in society at large, and on reflection we came to see that feminism has behaved like other political movements and special interests. It pursues a the-worse-the-better strategy, barely acknowledging women's considerable progress in the past few decades or even denying it altogether. It exaggerates to the point of absurdity the awfulness of men. And it enthusiastically indulges in the practice of "concept stretching" until terms such as rape or sexual harassment lose all definition and become mere signifiers of original patriarchal sin. The quite dreadful consequences of this last-mentioned habit—as manifest in legal transformations and destroyed lives—is beyond the scope of my talk here today.

Judging from our own observations and from the stories my coauthor and I heard from other disillusioned feminist faculty and students, we felt compelled to conclude that the propagandizing and scare tactics common in many women's studies classrooms have nothing to do with "education" in any meaningful academic sense. What students learn is that blame and accusation, self-righteousness and personal confrontations, so-called "political" criteria for deciding among different knowledge claims, and recrimination for "enemies" and pop-therapeutic group support for friends are habits prized and flaunted in the name of feminism. What students tend not to learn is that sound and unsound reasoning must be differentiated and that methods exist and can be taught for doing so. Asking of a pair of propositions, "which is the more 'feminist' of the two?" is, as it turns out, not a good guide to that differentiation.

In an effort to make our case as vividly as possible, but also to keep our spirits up, my coauthor and I presented the major excesses disfiguring many women's studies programs as a series of games. Games, of course, are utterly serious activities for those who play them. In a postmodernist age, every game within women's studies begins, naturally enough, with the very language in which the rules are laid down. WORDMAGIC—as we call women's studies' way with language—is always apt eventually to lead to the demand for censorship—which, if heeded, would make of the United States the first modern democratic country to do voluntarily what until now only dictatorships have done effectively. And why should it surprise any of us, by now, to see feminists indeed support demands for censorship in the name of making the world more "comfortable" for women?

But in writing our book, our main focus was on some of the more immediate threats to intellectual work now posed in the name of feminism. One of these is the game of TOTAL REJ, as we called it—rejecting everything tainted by masculinism. TOTAL REJ is often justified as "throwing away the master's tools," which may sound appealing when first encountered. But it has become abundantly clear by now that this attitude leads to the cultivation of ignorance, resulting, for example, in student papers crediting contemporary feminist novelists with a born-yesterday originality that fragments time, space, and character, and (so students confidently assert) sets women's writing apart from the "linear" narratives of males.

We give many examples of TOTAL REJ in our book, which range from students refusing to read male authors, to a student in a history class turning in a paper, ostensibly on Freud, containing the one liner: "Freud was a cancer-ridden cigar-smoking misogynist." The impact of TOTAL REJ on feminist attitudes toward science was of special concern to my coauthor, whose field is the philosophy of science. She once offered a women's studies course on feminism and science and discovered during the first class that almost all the women's studies students who signed up for it had no knowledge of science, hated it, and were enrolled in the course in order to get validation for the notion that they need learn nothing about it. She never offered that course again. For years it was distressing to me that life had come to imitate art: I had read dystopian satires of feminist societies run by know-nothing petty tyrants, and I took these, originally, as nasty misogynistic works. Imagine the shock of realizing that supposedly serious feminist writers often wrote in a very similar vein.

TOTAL REJ also promotes the game of BIODENIAL, an extreme form of social constructionism often espoused in women's studies programs. Defenders are quick to retort that since there is still much essentialism in feminist thought today, the charge of BIODENIAL must be false. But, as we point out in *Professing Feminism*, women's studies seems to have little trouble opportunistically switching from one order of explanation to the other. I have repeatedly heard students argue that everything that might be criticized in women is due to social construction while everything they admire is a mark of women's inherent nature. Men, of course, get the opposite treatment.

Another of the games that my coauthor and I discuss in our book is one we call GENDERAGENDA. It enables feminists who play it to reduce any and every question to gender, allowing them, for example, not only to criticize the traditional exclusion of women from science, but also to indict the scientific method itself as inherently masculine and thus inimical to women. But I sometimes wonder if the whole point of the feminist attack on male science and knowledge isn't precisely to allow feminists to say whatever they like, without being held to any standard of logic, thoughtfulness, or intellectual rigor—all of which, of course, can be (and have been!) readily dismissed as "masculinist."

The most pernicious game of all, however, the one that has contributed most to the unpleasant atmosphere found in many feminist circles—though not only in feminist circles, as you will all recognize—is one we call IDPOL. IDPOL is a particularly apt abbreviation because it can stand for both "identity politics" and "ideological policing." An example from my own local scene illustrates how it works in these two ways. I live in Amherst, Massachusetts, which is part of a very lively academic community that, within a ten-mile radius, comprises the University of Massachusetts and four private colleges: Amherst, Hampshire, Smith, and Mount Holyoke. A few years ago, feminist faculty from all five campuses met to discuss the possibility of establishing a five-college graduate program in women's studies. The minutes of this meeting record the request, made by an African-American faculty member, "that the white women present answer the question of what [they] personally were doing to dismantle [the] racial privilege in [their] outlook, teaching and research in Women's Studies." IDPOL thus serves some as a badge and bludgeon while serving others as an occasion to indulge feelings of guilt and shame. I have observed such tactics repeatedly used over the years and only rarely have I seen them challenged.

Some may say that my example is merely one more anecdote and has no general validity. And indeed that has been a main line of defense against the portrait of women's studies my coauthor and I present in our book. All over the United States, women are no doubt declaring that, in their programs, no such problems exist. It would, in fact, be of immense value to have a comprehensive empirical analysis made of women's studies programs. But given the disparagement of quantitative methods as "masculinist," notorious in feminist circles (whenever, that is, it suits immediate feminist purposes), and in light of their hostility to serious discussion of problems in women's studies, few programs would be likely to participate forthrightly in an appraisal of their activities and practices. Moreover, such an appraisal would be worth little if a program's success or failure were measured by internal feminist criteria, for these are quite unlike the indices of evaluation adopted elsewhere in the university.

But there is another way of getting a portrait of women's studies—and that is by its advocates themselves.

In *Professing Feminism* we analyzed some well-known writings produced by supporters of women's studies programs, writings that provide confirmation of the personal testimony we cite in our book. What these texts demonstrate is that the flaws criticized by us, and the virtues applauded by True Believers, are often the very same things.

A review of *Professing Feminism* underscored this point. The feminist scholar Carol Sternhell, writing in *The Women's Review of Books*, noted the congruence between our book and another volume published at about the same time (*The Feminist Classroom*), which dismayed her even more than ours because of its heady celebration of a feminist pedagogy all but devoid of intellectual substance. Sternhell tried to distance herself from both books by assuring her readers that none of these things went on at her university and that her faith in women's studies continued unabated.[2] What she revealed about the two books is very significant. It is that we, the critics, on the one hand, and the celebrants, on the other, write about the very same phenomena, though viewing them from different vantage points. Where many women's studies faculty see "politics" as what should be going on in institutions of higher learning, we see it as a danger to the process of learning itself. Where they see identity politics—IDPOL—as an appropriate corrective of, and atonement for, past discrimination, we see it as the seed of ever more conflicts since no one has an unassailable "identity." Where they see the therapeutic and supposedly "safe" classroom as a high achievement of feminist pedagogy, we see it as a mark of a debased education and note that only some people—those with "proper" feminist ideas, are in fact "safe" in these settings.

We said all this in our book, but most critics seem not to have noticed. We used documents emanating from women's studies itself to prove our point, but still our work got dismissed as "anecdotal" and unrepresentative. Nor have our critics commented on our documentation of women's studies' habit of carefully screening courses proposed for cross-listing, a habit prompted by the desire to ensure the ideological suitability of both course contents and instructors. On this point too our arguments continue to receive up-to-the-minute confirmation: In a posting a year or two ago on the women's studies e-mail list (WMST-L), a professor took the familiar line that it is not enough for a course to be "on women"; it must also incorporate a feminist perspective. At her school, a course on the psychology of women was not cross-listed because its instructor stated that she was not a feminist. The same e-mail message also had troubling things to say about the limited roles men might safely be allowed to play in women's studies. Indeed, there is considerable evidence that many feminist faculty count such restrictions a credit to their programs.

Nowhere in feminist rhetoric, incidentally, is there the slightest concern about making the classroom a "safe" place for male students. Instead, any and every challenge that a man might pose inspires IDPOL attacks. Consider this lengthy example (from our book), which illustrates how one male student's frank (and articulate) reports on his reading brought down the wrath of the graduate students who were team-teaching the course. We begin with the student's remarks on a reading assignment, followed by glosses by one or both instructors:

Student Comment #1:

I am dominant but I am not racist. This article denies that it is possible for me to overcome the prejudice with which I was programmed. This is why the Left is failing: because it reduces all of its subjects to simpering essentialist categories and fails to acknowledge that anyone—yes, even those nasty Anglos— can rise above their cultural morass and effectively reprogram themselves. I really resented this pandering, whiny article: it's Anglo angst in rare form.

Instructor:

How can you help but be—when you benefit and receive privileges from this racism? Your defensiveness has prevented you from understanding this article. One of the first signals to me that I have met a racist is when they insist that they are not.

Student Comment #2:

In this article, bell hooks once again proves her worth to the Black community and to the women's community.

Instructor:

Ugh! What a limitation on her contributions! Again, she is reduced to her race and gender. What a fine example of racism and sexism.

Student Comment #3:

To say that all one needs is to be good intentioned is, I think, ridiculous and harmful. Everyone needs to have some sort of theoretical basis from which their action springs, not just a visceral one.

Instructor:

Is this not reductionism at its finest and most limiting? Over time we have found that social change has occurred as a result of direct action resulting from emotional strength and courage. Often the theory comes afterward or gets in the way.

Second Instructor:

Yes—A very European-male opinion.

Finally, one instructor, reflecting the anti-intellectualism of much feminist pedagogy, commented on the student's reports as a whole:

> Again you have effectively avoided demonstrating any personal awareness or at least strategies for personal action. I can acknowledge your need to make sense of such a complex "paradigm"—but I have yet to see that you actually can make sense of it at a personal level. I'm sadly disappointed by your self-protected intellectualizations. I've met far too many white men who bend over backwards to protect their own racism and white supremacy and frankly I'm utterly bored.[3]

Imagine if women had been subjected to such comments by male instructors. I doubt they—the males—would still have jobs.

The breakdown of a working consensus about the importance of academic achievement is most notable in the classroom, where those professing feminism act out commitments to dismantle social hierarchies. Not surprisingly, feminist pedagogy encourages faculty to abdicate a "superior" role—though, as the example just quoted shows, only when it suits them. In the feminist classroom, some professors let undirected discussion go on for an entire semester (which certainly saves the professor much preparation time!). Even when feminist professors do not go to such extremes, many seem embarrassed at the thought that they have more knowledge than their students. They may work hard to disguise this fact, one technique for doing so being the affirmation that their students' experience is as valuable a form of knowledge as the intellectual training and specialized learning the professor has painstakingly acquired and is presumably being paid for. Such abdication of expertise, with its concomitant dissolution of identities and roles is, of course, connected to feminism's quite explicit assault not only on hierarchies generally, but also on the boundaries between the public and private spheres.

A posting on the WMST-L conveys the lengths to which some feminists in academe will go. In the course of a discussion of "intellectuals and elitism," a professor of philosophy saw fit to declare: "I have eliminated the term 'intellectual' from my vocabulary because it seems to me to suggest that some women are (not just different from others in a particular way but) superior to others." She went on to say: "To speak of intellectuals, I believe, tends to exclude and depreciate some women, to foster envy and competition, and to encourage conventional achievement within the mainstream." Such sentiments make it hard to imagine how she can in good conscience keep drawing a salary at a university.

In *Professing Feminism*, we commented on the problems created in women's studies programs by such efforts at "leveling," which display profound ignorance of the outcomes of some of the more damaging social and political experiments of the twentieth century. Feminists, above all, if they are serious about what they say, should be aware of the experiences of reforms and reformers in the past. But their passion for TOTAL REJ helps them economize on their efforts to inform themselves.

While denying the pervasiveness of feminism's own problems, women's studies advocates continue to tell us about the "chilly climate" alleged to exist for girls and women in North American schools. There's a slight hitch, however. Given the extraordinary successes of women in the past few decades, these advocates are being forced to scrape the bottom of the barrel for their evidence. Which is precisely what is done in the new report by the National Association for Women in Education (the same group that produced the 1982 report "The Classroom Climate: A Chilly One for Women?"). This new report finds evidence of women's continuing problems in academe in such subtle inequities as the supposed fact that professors "frown" more at female students than at males![4] Feminists apparently have no problem spotting the mote in someone else's eye.

But can feminists afford to keep denying and trivializing the problems within feminism instead of admitting and confronting them? Is—for example—the avoidance of women's studies by so many women professors on college faculties—not to mention the vast majority of women students—merely the result of "backlash"? I don't believe so. I think feminists are burying their heads in the sand. It is far easier to pretend that every failure is the result of a hostile outer world, one more instance of "backlash," than it is to attempt to fairly take account of what is actually going on.

When feminist faculty who have devoted years to women's studies are sufficiently discouraged to want to take "inner flight" or move full-time to other departments (as I and some of the women I interviewed have done); when programs are in danger of collapse not from outside attack or lack of support, as feminist faculty typically pretend, but rather from internal dissension and more-feminist-than-thou bickering; when proper search procedures are subverted (as I have repeatedly seen done) in the name of feminism; when normal academic critiques of a candidate's scholarship invariably lead to reductionist attacks by feminists on the very notion of scholarship and scholarly achievement; when programs and individuals committed to maintaining high intellectual standards are denounced as "elitist" or "careerist" (and all these are practices I have witnessed), we are clearly in trouble.

When feminist students hand in doctrinaire manifestos (as many feminist faculty report—though some seem to approve the practice)—repeating patently false or simple-minded assertions, utterly confident that they arise from fundamental feminist truths; when, for example, they insist that we live in a society in which women have no rights and are "forced" by men to conceive and bear children; when they affirm that nothing has really changed for the better in the last hundred or two hundred or three hundred years; when they announce that childbirth would be painless were it not for patriarchy, and that infant mortality was low before "men medicalized childbirth" (and all these are assertions made in my classes by women's studies majors in the past few years), it is clear that what they have picked up from their mentors is not education but indoctrination. When they are quick to point out which oppressed group is underrepresented on the syllabus of their imperfectly feminist professor; when they indulge in breast-beating over their own "white privilege" or in name-calling over the privilege they detect in others; when they readily believe the wildest statistics (like the graffiti on the toilet stall in the corridor outside my classroom saying that one out of two women will be raped in her lifetime) and show themselves incapable of establishing facts and exercising independent judgment on them; when any criticism of feminism is rejected outright as "backlash," how can I fail to conclude that feminism has lost its way? How can I notice that what is happening now in academe, which should have been one of feminism's most promising testing grounds, hardly gives cause for optimism?

When students with no knowledge of either geography or history parrot the current insistence on a "multicultural" perspective in their feminism while rarely bothering to learn a foreign language; when their curiosity about foreign cultures is satisfied by a course on "indigenous women in resistance" or other grab-bag courses about oppressed women from diverse parts of the world, about which the professor too usually has little knowledge, and all these heroic and victimized women become an indistinguishable mass; when to the students, Brazil and Bolivia are all the same—and they can't quite remember what country the inspiring third world feminist autobiography they're reading comes from (these too are real examples); when students are hostile to theory because it's "abstract" and not "political" enough; when they want their lives to be a seamless and coherent demonstration of their proper Feminist Consciousness; when they know the answers without even hearing the questions; when all these things go on in the name of "feminism," it is clear that students have absorbed attitudes and learned phrases, but have not developed the ability—because it is not demanded of them—to analyze what they think and say.

In my years in women's studies, I saw little ability on the part of feminists to work together; I saw women eager to claim the accolade of "activists" for themselves and putting down a colleague's work as "not real activism" the minute she left the room. I saw and heard a colleague criticized for wearing make-up—as if this were the definitive proof that she wasn't a "real" feminist—and saw another colleague ridiculed for going home to cook dinner for her family. I saw colleagues (myself among them) attacked for being racist whenever a decision did not go the way the most vocal women of color thought it should. I saw proper search procedures contravened and candidates who were not of the right activist mould grilled on their "politics." Everywhere I turned I saw identity politics taking over the program and pseudo-political rhetoric driving out serious educational efforts.

What I did not see was a group of women working together with mutual respect for their differences, with support, with generosity—though these are all the standard talk of feminism. And in particular I saw no tolerance for "differences." Where differences did exist, they tended to never get beyond competition for most-oppressed status; self-righteous stances came into play and the group as a whole divided between brow-beating and appeasing gestures, according to who claimed what identity and how aggressively.

In making criticisms of feminism, let me add that I do not want to see my comments used to defend a reactionary politics that I in no way support. But feminism has laid itself wide open to attack by its own exaggerations, its uncritical acceptance of the wildest statistics, its disdain for high standards of scholarship and logic, its double standards, and its petty and vindictive antagonism to men and to non-feminist women. In all this, feminism has been energetic but often unwise; it has been disdainful of the large numbers of women who might be very responsive to a movement that aimed to improve their lot while still respecting their choices—even the choice to have a traditional family life. And it has grossly caricatured men so that those male supporters who can stomach it are pushed into a posture of groveling assent—and even then feminists often snicker behind their backs.

By setting itself up as a movement of True Believers who have the right answers to everything—and quite regardless of the existence of debates within feminism—feminism has on the whole cut itself off from the large following it actually needs if it is to succeed as a mass movement. And why? Apparently (judging at least by what I've observed in academe) because there is some weird satisfaction in playing the eternal victim and feeling like one is part of the heroic few who have the truth, who are confident of their own superiority and righteousness and in fact find confirmation of that stance precisely in the distance between them and other people, mere mortals.

As for the university, and the objectionable practices of women's studies programs, I am convinced that the key problem is that feminists have undertaken to turn the academy into a political staging ground. The usual facile retort is that "education is always political"; but this is a disingenuous response. Intended to shut down discussion, this argument tries to ward off the all-important questions: Political in what way? With what aims? Leading to what results? At what cost? Bearing what relationship to other historical efforts to use education for purposes of indoctrination?

Of course, feminists today claim they lack the power to impose their vision on a society they still characterize as unremittingly patriarchal. But in certain areas—such as extending discussion of sexual harassment down through the school system into the playground—they have been remarkably successful. This is why I think what is needed now is vocal challenge to many feminist shibboleths and careful analyses of feminist claims. I am attempting to do this in two ways. One is through the project, mentioned earlier, on sexual harassment on campus. Using the model provided by sociologist Joel Best to study the creation of child abuse as a major social issue, I am analyzing what I call the "sexual harassment industry," which I believe is dangerously redefining social relationships in America. And that redefinition I see as part of a still larger project, which I characterize by the term "heterophobia"—fear of and antagonism toward the Other, that is, specifically toward men's difference from women.[5] I should make it clear that I am not blaming lesbian activists for this state of affairs; though there are famous and highly visible lesbian feminists on the cultural scene today. The suspicion of heterosexuality, and the antagonism toward it, could not have become an important factor without the acquiescence of great numbers of heterosexual women. At least in feminist circles, the apologetic heterosexual woman is a familiar figure.

It has been interesting for me to get feminist reactions to this heterophobia project from the women's studies e-mail list. When I first posted a brief announcement of this project, I got about a hundred denunciatory messages. Most intriguing, though, was that some people wrote that men deserved women's anger and hatred, while others wrote that women had no such attitudes toward men and that I was inventing it all. I also received many personal attacks, revealing an odd fantasy: that I was going to become rich and famous by criticizing feminism, and that feminist writers had no such access to the press or the best seller lists.

What this taught me is that over the past few years, feminists have managed not to hear what any critics say; many still pretend that women's studies programs are an endangered species and feminists a beleaguered group (quite absurd characterizations). This in turn leads to a trench warfare mentality with clearly demarcated zones for enemies and for friends. I find it ironic that contemporary feminism has taken such illiberal turns, since it is precisely the liberal values of tolerance and amenability to new ideas, including self-critical ones, that allowed feminism to gain a foothold in academe in the first place. Of course feminism is not unique in this respect. Still, I hold it to high standards, and I take seriously its claims to be paving the way for a better future. And by those very standards, it is surely to be found wanting.

Feminists should remember the categorical imperative and ought not to claim privileges in the university that they would in no way be willing to allow to other political groups. How many feminists would support a Christian studies program that advocated, rather than analyzed, fundamentalist religion? It is fatuous to argue that feminist politics alone deserve representation in academic forums (presumably because it is feminists alone who possess The Truth), yet many feminists—for whom women's studies programs are programs of feminist activism—hold precisely this view. A feminism pious and narrow, scornful and smug, dismissive of the past and derisive of those who dare to disagree—this is, I submit, not a feminism with a future.

NOTES

This essay was first presented as a talk at the Minnesota Association of Scholars annual meeting and banquet, University of Minnesota, May 8, 1997. Some sections first appeared in my article "What's Wrong With Women's Studies?" *Academe* (July-August 1995), 30-35. Reprinted with permission from the July/August 1995 issue of *Academe*, the magazine of the American Association of University Professors.

1. "Beyond Defensiveness: Feminist Research Strategies," *Women's Studies International Forum* 6:2 (1983), 177–189. The citation appears on page 179. The essay is reprinted in M. Barr and N. D. Smith, eds., *Women and Utopia: Critical Interpretations* (Lanham, Md.: University Press of America, 1984) and in R. L. Dudovitz, ed., *Women in Academe.* (Oxford: Pergamon, 1984).

2. Carol Sternhell, "The Proper Study of Womankind," *The Women's Review of Books*, December 1994, 1, 3-4.

3. Copies given to DP; emphases in original.

4. *The Chronicle of Higher Education*, March 1, 1996, A38.

5. The project was published as *Heterophobia: Sexual Harassment and the Future of Feminism* (Lanham, Md.: Rowman & Littlefield, 1998). Parts of this project appear as chapters 13 and 14 in this volume; chapter 17 in this volume is a more recent (2003) discussion of this theme.

10

Domesticating Tranquility

Carolyn Graglia's book *Domestic Tranquility* is, as its subtitle states, a brief against feminism.[1] That subtitle shows her lingering attachment to her original career, the law. The book is impressive in its energetic denunciation of feminist rhetoric and policy. Much of what Graglia writes about the excesses of feminism I agree with. And certainly she is correct in depicting the changes brought about in the last few decades as involving the "status degradation" of the housewife.

But Graglia's fundamental message seems to me an impossible one. I do not believe that women's ability to mother is destroyed by "too much emphasis on intellect."[2] In fact, Graglia in this and many other ways shares the ideas of some cultural feminists who seem to believe in an essential feminine way of being and want to see it elevated beyond all else. This is remarkably similar to the old idea that education would harm women's reproductive capacities by giving them a "wandering womb." It is astonishing to hear such notions espoused by a modern woman who did have a choice and who made it. Like the feminists she deplores, Graglia seems to want to keep other women from having such options. Her book was apparently written, relying heavily on her own case as exemplary, to convince other women and society at large that domestic life is the best life for a woman and to see social rules and laws implemented (or abolished, e.g.: of no-fault divorce) that will reinforce such a view. But we cannot turn the clock back; we cannot go back to "traditional families"—not, I think, for ideological reasons but because the world we live in today is a very different one than the world that encouraged the separate spheres Graglia celebrates. And that brings me to the first problem I see with Graglia's argument. It is fundamentally ahistorical.

97

Graglia seems to be denying both the character of the past and the character of our present society which, quite apart from feminist-inspired changes, is profoundly unlike what it was in, say, 1900. She avoids admitting that in the past women have indeed suffered from oppression, restricted opportunity, lack of political rights, and economic dependency on men. To Graglia economic dependency—to stick with the issue most crucial to her argument about male and female separate spheres—is not a problem but a fair deal, agreed to by two equally mature people following the dictates of their male and female natures. She uses her own generation and her own experience as a starting point, with some references to slightly earlier times. Does she really think there was no problem in women's lack of civic rights in the past? Is she unaware that women—even in the twentieth century in our country—have been told that a college education was wasted on them? Is the high illiteracy rate of women around the world today fine with Graglia? Is the extreme poverty of women without access to birth control of no concern to her? Or the sexual repression of women? Or the high infant mortality rate? Not to mention the high maternal mortality rate in some very traditional cultures that have resisted modernization? Is she really comfortable sharing the anti-Western bias I encounter all the time in a university world that, under the guise of "multiculturalism," in fact attacks the west? How does she feel about the Taliban's restriction of women's activities, which includes prohibiting a woman from standing in a window where, from the street, a man's view of her silhouette might inflame his passion? In that culture, the solution is for women not to be allowed to stand near windows that aren't heavily covered. Surely the difficult lives of all these women aren't due to feminism's misguided ideas but to traditional ideas that are, in fact, harmful to women and that sacrifice their interests to those of men.

So, strictly from a historical perspective, one can take issue with Graglia's representation of "traditional life" as necessarily a happy and complementary sharing of male and female spheres. I would suggest that her apparently happy marriage is not an appropriate basis for generalization.

A second problem I see is the hardly veiled condescension toward men in what Graglia writes. She speaks of "mastering a man"[3] and of what "we"— all of us women, I gather—supposedly want and know. The notion of "womb envy" goes back at least to Karen Horney's work in the twenties— and probably existed long before, though without a psychological label. I don't doubt that there's something to it. But Graglia's support is not merely for the important work women do as bearers of children; it is quite explicitly for the distinct roles embraced by the "traditional family." I would like to suggest that women and men may have distinct roles, at some points in their joint lives or perhaps throughout them, but that hardly means we can or should desire a return to the traditional family. One may *do* traditional things today, but that does not make one a traditional woman. Traditional women did not have Graglia's education and law career and certainly didn't have the choice of returning to domestic life, simply because they rarely had any other life available to them until modernization enabled the household economy to be replaced by a wage-earning husband and a stay-at-home wife.

Let me take an example from the work of a writer who, like Graglia, supported the traditional family with its clearly divided roles. Consider the family described by George Orwell in his 1939 novel *Coming Up for Air*. Yet even Orwell, ever nostalgic for the traditional domestic life of the lower-middle class before the First World War, described it in his novel in highly ambiguous terms. It was a way of life in which the mother rolled pastry as if celebrating a sacred rite—which in fact it was, George Bowling, the narrator of Orwell's novel, tells us. For in her kitchen she was in a world that she really understood. He says, "I doubt whether any time up to the outbreak of the Great War she could have told you who was Prime Minister. Moreover, she hadn't the smallest wish to know such things." George Bowling's mother, furthermore, is described as having tried to prohibit and control everything her sons and husband wanted to do. She lived in a female world of taboos, fears, and restrictions. And for all his idealization of this world, Orwell can only describe it with great distance and condescension: "The old English order of life couldn't change. For ever and ever decent God-fearing women would cook Yorkshire pudding and apple dumplings on enormous coal ranges, wear woolen underclothes and sleep on feathers, make plum jam in July . . . with the flies buzzing round, in a sort of cosy little underworld of stewed tea, bad legs, and happy endings."

This seems a far cry from the upper-middle-class life Graglia takes as the norm. Her comment that, in the United States, families claiming to need a second income in fact don't dream of depriving themselves of VCRs, color TVs, and other such goodies reminds me of similar criticisms made by well-off people of slum-dwellers in Brazil: They had color TVs! Evidence of their incompetence in deciding what is important. Yet the people making these criticisms invariably have such consumer items themselves, and it's only *other* people who are supposed to forego them for the sake of the exemplary life their betters sketch out for them.

In fact, people who study in developing countries tell us that the single most important correlate of a declining birth rate is education for women. And that education, available in this country on a mass scale throughout this century, in conjunction with the advent of reliable birth control, has created a situation in which women's "delight in their fertility,"[4] as Graglia puts it, is bound to be somewhat restricted. That fertility no longer produces say, ten pregnancies per woman, as was common at the turn of the century. Thus, women's "solid sense of irreversible achievement" (again,

Graglia's description of having and rearing children) occupies a different place in life than it used to. But Graglia doesn't discuss this. Modernization, declining birth rates, longer lifespans—none of these affect the portrait of life today that she seeks to paint. But these are the very factors that make a return to a "traditional life" simply impossible.

Still, I will grant that Graglia is right in objecting to feminists' extreme denigration of the family. I just don't think she's right in how she goes about suggesting an alternative vision. As an educated woman with a high-level profession who decided to give it up for the life of domesticity, she is hardly in the same position as the vast numbers of women who, absent feminism, would assume that that domestic life was their best shot at survival. Keeping men locked into their support of women (which Graglia construes as reinforcing their masculinity) strikes some women as demeaning. Some women are actually motivated by idealism—the desire for a partner who chooses to be with them and is not held there by fear of the law or the high costs of divorce or the unavailability of sex.

A third problem I see with Graglia's argument is that her housewife is very much an ideal type; it's surprising how specific are her comments about this woman's attributes.[5] Oddly enough, she earlier criticizes the insecurity induced in educated women by the professionalization of parenting, which made them doubt their own competency, no longer seeing it as simply "natural." Yet her own depiction of the successful housewife suggests that some very special characteristics, attitudes, and aptitudes are required, and that indeed this is not a type of life that would suit any and every woman. Not even perhaps most women. Graglia details the nurturing qualities of this ideal housewife: calm attention to others' needs and desires, and ability to be satisfied primarily by her family's well-being, of which she is the organizer and harmonizer.[6] Such a paragon does this ideal housewife seem that one begins to doubt whether she exists, any more than the "ideal executive" or "ideal office-worker" exists as more than an aspiration—or imposition.

Thus, Graglia raises the very specter she is trying to drive away: that the average woman may not, in fact, be cut out for such a role and that it might take an elaborate social apparatus to induce her to accept such a role and then to learn how to perform it.

Graglia's idealization of women is oddly reminiscent of cultural feminism's views of women as essentially nurturing, kind, peaceable—in fact, in many respects superior to men. In her description of women who are secure in their own importance and who humor their men by pretending their man is their lord and master as they send him out to do the hard work of the outside world, there's more than a little condescension, more than a bit of the Queen Bee syndrome. One can evidently be a feminist or a traditional woman, even an antifeminist, and still hold such views. Similarly,

Graglia's view of abortion as violence to a woman, like her criticism of sexual promiscuity, rather resembles that of anti-sex feminists (heterophobes, I call them), who see intercourse itself as degrading—and hence more intercourse as *more* degrading.

Of course, Graglia parts company from these feminists by making an exception for the one man in a woman's life with whom she forms a couple, a family unit. But her description of what that unit demands of women is not that far afield from that of feminists, especially cultural feminists, who argue that quilting, say, is as significant an art form as a painting by Titian. Graglia wants to defend such a view and perhaps would be surprised to know that many feminists agree with her about the devaluation of women's traditional skills and attributes.

Graglia attempts to explain why she must write as she does. She points out that when attacked by feminists, traditional women have no choice but to break the traditional pact by which women allow themselves to divide into distinct groups—most choosing the housewife role, some professional activities, and some a celibate life, with the tacit agreement among all that they will respect one another's choices. But was there ever such a "women's pact"? Surely we don't see much sign of it in the defensive and offensive behavior of bourgeois wives in traditional society. These women traditionally were actively antagonistic toward "loose women" and others who had not succeeded in making their particular kind of bargain with men. No friendly mutual respect was visible there, but rather shunning and ostracism. That seems to me the tradition that feminist extremists are carrying on.

As for Graglia's assessment of feminism's hostility to the role of housewife, I would in fact go further and say feminism is hostile to heterosexuality itself, without which there would be little in the way of housewifery. I agree with Graglia that feminism has been hostile not only to traditional women who choose to be housewives and mothers, but also in some cases to women who insist on continuing their heterosexual lives whether or not they are housewives. These heterophobes deny the desirability of any sort of heterosexual relationship. They don't all want to see women freed for greater sexual activity with men. In that respect Graglia, oddly enough, is on the same side as Andrea Dworkin, whose repulsive portrait of heterosex she seems to endorse except with that one special man with whom one forms a family unit in a monogamous relationship.

Interestingly, some feminists even criticize the housewife and mother routine when it is undertaken by lesbian couples. Radical feminist writers, in particular, are often hostile to women who adopt children to raise on their own or to lesbian couples that decide to have or adopt children. It's instructive to observe such situations and to note that even when leaving men out of the equation, the problem of family and domestic life continues—and here I am in sympathy with Graglia: Clearly, working women with young children have a hard time of it. Even same-sex couples these days are finding that some division of work roles makes sense when there are children. A few years ago, for example, I met a lesbian rabbi who had just had a child with her partner. Or, to be more precise, the rabbi's partner had had the child, and the partner—who was younger, less educated, and without a profession— was the housewife and mother in this couple, while the older, better-educated, and higher-earning woman neither bore the child nor was its primary caretaker. Nor is this the only such couple I have encountered.

What most puzzles me about Graglia, however (apart from some odd genuflection to traditional prejudices, as in her description of Jewish life as overvaluing the marketplace and mental abilities—all too reminiscent of the blame placed on Jews for—well, for everything, including communism, capitalism, whatever one wants to denounce), is that her own example suggests she appreciates the opportunity to utilize her energies outside the domestic sphere. And, like Phyllis Schlafly, whom she greatly admires, she exhorts other women to *not* follow her current example and not even be concerned about having the opportunity to do so (which after all requires education, sophistication, experience in the large world). Instead, she suggests that the satisfaction of being a wife and mother is enough. Meanwhile, her own actions show us that it's not enough, that even she (who is here with us today) wants to partake of what Charlotte Perkins Gilman called "the world's work." True, Gilman did attack housework, as Graglia describes in her book. And she apparently was a failure as a mother. But she still had some striking ideas and phrases, such as her desire to see women cease to be what she called "sexual specialists." Graglia thinks being a sexual specialist is a perfectly worthy destiny for a woman. Yet she has ceased to be that, no matter what she says.

But aside from my sympathy for Graglia's critique of the feminist attack on domestic life (to which I would add that the feminist conflation of the public and private sphere is also dangerous), I detect in her writing a strain similar to that which she deplores: a desire to see all women make the choices she has made and a disapproval of women who make other choices. We seem never to be able to escape from this tendency toward authoritarianism—as if it's impossible to have an idea without wanting to beat other people into submission before it. Modern women deserve better. I know some very accomplished women with young children who have recently decided to abandon their professions and stay home. I expect at some point—perhaps in five years, or ten—they will resume some professional activities. That doesn't strike me as a betrayal, as an unmanning of their husbands, as poor mothering, or as a capitulation to feminist orthodoxies.

Why should men bear the sole burden of economic support? Why not share it at certain times and stages in life, depending on one's situation, abilities, tastes? Isn't the whole point of progress to enhance people's options—so that we move from, say, arranged marriages designed to protect family property to a free choice of partner? Why not also a freer choice of activities, without the ill-concealed condescension of Graglia's phrase "market production," a phrase evidently chosen for its demeaning associations?

Work has many meanings, and Graglia ignores almost all of them. Work is not just serving others instead of one's own household (as she describes her own past work as a lawyer). Nor is it just about money. Work is a way of being in the world, using brain and heart, exploring different possibilities, and developing different talents. Certainly women have been restricted by their confinement to the domestic sphere. Perhaps not all women (Thomas More's daughters were reputed to be the best-educated women in sixteenth-century England!), but most. Most women who are housewives are not Carolyn Graglia. She is, and we are, among the privileged class who can move from one sphere to the other, finding success in both. But it may shock her to know that illiterate working-class women I interviewed in Brazil, who worked as domestic servants and earned sixty dollars a month, took pride in their work, as they also did in their families. Even in a society in which divorce (until twenty years ago) was not an option, women often encountered situations that required resourcefulness and energy in order to support themselves and their children. I doubt if their minds had been poisoned by feminism.

But these poor women too now live in a world in which, with a little luck, they will not have ten pregnancies. A modern woman has many years of life after her children are on their own. To dismiss any aspirations for a life outside the household as "fulfilling the market demands of strangers," as Graglia calls it, or equating the "materialistic pursuit of career achievement" with pornography in its compartmentalization of one's self, strikes me as a less than compelling argument.[7]

I don't think Graglia will convince women to flee the workforce. Feminist hostility toward the family—which means toward men and motherhood too—is unhealthy. So is Graglia's extreme animus toward women in the workplace—and her odd extension of this even to women's development of their intellectual abilities. I am most curious to see the voting on this issue that younger women are increasingly doing with their feet. For the first time in history (despite Graglia's assumption that women suffered no oppression in the past), young, educated women have the possibility of choosing from a range of options. This is more than men have at the moment. It will be intriguing to see what they choose to do, for how long, with what degree of satisfaction, and with what consequences for the society at large.

NOTES

This talk was presented at the annual meeting of the American Political Science Association, in Boston, September 1998.

1. F. Carolyn Graglia, *Domestic Tranquility: A Brief against Feminism* (Dallas, Tex.: Spence Publishing, 1998).

2. Graglia, *Domestic Tranquility*, 371.

3. Graglia, *Domestic Tranquility*, 144.

4. Graglia, *Domestic Tranquility*, 148.

5. Graglia, *Domestic Tranquility*, 95–96.

6. Graglia, *Domestic Tranquility*, 95.

7. Graglia, *Domestic Tranquility*, 146.

11

Will the Real Feminists in Academe Please Stand Up?

What's going on in women's studies?

The sociologist Joan D. Mandle relates a telling anecdote in her recent book, *Can We Wear Our Pearls and Still Be Feminists?: Memoirs of a Campus Struggle.*[1] In the mid-nineties, some female students from Colgate University attended a conference on global feminism at the State University of New York at New Paltz. Staying with local women's studies students, the Colgate women found themselves talked down to by the more assertive SUNY feminists, who fined them (as they did one another) twenty-five cents for every politically incorrect word uttered, words like "guy," "history," and "straight" (as in giving directions—"just go straight," which cost a three-word, seventy-five-cent fee). Many of the Colgate students were intimidated but also impressed. Their own feminism seemed pale by comparison. Colgate, they decided, was "not feminist enough."

In women's studies these days, Mandle counts as a heretic. She believes that all kinds of faculty members ought to teach women's studies and all kinds of students ought to study it. Her approach is inclusive and outreaching. What could make such nice liberal ideas heretical? Only the context in which they are offered.

For six years (1991–1997), Mandle was director of the women's studies program at Colgate before, she tells us, being replaced without notice while away on leave. What were her sins? Rejecting the proposition that separatist "safe spaces" and so-called therapeutic classrooms are legitimate academic goals, she tells us. Believing that women's studies should reach out to members of sororities, to men, to all parts of the university without restriction. Above all, insisting on high academic standards and exhibiting a low tolerance for feminist orthodoxies.

Mandle's book is important because it gives us a more accurate, less idealized version than the vast majority of accounts of the sorts of struggles that have—and continue to—beset women's studies programs. Such struggles are not so much against grudging outsiders as among women for whom the overriding bone of contention has often been the question: What sort of feminists are we?

A "founding mother" of Sociologists for Women in Society in 1972, Mandle arrived at Colgate with a background in civil rights and New Left activism. Unafraid of leadership and responsibility, unapologetic about using "I" instead of the politically preferred feminist "we," critical of the "consensus" model that can paralyze an organization, impatient with the constant appeals to "community" and "support," she was bound to arouse hostility. She was also enormously successful in making women's studies a major presence at Colgate. When ideological purity is the name of the game, however, academic success doesn't count for much. Thus, Mandle's narrative is a troubling story of how the self-created marginalization and isolation of some women's studies scholars have served to affirm their identity as "real" feminists and made them fiercely resentful of any encroachment on their turf.

Mandle shared with most feminists the belief that the disadvantages suffered by women justified a separate women's studies program, and she urged students to develop the organizational skills they would need to go out and change the world. But that was not enough to salvage her position as battles raged over who "owns" women's studies. Mandle incorporated the Women's Resource Center, run by students, into a new Center for Women's Studies, whose mission was to be primarily academic. She was critical of a feminist "theme" dormitory whose ever-dwindling members saw themselves as the only true feminists.

Mandle's account of her talks with other women's studies directors (in particular, at the meeting of the National Women's Studies Association in 1998, where a number of women acknowledged the internal difficulties besetting their programs) confirms the frequency of internal discord. At the time, what set Mandle apart from her colleagues was not her concerns but her willingness to go public with them, defying the accepted adage that airing dirty linen in public would aid women's studies' enemies.

Most of the conflicts that Mandle discusses in her book concerned one essential question: Is women's studies an integral part of academe, or should it embrace permanent outsider status? That is far from an abstract matter. It raises such concrete questions as: Must women's studies adhere to the same standards and goals as those of the rest of the university? Should it create a noncompetitive alternative for women, in which the key values are promoting a sense of community and providing a nurturing environment?

As Mandle rightly observes, it's one thing for young female students to be caught up in heated debates over identity and legitimacy, but quite another for female faculty members, supposedly wiser and more knowledgeable, to be forever embroiled in them. There's more than a touch of immaturity to be found in students' and faculty members' reinforcing in each other a combative understanding of feminist identity that, on the one hand, wallows in self-pity and vastly exaggerated perceptions of victimhood and, on the other, makes grandiose claims to be creating a new and better world.

The deep and contentious conflicts over who is what sort of feminist have been a staple of women's studies. Six months ago, on the women's studies' e-mail list (WMST-L), some critical remarks of mine were parried by the usual personal attacks and charges that I was misrepresenting the field. I was intrigued, therefore, that several women who followed the exchange chose to write to me privately about their own experiences.

A literature professor who has published extensively on female authors wrote that she once dismissed criticisms of the current feminist movement as right-wing distortions of the extremist views of only a few. No longer. A graduate student who has been teaching an introductory women's studies course for several years noted her dismay at being expected to disabuse her students of the notion (with which they all entered class) that they are fully equal to men and to teach them instead that they are oppressed victims. She said the texts she works with are all slanted toward the view that gender is entirely a social construct, that too many courses focus on feminist ideology, playing down detailed research on women. An instructor in women's studies wrote of being tired of having her feminist credentials constantly scrutinized and of having to defend her decision to allow men to speak up in her class.

Clearly, the conflicts and unpleasantness experienced by Mandle in the early and mid-nineties continue.

Joan Mandle's depictions of the contentious milieu generated by feminists is confirmed by another recent book on women's studies programs—although nothing could be further from the book's intent. Excitement, exhilaration, nostalgia—all are present in the just-published *The Politics of Women's Studies: Testimony from Thirty Founding Mothers,*[2] edited by the feminist dynamo Florence Howe, who this year is stepping down as head of the Feminist Press, which she cofounded thirty years ago. In many ways, this book about "scholars and activists in the patriarchal halls of 1970's academe" (as the back cover puts it) is an inspiring story of the individual commitment and institutional transformation that have fundamentally altered education in the United States. The recollections gathered here paint a vivid scene in which male allies and institutional receptivity allowed feminist activism to transform the academy through the creation of women's studies programs. Why, then, do many feminists today insist that universities in the seventies were (and still are) riddled by "systemic sexism"?

We are now entering the fourth (or fifth—if one starts counting from the late sixties, when the first women's studies courses were created) decade of the enterprise, but feminists still routinely refer to the "chilly climate" supposedly undermining women in schools and universities—and this despite the extraordinary achievements not only of women in higher education but also of feminist scholarship. The remarkable fact is, indeed, that feminists— black and white, gay and straight—have succeeded spectacularly.

Howe's book reminds us of some well-known statistics. Within the first decade (1970–1980), about 350 programs—that is, more than half of the currently existing women's studies programs—were set up. Resistance and opposition certainly occurred at times, but the "politics" of the book's title is rarely depicted by its authors, beyond axiomatic references to "patriarchy." Consider the testimony of Mariam K. Chamberlain, a former project officer at The Ford Foundation and the sole nonacademic in the Howe volume. She tells us that, between 1971 and 1981 (when she left Ford), the foundation gave grants totaling more than $9 million to support women's advancement, over half going to women's studies programs. Why did the patriarchy not defend its bastions? Clearly, the seventies was a time and the American university was a site prepared for, and in fact embraced, change.

But the personal stories in Howe's book do not acknowledge that favorable climate, although they reveal its presence. Instead, they seek to convey struggle and effort—on a heroic scale and against formidable and entrenched forces. Seldom is reference made to internal conflicts among female faculty members or to the many women in academe, past and present, who wanted no involvement with women's studies. There's a tendency to oversimplify and to gloss over serious intramural conflicts concerning the meaning of feminism. The one exception is the complaint, which we hear a lot about, that women's studies was originally "white women's studies" (a charge several essays in the book actually suggest is unfounded).

Most interesting are the authors' descriptions of steps taken to dismantle inequality and break down hierarchy. Classes sat in a circle; teachers overtly renounced their authority (though a few came to regret that later); teaching collectives and participatory governance structures (made up of students and faculty, staff, and sometimes "community" members) were set in place; political conformity was promoted, often to something vaguely called "socialism"; experience, rather than knowledge, was given a place of honor; the need for role models was stressed.

Above all, the authors in *Testimony* clearly placed great importance on developing in students the correct awareness of gender, race, class, and the ever-growing list of politically charged identities. Always, they emphasized that women's studies was not merely an intellectual or scholarly pursuit but a program fervently committed to feminist activism.

Only two or three chapters in the book (which, incidentally, contains no contribution by a scientist) present dissenting ideas. Inez Martinez, a professor of English at the City University of New York's Kingsborough Community College, writes of rejecting the posture of "no hierarchy" in her classroom, recognizing that if professors pretend to know no more than their students, there cannot be any education. Yet she too ends her piece by celebrating women's activism and the gains made by teaching students how victimized women have been. An even more unusual voice is that of Mimi Reisel Gladstein, an English professor and associate dean at the University of Texas at El Paso who, as an Ayn Rand enthusiast, sees Rand as a positive model for women, even though Rand's opposition to collectivism has made her anathema to feminist academics.

The lone contributor to question the key ideas and practices of women's studies is Nona Glazer, now retired, who was a professor of sociology at Portland State University. She says she disliked many aspects of feminist pedagogy. An advocate of liberal education, Glazer, by her own account, often went "against the grain of feminism." She disliked the drift of the program she cofounded at her university: the "vacuous psychologizing about men," the "whimpering," the "mixing psychobabble with social analysis," the tendency of many younger scholars simply to repeat earlier feminist work.

Glazer criticizes the antagonism to intellectual work heard at women's studies conferences. And she declares herself reluctant to see women's studies, with its separatism, "become permanent and institutionalized." Instead, she looks forward to a time when we can have "people's studies." That sentiment puts her at odds with the many feminist faculty members worried that the feminist edge of women's studies might become muted as some institutions rename their programs "gender studies." Glazer is also the sole writer in this 400-page volume to question the feminist mantra of an "integrated analysis" of race, class, and gender and other group markers. ("I never worked through to my satisfaction how to talk or write cogently about gender, race, ethnicity, sexual orientation, and class simultaneously," she admits.)

Still, she makes clear that, having distanced herself from her own women's studies program, she invariably returned to support it in times of crisis. And, though she remains unhappy that feminism has not "produced an intellectual revolution" capable of completely transforming the curriculum, Glazer considers women's studies to have been her "salvation."

Most tellingly, almost every author in the Howe volume prides herself on the political direction taken by women's studies, especially its close association with women's centers and support groups on campus. Joan Mandle would have found most of these founding mothers of women's studies siding with her opponents.

The explicit use of the classroom for purposes of indoctrination is enthusiastically promoted in another recently published book: Paula S. Rothenberg's *Invisible Privilege: A Memoir about Race, Class, and Gender*.[3] This is not a memoir in the conventional mode. It is a narrative locked into the iron grid of race, class, and gender. The author adopts an attitude of public self-criticism for the "invisible privilege" she has enjoyed in the first two categories, which contrasts with the lack of privilege she has experienced as a woman.

Unlike Nona Glazer, Rothenberg, a professor of philosophy and women's studies at William Paterson University of New Jersey, judges the analysis of the "intersections of race, class, and gender privilege" to be an unfailing intellectual and political tool. She must be gratified to see that belief now officially inscribed in a large number of women's studies "mission" statements and course descriptions, and indeed in many universities' general education requirements.

What emerges from Rothenberg's book is a world in which only group identity counts, and individuals, even those close to her, are of interest merely as exemplars of those groups. *Invisible Privilege* lacks human warmth, most shockingly in an epilogue in which the lingering deaths of Rothenberg's parents, treated and mistreated by nurse's aides and other women of color, are served up to make some closing comments about race, class, and gender.

Given that Rothenberg is a prominent advocate of multiculturalism who has edited several widely used feminist and multicultural anthologies, it's disturbing that her avid defense of those isms comes down to a few fundamentally anti-intellectual and downright ignorant views. Consider her description of her own experience decades ago in a high school English class, as rescripted from her present point of view. She and her fellow students were required to write book reports, which were supposed to end with "a mandatory discussion of the universal themes in the work" they had read by English and American writers.

"In this way, we came to understand that novels and short stories about the trials and tribulations of well-to-do, white men were universal and timeless," Rothenberg tells us. "In this way, we came to own Ernest Hemingway, Herman Melville, Samuel Butler, William Shakespeare, and a host of other similarly situated writers and adopt their Eurocentric and privileged male view of life and the world as though it were coextensive with reality."

I can think of few more powerful indictments of Rothenberg's ideas about education and the curriculum than that confused statement, which makes a mockery of decades of serious feminist scholarship that attempts to get beyond such stereotypes. Among other objections, such language should raise the question of whether someone who lumps together the above-named writers as "well-to-do, white men" with a "privileged male view of life" should be teaching at all, let alone be director of the New Jersey Project on Inclusive Scholarship, Curriculum and Teaching, which provides resources to all colleges in the state.

In further illustration of her pedagogy, Rothenberg recalls an episode in which her black students, in an introductory college philosophy class, confessed to her that they could make no sense out of Descartes's radical doubt. The incident, she says, "proved to be another turning point in my intellectual life," because it taught her "to operate from the premise that their [the students'] discomfort was a sign of Descartes's inadequacy." Still, she didn't want to dismiss Descartes altogether. So she informed her students about his poor eyesight and the privilege reflected in his worldview. "By constructing a curriculum—worse yet, a culture—around such an idiosyncratic worldview and then calling it knowledge, we have privileged the distorted perspective of an infinitesimal fraction of the world's population," she writes. Her pedagogy, she believes, communicated ideas "in ways that empowered" students.

Rothenberg goes on for pages about the "sham" of multiculturalism "undertaken to placate, not educate." She decries "curricular affirmative action" that amounts to giving little more than lip service to multiculturalism; she pleads for "another way"—a "more inclusive curriculum" that "acknowledges the race, gender, and class differences that have shaped every aspect of the world we live in today."

I agree that much of what is called multiculturalism is a pious fraud. However, this fraud, now perpetrated at virtually all levels of education, ought to be seen as a response to insistent demands like Rothenberg's for multicultural and multidisciplinary teaching in all courses, no matter how unsuitable. It is such demands that force teachers with scant or no training in what they must add to their courses to become purveyors of perfunctory and largely vacuous multiculturalism.

Rothenberg—like almost all of the authors in the Howe volume—evinces no doubts about using the classroom for the promotion of political commitments. Add to that Joan Mandle's failed attempt to turn women's studies into serious education and one can begin to see what's going on in women's studies today. Feminist faculty members and their sympathizers on campuses (some of whom may merely be afraid of crossing feminists) have done their best to dissolve the boundaries between education and indoctrination. Surely those should be sharply drawn in a democratic society.

Far from being a small band making a brave stand against the patriarchal and racist university, many scholars in women's studies are, in fact, well situated, influential, and very busy. What long-term impact they will have on student views and behavior remains to be gauged. Perhaps it will not be much. But in the meantime, these feminists have succeeded both in remodeling the

program of studies at many universities to conform to their often questionable aims and in transforming—not always for the better—the environment
for the men and women who learn and teach there.

NOTES

This essay first appeared in *The Chronicle of Higher Education (The Chronicle Review),*
October 6, 2000, B7.

　　1. Joan D. Mandle, *Can We Wear Our Pearls and Still Be Feminists?: Memoirs of a
Campus Struggle* (Columbia: University of Missouri Press, 2000).
　　2. Florence Howe, ed., *The Politics of Women's Studies: Testimony from Thirty Founding Mothers* (New York: Feminist Press, 2000).
　　3. Paula S. Rothenberg, *Invisible Privilege: A Memoir about Race, Class, and Gender*
(Lawrence: University Press of Kansas, 2000).

12

Whose Truth? Iconicity and Accuracy in the World of Testimonial Literature

A SAINT'S LIFE

In an essay on teaching *I, Rigoberta Menchú*, a North American university professor explains her dismay at her students' criticism of the book by telling us that, for her, Rigoberta's text is "sacred" and "untouchable."[1] Arturo Arias, in the same volume, tells us that Rigoberta has, for good or ill, become a "living icon" in Guatemala and that her receipt of the Nobel Peace Prize in 1992 "singlehandedly changed the configuration of Guatemalan politics."[2] Here, I suspect, is the heart of the problem. In the hostile responses that have greeted David Stoll's book, *Rigoberta Menchú and the Story of All Poor Guatemalans*,[3] there is revealed a depth of commitment on many readers' parts to Rigoberta[4] that is closely akin to hagiography and the absorption of it by the faithful.

The comparison is suggestive. The adventures of medieval saints are for the most part fanciful, and in any case cannot ordinarily be verified by scholarly research. But to the pious reader, the historicity of these incidents is unimportant because both the lives and reading about them are acts of faith. In their brave deeds, above all in their passions, saints and martyrs demonstrated the truth of their religion, so it hardly matters to the devout reader whether a particular story is historically accurate or not. The saint's life, told reverently, is an exemplary narrative. It is taken to embody a higher kind of truth to which its hero is the witness.

Our secular world too has its rites of unquestioning reverence. Is there not something indecent about quibbling over evidence when the subject is suffering and oppression? The case of Tawana Brawley some years ago—the African-American teenager who claimed to have been assaulted and raped by six white men—is instructive. When the girl's story was shown to lack any foundations, attorney William Kunstler asserted that "it makes no difference anymore whether the attack on Tawana really happened. It doesn't disguise the fact that a lot of young black women are treated the way she said she was treated."[5]

A continent away and more than a decade later, the same apologia has been offered by different people, inside Guatemala and out, who have sought to discredit David Stoll and minimize what they have perceived as the political damage done by his carefully documented challenge to Rigoberta's famous *testimonio*. In the face of Stoll's evidence showing that Rigoberta's brother did not die as she said he did and that, furthermore, contrary to her horrifying account, she had not been a witness to his death, the Guatemalan Dante Liano asks rhetorically: "At any rate, is a death by bullets better than one by burning?"[6] And to Rigoberta's false claim that she learned Spanish only a few years before her meeting with Elisabeth Burgos in 1982, Dante Liano merely rejoins: "Is partial illiteracy better than total ignorance?" Rigoberta is being subjected to a "smear campaign," he charges, the real object of which is to exonerate Guatemala's ruling oligarchy. His conclusion is uncompromising: "To say that Rigoberta Menchú has lied is taken to mean that no social injustice has taken place in Guatemala."[7]

In the United States too many academics have leaped to Rigoberta's defense. One of them, Marjorie Agosin, chair of the Spanish Department at Wellesley College, told a reporter for *The Chronicle of Higher Education* that criticisms of Rigoberta serve only to attack multiculturalism. As to trust in Rigoberta, Agosin sidestepped the issue: "Whether her book is true or not, I don't care. We should teach our students about the brutality of the Guatemalan military and the U.S. financing of it." Besides, says Agosin, "Even if she didn't watch her little brother being murdered, the military did murder people in Guatemala."[8]

Speaking for myself, I am deeply skeptical about the motives underlying such a defense (the tactical aspects of which Stoll addresses in his book). I am certain that, were the object of this controversy not a figure revered by leftists but one out of favor with them, the reaction to half truths, misrepresentations, and outright falsehoods would be very different. What this tells me is that "truth"—with or without scare quotes—is in this case (as in so many others) being made subservient to politics. And that is a dangerous, if hardly original, stance for intellectuals to take. For what is the value of a human rights activism that is driven by an a priori loyalty to certain political causes and not to others, rather than being rooted in a commitment to the defense of human rights wherever they are abused? Of what merit is it for academics to praise some *testimonios* as heroic literature, when other testimonies, those that offend their own politics—the many, for example, that have been written by dissidents persecuted in Castro's Cuba—are ignored? This double standard, the existence of which is easily exposed by a survey of the literature, is enough to demonstrate the political corruption at the heart of the prolific academic industry on *testimonios*.

WHOSE TESTIMONY?

When, one might therefore ask, is a *testimonio* not a *testimonio*? Answer: when it attacks a sacred idol of the left.

A review of some of the most often-quoted definitions of *testimonio* makes the ideological triage at work here abundantly clear. In a well-known essay, "The Margin at the Center: On *Testimonio* (Testimonial Narrative)," John Beverley defines *testimonio* as "a new form of narrative literature in which we can at the same time witness and be a part of the emerging culture of an international proletarian/popular-democratic subject in its period of ascendancy." It is a form of writing, he says, that engages readers in the struggle of particular communities and involves them in significant human rights and solidarity movements. *Testimonio*, according to Beverley, arises from "an urgency to communicate, a problem of repression, poverty, subalternity, imprisonment, struggle for survival."[9]

Interestingly, when writing this essay in the late eighties, Beverley had not excluded *testimonios* such as Armando Valladares's *Against All Hope*, chronicling his twenty-two years in Castro's prisons. The theme common to all *testimonios*, including those, such as Valladares's, that Beverley labeled as coming from the "political Right," was "the need for a general social change in which the stability of the reader's world must be brought into question."[10] Beverley had stressed the "urgency" of *testimonio*, its concern with "sincerity" rather than literariness, and the fact that "it is not, to begin with, fiction." And, like other commentators on *testimonio* as a genre, Beverley emphasized that in *testimonio* the narrator always represents or speaks for a community or a group.[11] He had also made the extremely astute observation (in light of what Stoll would later disclose) that the episodes in which Rigoberta describes "in excruciating detail" the torture and murder of her brother and mother differed markedly in tone from the rest of her account, expressing a "hallucinatory" intensity that Beverley labeled "magic realism."[12]

By the mid-nineties, however, Beverley had grown more restrictive in deciding what to count as a proper *testimonio*. In his 1996 essay "The Real Thing," he calls *testimonio* "the voice of the body in pain, of the disappeared," and then adds: "of the losers in the rush to marketize."[13] More significant, Beverley now takes an entirely new approach to the question of authenticity in Rigoberta's story. Having in the meantime become aware of

Stoll's work, he begins to treat Rigoberta as a sophisticated author. She is no longer limited to being a mere witness to events, as anthropologists would like to have it. Instead, Beverley—no doubt aided by his self-critical account of how "literature and the university are among the institutional practices that *create* and sustain subalternity"[14]—now sees testimonial narrators as possessing, as he puts it, the "power to create their own narrative authority and negotiate its conditions of truth and representativity."[15] Perhaps hoping to clinch his argument, he adds that Stoll can only replace Rigoberta's narratives with other narratives he has gathered, as if the problem of truth and accuracy could be dismissed as nothing more than an infinite regress. *Testimonio*, in Beverley's new understanding, "is both an art and a strategy of subaltern memory."[16]

To speak here of "strategy" is, in effect, to redeem Rigoberta from the consequences of her misrepresentations by suggesting that these falsehoods were tactical choices with no bearing on the deeper questions of truth and trust. Postmodernist obfuscations notwithstanding, however, it is a fact that commentator after commentator has praised the reliability of Rigoberta's plain-spoken narrative, treating as axiomatic the truth of what she recounts. It is this supposed authenticity that has made the book a staple in the classroom, where scores of teachers have, by their own reports, taught it as real history and *not* as a version of "truth" to be read like poetry and the novel, from which students are to draw no precise historical conclusions. Only when challenged on their interpretive shifts do such professors retreat to oracular equivocations about the indeterminacy of truth and the ambiguities of narrative.

Before Stoll, why did none of the many celebrants of Latin American *testimonio* think to question basic elements of Rigoberta's narrative? Clearly it is because they wanted the story to be true in all its painful details, believing that the more graphic the suffering depicted, the more impressive—and useful—the story and its protagonist. A rather different attitude is adopted toward testimonial accounts that do not support these readers' own political commitments. In other words, there is presumption of truth telling in the testimonies of "subalterns" and suspicion of unreliability for everyone else. Given this permissive reception of her story, Rigoberta's narrative elicited little distance, few doubts. Instead, in academic circles, she became an epistemologically privileged spokesperson whose status as a perfect Other was powerfully reinforced by her North American readers.

What Stoll undertook to do, and what many cannot forgive him for, was intervene in Rigoberta's story. As he tells it, he did not set out to destroy her. But scholarly rigor made it impossible for him to avoid asking basic questions once he became aware of the many discrepancies in her story. These are the sorts of questions we should always ask of accounts claiming to be a true reflection of events on the basis of which we are asked to engage in political action: Did they really happen? Is the teller trustworthy? Is there corroborating evidence? Philosophical speculations about the nature of truth or the reliability of our senses are irrelevant to this level of investigation, which concerns the degree of agreement between what is told and what actually occurred. Certainly such questions must be asked if political programs and actions are contemplated.

It is true that oral histories of the "life history" type—which is what Rigoberta's original story is (notwithstanding the distinctions sometimes drawn between oral history and *testimonio*)—tend to be taken at face value. Indeed, this is one of the criticisms directed at oral history methodology: Too often it does not attempt to ascertain the truth or falsity of what is told. The usual answer to the question of facticity and accuracy in oral history is: There are no lies in oral history. This assertion, however, has a very specific and limited meaning. It refers to the proposition that in "constructing a self," the speaker reveals her intentions, her projection of the self she wants to present to the world, regardless of its conformity to the objective facts of her life. And in that sense, her self-portrait is indeed "true"—truly reflective, that is, of the self she is offering up to the world. Rigoberta, for her part, presents a self that is a victim. She is one of the oppressed. But above all she is a proud fighter for her indigenous identity. The distortions in her story serve to advance the creation and acceptance of this double image. Its persuasiveness outside her own country has, in turn, been much enhanced by a notion pervasively present in the scholarly and academic world of North America, that of "the authority of experience." This oft-repeated and versatile shibboleth has it that when one of the oppressed—especially a third world woman or a woman of color—tells her story, she herself is the authority on that experience, and what she says should remain beyond challenge. The truthfulness of any specific allegation can thus always be validated by an implicit appeal to the broader experience of the group. Raising questions, let alone testing the allegation for its specific accuracy, becomes that much more problematic.

CONSTRUCTING A SELF

"Inaccuracies are common in oral history interviews," William Cutler III has written; "but if the researcher can identify them, especially those resulting from dishonesty or reticence, he can profit handsomely, for sometimes they provide an important avenue of insight into a respondent's state of mind."[17] It is in this sense, as I have explained above, that one can say that there are no lies in oral history—which is not to claim that all statements are accurate, but to say only that all statements are meaningful and reflect pertinently on the speaker. In a far more sophisticated treatment of the same issue, Agnes Hankiss, in her essay "Ontologies of the Self: On the Mythological Rearranging of One's Life-History," discusses the way in which, in the narration of a life history, certain episodes are endowed with a symbolic significance that in effect turns them into myths. She tells us that this is a never-ending process, for an adult constantly selects new models or strategies of life, by which the old is transmuted into material useful for the new—the new self and the new situation. Everyone attempts, "in one way or another, to build up his or her own ontology."[18] Hankiss discusses four strategies for doing this; of these Rigoberta clearly chose the one in which the scenario of a bad image of childhood is shown to lead to a good image of the present self.[19] From the point of view of an effective narrative, Rigoberta's embellishment of her experiences, to make them harsher and crueler than they really were, causes her adult heroism to stand out all the more strongly.

As I wrote in *Brazilian Women Speak: Contemporary Life Stories*, the very act of telling one's life story involves the imposition of structure on experience. In the midst of this structure, a subject emerges that tends to be represented as constant over time. Concerning "the truth" of the accounts we (as intermediaries) record, I wrote the following, reflecting on my own experience interviewing sixty women in Brazil:

> While I cannot address this issue with any certainty, I am satisfied that the women who talked to me were telling me a truth, which reveals what was important *for them*. This does not, of course, exclude the possibility of intentional misrepresentation, self-censorship, or unintentional replication of a given society's myths and cherished beliefs about the world, itself, or the roles that distinctive individuals or groups play.[20]

Perhaps not coincidentally, Rigoberta chose to defend her book on similar grounds. It was "my truth," she said, that she had told to Burgos.[21] This was, however, Rigoberta's second line of defense, following the collapse of the first, which was simply to blame Burgos for any inaccuracies in the account. But what is most telling in the current debate is that Rigoberta at some point began to use the language of intellectuals schooled in postmodernist evasions. She seems to know the rhetoric of truth as contingent. This is part of her careful crafting of an identity likely to be pleasing to her academic supporters.

These supporters have staunchly affirmed Rigoberta's early assumption of another posture, one they would never willingly grant to most speakers in our own culture: that of spokesperson for "her people." On the very first page of *I, Rigoberta Menchú*, Rigoberta confidently announces that her tale is that of all her people. It is also on this very first page that Rigoberta tells us she received no schooling—a false assertion, as Stoll has established. The predictable rejoinder that such falsehoods result from Burgos's emphasis in editing the book or from Burgos's mistaken conflation of a number of different stories told to her by Rigoberta has already been neutralized by Stoll's discovery that Rigoberta set forth the basic outlines of her public persona before she ever met with Burgos. Stoll located a narrative, dating from 1981, in which Rigoberta lays out the pivotal tale of her father's brave resistance to the "landlords," and the torture and death of her brother Petrocinio and of her mother. Equally important, Stoll found that the representational stance Rigoberta took in her interviews with Burgos had also been anticipated in that earlier narrative: "My sorrow and my struggle are also the sorrow and struggle of an entire oppressed people who struggle for their liberation."[22] There is every reason, Stoll concludes, to believe that *I, Rigoberta Menchú* is indeed Rigoberta's own account of her life, not a tale distorted by Burgos.[23]

It is interesting to note how Rigoberta's initial attempt to blame Burgos feeds into the lengthy debates in certain intellectual circles about who controls the story. There have been some notable conflicts over this issue between ethnographers and storytellers. A famous case is that of Adélaïde Blasquez , who published a book called *Gaston Lucas, serrurier: chronique de l'anti-héros* (1976). The French scholar Philippe Lejeune called this book a masterpiece of ethnographic truth telling—until he learned that Blasquez had erased each interview with Lucas after transcribing it. When Blasquez's publisher invited Lejeune to interview Blasquez for a video, Lejeune suggested that Gaston Lucas, who was still alive, should be included. Blasquez refused, insisting that the living Gaston Lucas had nothing of value to say. Rather, she asserted, he truly existed only as a character that she, through her art, had created.[24]

Closer to Rigoberta's situation is a conflict between ethnographer and narrator discussed by Sondra Hale in an essay describing her problematic relationship with a Sudanese communist named Fatma Ahmed Ibrahim, Sudan's most visible woman politician and for more than thirty years a leading activist. In the course of their interview, Hale's Western feminist expectations of sisterly exchange and mutual recognition turned to disillusionment as Fatma presented her with a carefully contrived account in which she revealed only what she considered strategic to her political objectives, for which she clearly expected Hale to be her mouthpiece.

Hale is unusually forthright in describing how this meeting upset her. She felt relegated to the category of "mere listener."[25] Her own long residence in the Sudan, and her status as a "sister feminist" from the west, seemed to count for nothing, "My 'dream of a common language,'" she confesses, "had been dashed by the interview, but perhaps that was because, although I had remembered a form of 'feminism,' I had forgotten some anthropology, politics, and history."[26] She is certainly correct in this suspicion. And Rigoberta's case makes it even more clear how strongly North American responses to this "subaltern" narrative have been shaped by politics and iconicity, rather than by the search for accuracy and truthfulness. The fervor of these responses can be gauged from the extremely hostile reaction Stoll's work has generated, because Stoll, though warmly sympathetic to both Rigoberta and her cause, is above all committed to scholarly standards not subjected to political oversight.

LYING

Sissela Bok has argued that lies (even so-called "white lies") have consequences and that lies tend to spread by repetition. It is not surprising, then, that Rigoberta's lies are regularly repeated in the literature about her. In a children's book about Rigoberta, for example, published in 1996 by Brill, we find all her exaggerations and distortions recycled: Her older brother is tortured and burned to death before her eyes; her younger brother succumbs to starvation; she is deprived of education and spends her childhood laboring on plantations; and, of course, the foundational tale—key to the mythic view of community of which so many U.S. academics are enamored—is her father's conflict with Ladinos over land in Chimel, these Ladinos being described as "rich landowners," always the enemy in this children's book.

What exactly is the nature of Rigoberta's "misrepresentations" (as some have discretely called them)? Unlike "white lies," which typically attempt to spare someone else's feelings, or otherwise innocuous fibs (though even those are not necessarily without negative effects, as Bok argues), Rigoberta's distortions seem motivated predominantly by a political purpose. But this represents an altogether different order of dishonesty, for—as Bok points out—such dishonesty has the unavoidable consequence of destroying trust. Thus, lies that are told originally in order to increase the power of their teller (or of the teller's cause), paradoxically, when exposed, have the effect of decreasing that power, and replacing it with mistrust.[27]

The specifics of some of Rigoberta's lies also carry some unexpected implications. By inflating her own agonies, especially in falsely describing herself as a witness to the burning to death of her brother, Rigoberta suggests, implicitly, that her actual sufferings were insufficient to make the kind of powerful impression she wants to leave with her readers. Given her eagerness to win support for the guerrilla cause, it is perhaps understandable that she should have made this decision. But it also shows that she was consciously constructing a story that would be useful for her immediate purpose—which was a political one. Until Stoll wrote his book, few readers had bothered to notice the agenda she was promoting in her conversations with Burgos—or, rather, many academic readers seem to have automatically assented to that agenda and hence avoided subjecting it to critical scrutiny. Post-Stoll, of course, the rhetoric about Rigoberta has changed. Even John Beverley now suggests that we should "worry less about how *we* appropriate Menchú, and . . . understand and appreciate more how she appropriates us for her purposes."[28]

Perhaps nothing in Rigoberta's account is quite as revealing of the artful construction of her life story as her representation of herself as an unschooled person with only broken Spanish recently learned. This lie (she had in fact been a well-regarded pupil in a nuns' school) is of a somewhat different order than her misrepresentation regarding Petrocinio's death or the equally politically motivated cover-up of the land struggle between her father and his in-laws. Here Rigoberta attempts to manipulate the reader's take on her whole person, and clearly she knew what counts as positive in the "outside world" of her readership. Most people lie by inflating their accomplishments. But Rigoberta does the reverse, as if she were wise to the strange competition going on in the contemporary world over what groups are to be accorded most-oppressed status. As Stoll comments, Rigoberta's denial of knowledge of Spanish and literacy should be seen as "a preemptive defense of her authenticity." Why? "It is not true," writes Stoll, "that solidarity activists require their Indians to be barefoot and illiterate. But it is not hard to find people in the left and on the fringes of anthropology who disparage Indians wearing a tie as inauthentic."[29]

Here too—and as noted before—the main damage done by Rigoberta's misrepresentations is to the cause of human rights. It cannot help human rights activists to be reminded that their witnesses are apt to deceive them. And it can only diminish the public's humane responses to repression and privation to discover that a leading icon of the international struggle to improve the human lot has built her reputation at least in part on falsehoods.

TEACHING RIGOBERTA

I once made the point, based upon sad personal experience, that in the field of women's studies, "empowerment" means the equal disempowerment of each by all. The major exception to this is women of color and third world women, who have come to occupy a special status within feminism. When we are being urged to believe in the privileged consciousness of non-white narrators, it becomes risky at times for scholars to defend objectivity and common sense. Nowhere is this risk more apparent today than in the classroom.

An entire volume has been devoted to the teaching of Rigoberta's book: *Teaching and Testimony: Rigoberta Menchú and the North American Classroom,* edited by Allen Carey-Webb and Stephen Benz.[30] Its twenty-eight chapters, in addition to showing how widely used a text *I, Rigoberta Menchú* has become in colleges and universities, make abundantly clear how readily many professors and students seem to accept Rigoberta's account as a true one, and how frequently it is precisely the harrowing episode of her brother's torture and death that particularly impresses students.

Rigoberta's book was a required text in a first-year general education core course at Mount Vernon College, a small liberal arts college for women in Washington, D.C. A teacher comments: "Only after they read Rigoberta's moving accounts of the torture and death of her sixteen-year-old brother burned alive in front of his family and of the kidnapping, torture, rape, and murder of her mother . . . did many students grasp fully the meaning of the term *human rights violations* that had figured centrally in the history outlined for them."[31]

Other contributors report similar experiences. Catherine Ann Collins and Patricia Varas, who used Rigoberta's book in an obligatory freshman "world views" course taught at Willamette University, in Salem, Oregon, quote a colleague who complained that "students wanted to believe [Rigoberta] literally, rather than metaphorically" and was dismayed that when students realized something was not literally true, "it tended to discredit her."[32] The teachers here criticize their students for insisting on the "facts" and blame this on the influence of Western narratives that—so the essay informs us— condition students to be "in search of an authoritarian, first-person hero/heroine who controls the narrative and talks directly to the reader. If that hero/heroine isn't present, they can feel betrayed."[33] That sort of voice is, of course, very much in evidence in Rigoberta's account, and it appears to be the professors who cannot hear it. They insist that Rigoberta is "voiceless"—following Gayatri Spivak's much-touted contention that the "subaltern cannot speak"[34]—and disparage their students' view of her as an extraordinary person, winner of the Nobel Peace Prize. Their students' problem, Collins and Varas say, is that their reading of *I, Rigoberta* "has not developed the necessary relationship to testimony as a discourse that (1) moves the reader toward change; (2) gives voice to the voiceless, especially women; and (3) questions 'not only Western versions of what is true, but even Western notions of truth.'"[35] Unlike their students, Collins and Varas regret what they take to be the typical Western emphasis on individual effort and use the occasion for a trendy blast at their own culture: "The collective voice of the testimony, again, is undermined by Western notions of truth and objectivity."[36]

Yet another essayist, Robin Jones, who taught the book in a course on women writers at the University of Colorado at Boulder, was initially taken aback at her students' skepticism about Menchú's narrative. It is Jones whom

I quoted at the beginning of this essay as stating that "the work to me had taken on sacred dimensions and had become untouchable."[37] She tells of a student who, by focusing on environmental issues in Rigoberta's book, was "avoiding" the issues of ethnicity and gender.[38] Jones, too, makes much of the episode of Rigoberta's brother's death and of her own difficulty in teaching "such a personal and painful work" (which she likens to teaching about the Nazi-inspired Holocaust).[39] Her students'

> main reaction to the violence was that Menchú was being "too graphic." If she wanted to arouse sympathy she should have "softened" the images. In other words, she should have retold the story in a gentler fashion so the reader could stay within the story. Students did not feel horrified as much as manipulated, as if this was indeed a slasher movie, not a real account of the death of a family member.[40]

Needless to say, Jones was "disappointed" at this reaction.

Jones also provides a clear example of the multicultural mode now current in North American pedagogy: "I suggest that when students describe a work as 'too depressing,' this statement be interrogated to find out which element of the story they find most depressing. I suspect that what is really at stake is the student's reaction to being decentered as a subject and feeling disempowered by the strength of an unfamiliar life experience. I am still troubled," she concludes, "by the students' resentment towards Menchú and her work, reflecting a backlash against multiculturalism and an unexamined response to the politics of 'political correctness.'"[41] She promises to give her students more historical preparation in the future.

In another essay Mary Louise Pratt tells us that, in teaching Rigoberta's book, she instructs her Stanford students as follows: "Take notes about where you find yourself resisting its force, where it forces you into rejection or denial."[42] She teaches the book, Pratt explains, not in order to get her American students to change Guatemala, but "to do something about North America."[43]

For her part, in an essay in the same volume, Meri-Jane Rochelson addresses the importance of finding an "authentic voice in making one's history known." Rochelson, like most commentators, highly approves of Rigoberta's "repeated insistence that she was speaking for her group rather than for herself," and accepts this "as part of the revolutionary status of her *testimonio.*"[44] We have seen this proposition asserted by critics such as John Beverley who deem it characteristic of *testimonio*, thereby elevating it to a status superior to that of the individual memoir, dismissible as a bourgeois-individualist exercise.

Doris Sommer, whose work on Rigoberta is, like Beverley's, frequently cited, speaks in an essay entitled "Not Just a Personal Story: Women's *Testimonios* and the Plural Self"[45] of the "helpless solitude" that she thinks plagues

Western women, in contrast to the "collective self" evidenced by *testimonios* such as Rigoberta's. Along with many of her colleagues, Sommer too feels compelled to parade her postcolonialist, anti-Western attitude, as when she laments that even the collective subject bears witness to "Western penetration" when it is expressed through the individual *testimonio*.[46]

It is intriguing to contemplate these critics' patronizing view that "non-hegemonic" people somehow cannot possess (or at least do not have the poor taste to display) an individual sense of self. And it is even more fascinating to speculate on why such high-profile academics express so much disdain for the intellectual values that have bestowed so many honors and rewards on them. The work of these writers is filled with unexamined *obiter dicta*—for example, Sommer's statement that "historical change cannot [sic] be mandated from the top down"[47]—and modish declarations, such as the oft-reiterated doctrine that "community" and "communal values" are necessarily more desirable than "individuality."[48]

This latter assertion, in particular, is an astonishing belief to be professed by someone living today, when so many horrors have been committed worldwide in the name of some community or other in the service of its vaunted ideals. Consider a kind of *testimonio* that is rarely heard in the classrooms where Rigoberta is celebrated: Ana Rodríguez's *Diary of a Survivor: Nineteen Years in a Cuban Women's Prison*. Rodríguez, like many Cuban dissidents of her generation, was first anti-Batista, then anti-Castro, and at about the age of twenty was imprisoned. Describing Cuba's Reeducation Program (renamed the Progressive Plan in the late sixties), she sheds quite a different light on "community" and the obligations it imposes on the individual.

> To me it looked like the same old Orwellian stuff. You signed a confession of your sins against the Revolution, implicating others to prove your sincerity; with other prisoners, you went to "self-criticism" sessions . . . and you performed slave labor to show your gratitude for the whole process. [There was also] . . . mandatory participation in the idiotic Spoken Choruses. These consisted of groups of prisoners chanting in unison musty passages from Castro's speeches and letters. Perfect Communist art: It required neither talent nor imagination.[49]

One wonders what personal experiences with "community" American academics have had that lead so many of them to laud communal over individual values.

CONCLUSION

The saga of Rigoberta's status is a morality tale for our time. Whom can we trust? Whom do we celebrate? Must we mythologize figures in order to respect them? Is truth a Western ploy? What are the obligations of intellectuals—especially those fortunate enough to live in countries where they are free to pursue their vocations?

It seems to me that, at the present moment, demystifying Rigoberta is an important part of answering these questions. Opposition to human rights violations should not depend upon misrepresentation—whether it is about land conflicts, one's family history, one's own education, or who did what to whom, and who was there to see it. Truth and integrity matter, and we should not rush to give willing credence to stories just because they fit our preconceived ideas, all the while insisting on sound evidence only for those that do not.

As far as Rigoberta's own role is concerned, a simple and probable explanation exists for the choices she made in presenting herself to the world, and it is an explanation that makes short work of the endless rhetoric about *testimonio* and collective voices, which no doubt tells us more about first world intellectuals' needs and longings than about third world testimonials. Rigoberta had, as Stoll's work makes convincingly and sympathetically clear, mixed motives. She wanted to promote her cause *and* she wanted to project a certain image of herself. Both objectives were served, in her view, by distorting her life story and even lying about it when that seemed expedient. When confronted with evidence of her falsehoods, she sought to blame others, as many have done before her. Why should this surprise us? It should not—unless we have fallen in thrall to notions about the superior virtues of the oppressed, or have come to imagine, or hope, that by idealizing the "subaltern," some of their charm will rub off on us.

As for scholars, clearly it is their duty to put scholarship first in their work and "advocacy" second. There is life outside the university, and plenty of time for acting on one's political commitments without turning either one's scholarly writing or one's teaching into propaganda. Is there anyone left on the left, I have wondered in recent years, who is prepared to defend the autonomy of intellectual work and hence disinclined to reduce all questions to political bottom lines? Is no one on the academic left concerned about the perils of conflating political and intellectual goals?[50] Must everything we do be absorbed into politics and be justified by the pretense that we (we academics) become "activists" every time we write another essay about the "oppressed"? Have we made the study of "subalterns" into a holy relic by association with which we hope to gain absolution from our sinful state as "oppressors"?

David Stoll addresses this delusion in his book and illustrates it with a telling quotation from Bertrand Russell:

> The stage in which superior virtue is attributed to the oppressed is transient and unstable. It begins only when the oppressors come to have a bad conscience,

and this only happens when their power is no longer secure. . . . Sooner or later the oppressed class will argue that its superior virtue is a reason in favor of its having power, and the oppressors will find their own weapons turned against them. When at last power has been equalized, it becomes apparent to everybody that all the talk about superior virtue was nonsense, and that it was quite unnecessary as a basis for the claim to equality.[51]

Only one thing is missing from this passage. Russell could not have imagined that in our time self-proclaimed "oppressors" would tirelessly insist on the superior virtue of the oppressed, and that bizarre internecine disputes would ensue over who should be granted the distinction of this honorable status. Much less did he foresee that academic reputations would be made and unmade in the course of waging this unseemly quarrel.

NOTES

This essay was originally written for the volume *The Rigoberta Menchú Controversy*, ed. Arturo Arias (Minneapolis: University of Minnesota Press, 2001), 270–88. Reprinted by permission. It draws also on my essay "Rigoberta Menchú and the Politics of Lying," in *Human Rights Review* 1:1 (October 1999), 78–85. My thanks to Wilfrido H. Corral for his comments on the issues raised by the Menchú-Stoll controversy and for supplying me with Spanish-language articles.

 1. Robin Jones, "Having to Read a Book about Oppression: Encountering Rigoberta Menchú's Testimony in Boulder, Colorado," in *Teaching and Testimony: Rigoberta Menchú and the North American Classroom*, edited by Allen Carey-Webb and Stephen Benz (Albany: State University of New York Press, 1996), 149–62.

 2. Arturo Arias, "From Peasant to National Symbol," in *Teaching and Testimony: Rigoberta Menchú and the North American Classroom*, edited by Allen Carey-Webb and Stephen Benz (Albany: State University of New York Press, 1996), 29–46.

 3. David Stoll, *Rigoberta Menchú and the Story of All Poor Guatemalans* (Boulder, Colorado: Westview Press, 1999), 183.

 4. John Beverley, "The Real Thing," in *The Real Thing: Testimonial Discourse and Latin America*, edited by Georg M. Gugelberger (Durham, N.C.: Duke University Press, 1986), 266–86, has written at some length about the practice of referring to Rigoberta by her first name, making the predictable comments about the familiar usage. I nonetheless follow it. It is common practice in Latin America to refer to famous figures by their given names—for example, "Getúlio" for Getúlio Vargas, "Fidel" for Fidel Castro, "Clarice" for Clarice Lispector, and so on.

 5. Fred Siegel, "Taking it to the Streets," *Reason* (June 1998), 72–73.

 6. Dante Liano, "I, Rigoberta Menchú? The Controversy Surrounding the Mayan Activist," translated by Will H. Corral, *Hopscotch* 1:3 (1999), 96–101.

 7. Stoll in fact put off publishing his work for several years, until the end of the war in December 1996, when the Guatemalan government and leftist rebels signed a peace treaty.

8. Robin Wilson, "Anthropologist Challenges Veracity of Multicultural Icon," *The Chronicle of Higher Education* (January 15, 1999), A14.

9. John Beverley, "The Margin at the Center: On *Testimonio* (Testimonial Narrative)," in *De/Colonizing the Subject: The Politics of Gender in Women's Autobiography*, edited by Sidonie Smith and Julia Watson (Minneapolis: University of Minnesota Press, 1992), 91–114. Beverley's essay first appeared in *Modern Fiction Studies* 35:1 (Spring 1989).

10. Beverley, "Margin at the Center," 103.

11. Carmen Ochando Aymerich, in "De la representatividad literaria a la politica." *Lateral* (Barcelona) VI:52 (April 1999), 31, discusses the limited ideological horizon that defined testimonials that, like Rigoberta's, received literary awards from Cuba's Casa de las Américas. She warns readers about the dangers that lie behind the assumption of "representativity" accorded such works, which can lead to what she calls a totalizing discourse, one that fails to recognize that people can be victimized by a variety of political commitments.

12. Beverley, "Margin at the Center," 101.

13. Beverley, "The Real Thing," 281. Interestingly, despite entitling his essay "The Real Thing," he makes no reference to Henry James's short story of the same name, which brilliantly depicts the problems confronted by a painter when a "gentleman and a lady," fallen on hard times, wish to sit for him as models. The story recounts the painter's increasing discovery that the "real thing" cannot successfully represent the real thing, which the painter's usual declassé models can do to perfection. As James's artist-narrator puts it, he had "an innate preference for the represented subject over the real one: the defect of the real one was so apt to be a lack of representation. I liked things that appeared; then one was sure. Whether they *were* or not was a subordinate and almost always a profitless question" [emphasis in original].

14. Beverley, "Real Thing," 271 [emphasis in original].

15. Beverley, "Real Thing," 276.

16. Beverley, "Real Thing," 277.

17. William Cutler, III, "Accuracy in Oral History Interviewing," 84, in *Oral History: An Interdisciplinary Anthology*, edited by David K. Dunaway and Willa K. Baum (Nashville, Tenn.: American Association for State and Local History, 1984), 79–86.

18. Agnes Hankiss, "Ontologies of the Self: On the Mythological Rearranging of One's Life-History," 204, in *Biography and Society: The Life History Approach in the Social Sciences*, edited by Daniel Bertaux (Beverly Hills, Calif.: Sage Publications, 1981), 203–09.

19. Hankiss, "Ontologies," 204.

20. Daphne Patai, *Brazilian Women Speak: Contemporary Life Stories* (New Brunswick, N.J.: Rutgers University Press, 1988), 18.

21. See Julia Preston, " Guatemala Laureate Defends 'My Truth,'" *New York Times*, (January 21, 1999), A8. Stoll offered similar defenses in the Latin American press when news of his work broke in December 1998.

22. David Stoll, *Rigoberta Menchú and the Story of All Poor Guatemalans*, 183.

23. Stoll, 183. See also Luis Aceituno, "Arturo Taracena rompe el silencio," *El Acordeon* (January 10, 1999), 2B, reporting that Arturo Taracena, who had introduced Rigoberta to Elisabeth Burgos and participated in the editing of her interview, also states that, though the Guatemalan press had insisted it was Burgos who wrote

the book, this is entirely false. Burgos merely edited it, Taracena says, with his help. The book, according to Taracena, "is completely Rigoberta's narration, with her own rhythm, her own inventions, if there are any, her own emotions, her own truths. What the rest of us did was editorial work" [translation by DP]. For a more detailed account of explanations and defenses of Rigoberta, by herself and others, see Patai, "Rigoberta Menchú and the Politics of Lying" (1999).

24. Paul John Eakin, Foreword to Philippe Lejeune, *On Autobiography*, edited by Paul John Eakin, translated by Katherine Leary (Minneapolis: University of Minnesota Press, 1989), xvii–xix.

25. Sondra Hale, "Feminist Method, Process, and Self-Criticism: Interviewing Sudanese Women," 131, in *Women's Words: The Feminist Practice of Oral History*, edited by Sherna Berger Gluck and Daphne Patai (New York: Routledge, 1991), 121–36.

26. Hale, "Feminist Method," 134.

27. Sissela Bok, *Lying: Moral Choice in Public and Private Life* (New York: Vintage Books, 1978), 27.

28. Beverley, "Real Thing," 272–73.

29. Stoll, *Rigoberta Menchú*, 195.

30. Allen Carey-Webb and Stephen Benz, eds. *Teaching and Testimony: Rigoberta Menchú and the North American Classroom* (Albany: State University of New York Press, 1996).

31. Johnie G. Guerra and Sharon Ahern Fechter, "Rigoberta Menchú's Testimony as Required First Year Reading," 265, in *Teaching and Testimony: Rigoberta Menchú and the North American Classroom*, edited by Allen Carey-Webb and Stephen Benz (Albany: State University of New York Press, 1996), 261–70.

32. Catherine Ann Collins and Patricia Varas, "The Freshman Experience at Willamette University: Teaching and Learning with Rigoberta Menchú," 144, in *Teaching and Testimony: Rigoberta Menchú and the North American Classroom*, edited by Allen Carey-Webb and Stephen Benz (Albany: State University of New York Press, 1996), 133–47. See also my essay, "Who's Calling Whom 'Subaltern'?," included as chapter 7 in this volume.

33. Collins and Varas, " Freshman Experience," 144.

34. Gayatri Chakravorty Spivak, "Can the Subaltern Speak?," in *Marxism and the Interpretation of Culture*, edited by Cary Nelson and Lawrence Grossberg (Urbana: University of Illinois Press, 1988), 277–313.

35. Collins and Varas, "Freshman Experience," 144, quoting from Georg Gugelberger and Michael Kearney, "Voices of the Voiceless: Testimonial Literatures in Latin America," *Latin American Perspectives* 18:3 (1991), 9.

36. Collins and Varas, "Freshman Experience," 144.

37. Jones, "Having to Read," 158.

38. Jones, "Having to Read," 155.

39. Jones, "Having to Read," 159.

40. Jones, "Having to Read," 159.

41. Jones, "Having to Read," 160–161.

42. Mary Louise Pratt, "Me Llamo Rigoberta Menchú: Autoethnography and the Recoding of Citizenship," 57, in *Teaching and Testimony: Rigoberta Menchú and the North American Classroom*, edited by Allen Carey-Webb and Stephen Benz (Albany: State University of New York Press, 1996), 57–72.

43. Pratt, "Me Llamo Rigoberta Menchú: Autoethnography and the Recoding of Citizenship," 71.

44. Meri-Jane Rochelson, "'This is My Testimony': Rigoberta Menchú in a Class on Oral History," 248, in *Teaching and Testimony: Rigoberta Menchú and the North American Classroom*, edited by Allen Carey-Webb and Stephen Benz (Albany: State University of New York Press, 1996), 247–57.

45. Doris Sommer, "Not Just a Personal Story: Women's *Testimonios* and the Plural Self," 110, in *Life/Lines: Theorizing Women's Autobiography*, edited by Bella Brodzki and Celeste Schenck (Ithaca, N.Y.: Cornell University Press, 1988), 107–30.

46. Sommer, "Personal Story," 111.

47. Sommer, "Personal Story," 114.

48. Sommer, "Personal Story," 123.

49. Ana Rodríguez and Glenn Garvin, *Diary of a Survivor: Nineteen Years in a Cuban Women's Prison* (New York: St. Martin's Press, 1995).

50. See my essay, "When Method Becomes Power," in *Power and Method: Political Activism and Educational Research*, edited by Andrew Gitlin (New York: Routledge, 1994), 61-73.

51. Bertrand Russell, "The Superior Virtue of the Oppressed," in *Unpopular Essays*, 58–64 (New York: Simon and Schuster, 1950), quoted in Stoll, 194.

III

HETEROPHOBIA

13

Heterophobia: The Feminist Turn against Men

Something strange happened toward the end of the twentieth century. Women turned against men. Lives of human complexity, filled with both affection and antagonism, slowly began to be perceived as intolerable, perhaps despicable. Heterosexual intercourse was reclassified as "rape," and women's power to "consent" dismissed as powerlessness to resist patriarchal impositions. Even Simone de Beauvoir, formerly seen as a feminist heroine, a fighter for women's rights, became suspect because of her attachment to Jean-Paul Sartre. Intellectual companionship and lifelong love and friendship were recast as subservience as feminist critics scurried to deal with the discovery that their former idol had failed to lead the exemplary life they prescribed for her.

Heterosexuality has gone from being the norm to being on the defensive in the face of the phenomenon I call *heterophobia*—fear of difference, fear of the "other"—a term I use to refer specifically to the feminist turn against men and against heterosexuality. Of course, these attitudes are not held by all women, not even, perhaps, by many women, though certainly they are found among many feminist women. Nor is heterophobia solely the creation of lesbians, since they, vastly outnumbered by heterosexual women, could never have imposed such an agenda had it not been acceptable to heterosexual feminists as well. But if homophobia is still a problem for society at large, heterophobia is now feminism's own predictable reversal of that problem.

Heterophobia is by no means an entirely new phenomenon, though never has it gone so far or gained such notoriety as it has in the past couple of decades. When Mona Caird in the 1880s agitated against marriage, or when Cristabel Pankhurst published *The Great Scourge* in 1913 and described men as repulsive carriers of venereal disease, these women were combating particular social conditions. Their attacks were often immoderate, and there is in early feminism a strong and well-known antisexuality bias. Some women engaged in purity campaigns and argued for chastity, for both men and women. They opposed legalization of prostitution; some called for censorship of written materials and of art work depicting nudity. They judged male politicians on the basis of sexual morality, as did Lucy Stone in opposing Grover Cleveland's candidacy in the presidential election of 1884 because he had fathered—and taken responsibility for—an illegitimate child.

Yet these nineteenth- and early twentieth-century women did not support any sort of double standard that would have encouraged and promoted homosexual sex, while seeing only heterosexual sex as corrupting and deplorable. Living at a historical moment when women were struggling to win basic political rights—and were resting their claims on arguments that they had the *same* intellectual and moral capacities as men—they clearly saw that heterophobia could not be a winning tactic. The relative restraint of most early feminists is actually surprising, for they certainly would have been justified in taking a more aggressive stance on women's relationships with men at a time when those relationships were characterized above all by women's civic inequality, extreme economic dependence, lack of education, vulnerability to constant pregnancy and its attendant dangers of increasing pauperization, ill health, and death.

We in this country hardly live in that sort of world—feminist scare statistics notwithstanding. Most (though not all) women in America today have many options, due principally to their access to education and birth control and their resulting position in the labor market. And perhaps it is precisely because of these shifts, which have enormously increased women's autonomy and life opportunities, that heterophobes wishing to attack men must find ever new and more dramatic grounds for doing so.

In working on a book on the phenomenon of heterophobia, I am particularly interested in how heterosexual feminists experience being both feminist and heterosexual at a time when the two categories are often presented as antithetical and when heterosexual women's sexual preferences and experiences are being redefined and debased by rather silly, but nonetheless influential, ideas put forth in the name of feminism.

What, for example, is a heterosexual woman to do in a climate that tells her that male potency is a threat? That the penis is an instrument of domination? How many hetero feminists fail to challenge heterophobia out of a secret belief that only lesbian feminists are "the real thing"? How common is it for heterosexual women who call themselves "feminists" to find their heterosexuality complicated by their feminism? How productive are such tensions? Do they lead to inhibition and awkwardness as the "heterosexual body" comes under postmodernist scrutiny? How do women negotiate the ensuing problems? How do they compare the difficulties they encounter with the gains they feel they have made because of feminism? How frequently are they turned off of feminism or find that the word itself does nothing for them? And, a very important question, how much of a role does heterophobia play in "ordinary" women's alienation from feminism? Far from being the result of "backlash" or bad public relations, such alienation, in my view, is a legitimate perception of much that is wrong with feminist discourse.

Somewhere along the line, the criticism of patriarchal institutions derailed into a real, visceral, and frightening antagonism toward men and a consequent intolerance toward women who insist on associating with them. I'm amazed, as I think about it, that hetero women have submitted to this stigmatizing of their sexual desires and personal relations, but without question many of them have done so. A few examples follow.

While interviewing students for a book I wrote in 1994 (with Noretta Koertge), *Professing Feminism: Cautionary Tales from the Strange World of Women's Studies,* I was told by a women's studies major that one of her teacher's habitually referred to her "partner," without ever using any pronoun. Assuming, along with the whole class, that she was a lesbian, the student was shocked—and felt deceived—when she accidentally discovered that her professor was in fact heterosexual, was married, and had a child. My question is: Why does a women's studies teacher feel obliged to engage in such a cover-up? Another instance, small but telling: Following the publication of one of my early articles criticizing feminist excesses, I received a letter from a male academic who told me that he and his wife, also a professor, had been very active in setting up a women's center on their campus. When it came time to celebrate the center's anniversary, his wife had asked him not go to the event, saying: "I don't want to flaunt my heterosexuality." A final example, from my own experience as a teacher: In my courses on women's utopian fiction I have regularly taught lesbian utopian novels without ever uttering a word of criticism to suggest that their visions offered no hope for heterosexual women. Only after I had done some thinking about heterophobia did I begin to perceive the message I was inadvertently reinforcing to my students.

How heterophobia works out at the level of social behavior is often bizarre. I remember a meeting of some women faculty who got together weekly for lunch at a university where I was on leave in the mid-eighties. One day one of the members of the group announced that she was going to be married. There was an absolute dead silence in the room. Obviously we feminists (both lesbian and straight), were far too sophisticated to shriek and gush happiness, and no one knew what response to make as an alternative. So, stunned silence for far too long greeted her declaration. I have no doubt that if her announcement had been that she'd fallen in love with a woman and was about to move in with her, the reaction would have been quite different.

It seems that much of the present passionate rejection of men is explained, only apparently paradoxically, by feminism's embrace of "difference." This embrace has led to such a splintering of identity that the category "woman" can hardly be used without embarrassment. There are so many newly emergent identities to which any one group of feminists need feel inferior: white women vis-à-vis women of color; heterosexual women vis-à-vis lesbians; women of privilege vis-à-vis poor women (though, characteristically in American society, this theme seems to be of less importance than the others). The fact is that feminism is fragmented by all these divisions, which have created something that, in our book *Professing Feminism*, my coauthor and I referred to as the "oppression sweepstakes." I believe this jostling for place creates so much tension within feminism that it is barely able to sustain itself as a movement in which separate identity groups keep speaking to one another. But there is one thing that, apparently, can save the day for them all, and that is hostility to men.

The crude attack on men as a group provides some psychological ballast to feminists otherwise pulled in different directions by the highly politicized atmosphere in which they live. One lesbian I know deplores the heterophobic trend within feminism and has written to me that this amounts to casting men as what she calls "the universal scapegoat." Of course, on reflection, this requires further qualification, since women of color and women from other parts of the world at times argue that their struggle is "together with our men." From my observations, however, the white women who put up with such talk don't really like it, and only the heavy hand of racial or ethnic identity politics keeps them from directly challenging it. So it is white men who are indisputably at the pinnacle of the hated heap—as dishonest as it is to put them there, given that significant social divisions and highly variable behavior exist among white males as they do within any other human group.

No one acquainted with women's studies programs or feminist circles generally will be unaware that some of the most widely taught and read figures are the notorious heterophobes Catharine MacKinnon, Andrea Dworkin, and Mary Daly. I cannot bring myself to call these women "radical" feminists, as they are so often labeled, because I do not believe they go to the "root" of anything. Instead, I believe they manifest a pathological aversion to men, and I hold that their views have had a strong and negative influence on feminism and its future, in the classroom and out. One could, of course, argue that some of their extreme positions, such as that intercourse is indistinguishable from rape, or that all men are potential rapists, are useful as rallying cries for necessary social change, creating an audience capable of demanding that rape should never happen, that no woman should ever be the victim of sexual assault. And I think, in fact, that something must be conceded to such an argument. But more than this must be said, for how can one view with equanimity an agenda whose spokeswomen feel free to make grossly demeaning generalizations about half the world? Consider the following examples:

A year ago, on FEMISA, which is an e-mail list devoted to issues of gender and international relations, someone announced that she was preparing a paper contending that fathers are necessary for children's development. But, she said, "I would be helped by arguments that proved the opposite: that men are unnecessary for a child to grow into mature adulthood." Quite a few people were happy to oblige. One wrote:

> Men, as a group, tend to be abusive, either verbally, sexually or emotionally. There are always the exceptions, but they are few and far between (I am married to one of them). There are different levels of violence and abuse and individual men buy into this system by varying degrees. But the male power structure always remains intact.

Another poster wrote a long message in the same vein:

> Considering the nature and pervasiveness of men's violence, I would say that without question, children are better off being raised without the presence of men. Assaults on women and children are mostly perpetrated by men whom they are supposed to love and trust: fathers, brothers, uncles, grandfathers, stepfathers.

Disregarding the ample evidence, readily available, that women too are responsible for child abuse (and even child murder), this message continued:

> I agree with the many feminists who have argued that the role of fathers as perpetrators of sexual, emotional, and physical violence against female children is absolutely critical to the maintenance of male supremacy. Through incest, girls learn about subordination on the most basic level, and are thus prepared for their proper roles as women in this society.

In a stunning example of concept stretching, this last poster explained that when she uses the word "abusive," she means "to include the assertion of male dominance." The number of men who do not fit this profile, she wrote, is so small as to be "negligible." Though the FEMISA list is supposed to maintain an "international" perspective, these posters did not bother to qualify their statements, presumably intending them to characterize all males in every country in the world. When a few men on FEMISA did protest the male-bashing going on—not considered "flames," but perfectly appropriate messages—it was they who were summarily removed from the list.

When I become aware of such mind-numbing caricatures of male behavior, I am often reminded of a scene I repeatedly witnessed years ago when I was living in Paris. At the post office, at the end of the week, working-class men who were obviously immigrant laborers in France (Greek and Turkish men mostly, at that time) used to line up to send their money home, often to places so remote that long discussions ensued as the clerks tried to figure out just which particular village or island was addressed. I used to stand in line behind these men, week after week, asking myself: What keeps them coming back here? Badly dressed, surely living in poor accommodations, yet faithful, determined to support their families, why do they do it? Nothing in the extremist feminist vision allows one to understand the behavior of such men—except, of course, the gross supposition that what they are really manifesting is their economic power so that one day they can go home and resume tyrannizing their wives and children.

At about the same time that I was observing and wondering about these men, a woman in the United States was composing what later became a famous "feminist" document. She wrote:

> Life in this society being, at best, an utter bore and no aspect of society being at all relevant to women, there remains to civic-minded, responsible, thrill-seeking females only to overthrow the government, eliminate the money system, institute complete automation, and destroy the male sex.

This statement comes, of course, from Valerie Solanas, whom some readers may remember as the author, in 1968, of the *SCUM Manifesto*, and who moviegoers can now see as the heroine of a recent film. By being SCUM—members of the Society for Cutting Up Men—Solanas argued, women could quickly take over the country. Foreshadowing the intense animosity between many feminist women and their non-feminist sisters, she pinpointed the real conflict as not that between females and males, but between SCUM—whom she defines as women who are dominant, secure, proud, independent—and those she contemptuously labels "approval-seeking Daddy's Girls." Among the things SCUM will do when it takes over is "destroy all useful and harmful objects—cars, store windows, 'Great Art', etc." "SCUM will couple-bust," Solanas ominously announced; it will "barge into mixed (male-female) couples, wherever they are, and bust them up." And, in case anyone remains in some doubt as to what SCUM had in mind for men, Solanas spells it out (showing that Mary Daly and Andrea Dworkin are mere latecomers and also-rans): "SCUM will kill all men who are not in the Men's Auxiliary of SCUM. Men in the Men's Auxiliary are those men who are working diligently to eliminate themselves."

Solanas can probably be dismissed as part of the lunatic fringe. Some have tried to deal with the problem posed for feminists by her manifesto by labeling it satire. But such a view is belied by Solanas's own actions. She is, after all, the woman who, in June 1968, shot and nearly killed Andy Warhol (and one of his associates) over Warhol's apparent lack of interest in a film script entitled "Up Your Ass" that she had submitted to him. And what is one to make of Solanas's feminist champions, such as the two representatives of NOW, Ti-Grace Atkinson and the attorney Florence Kennedy, who accompanied Solanas to court? According to Victor Bockris's book *The Life and Death of Andy Warhol* (1989), Atkinson said at this court appearance that Solanas would go down in history as "the first outstanding champion of women's rights," while Flo Kennedy called her "one of the most important spokeswomen of the feminist movement." Such views are echoed by feminist writer Vivian Gornick. In her long introduction to the 1970 edition of the *SCUM Manifesto*, Gornick called Solanas a visionary who "understood the true nature of the struggle" for women's liberation. One can well imagine the reaction of feminists if a male would-be murderer of women were honored in this way.

But even if one grants that Solanas is an extreme and atypical case (and the movie *I Shot Andy Warhol* clearly portrays her descent into madness), what shall we say of Sally Miller Gearhart, a professor of communications who, nearly fifteen years after Solanas, wrote an essay entitled "The Future—If There Is One—Is Female"?[1] Gearhart's argument, like Solanas's, is simple: The future must be in female hands, women alone must control the reproduction of the species (with men given no say in it whatsoever), and only ten percent of the population should be allowed to be male. Gearhart plays a few notes of sweet reason, granting that, since we cannot be sure that men are inherently destructive or women naturally nurturing, men should not be eliminated altogether.

Like Gearhart, I myself used to believe that women should run the world. Even if we couldn't be sure what women *would* do, it was reasonable, I used to argue, to expect that we would make no worse a job of it than men had done. That was before I spent years in a women's studies program and saw for myself how, in practice, women deal with conflict. It was an experience that convinced me that women are in no way superior to men in political virtue, kindness, or even plain good sense. It also persuaded me that we should keep muddling on toward equality between the sexes and that an important aspect of pursuing this goal is to avoid the language of hate.

But this is not what feminist extremists have in mind. Like Valerie Solanas and her *SCUM Manifesto*, Professor Gearhart calls upon men to participate in their own demise by voluntarily assisting in a program of reducing their own numbers (she makes reassuringly clear that she does not contemplate mass murder but rather slow attrition through new reproductive technologies and support from men for feminist goals). And from what I see on the feminist e-mail lists, there are groveling males in the world who would gladly go along even with this policy for the sake of maintaining their cherished but never entirely secure status as "feminist men." It appears that not only women are inclined to knuckle under to strong speech and intimations of power.

Gearhart's essay on the female future in fact reveals that in her view not all women are equally qualified to build the better society to come. One would, of course, want to know at the outset how conflicts among women are to be resolved in Gearhart's vision. But she has nothing to say about this problem. As a lesbian-feminist activist, she does, however, know which women can—and which can *not*—be permitted to exercise power. Women who might not go along with her views are, she says, "enslaved by male-identification and years of practice within the system." No attention need be paid to them. Such women, along with men, will need to be subjected to "education" in the "voluntary [sic] and vast changes that must take place."

The claim that women's rule would necessarily lead to peace and order in the world (a staple of feminist utopian fiction, a subject I have been teaching for years) and that political in-fighting would vanish is, of course, nonsense. It is a childish dream, perhaps a touching one, but still nothing more than a dream. Let us ignore, for the moment, the fact that women as a group do not see eye to eye or hold identical ideas (how could they?). Women are not, after all, natural socialists or born egalitarians, though many feminist writers like to pretend that they are. What do we find when we actually investigate how women handle conflicts? One woman, Rachel Bedard, who became a lesbian separatist for a while after her marriage failed, has left this account:

> I moved into a separatist house with tremendous expectations of feminist support and nurturance. But within weeks we were divided over everything from dinner hour to cats to who owned which soap in the bathroom.[2]

No doubt feminist extremists will blame this discord too on The Patriarchy. In any event, Bedard's household broke up, and she, though ostracized by feminist friends for doing so, eventually returned to heterosexuality. Bedard, tellingly, titled her account of these experiences "Re-entering Complexity."

If we reject—as it seems obvious we must—the notion that a world ruled by feminists would necessarily be a superior one of peace and harmony, we have the right, even the obligation, to ask what sorts of political processes feminists will set in place instead of the much despised masculinist ones. And how will the feminist future deal with dissenters? On this subject feminist utopian fiction should have something to tell us. But it does so only too rarely. Even my undergraduate students notice that Charlotte Perkins Gilman's utopian novel *Herland* (1915), which describes an all-female society, presumes lack of conflict rather than outlines mechanisms for dealing with it. And they recognize too the coercive manipulations that subtly underlie that society: the pressure brought to bear on women who are not—by the society's eugenic standards—deemed worthy of reproduction (accomplished through parthenogenesis in the novel). And if social pressure fails, the novel tells us, more stringent measures are taken. These measures, however, are not described, so we are left to wonder: Do the uncooperative women undergo forced abortions?

In many ways, the anti-sex rhetoric (and, more generally, the anti-male campaign) of contemporary heterophobes is an assault on the private sphere. And it makes sense that extremists should go after the private sphere, for it is in the realm of the personal that their ideas are most vulnerable. Not surprisingly, perhaps, feminist extremists at times exempt themselves from the behavioral norms they wish to impose on all other women. In practice, they often carve out little pockets in which their particular personal lives and tastes can continue untainted, and it is only other women whose lives need to be scrutinized, regulated, and—if they do not measure up—scorned. How else explain that Andrea Dworkin, with her notoriously hateful and obscene writings about men and heterosexuality in general, has also written lovingly about her own father, a feminist man to whom she says she owes her passion for writing and her independent spirit? And how else explain Catharine MacKinnon's apparent belief that while other women cannot give informed consent, she herself can? This seems a fair inference to draw from those affectionate photographs seen a few years ago of MacKinnon arm-in-arm with her then-fiancé, Jeffrey Masson. Clearly, these women are prepared to impose their views on others, while, for themselves, they maintain the rights belonging to autonomous adults. This is the standard tactic of authoritarian leaders.

Faced with the incontrovertible fact that many women who are economically independent nonetheless seem to like living with men, heterophobes have had to bring out their heavy artillery. The older of the two main tactics is simply to unleash the language of hate against men, to heap such scorn on them that it becomes difficult for self-respecting women who consider themselves feminists to associate with males.

A newer tool in the feminist arsenal is the postmodernist obfuscation or "problematizing" of not only gender but also sex, which are represented as entirely imaginary constructs that—once we see them for what they are—will cease enslaving us. In other words, once we learn that "sexual preference" and even our own "sexual identity" are "social constructions," the products of social conditioning that force us to limit our lovers to a particular group of people, heterosexual relations as we know them will come to an end, along with all questions of sexual identity and preference or orientation. For in this view, not only gender but even sexual identity is performance; it is ideology, but it is certainly not an essential part of the self-definition of free and thoughtful human beings who actually are born female and male.

Some of the reasons for advancing these extraordinary arguments are, of course, easy to understand. Some proponents may honestly think that it is not possible to gain civil equality for gays and lesbians except by stigmatizing heterosexuality or at least by "problematizing" it. In this view, gay-rights activism, like feminism, is a zero-sum game: Whatever I win, you lose. If my being homosexual is to be valued, your being heterosexual must be debased. But this seems a doomed strategy, since such theorizing will have little effect on the vast majority of people, who will no doubt go right on being stubbornly heterosexual while feeling nothing but alienation from the sort of feminists who tell them they shouldn't be doing what they're doing, and certainly should not consider it "natural."

A dismal example of postmodernist approaches to sexuality—and a textbook case of heterophobia at work—is provided by a recent article entitled "The Medicalization of Impotence: Normalizing Phallocentrism," by Lenore Tiefer.[3] Its abstract states the following:

> Today, phallocentrism is perpetuated by a flourishing medical construction that focuses exclusively on penile erections as the essence of men's sexual function and satisfaction. This article describes how this medicalization is promoted by urologists, medical industries, mass media, and various entrepreneurs [offering treatments for impotence]. Many men and women provide a ready audience for this construction because of masculine ideology and gender socialization.

In this view, nobody really needs an erect penis. Presumably, the author of this article would prefer to live in the world of Sally Gearhart's 1979 feminist utopia *The Wanderground*, where the women's only male allies (of whom they're nonetheless suspicious) are the gay men, called "gentles," who have voluntarily accepted impotence. In other words, the only good man, it seems, is an impotent man.

Such thinking is admittedly a minority position within the larger sphere of feminism, but the language of hate, which is embodied and prevalent in many feminist writings, should be taken seriously. It ought to be no more acceptable in the mouths of women than in the mouths of men, no more tolerable coming from feminists than from the Ku Klux Klan. And we must consider the kinds of power feminist ideas have indeed actually achieved. The relations between men and women have become "problematized," so much so that any word or gesture may these days give offense to women. If, in the old days, women's complaints against men's abusive behavior were seldom taken seriously, today things are quite different. Nor is this just a matter of social norms, of casual office behavior. There are men who have lost their jobs, certainly in academe which is the area I know best, because of flimsy allegations of sexual harassment. Men are being deprived of due process. And many feminists quite explicitly and seriously consider that this is the way things should be. In their view, due process is merely one of the patriarchy's power tools, like freedom of speech.

Feminism has in fact been remarkably successful in creating a climate in which men's words and gestures are suspect and in which it is now women's charges that are given quick credibility or at least the benefit of the doubt. Tell an innocent man who has lost his job in a university (and cannot get another one) because of a charge of sexual harassment that feminists don't have power. But it is not only men who are the victims of such accusations. Women in academe too, though much more rarely, are being accused of sexual harassment when it suits the agenda of others, even of so-called feminists.

It is frightening to see a society unleash against its own citizens codes of speech and behavior that can ensnare just about anyone and that have as their rational underpinning nothing more than a woman's sense of "discomfort" around certain phrases or deeds. To conflate this with serious acts of sexual harassment and abuse is to invite totalitarianism—the heavy hand of authority everywhere in the private sphere, until there is virtually no private sphere left. Is this an enactment of the feminist vision? It sounds more like the dystopias we're all familiar with from the novels of Zamiatin and Orwell, in which political control of sexuality is closely linked to the creation of an atmosphere of hysteria that has as its aim the suppression of the private sphere while redirecting of individuals' energy toward state goals and definitions.

Consider, as well, the truly bizarre and frightening climate surrounding child sexual abuse and "recovered memories," as they are called. Innocent people are in prison as I speak because of so-called "evidence" that any sane society would have laughed out of court. Tell those victims that contemporary feminist ideas about the protections we all need from the demon of sexuality (which is always above all heterosexuality) have not had any effect. Or consider the affront of "visual harassment"—which is what one Minneapolis construction supervisor called it when urging his crew not to look at women passers-by.[4] And what about the absurd suspicion that massive sexual harassment is going on in school yards, and the demand of grown women that little boys be made to face up to it and reform?

The writings of the most notorious and least responsible among heterophobes have enormously contributed to the creation of a "gotcha" atmosphere in which individual autonomy and its sexual manifestations in particular are under attack. And what is the justification for this assault? It is being waged "for our own good," and such niceties as democratic processes and First Amendment rights may just have to be sacrificed.

It is to protest this state of affairs that I am speaking about heterophobia. Despite its apparent relationship to the long tradition of sexual repression in America, heterophobia, should not be mistaken for a nostalgic return to Victorianism. On the contrary, its best fit is with the dismaying history of twentieth-century totalitarianisms. A tendency toward totalizing pronouncements and an absence of respect for the political process—the essence of which, after all, is compromise—are quite blatant among feminist extremists. But we all bear responsibility for it if we do not speak out against it and against the indignities and falsehoods that feminist rhetoric heaps upon men as a group—a tactic that, these days, would not for an instant be tolerated if it were directed against, say, blacks, or Hispanics, or Jews,[5] or women as a group. It is absurd to characterize every man who will not agree with feminist positions as a throwback who is, by his very disagreement, demonstrating the male drive to dominance and the desire to keep women barefoot and pregnant.

It is astonishing that decades of progress for women, decades of denunciation of misogynist ideas, should have brought us to the point where a mere reversal—a resort to misandry instead of misogyny—should count as serious feminist thought and should be taught and promoted in the name of feminism. Thus the historical spectacle of sex antagonism continues, with no hope that it will ever be superseded. By fanning the flame of this antagonism, feminists prove, ironically, that they are no different from their masculinist counterparts.

Feminist extremism has brought about very negative results—such as the exorbitant sexualization of all interactions between men and women, the vigilante mentality, the vocabulary of sexual harassment even at the kindergarten level, the denial of due process to men (and occasionally to women) accused of sexual misdeeds at universities and in the workplace, the attack on the rights of fathers, and so on. But at the same time I am suggesting that this vindictive sort of feminism has nowhere to go because it alienates many women—and, of course, men too. So which is it? Has heterophobia succeeded or is it doomed to failure? The two views can, I think, be reconciled. We need to acknowledge that the negative consequences are real and are being felt—in unjust and frivolous accusations against men (and against women too), in the resulting loss of reputation and even of livelihood, in a strained atmosphere between the sexes, in assaults on freedom of expression and association.

All these are short-term results. They lead so clearly to a worse world that they cannot possibly endure. Other, more tyrannical and much more powerful ideologies have self-destructed; so will this. And when that happens, the damage done to feminism in the eyes of millions of potential supporters will be clearly felt. For the feminism that aimed at promoting justice and equality, not anger and revenge, will have been tainted as a far-out movement dominated by the male-bashers (who are indeed often the loudest among feminist spokespersons), and enormous effort will be required to restore feminism to the dignity that it deserves. Because feminist extremism is creating a well-earned bad name for itself, and because it is genuinely harming people, women and men who want a better society must speak out against it. And they must do so, I think, without allying themselves with reactionary forces that truly do desire to see women under men's thumbs once again.

Yet at the moment, the dominant trend within feminism still seems remarkably resilient to any self-criticism. When, in May 1996, I posted an announcement about my heterophobia project to the women's studies e-mail list, inviting reactions, scores of hostile replies poured in from women telling me my project was dangerous and ill conceived. Ironically, they seemed divided between those who argued that there was no such thing as heterophobia within feminism and those who felt it was justified by men's behavior. Many of the respondents, furthermore, cast aspersions on my motives in pursuing this subject and criticized my "methodology" for inviting anecdotal evidence to confirm what they considered to be an invalid and ideologically biased project (a most interesting criticism, coming from feminists). Even the feminist novelist Marge Piercy, who, I assume, would not take kindly to suggestions that she recast her writing according to someone else's views, urged that I reconsider or redefine my project.

There have always, of course, been sane feminists who have seen the dangers of the domination of either sex over the other. One such figure was the British writer Katharine Burdekin (1896–1963) who, in the thirties, wrote a series of remarkable feminist-inspired utopian and dystopian novels. In a novel called *Proud Man*,[6] Burdekin outlined her critique of a world run by women. The narrator of the novel, an androgynous being from a future that it calls *human*, observes life in England in the 1930s and comments on the behavior of us *subhumans*, still living in "the childhood age":

> If women retain their biological importance, and become pleased with themselves from birth, and learn to associate power with the womb instead of with the phallus, a dominance of females over males is not only possible but likely. Their self-confidence, which would be rooted as deep as the old male jealousy, would cause in them a tremendous release of psychic power with which the males would be unable to cope. Naturally a female dominance would make the race no happier, nor bring it a whit nearer to humanity. The privilege would merely be reversed, and possibly it would be more oppressive and more cruel.

Twenty years ago I would never have suspected that we, today, would need to hear such a warning. That heterophobes, at the moment, lack substantive political power should not deceive us about the kind of world they clearly want to bring about—and would if they ever gained the means to do so. As I have argued, they have succeeded in introducing an element of genuine paranoia into the relationships of ordinary men and women, and this achievement—backed up as it is by changes in the law—should not be taken lightly. Their ideas need to be seen for what they are: a project posing as utopian that, were it ever to become reality, would instead be a nightmare.

NOTES

A version of this essay was first presented as a talk at the Women's Freedom Network conference in Washington, D.C., on October 15, 1995. It was then published in *Partisan Review* 4 (Fall 1996), 580–594, and thereafter became the core of my book *Heterophobia: Sexual Harassment and the Future of Feminism* (Lanham, Md.: Rowman & Littlefield, 1998).

1. Sally Miller Gearhart, "The Future—If There Is One—Is Female" in *Reweaving the Web of Life: Feminism and Nonviolence*, ed. Pam McAllister (Philadelphia: New Society Publishers, 1982), 374–84.

2. Rachel Bedard, "Re-entering Complexity," in *Reweaving the Web of Life: Feminism and Nonviolence*, ed. Pam McAllister (Philadelphia: New Society Publishers, 1982), 401.

3. Lenore Tiefer "The Medicalization of Impotence: Normalizing Phallocentrism," *Gender and Society* 8:3 (September 1994), 363–77.

4. As reported in the Minneapolis *Star-Tribune*, August 5, 1995.

5. Note added in 2007: How rapidly things change. It is less than fifteen years since I wrote the above words but, at the present time, attacks on Jews are once again acceptable. Islamism, with its conflation of anti-Israeli, anti-Western, and anti-Jewish attitudes, has spread not only throughout Europe but also throughout the United States and is routinely visible in the academic world.

6. *Proud Man* by Katharine Burdekin (London: Boriswood, 1934) was originally published under the pseudonym Murray Constantine. I discovered the author's real identity in the 1980s and the book was reprinted with both names by the Feminist Press in 1993. This note refers to the later edition which includes the foreword and afterword I composed for the edition.

14

Casting the First Stone

Halfway through her book *The First Stone: Some Questions About Sex and Power*,[1] Australian writer Helen Garner contemplates how institutions can inspire such deep feelings in men that they, as she writes in italicized wonder and admitted distaste, "fall in love with an institution *for life*." Such loyalty, she notes, "might unsettle [one's] broader ethical judgments."[2] Her case in point is the dismissal of the Master of Ormond College, a residential college at the University of Melbourne, after he had been accused of groping two female students at a College celebration.

Yet Garner herself has experienced a comparable falling in love. This is never stated explicitly in the book, but it is implicit throughout by her deep sorrow at the loss of her faith in feminism's capacity to make the world a better place.

Perhaps it is this tone of loss, which provides a dark backdrop to the "quiet, thoughtful" book Garner had hoped to write, that led Janet Malcolm, with her keen ear for the scathing put-down, to characterize Garner's book in *The New Yorker* as the "ravings of a rejected lover"[3] But Malcolm is wrong on both counts. There are no ravings here: there is sadness and bewilderment, and now and then a flash of deep anger (is only feminist anger at supposed male privilege legitimate?).

Nor is Garner the "rejected lover," despite her increasing frustration at being denied access to the two women who brought the charges. Hers is the voice of an older-and-wiser feminist who discovers suddenly that she cannot tolerate the denial of fairness, justice, and common sense, even when it is perpetrated in the name of feminism, and who now looks wistfully at the affection, trust, and hope of her earlier affair with feminism. And like men's passion for institutions, commitment to feminism, she now sees, can warp one's judgment of individual cases.

The course of events leading to Garner's critique is told in this very personal account of what happened in Melbourne starting in October 1991. It is a rather typical male/female conflict, a conflict classified, as so often these days, by the label "sexual harassment." Such cases increasingly take on the dramatic form of a morality play, dividing their audiences, turning friendship to hostility, and ultimately raising questions about who and how we are in the world.

Garner pursues two main questions. First, why did the two students decide to go to the police to press charges of indecent assault rather than attempt to settle the matter in less adversarial ways? She never quite reaches an answer, though it seems that it had much to do with both feminist rhetoric and the instant support given to the students by other women in the College, who resisted more informal solutions. It is this sequence of events—"He touched her breast and she went to the *cops?*"—that shook Garner's commitment to feminism to the point of sending a letter of sympathy to the accused, expressing her dismay at the "ghastly punitiveness." and "warfare" directed against him.[4] This letter, once circulated, made Garner the target of antipathy by feminists within and without the College, which explains the complainants' persistent refusal to discuss the case with her when she subsequently tried to interview them. The second main question Garner addresses is: Why did the Master—who repeatedly denied the allegations—lose his position even though on appeal he was found not guilty of the charges? While Garner seeks an explanation primarily in terms of the personalities, history, traditions, and ethos of the College, I suspect (given what I know of similar outcomes in very different places) that the force of feminist ideology played an important role.

But Garner's book is not a simple tale of feminist justice gone awry. As a long-term feminist, who had her own experiences with unwanted and offensive sexual overtures, she is sensitive to the students' allegations and offers interesting reflections on the odd passivity that keeps women from handling such situations on their own. She is also aware of the real violence to which women are subjected, and episodes of it intrude into her narrative. In April 1993, for example, while working on her book, Garner hears about a fourteen-year-old girl who, on her way to school, was raped at knifepoint in a public toilet:

> I thought . . . that our helpless rage and grief at this eternally unpreventable violence against women and girls—our inability to protect our children from the sickness of the world—must get bottled up and then let loose on poor blunderers who get drunk at parties and make clumsy passes. . . .[5]

It is a revealing passage. First, many feminists would denounce Garner's "sickness of the world" as a weak euphemism for "the sickness of men," a condition demanding correction and control. Second, the pronouns hint that Garner does not see herself as one of the potentially raped, as one of the victims. By contrast, many feminists who clamor for drastic measures against sexual harassers do identify with the offended parties, do see themselves as sufferers, indeed see all women as men's victims. Given that much feminist discourse has been devoted precisely to eliding the distinctions between types of offenses and degrees of suffering, this identification should come as no surprise.

Therefore, when Garner concludes: "But the ability to discriminate [between attacks and clumsy overtures] *must be maintained*. Otherwise all we are doing is increasing the injustice of the world,"[6] she asserts a proposition that not only has never won general agreement in feminist circles, but is expressly denied and actively contested by some of the most vocal feminist writers.

For my part, I concur with Garner. Distinctions are of the utmost importance. Unfortunately, we live in a climate (and evidently so does Garner) in which many women are doing their best to prevent nuanced thinking from dissolving their caricature of the undifferentiated male menace, so that the smallest offense can be represented as "as bad as" or "not fundamentally different from" the most heinous. Is it any surprise that feminism strikes Garner increasingly as "priggish, disingenuous, unforgiving"?

Garner rejects the view that sees male power at work in all heterosexual exchanges. She worries that "Eros, 'the spark that ignites and connects,'"[7] will be extinguished by the new dispensation with its ferocious insistence on conflating "harassment" and "violence."[8] But even Garner occasionally genuflects to feminist discourse, as when she describes sexual harassment as "bullying"[9]—forgetting her own arguments elsewhere that a provocative word or gesture may be a positive expression of desire, even awe, when encountering female beauty and vitality. Why, she asks more reasonably, must flirting be harmful? Why must it mean something beyond itself? "It's play. It's the little god Eros, flickering and flashing through the plod of our ordinary working lives." She concludes: "Feminism is meant to free us, not to take the joy out of everything."[10]

But the problem is that what she calls "joy" and "play" have been reconceptualized by many feminist theorists as patriarchy's perpetuation of its oppression of women. So, unless a great many women step forward to support Garner's call for reasonableness—to declare that the inconvenience of an unwanted sexual overture is a small price to pay for freedom of expression and association, and to reject a world in which sexuality is banished from school and workplace in the name of avoiding any possible offense—the theoretical battle will continue to be won by those who talk the most and the loudest.

The battle is between two fundamentally opposing worldviews. One sees sex (especially male sexuality) as a perpetual danger; the other, as primarily a source of pleasure for both women and men. Garner's version of the world is an irritant and a threat to the sex police who would leave nothing to chance, risk no unpleasantness, opt always for safety and certainty over improvisation and possible accusations of abuses of power.

Garner suspects that much of the conflict between herself and the younger women who supported the complainants may be due to differing generational perceptions. In light of what I have seen of sexual harassment cases in academe, I doubt it. Older women who have absorbed and sustained the "punitive feminist" (Garner's term) line on sexual harassment are likely to be as vindictive as the students to whom they teach that line.

What is most significant about *The First Stone* is its commentary on the implications—for women, for feminism, for men—of the new dispensation that pits women against male sexuality. In no uncertain terms, Garner deplores the atmosphere created as a result of the wide acceptance of a punitive feminism that insists on seeing women as victims.

Once *The First Stone* was published in Australia, Garner's dismay was compounded, as is made clear in an afterword to the North American edition, in which she reflects on the reaction to the book itself and to her personally. Like other women who have written critically of feminism, she found herself vilified and turned into an official enemy, her motives presumed mercenary, her words and views distorted. Janet Malcolm, for example, contemptuously dismisses Garner's suggestions for "less destructive responses" to harassment (such as letting one instance of groping pass with a warning). "This isn't good enough," Malcolm admonishes. "This is closing ranks with the abuser. . . . Sexual harassment isn't sexual abuse—exactly. It lies on the border between a crime and a mistake."[11] Malcolm wilfully ignores Garner's call for responses suitable to borderline situations, that is to say, for measured reactions to highly diverse episodes, all of which are today viewed strictly through the distorting prism of "power," a term beloved by practitioners of feminist discourse. But Garner also received hundreds of letters (about two-thirds of them from women), expressing relief that someone was at last saying that daily life is not as horrible and destructive to women as feminist orthodoxy insists it is.

One of the most illuminating lines in the book comes from the Ormond Master's wife, who is the subject of a sympathetic chapter. "Deep down," she says, "under this extraordinary pain I feel, there's a sense of the *triviality* of this destruction."[12]

Garner's is a brave and mellow book. It recognizes the legitimate grievances of women, but also the power of youth and beauty and the unpredictability of Eros. It insists on a sensible approach to complex, problematic human interactions, rather than vigilantism and retribution. That this posture makes its author, in many eyes, an enemy of feminism is a sorry reflection on the state of feminism in the English-speaking world.

NOTES

A version of this essay was first published in *The Women's Freedom Network Newsletter*, vol. 4, no. 4 (Fall 1997).

1. Helen Garner, *The First Stone: Some Questions About Sex and Power* (New York: Free Press, 1997; first published in Australia in 1995). All italicized words in quoted phrases are Garner's.
2. Garner, *The First Stone,* 111
3. Janet Malcolm, "Review of *The First Stone*" (*The New Yorker*, July 7, 1997, 75).
4. Garner, *The First Stone,* 15–16.
5. Garner, *The First Stone,* 120.
6. Garner, *The First Stone,* 120.
7. Garner, *The First Stone,* 112.
8. Garner, *The First Stone,* 100.
9. Garner, *The First Stone,* 103.
10. Garner, *The First Stone,* 112–13.
11. Malcolm, "Review of *The First Stone*," 75.
12. Garner, *The First Stone,* 140.

15

Politicizing the Personal

Imagine the following scenario: A coup against the president of the United States, aimed at deposing him, is led by a war-hero general who deplores the president's peaceful policies. In a desperate situation, the president discovers an unexpected means of bringing down his opponent: a cache of love letters written by the rebellious general to his mistress, evidence of an adulterous affair. Confronting the traitorous general, the president asks for his resignation. The general refuses, attacks the president for his weakness, and threatens to take his case to the people, via a television address. Imagine the president at his desk, looking down at the sheaf of love letters in a half-open drawer. Will he use them to blackmail his opponent? Coming to an unspoken decision, he shuts the drawer. He then fights his opponent on political grounds—and wins, thwarting the coup.

It may be remembered that this is the plot of the 1964 film *Seven Days in May*, based on the novel of the same title by Fletcher Knebel and Charles W. Bailey II. Today, of course, the serious charge of treason could be easily subsumed, and dealt with, by the more fashionable accusation of sexual impropriety. The love letters would be leaked to the media, the general—and his cause—discredited.

In the thirty-five years since *Seven Days in May*, codes of behavior and the choice of political weaponry have undergone a profound change. But it is not generally understood that this change must be credited to—or blamed on—the success of feminism in promoting the notion that "the personal is political" and that boundaries between the private and public spheres must and should be effaced.

To grasp precisely what politicizing the personal can lead to, let's reverse the film's plot. Now the president is the one with the extramarital affair. His enemy, the sexually pure general, attempting a military takeover, gets hold of the president's letters to his mistress, an effective instrument for bringing him down. The reversal highlights what should by now be clear to us all: The "personal" is a very powerful weapon, but that tells us nothing about the "political" in the name of which it may be used.

Whose interests are served by dismantling the boundaries between public and private life? The answer appears to be political opponents of every type, who find in this erosion a deadly assault weapon from which few are safe. We might wish that all people never behaved in a less than honorable manner, but are we really ready for a society in which no one dares do anything wrong, in which bright light is focused on every single aspect of private life?

Of course, as we become more deeply embroiled in a political climate in which no private arena is safe from scrutiny, it's worthwhile recognizing that there is nothing new about men using women as weapons against other men. What is startling is the realization that feminism has had a major role in bringing this situation about, for it is feminism that has given us the concept of sexual harassment, without which the relations between men and women would not have become such dangerous territory. By now there is a substantial feminist literature that takes as axiomatic the notion that heterosexual behavior is how men keep women in an inferior position. This concept has proved so expansive that today, the expert literature informs us, sexual harassment can range from a look to rape. This is the same feminist framework that has led to the obsession with "power differentials," which in their extreme form enormously limit the range of permissible relationships and lead ultimately to the notion that women in a patriarchal society cannot give "informed consent" to heterosexual relations.

As we are now discovering, effacing the boundaries between the public and the private is a game anybody can play. As more and more charges and confessions flood the public sphere, it has become clear that few are immune; all people in the public eye can be brought to heel by fear of exposure.

There are, however, some other surprising beneficiaries to the merging of public and private spheres. In earlier times it was mostly women who bore the stigma of sexual misconduct. But now it is men who have to run scared. Not all women are wives, trying to keep their husbands in line. Mistresses and girlfriends may also benefit from the new dispensation, since they now control a man's fate far more than in the past.

But the harsh light of exposure doesn't usually stay put; it has a way of running amok, which in the long term can only mean that both men and women find their most personal sexual impulses under scrutiny. The attack on the private sphere in fact threatens everyone—except perhaps those bland folk who, devoid of personal habits that could ever be used against them, might rise to high public office on a platform of personal purity. This sort of rectitude may or may not be accompanied by any political talent— but if, indeed, "the personal is political," does it matter? Surely absence of political ideas and skills is of little consequence once we know that our politicians lead unblemished private lives or perhaps have no private lives at all. But should we really assume that the best political leaders are those whose personal record is blameless, and who therefore have nothing to fear from the politicization of the most private and vulnerable arena of all—that of sexual desire?

Yet another group of beneficiaries of sexual policing is those feminists whose antagonism to men, and in particular to male sexuality, is generalized into an attack on all males and on women's relationships with them. For such heterophobes, ever on the lookout for a suspicious word or gesture, sexual harassment law and the climate it has created are powerful new weapons to wield in their effort to place obstacles in the personal relations between men and women. Yet it cannot serve the interests of most women to have men be afraid of involvement with them.

Ironically, it seems highly improbable that the current demands for personal probity on the part of public figures will lead to a better world. Why? Because the type of vigilance necessary to ensure a life entirely free from reproach will create a social climate so unpleasant, and ultimately so repressive, that the cure will be much worse than the disease. Signs of precisely such a climate are everywhere around us, as politicians, employers, and even college presidents mouth platitudes about "power differentials," as if the new orthodoxy were beyond question.

This vigilantism should worry us all. When the private becomes public and the personal is seen as political, anyone can be targeted. As for the realms of actual politics and public life, these deteriorate into prurient squabbles and competition over moral one-upmanship. Just read any newspaper.

NOTE

First published in the *Women's Freedom Network Newsletter* 5:6 (November/December 1998), 3, 7.

16

Do They Have to Be Wrong?

On Writing about Rape

There are subjects that are difficult to write about because they arouse strong feelings and involve pain and suffering. Rape is obviously such a subject. In the mid-seventies, I served on the editorial board of a feminist arts journal called *Aphra*, founded and edited by Elizabeth Fisher. I recall that a short story was submitted to us—an account of a rape experience—and to me fell the task of writing the author a rejection letter, since everyone agreed that the story was poorly done. I still remember how difficult it was to do something as formal as send a letter of rejection to the woman who had written such a personal tale. Yet, we had no choice. The magazine (which published early works by many women who went on to become important figures in feminism and contemporary literature) could not simply print every heart-rending account regardless of its literary merits.

Though the issue is not one of literary merit in the case of scholarly studies of rape, the subject remains an awkward one to discuss in measured tones. It is hard to read a book such as Randy Thornhill and Craig T. Palmer's *A Natural History of Rape: Biological Bases of Sexual Coercion*[1] precisely because so wide a discrepancy separates the cool discourse of scholarship from the anguished emotions evoked by the experience or even second-hand knowledge of real rape. Yet, again, there is no choice. Scholarship gains little, and perhaps loses much, when it is mired in emotional exhortations and the rhetorical gestures these require. To attempt to understand a subject always means standing at some slight remove from it, not allowing feelings to overwhelm one to the point of obscuring critical assessment. But because this is difficult—and to some people dangerous, as if explanation and understanding necessarily imply legitimization or even endorsement—the negative reactions to this book should not come as a surprise. Feminists, in particular, have urged a conflation of emotion and reason (when not dismissing reason altogether as "masculinist"), though one suspects they might not wish such a conflation to beset surgeons about to perform delicate operations. But one does not have to be a feminist to find it hard to keep one's passions out of a discussion of rape and rapists.

Still, it is unusual that a biologist and an anthropologist, who between them have published dozens of articles in scholarly journals—journals such as *Ethology and Sociobiology, Journal of Comparative Psychology, Animal Behaviour, American Naturalist, Behavioral Ecology and Sociobiology, Jurimetrics, Advances in the Study of Behavior, Human Nature, Evolution and Human Behavior, American Scientist, Biological Reviews, Behavioral and Brain Sciences, Ethnology, Journal of Sex Research, Aggressive Behavior, Annual Review of Ecology and Systematics*, and *Human Organization*—should find their work labeled "scientific pornography." But this is precisely how Steven Rose, in a recent review in the *Times Literary Supplement*[2] bristling with antagonism toward what he judges to be genetic determinism, has characterized the new book by Thornhill, a specialist in scorpion flies who is Regents' Professor and professor of biology at the University of New Mexico, and Palmer, instructor of anthropology at the University of Colorado in Colorado Springs. Perhaps the authors should be grateful for small favors: Rose did not write "pseudoscientific pornography," thus at least granting one important feature of the book: its grounding in widely accepted evolutionary theory.

Thornhill and Palmer argue that rape is a natural and biological phenomenon whose ultimate (not proximate) cause can be traced to our evolutionary heritage. They insist that efforts to prevent rape can only benefit from taking this knowledge into account. Jerry Coyne, professor at the University of Chicago and himself an evolutionary biologist who works on the fruit fly, declares the book's thesis to be nothing more than a banal tautology, one few biologists would object to. After all, he states, all behavior originates in our having brains that result from natural selection, but this is a "crushingly trivial" explanation.[3] Coyne calls Thornhill and Palmer's work "unscientific," and "an embarrassment to the field," and focuses in particular on the second part of their thesis, which argues that, far from being a mere evolutionary byproduct, rape is a "direct adaptation" by which natural selection allows "sexually disenfranchised" men (those not likely to be selected as partners by females) to reproduce their genes. He rejects their work because it is "utterly resistant to scientific refutation."

Though Thornhill and Palmer refer to a large body of evidence of rape in other species and in all human societies, their work raises many still unanswered questions. Even if seventy percent of reported rapes indeed involve women of reproductive age, what about the other thirty percent? And what about male-male rape, a commonplace in prisons? Perhaps Thornhill and Palmer are right in arguing for reproductive advantage as the ultimate cause of rape. Perhaps they are wrong. Either way, hostility to their book seems a futile and empty gesture. Why would feminists, in particular, not embrace this addition to the arguments supporting their agenda of stopping rape? The reasons are clear: First of all, after thirty years of feminist-inspired nonscientific work telling us that rape is "not sex," but rather violence and power, here come two scholars challenging this orthodoxy and doing so with impressive documentation. Second, Thornhill and Palmer's challenge is based on evolutionary biology (the field that used to be called "sociobiology"), a special bane to most feminists. The two authors contend that natural selection and the competition among individuals within a species to reproduce their genes has made rape one evolutionary strategy, the effects of which are still observed today. To make matters even worse, they include in their study a detailed demonstration of the contradictions and confusions besetting the feminist line on rape, rooted as it is in what professors of psychology Martin Daly and Margo Wilson, in a similar evolutionarily inspired study of homicide, called "biophobia."[4]

In an essay called "Is Darwinism Sexist? (And If It Is, So What?),"[5] Michael Ruse, professor of philosophy and zoology at the University of Guelph, writes, "To say that evolutionary theory—Darwinian evolutionary theory in particular—comes saddled with a bad reputation among feminists is akin to saying that Hitler had a thing about the Jews. For about 20 years now, since the human sociobiological controversy of the 1970s, Darwinism—the theory of organic evolution through natural selection— has been right at the top of the feminist hate list." My own experience in academic feminism certainly bears out this charge. I am perhaps a typical product of the women's studies revolution of the past few decades. I was trained in literature and wrote a dissertation in the mid-seventies that was influenced by both the Marxist and the feminist ideologies current at the time. Science was always another world to me, one that I knew very little about and that I considered largely outside my scope. As a professor with a joint appointment in women's studies from the mid-eighties to the mid-nineties, I taught feminist theory and did not hesitate to repeat the standard (then and now) feminist line on issues such as gender roles (socially constructed), abortion (every woman's right), and rape (an expression of male violence and power). No doubt my limited understanding of biology shaped my teaching, which was buttressed by the belief that we were doing something entirely new and "multidisciplinary" and premised on the rejection of conventional academic values, as part of The Patriarchy.

As I grew dissatisfied with this kind of teaching and with the predictable mindset of my women's studies students (which led them to make silly assertions such as that there was little infant mortality until "men medicalized childbirth"), I noticed that no one in our women's studies program had a background in science, nor was this considered a problem. Expertise, especially in scientific fields, was under suspicion, and women's "author-ity of experience" was celebrated instead.[6] The texts we taught, feminist bottom-line articles on complex questions such as violence, rape, maternal "instinct," sexual orientation, and the like, typically included denuncia-tions of science. When we once considered pursuing a visiting appoint-ment in "science," it was Carolyn Merchant (author of the 1980 book *The Death of Nature*, which argued that modern science has treated the natural world as nothing more than a woman to be raped) whose name immedi-ately came up as the ideal candidate.

I remember a dinner party at which I felt profoundly injured because the wife of a physicist agreed with her husband that some basic brain differ-ences exist between males and females and that these differences probably explain men's greater gift in higher mathematics. In retrospect, I wonder at the passion I brought to that discussion, though its causes are not difficult to discern. Any recognition of women as different from men seemed to threaten the drive for women's equality since it could be used as a pretext to "keep them in their place." It was feminism's political agenda that ex-plained its hostility to biology. Of course, like other feminists, I was incon-sistent in my application of such tenets and inclined to see women as "nat-urally" better than men in a variety of respects.

Now, several years after parting company from women's studies, I can still, while reading Thornhill and Palmer's book, easily run a feminist script through my mind and reject outright what they have to say. Thus, I am by no means surprised at the antagonism and contempt their work has aroused. They of course foresee and address the predictable negative reac-tions from feminists and social scientists. They call attention to the "natu-ralistic fallacy," by which explanations for human behavior attributed to na-ture or biology are feared because they may be used to condone or legitimize those behaviors. From this point of view, the danger of even ap-proaching a subject such as rape from the perspective of evolutionary the-ory is that rape may thereby be treated as inevitable and men who rape ex-culpated. But nothing could be further from Thornhill and Palmer's intent, and it is therefore fascinating to see that none of their clear statements about these issues has put off their detractors, who in often hysterical tones accuse them of "blaming the victim."

Could these detractors be right? Isn't it possible that some politically committed interests might take this book and run with it? Although authors cannot control the uses to which their work is put, Thornhill and Palmer have attempted to set obstacles in the way of misuse of their book. Repeat-edly they stress that by understanding the ultimate causes of rape we may be better able to prevent it. At the same time, they have also very thoroughly dissected feminists' pronouncements on rape, pointing out their ideologi-cal underpinnings, their hostility to scientific method and the research findings it has generated, and the inevitable contradictions arising from arguments resting not on evidence but on ideology.

Feminist antagonism to biological approaches to sexuality has many and deep roots. As noted earlier, there is the fear that *tout comprendre, c'est tout pardonner*. As a political movement, feminism has necessarily had a strong commitment to a social constructionist worldview, which has taken feminists far in their analyses of gender roles. But what if there is a biological basis for gender? Doesn't this threaten the feminist plan for universal reform? Feminists have tried to fend off this danger by means of a simple ploy: Whereas they originally distinguished gender (which they argued is socially constructed) from sex (biological), increasingly over the past two decades, they have expanded their analyses so that sex itself has come to be seen as something other than a biological reality. Anne Fausto-Sterling, for example, argues that, far from having significant biological components, our apparent sexual dimorphism is itself a social construct.[7] And this argument has served the significant feminist purpose of interfering with most women's tendency to assume that "sleeping with the enemy" is an entirely natural thing to do. Clearly an attack on biology is necessary if heterosexuality itself is to be presented as a social construction.

Instances of this agenda are readily found in feminist literature.[8] A recent volume edited by Wilma Mankiller et al., entitled *The Reader's Companion to U.S. Women's History*, contains some four hundred articles by three hundred contributors yet presents very little variety in the message about sexuality. Consider the following examples. In an entry about celibacy, Sally Cline states: "Our society assumes that women in particular should be eager consumers of preferably heterosexual activity which, along with beauty products, diets, low wages, and violence, is part of the contemporary culture that aims to limit women's power." Cline refers to the "genital myth" that, she says, "prescribes genitally active behavior."[9] Charlotte Bunch's article on heterosexism reassures us that the term "does not imply that heterosexuality is innately bad. . . . Rather, it refers to the structural and attitudinal ways in which one form of sexuality has dominated and distorted others."[10] But E. Kay Trimberger's entry on heterosexuality is blunt: "Sexuality is not private, but is political and related to power. 'Compulsory heterosexuality' is part of a power structure benefiting heterosexual males at the expense of women and homosexuals." What is the point of such declarations? Trimberger spells it out: "If our sexuality is socially constructed it can also be de- and reconstructed."[11] In the same volume, an article on rape is situated as a subcategory of a long entry on violence against women. This latter entry begins with the bizarre statement: "Western society identifies gender, class, race or ethnicity, and sexual orientation as significant social categories"[12]—as if this were some peculiarly Western failing. Jennifer Wriggins's main entry on rape gives pride of place to Susan Brownmiller's *Against Our Will: Men, Women and Rape* (1975), saying: "Feminists reconceptualized rape as a crime of violence and as part of a range of violence against women." To her credit, Wriggins at least adds, "This approach gained wide acceptance, although some feminists believed that the specifically sexual aspect of rape should be emphasized more."[13]

Thornhill and Palmer note that Catharine MacKinnon too has insisted on the sexual aspect of rape. However, as they correctly explain, it's not that MacKinnon can see the sex in rape, but rather that she sees (or argues for) the rape in virtually all (hetero)sex. Thus, while apparently taking a position somewhat different from that of many feminists, MacKinnon has in fact helped move the entire discussion toward a radical pole in which heterosexual intercourse is increasingly indistinguishable from male violence against women. By now she is in the company of many other feminists who see heterosexuality as socially constructed and serving the interests of men. The classic statement of this position is Susan Brownmiller's pronouncement: "From prehistoric times to the present, I believe, rape has played a critical function. It is nothing more or less than a conscious process of intimidation by which *all* men keep *all* women in a state of fear."[14] In Brownmiller's view, marriage is nothing more than a con game designed by men to control women.

Brownmiller's view of rape is cited—and rejected—by Donald Symons in his 1979 book *The Evolution of Human Sexuality*,[15] clearly an important influence on Thornhill and Palmer. Symons asserts that the real feminist contribution to an understanding of rape is "the thorough documentation of the victim's point of view."[16] And no doubt this is one reason why Thornhill and Palmer's cold-blooded chapter called "The Pain and Anguish of Rape," arguing for an evolutionary explanation of women's reactions to rape, arouses special venom in readers. But feminist scholarship has not been content with illuminating women's experience, nor with the revision of rape law and the improvement of social services that feminist activism has indeed brought about. The antagonism toward heterosexuality that underlies much feminist discourse inevitably makes evolutionary arguments (which presuppose heterosexuality as natural) anathema to feminists. This perhaps explains the contemptuously dismissive comments made about Thornhill and Palmer's work. Brownmiller, for example, in an NPR interview, ridiculed the authors as "a couple of guys with a crackpot theory," and in the on-line law journal *Jurist*, she gloated that between her feminist and her scientist allies, "we've destroyed Thornhill."[17]

What is more interesting, however, is that so many scholars who surely do not participate in the extremist feminist attack on heterosexuality nonetheless feel compelled to reject evolutionary arguments about sexual behavior out of fear that they will invariably lead to retrogressive social policy. In their book *Homicide*, Martin Daly and Margo Wilson refer to the apparent need of social scientists to see "our social natures [as] pure cultural artifacts, as arbitrary as the name of the rose, and [to argue] that we can therefore create any world we want, simply by changing our 'socialization practices.'"[18] Why do so many American social scientists fear and despise biology, though few have troubled to study the field? Because, say Daly and Wilson, these social scientists hold the misguided view that "biological" is equated with "invariant" or "genetic" or "instinctive"—all of which contrast with social scientists' preferred explanatory terms: "social," "cultural," and "learned." Such a usage, Daly and Wilson state, "betrays an incomprehension of the domain of biology."[19] What biology provides, they argue, is "an encompassing *conceptual* framework, which the social sciences ignore to their disadvantage."[20] They refute the common misapprehension that a Darwinian view of the human animal is "pessimistic," commenting: "As if ignorance of our natural selective history will somehow make us free!" They conclude:

> Ironically, the model of humankind that is really pessimistic is the one that is usually stated as an alternative, namely that man *has* no nature and is therefore limitlessly malleable by the forces of "conditioning" and "behavior modification." Extreme versions of this view would deprive the individual of any stable self-interest, making him putty in the hands of "educators," a totalitarian's dream. Fortunately, this pessimistic antibiological denial of human nature and human dignity is false. The endemic fact of conflicting interests has been the selective milieu for a human psyche that is buffered against manipulation and deception—a psyche that is capable of discerning its own interests and acting both individually and collectively to advance them.[21]

This was published in 1988. Yet the familiar attacks on biology, and evolutionary psychology in particular, surface in more recent work, so that Thornhill and Palmer have to repeat essentially the same arguments. Apparently years of research have done little to diminish the hostility evolution arouses in many quarters when it is applied to human beings. In another dismissive review of Thornton and Palmer's book, in the *Times Literary Supplement*, Sue Lees, automatically endorsing the Brownmiller approach, censures the authors for promoting "myths" about rape and compares their prescriptions for avoiding rape to policies imposed by the Taliban in Afghanistan.[22] This is quite an accusation and demonstrably false. Like Camille Paglia, whom they cite, Thornhill and Palmer urge women to use caution in how they dress and where they go. But they also press for harsher penalties for rape and for better education of young men. It may be that their more unforgivable sin is to note that dismantling traditional gender roles has the likely effect of increasing women's vulnerability to rape.

Jerry Coyne, in his *New Republic* review, asks the relevant question: "Can knowledge about evolution play a useful role in reforming society?" He doubts it. He sees Thornhill and Palmer's larger aim as being "the engulfment of social science and social policy by the great whale of evolutionary psychology," a takeover he dates back to E. O. Wilson's 1978 work, *On Human Nature*. Coyne calls this campaign the "Darwinization of Everything," that is, the attempt to annex "all human experience to evolutionary psychology," a project he judges to be megalomaniacal. And perhaps he is right to object. One should always be suspicious of totalizing explanations. Feminists, however, are not in a good position to cast this particular stone, since their resort to "patriarchy" and "oppression" as ultimate explanations is at least as global in its intended reach.

If Thornhill and Palmer err in judging rape to be primarily an evolutionary adaptation and not an expression of rage or power, feminists have erred in the opposite direction. But there is an important distinction to be drawn. Susan Brownmiller's book was and still is celebrated. It has led to the establishment of a feminist orthodoxy. To this day it provides the framework within which rape is discussed in both academic circles and the popular media. By contrast, Thornhill and Palmer's work is encountering massive opposition and painstakingly detailed criticism. Ironically, the very attention given to the book is likely to end up reinforcing feminist axioms about rape, for, implicitly if not explicitly, Thornhill and Palmer lend support to the view that all men are potential rapists.

But is their argument for the ultimate evolutionary causes of rape in fact inimical to feminist interests? It would seem not. Much of what they say is compatible with the feminist emphasis on anger and domination as factors in rape. It is indeed probable that men who fail to measure up in the mating competition should feel anger toward women, and this anger may translate into violent attack under certain circumstances. There may well be cases in which these drives are more salient than sexual ones—or interact with sexual motives in complex ways. The feminist tendency toward stretching the concept of rape to encompass ever more aspects of male sexuality does not help in addressing the problems of real rape. Nor does feminists' attribution of rape to "patriarchy" take us very far. Rape is dreadful, and among the many people writing against it are Thornhill and Palmer. An interdisciplinary approach should be welcomed. Animal studies show us that there is more than one way to be successful reproductively: The alpha male tactic and the indirect and sneaky non-alpha approach can both promote reproductive fitness. Perhaps there are other tactics as well. Far from denouncing work that doesn't suit their immediate anti-male agenda, feminists should welcome research that places a high priority on understanding rape.

NOTES

This essay appeared in *Gender Issues* 18:4 (Fall 2000), 74–82. Reprinted with kind permission of Springer Science and Business Media. My thanks to Marc Defant of the University of South Florida and to Noretta Koertge of Indiana University, Bloomington for a lively correspondence on the issues raised by Thornhill and Palmer's book.

1. Randy Thornhill and Craig T. Palmer, *A Natural History of Rape: Biological Bases of Sexual Coercion* (Cambridge, Mass.: The MIT Press, 2000).

2. Steven Rose, "The New Just So Stories: Sexual Selection and the Fallacies of Evolutionary Psychology," *Times Literary Supplement*, July 14, 2000, 3–4.

3. Jerry Coyne, "Of Vice and Men," *The New Republic*, April 3, 2000. Available at www.tnr.com/040300/coyne040300.html.

4. Martin Daly and Margo Wilson, *Homicide* (New York: Aldine de Gruyter, 1988). Noretta Koertge and I, unaware at the time of Daly and Wilson's work, used the term "biodenial" in our critique of women's studies programs, *Professing Feminism: Cautionary Tales from the Strange World of Women's Studies* (New York: Basic Books, 1994).

5. Michael Ruse, "Is Darwinism Sexist? (And If It Is, So What?)," in *A House Built on Sand: Exposing Postmodernist Myths about Science*, ed. Noretta Koertge (New York: Oxford University Press, 1998), 119.

6. My personal impression on this point is confirmed by a recent book of testimonies by thirty "founding mothers" of women's studies—not one of them a scientist. See Florence Howe, ed., *The Politics of Women's Studies: Testimony from Thirty Founding Mothers* (New York: The Feminist Press, 2000); my essay on this, "Will the Real Feminists in Academe Please Stand Up?" *The Chronicle of Higher Education*, October 6, 2000, B7–9 (chapter 11 in the present volume); and other recent books on women's studies.

7. See Anne Fausto-Sterling, *Myths of Gender: Biological Theories about Men and Women* (New York: Basic Books, 1985) and her essays, "How Many Sexes Are There?" *New York Times*, March 12, 1993, A29; and "The Five Sexes, Revisited," *The Sciences* (July/August 2000), 19–23. Fausto-Sterling has argued that a less patriarchal society would accommodate many more than two sexes. See also her essay, "How to Build a Man," in *Constructing Masculinity*, ed. Maurice Berger et al. (New York: Routledge, 1995), 127–134, the point of which is to dismantle as mere "narrative" (male) scientists' linking of biology with gender.

8. For many other examples of feminist antagonism toward heterosexuality, see my book *Heterophobia: Sexual Harassment and the Future of Feminism* (Lanham, Md.: Rowman & Littlefield, 1998).

9. In Wilma Mankiller et al., eds, *The Reader's Companion to U.S. Women's History* (Boston: Houghton Mifflin Co., 1998), 79.

10. Mankiller, *The Reader's Companion*, 254.

11. Mankiller, *The Reader's Companion*, 255.

12. Mankiller, *The Reader's Companion*, 602.

13. Mankiller, *The Reader's Companion*, 613.

14. Susan Brownmiller, *Against Our Will: Men, Women and Rape* (New York: Simon and Schuster, 1975), 15; emphasis hers. (For a detailed discussion of Catharine MacKinnon's views on heterosexuality, see chapter 18 in the present volume.

15. Donald Symons, *The Evolution of Human Sexuality* (New York: Oxford University Press, 1979), 279.

16. Symons, *The Evolution*, 279.

17. The NPR interview is cited by Steve Wilson, "Furious Debate Clouds Usefulness of Rape Theory," *The Arizona Republic*, April 11, 2000. The *Jurist* interview, vol. 3, no. 3 (March 2000), is available at: www.jurist.law.pitt.edu/lawbooks/intervw .htm.

18. Martin Daly and Margo Wilson, *Homicide* (New York: Aldine de Gruyter, 1988).

19. Daly and Wilson, *Homicide*, 154.

20. Daly and Wilson, *Homicide*, 154–155; emphasis theirs.

21. Daly and Wilson, *Homicide*, 296–297.

22. Sue Lees, review of *A Natural History of Rape: Biological Bases of Sexual Coercion*, by Randy Thornhill and Craig Palmer, *Times Literary Supplement*, March 17, 2000, 12.

17

Women on Top

We made this law up from the beginning, and now we've won.

Catharine MacKinnon[1]

Nadine Strossen, head of the American Civil Liberties Union, refers to sexual harassment law as a "Trojan horse" by which radical feminists, having failed in their anti-pornography efforts, have found another means to impose censorship on school and workplace. The appalling results—guarded speech, wary interactions, general suspicion, vigilantism, and abuses of due process resulting in lost reputations and livelihoods—are all around us. But this is of no concern to feminists such as Catharine MacKinnon, godmother of sexual harassment law, who has argued that sexual harassment turns women into "pornography."

Sexual harassment became illegal because feminists convinced the government that it is a form of "discrimination" in that it alters for the worse the conditions under which women work and study, and thereby puts them in a disadvantageous position vis-à-vis men. Though the ensuing laws have on occasion been applied against women harassing men and same-sex harassers, their main targets are and have always been men. Studies tell us that the vast majority of sexual harassment charges today fall into that amorphous and omnibus category known as hostile environment harassment. By contrast, accusations of quid pro quo harassment—basically sexual extortion—are rare.

Mostly unnoticed in the feminist effort to ferret out ever more instances of hostile environment harassment is the inconvenient fact that this form of behavior is often indistinguishable from the exercise of free speech, on the one hand, and from romantic overtures or bantering pleasantries, on the other. Riding high on the crest of its successes, the burgeoning "sexual harassment industry" (SHI), as I have called it—made up of feminist activists, lawyers, counselors, trainers, policy advisors, and enforcement officers in schools and workplaces—has made it clear that micromanaging men's behavior and attitudes is its major goal and women's "comfort" level its main criterion for intervention.

How can we try to understand laws and court decisions that have led us to a situation where—as numerous SHI books openly insist—classroom comments, an overheard joke, "elevator eyes," a casual touch, a brief gaze, or a repeated request for a date can lead to serious sanctions and litigation? Several recent books attempt to guide us in thinking our way through the thicket of rules, regulations, and rationales that today make up the corpus of sexual harassment law. One of them urges us to be skeptical about the law; the second offers a somewhat mixed message but ultimately, like the third, invites adherence and support.

I

Mane Hajdin, a philosophy professor who has written extensively on ethical theory and philosophy of law, has for some years been publishing critiques of sexual harassment law. He has now produced a comprehensive book on the subject, *The Law of Sexual Harassment: A Critique*,[2] which identifies as the key question: Is sexual harassment law morally justified? Hajdin's conclusion—made clear from the outset—is that it is not. But it is the thoughtful and graceful analyses by which he arrives at this conclusion that make the book such an important contribution.

Hajdin begins with a compelling observation: Sexual harassment law, which has existed for three decades, has never been subjected to the kind of public debate that has accompanied proposed changes in the law on comparable public policy issues such as abortion, affirmative action, gun control, or pornography. And yet sexual harassment law affects our daily lives far more than laws in these other areas. This failure to have a public airing is partly explained by the fact that sexual harassment law was created not through congressional vote preceded by open hearings but largely through action by the judiciary. It "sneaked into existence quietly on 20 April 1976 in a decision of the federal district court for the District of Columbia." Seemingly nothing more than an application of Title VII of the 1964 Civil Rights Act, which prohibits discrimination in the terms or conditions of employment, the court's decision in *Williams v. Saxbe*, treating sexual demands in the workplace as terms or conditions of employment, was, in fact, to have enormous significance.

Moreover, current sexual harassment law is the result of gradual development, an accretion of numerous judicial decisions handed down over the past few decades. The cumulative effect of these decisions is that the law has become ever more elaborate and has come to cover an ever greater range of behavior. In addition—and this is an important insight—what is now called sexual harassment overlaps with many kinds of conduct that people have long regarded as "wrong." Conventional morality thus prevented people from noting what was really new about sexual harassment law. For all these reasons, despite an immense academic and scholarly literature on the subject, to this day, Hajdin notes, the necessary public debate about sexual harassment law has not taken place.

Hajdin's opening chapter attempts to disentangle some of the conflated issues that make it difficult to appraise whether sexual harassment law is morally justified. First among these issues is "legal moralism," the view that immoral conduct ought to be prohibited precisely because it is immoral. Hajdin argues that although legal moralism, these days, is not endorsed by most of us, policies and training programs on sexual harassment law are designed to maximize compliance and do not promote critical thinking about the law. Hence people do not realize that if they wish to justify sexual harassment law, they must do so on grounds independent of the adulterous, promiscuous, insensitive, or vulgar character of the conduct they are incensed about. They cannot expect to prohibit conduct that merely "overlaps" with the conduct they consider immoral. Legal moralism, then, cannot in itself provide a justification for sexual harassment law. Our laws do not normally jumble together dissimilar acts, yet sexual harassment law works in precisely this way, as a sort of patchwork. Even if individual patches are morally wrong, Hajdin argues, the patchwork as a whole lacks unity. The law needs to explain why various sorts of prohibited behavior have been brought together, and sexual harassment law does not do so.

Hajdin devotes two chapters to the "demarcation problem," showing that sexual harassment law fails to provide a workable criterion of demarcation between sexual interaction that is harassment and that which is not. At this point one begins to see clearly the parting of the ways between Hajdin's logical analysis and the approaches of some feminist jurists and legal philosophers who defend sexual harassment law. Hajdin contends that if no such demarcation is made, and any and all sexual interaction in the workplace is prohibited, the law is obviously unjustified and would elicit public opposition. But, as we shall see below, some notable feminists wish precisely for this result, for Hajdin's argument—that the lack of demarcation of prohibited behavior means in effect that all behavior of a sexual type must be avoided—fits perfectly with the ideological aim of much feminist writing on the subject.

By contrast, Hajdin argues that since adults have an interest in seeking partners, a ban on all workplace sexual activity (in order to be sure of catching in the net that part of it that is unwelcome or offensive) would reduce their opportunities for finding partners. Such a prohibition would in any case be impossible to enforce. If, on the other hand, a general prohibition against all sexual interaction in the workplace is not what sexual harassment law aims at, the law itself must allow people to distinguish between harassing and non-harassing sexual interactions. And this it fails to do.

One of Hajdin's key contributions is his analysis of the two-tiered system through which sexual harassment law functions. Because the law rests on the notion of discrimination, it is addressed primarily to employers—those whose discriminatory acts have real consequences—requiring them to see to it that sexual harassment does not occur. The legal instructions aimed at employers constitute the "upper level" at which sexual harassment law operates. But there is also another level, operating within the workplace, where employers enact regulations to induce compliance with upper-level requirements. These regulations, and the mechanisms on which they depend, constitute the "lower level."

The significance of Hajdin's delineation of these two levels lies in his perception that two different processes of adjudication result from this two-tiered system. At the upper level, courts of law adjudicate and may impose sanctions on employers; at the lower level, however, the employer sets up offices and mechanisms and it is the employer who will, in order to avoid liability, impose sanctions ranging from prohibitions against certain magazines or photographs on a desk all the way to demotion or firing. The upper level requires that the employer set in place the lower level of sexual harassment law. Criteria such as "severe or pervasive," for judging whether words and/or behaviors are actionable, pertain to the upper level. But long before a case rises to that level, employers will have imposed regulations that seriously interfere with their employees' speech and conduct. As Hajdin puts it: "The lower-level regulations thus, if they are to enable the employer to avoid the upper-level liability, have to make internally actionable offensive conduct of a sexual nature even if that conduct is, on its own, neither severe nor pervasive." This is why the many manuals produced by the SHI typically tell us that sexual harassment can be anything from a look to rape. They make it clear that even an off-color joke or a one-time amorous gesture can have serious consequences for the employee.

Given that employers want not merely to be able to win lawsuits but to minimize the likelihood of being sued in the first place, their incentives are to show potential plaintiffs that they have no case. This can most effectively be accomplished by harsh penalties at the lower level. In addition, since these are not criminal charges, a far lower standard of evidence prevails than would in criminal court, where due process and traditional legal protections exist. Because employers these days fear suits primarily in one direction (not from the accused), they experience little pressure to refrain from overreacting to minor offenses. All this means that employers have motivation to prohibit and punish conduct that is far from satisfying the definitions that operate at the upper, juridical, level.

The result is an atmosphere in which one alleged offense can unleash the entire defensive institutional apparatus, where it is always the rights of the complainant, not of the accused, that matter. Offenders lucky enough not to be fired hasten to make abject apologies, agree to attend workshops and take "sensitivity training," and go through other humiliations that—I would argue—have no place in a free society. In turn, sexual harassment charges become a powerful weapon that ambitious and resentful people can—and do—utilize, whether to oust an irksome colleague from a job, move up in the ranks, act out a political agenda, or seek revenge for a real or imagined slight or a relationship gone awry.

As critics such as Harvey Silverglate and Alan Kors (authors of *The Shadow University*[3]) have also argued, sexual harassment policies on college campuses violate First Amendment rights because they routinely include "verbal acts" among proscribed behavior and are not content-neutral. They are, in fact, speech codes in disguise. Hajdin makes a further point. Although the government does not have the power either to prevent people from speaking or to force them to speak in a particular way, sexual harassment law subverts this principle. It is not enough for employers to have sexual harassment regulations "on the books" and to enforce them as they are invoked by complaints; court decisions have demonstrated that upper-level legal liability cannot be avoided in this way. Guidelines promulgated by the Equal Employment Opportunity Commission compel employers to speak out on the issue of sexual harassment and express "strong disapproval" of it. This, Hajdin argues, ought to raise freedom-of-speech concerns, for it forces employers to express one specific viewpoint. They cannot criticize the government's position on sexual harassment but they also cannot remain silent, in clear opposition to the First Amendment.

II

Whereas Hajdin argues that different kinds of wrongful acts should not all be squeezed into the same area of the law or into one conceptual framework, it is precisely such squeezing that appears in two other recent books, as writers seek large all-inclusive explanations for the essential wrongness of sexual harassment in all its manifestations.

Margaret Crouch's book *Thinking About Sexual Harassment: A Guide for the Perplexed*,[4] while informative and useful in content and often thoughtful and lucid in tone, ultimately falls into this trap. A professor of philosophy, Crouch attempts to think through the competing views of sexual harassment law and arrive at a unified analysis. She presents a detailed reading of the controversies surrounding the law, richly illustrated with extensive quotations from critics with a variety of perspectives, and she also includes information about how sexual harassment is dealt with in other countries.

Creating divergent arguments—pro and con—about sexual harassment law (including some of Hajdin's) with seriousness and respect, Crouch makes clear her own view that prohibition of all sexual interaction at school and work is an unreasonable as well as undesirable goal. She delineates three conceptual (and not mutually exclusive) frameworks underlying distinct approaches to sexual harassment: the natural/biological (that is, evolutionary psychology's view that sexual harassment is the expression of age-old strategies designed to enhance reproductive success), the liberal (committed to freedom and equality), and the sociocultural (the "male dominance" framework asserted most vigorously by radical feminist ideology).

Crouch states that she cannot decide among these several explanatory frameworks and says, "There is no way of determining which of the three perspectives . . . is 'true' without begging the question against the others. There is no neutral position from which to judge them." She attempts to justify this agnostic position by claiming that "empirical data will not settle the issue, since such data are not free of value judgments." But while it is certainly true that empirical data are sometimes insufficient to ground a choice among theories, it is absurd to claim that the choice can never be made on the basis of evidence. If we could not reject on empirical grounds the hypotheses that the cause of milk going sour is the gaze of a witch or that women can't study while menstruating, imagine the position of women today! Indeed, Crouch's dismissal of empirical data merely because they are vulnerable to the intrusion of values is not only implausible but pernicious.

I believe Crouch's desire to claim neutrality on her three conceptual frameworks is not mysterious. Many feminist scholars are aware these days that existing law is not a broad enough ground for banning all the behaviors feminists wish to count as harassment. They therefore seek to amplify or reconfigure sexual harassment law so as to allow it to cover a variety of attitudinal and ideological offenses, but this threatens to become the incoherent legal patchwork of which Hajdin speaks. They therefore need an overarching unified theory. The structural or sociocultural "dominance" approach, however, which is preferred by these feminists, rests on dubious categorical assertions, such as that men as a group express and impose the view that women are their inferiors and that this is a wrong in itself that the law must right. Since Crouch in practice opts for this approach, her dismissal of empirical grounds on which to decide among the competing frameworks seems intended to shield the sociocultural approach from rational criticism.

Crouch makes it clear that she's looking for a way to show that quid pro quo harassment is not merely coercion or extortion, but "sex discrimination" as conceived by the "dominance" approach. Thus, she (like Catharine MacKinnon) disagrees with Ellen Frankel Paul, who has argued that sexual harassment as sex discrimination is in fact a defective paradigm and that it should be a tort instead. Paul's view is unsatisfactory to "dominance" feminists because it blames the individual harasser, not the social structure as a whole. Crouch believes that when a person discriminates (in the sense of distinguishes) between the sexes, motivated by sexual desire, this in itself is not wrongful discrimination. She cites Hajdin on this point, but misstates his position by claiming that he accepts quid pro quo harassment as wrongful discrimination (a view he explicitly rejects), which, according to Crouch, doesn't go far enough. What she claims is that gender is not incidental to this kind of discrimination; that is, she wants to preserve quid pro quo harassment as sex discrimination specifically committed by men against women.

Thus Crouch agrees with scholars who have argued that women as a group are affected differently by quid pro quo harassment than are men as a group. Laws against quid pro quo harassment, according to this view, need not rest on the claim that this form of harassment discriminates on the basis of sex, but rather that it constitutes an assault on all women by reinforcing harmful stereotypes about them. No similar stereotypes stigmatize men. (To the contrary, I would argue that the actual effect of sexual harassment law is not only to threaten men's livelihood but to confirm the formulaic view that men in general are sexual predators and oppressors, the very view underlying the "dominance" perspective.) Crouch therefore supports Anita Superson's argument (discussed below), that sexual harassment in general harms women because it perpetuates and expresses the view that they are inferior to men. And from this it follows that when women act like men, what they do cannot be sex discrimination or harassment. As MacKinnon states in *Feminism Unmodified* in 1987: "Basically, it [sexual harassment] is done by men to women regardless of relative position on the formal hierarchy."

Where Crouch significantly parts ways with feminists such as MacKinnon is in their assertion that heterosexuality itself is a pernicious social construct by which men impose their dominance. Thus, for example, although Crouch believes that consensual relations in "asymmetrical" situations should be banned, her reasoning is unlike that of Billie Dziech and Linda Weiner (authors of *The Lecherous Professor*), or MacKinnon, who hold that women cannot give meaningful consent without absolute equality—a principle Crouch considers "ultimately unintelligible." Her grounds for wishing to ban relationships between professors and students (while the latter are in the former's classes, she specifies) rest on the problems raised by conflicts of interest and favoritism. However, this argument ignores the reality that professors regularly face—and deal with—these and other ethical issues in situations quite unrelated to sexual or romantic relationships.

Crouch's "unified" approach would treat both quid pro quo harassment and hostile environment harassment as inflicting a variety of harms upon women, beyond mere discrimination. She supports retaining the term sexual harassment, actionable under Title VII and Title IX, for quid pro quo harassment, while reconceptualizing hostile environment harassment as "gender harassment." Such a move aims to make it not sexuality that harassment law targets but rather "gender" inequality—again the view that women are inferior both in the workplace and in educational environments. She considers it an advantage of her analysis that men's claims to have been sexually harassed by other men would be limited to those situations in which (as in *Oncale v. Sundowner Offshore Services, Inc.*) the victim is seen by his tormentors as "inferior" by virtue of being insufficiently "masculine." This, as noted, is part of the continuing feminist effort to safeguard harassment law as a weapon primarily for women to use against men.

While trying to resist the puritanical and anti-sex aspect of current sexual harassment law by this reconfiguration, Crouch nonetheless aims to extend the reach of the law so that it will not be constrained by the present definition, which makes harassment actionable only if it constitutes discrimination on the basis of sex. That definition, as many critics have noted, leads to problems (which feminists have been attempting to get around) regarding same-sex and bisexual harassment. Unfortunately, Crouch's clarification—that both quid pro quo and hostile environment harassment "express and perpetuate the view that women are inferior workers or academics"— turns out to have as many problems as the original concept, not the least of which is that someone will have to decide when a man is merely expressing sexual interest and when he is manifesting unacceptable views or beliefs about women. Note that it is not only actions but also attitudes ("views") that will be punished. Crouch ends her book with the affirmation that "to categorize both quid pro quo and hostile environment sexual harassment as *sexual* harassment perpetuates two errors in thinking: (1) thinking that harassment that is sex discrimination is *sexual,* and (2) thinking that all *sexual* expression and conduct is harassment."[5]

One could, however, plausibly argue that the entire sociocultural case for which Crouch speaks itself rests on a "view" of men as inferior to women in a significant sense: as having fundamental moral defects. Ironically, Crouch has no trouble abandoning "neutrality" in her adherence to such a view, to which I now turn in greater detail.

III

Though its conclusions are unconvincing, Crouch's book is a far more insightful and serious work than Leslie Pickering Francis's *Sexual Harassment as an Ethical Issue in Academic Life.*[6] I have no objections to books that take strong positions and argue them well. What I do object to is the pretense— both on Francis's pages and in a blurb on the book's back cover—that hers is a "lucid and balanced treatment of sexual harassment grounded in clear and concise legal theory." It is nothing of the kind. Francis, a professor of philosophy and law, nowhere questions the premises of sexual harassment law. Nor does she seriously address the harm done to the falsely or trivially accused. She gives much more space and credence to feminist defenses of sexual harassment law than she allots to its critics (feminist and other). She accepts the usual conflation of sexual harassment with rape and sexual assault (which are criminal offenses). And she gives short shrift to the issue of First Amendment rights.

Arguing that social reform is a significant goal of higher education, Francis dismisses as "conservative" (and therefore unsatisfactory) the mere transmission of knowledge. Her convictions on this point govern her account in part I of her book, as well as her selection of texts for part II, which comprises previously published essays by Catharine MacKinnon, Billie Dziech and Linda Weiner, Nancy Tuana (who argues that offers of rewards for sex are coercive), Ellen Frankel Paul (mentioned above), Anita Superson (to be discussed below), Robert Holmes (for whom sexual harassment is an invasion of privacy), Jane Gallop (who defends the "erotics" of pedagogy while claiming that women by definition cannot commit sexual harassment), Linda Fitts Mischler (arguing that bans on relationships between attorneys and clients deprive women of autonomy), and David Archard (who argues the contrary and sees such relationships as resting on "exploited consent"). The volume concludes with a thirty-page selection of sexual harassment policies from seven schools, the longest of these being Antioch College's notoriously thoroughgoing code, which stipulates that explicit verbal permission must be given at each stage of sexual contact "in any given interaction."

The "balanced treatment" offered by Francis can be gauged by her discussion of the problem of false positives (innocents nonetheless found guilty) and false negatives (genuine victims who are not believed or cannot prevail). Both errors, Francis avers, may have "major, ongoing life consequences," but it is better to err on the side of false positives, for "there is a sense in which all those in a position of power—potential victimizers, as it were—bear some responsibility for an ongoing campus climate in which harassment flourishes." Acknowledging that this contravenes "the standard assumptions of criminal law," she suggests that we move away from the criminal law paradigm and toward greater education (for faculty) and support (for students).

Francis's basic strategy in her book is a simple one: To the most disparate instances of sexual and gender awareness in academic life—whether injurious or not—she applies language about the right to an "equal education."

Though she concedes that social relations may well be an important part of university life for many people, this acknowledgment is offered merely as a counterargument, to be rapidly dismissed. While Hajdin's analysis—as noted—rests on the view that women as well as men have a stake in access to potential partners and that one cannot discipline these interactions without damage to the vital interests of a free people, Francis insists that "where seduction is unreasonable because it is clearly unwelcome or because of the circumstances, it should be disciplined by the university," going on to amend this assertion to state that even where "seduction" is not "recognized as unreasonable," universities should work to inhibit it because it "reduces the recipient's educational effectiveness and opportunity."

As Hajdin points out, however, even the "reasonable woman" standard in judging "welcomeness" in effect makes any sexual overture or bantering impossible. In the absence of any way of knowing in advance what may be acceptable to a given woman, we arrive at the problem Hajdin labels "infinite regress," by which every effort to use words to make such inquiries might in turn be construed as sexual harassment. In Francis's sole mention (in an endnote) of Hajdin's work, she dismisses this concern, saying only that he does not understand the standard of "welcomeness."

Like Margaret Crouch, Francis supports the "sociocultural" view of harassment as resting on women's subordination and powerlessness. This view is forcefully articulated in Francis's volume by Anita M. Superson's 1993 essay "A Feminist Definition of Sexual Harassment" (also substantially endorsed by Crouch), which is therefore worth looking at in some detail.

Superson begins by declaring that sexual harassment is "by far the most pervasive form of discrimination against women," a statement that should make feminists everywhere rejoice since this would seem to imply that other problems have been substantially resolved. Because sexual harassment is so pervasive, she asserts, existing law is too tolerant of it and women lack sufficient legal recourse. The underlying problem is that sexual harassment is currently defined in "subjective" ways that disguise the "more subtle but equally harmful forms" of it that escape the law.

The solution is to seek an "objective" definition of sexual harassment. What follows, in Superson's essay, is the sociocultural "power" analysis that sees sexual harassment as verbal or physical behavior by means of which a dominant class member directs at a subjugated class member the attitude that the latter is inferior because of her sex. It has nothing to do with sexual desire and is not about seduction but is, rather, "about oppression of women."

Despite women's dire plight in this scenario, they for a variety of reasons reject the burden of denouncing their oppressors and may even fail to recognize harassment when it occurs. It follows that what women report cannot be the basis for judging whether sexual harassment has indeed occurred, nor is an individual woman's reaction significant. Instead, sexual harassment becomes an "objective" harm inflicted on all women—and any example of a negative view of women would therefore be an instance of it.

Such claims are an important (and not unusual) move on the part of some feminists precisely because they eliminate qualifying terms such as wanted, unwanted, welcome, severe, pervasive, and so on, all of which hamper feminist efforts to expand existing sexual harassment law.

Superson's conclusion that sexual harassment "should be treated no differently than crimes where harm to the victim is assessed in some objective way, independent of the perpetrator's beliefs," merely replaces "belief" with "attitude." She asks only whether the behavior "expresses and perpetuates the attitude that the victim and members of her sex are inferior because of their sex." She recognizes that in a reversed world, women could do this to men. But she is firmly convinced that, in our world, while every offense to a woman is directed at all women, by contrast, whatever harm women might do to individual men, "women cannot harm or degrade or dominate men *as a group*."[7] Not for an instant does she entertain the notion that our society may already be one in which different groups compete for their own avenues to domination, as much feminist jurisprudence (as well as critical race theory) reveals.

To my mind, Superson's "objective" view is based on nothing more than the subjective ideology espoused by certain feminists, asserted as axiomatic. Inasmuch as she is herself a member of the subjugated class, Superson's low estimation of women's ability to appraise and act on their own experience cannot be considered harassment. But were we to suddenly discover that Superson is a man, her characterization of women would become, by her own account, a clear example of "objective" sexual harassment.

Ideas like Superson's open the way to tyrannical law and to sweeping feminist oversight of men's words, gestures, expressions, and even thoughts. Now that "third party harassment" is taken to be a legitimate concept, even women who find men's attentions or sexual references welcome have no right to them since another woman in the vicinity may be offended. Third party harassment turns out to be a device placing us all squarely in Superson's hands, for this third person would presumably be the "objective" observer such as Superson, able to gauge the precise quality of a man's "attitude."

As for Leslie Pickering Francis, she concludes part I of her book with what might seem a reasonable, indeed conciliatory move, suggesting that "education" on this issue is crucial and that informal resolution is better than formal complaints. This, of course, disregards the anti-male bias in existing "informal" procedures. But, more importantly, why does she think this a better route? Because it will facilitate complaints. Francis's concern to find procedures that further encourage charges and accusations exemplifies an oddity of much feminist writing about sexual harassment and other "pervasive" wrongs against women. Absence of complaints invariably is taken to mean that women are constrained from reporting the offenses that abound. By this definition, a policy that works well is one that generates a great many complaints. This, in turn, is part and parcel of the notion not only that "women don't lie," but also that they need perpetual prodding to make public the harms they constantly experience at the hands of men.

IV

For the reasons Hajdin explains so thoroughly, the typical sexual harassment policy in the academy is heavily weighted in favor of the alleged victim and says not a word about false or trivial accusations. Even if charges against someone are dismissed (usually years later) and are clearly demonstrated to have been maliciously or opportunistically made, the accuser faces no consequences, while the destroyed reputations and wrecked careers of the accused remain. Furthermore, "moral" charges have an odd way of scaring off friends and colleagues who fear contamination. For the accused, "due process" is a rare experience. Sometimes the same feminist staffers who promote training sessions and propagandize the endless harms purportedly done to women on campus are the very officials who "investigate" the charges. Universities' own procedures (including deadlines) are typically bypassed and violated—always in the direction of favoring the complainant. Prohibitions against "retaliation" (intended to keep an employer from firing an employee who has made sexual harassment charges) are used to isolate and disempower the accused; they also function to provide individuals anticipating poor grades or performance evaluations with strong incentives to make false charges. Often the "victim" advocate (a university employee) makes great efforts to locate other people willing to talk against the accused, while finding reasons to exclude the accused's own witnesses. At times the accused cannot even get a statement of the accusations and the names of the accusers until late in the process. "Victims" are provided with books to read that teach them how to reconceptualize what may be minor slights or misunderstandings into serious harassment allegations. Some complainants, of course, are after the quick cash settlement universities will offer to avoid the costs and publicity of protracted lawsuits.

I believe that only when those who are opportunistically and falsely accused start to sue their employers, in large numbers and for hefty damages, will the situation begin to change. Why, then, do they not often take action? The following example helps us understand their hesitation.

At the University of Wisconsin, Milwaukee, in the early nineties, a female faculty member made sexual harassment charges against three male colleagues (all of whom had supported her for tenure). Initially she claimed to have "recovered" a memory that one of these men had left on her doorstep a pornographic book whose heroine's name was the same as hers, but she could never produce the book. Eventually the men were exonerated of this and other charges. Does this mean the university's sexual harassment procedures "worked" in a fair way? Hardly. Professor Stan Stojkovic, a specialist in criminal justice, was one of the accused. Here is his explanation—given to me recently—of why he did not sue the university for its gross mishandling of this case:

> Regarding civil actions against the university, we did not sue the university largely because we had already spent two and a half years in and out of court trying to get a due process hearing [as required by the university's own procedures], and once we got the hearing, after spending $50,000.00 in legal fees, we were exhausted. For us to go after the university further would have required another $50,000.00 (according to our lawyers) and much more emotional and physical effort than we could muster. We finally received the hearing our policies at the time stated we were entitled to, and at that hearing we were vindicated after a forty-minute discussion.

> The reason people don't fight the administration is that it is too time consuming and costly, and the university goes back and does what it wants anyway because nobody is holding them accountable. University officials have no loss to their reputations or pocketbooks when issues are addressed in court. The litigants, on the other hand, can lose potentially everything. After our case, the administration went back and did what it always had done and other alleged sexual harassment perpetrators either accepted their punishments or left the university. The number of such cases where people were forced out is large.

This is part of the reality of academic life in America today, a reality ignored by supporters of sexual harassment law who are doing what they can to extend the law's reach in the untiring search for evidence of the wrongs done to women.

While I appreciate the complexities of the arguments that underlie sexual harassment law, I have no difficulty in seeing that Hajdin's is a more reasonable, logical, and empirically based appraisal than those of the two other authors discussed here. It is less mired in ideology. It is more suitable for this world, not keyed to some imaginary one in which men have to be constantly held in check by vigilante feminists acting on behalf of frightened women too compromised to realize the harms they constantly suffer. If one adopts the "dominance" view articulated by MacKinnon and her epigones, double standards are needed as a corrective. But once this view is disputed—and there are many grounds for doing so—the numerous inconsistencies, paradoxes, and injustices spawned by sexual harassment law and

incorporated in its two levels of implementation come into focus, and with
them the urgent need for public exposure and protest.

NOTES

First published *in Academic Questions* 16:2 (Spring 2003), 70–82. Reprinted with
kind permission of Springer Science and Business Media.

1. Catharine MacKinnon, on the occasion of the 1986 U.S. Supreme Court decision, in *Meritor Savings Bank v. Vinson*, accepting the EEOC guidelines that created
the category of "hostile environment" harassment—harassment even without economic harm to the plaintiff.

2. Mane Hajdin, *The Law of Sexual Harassment: A Critique* (Selinsgrove, Pa.:
Susquehanna University Press; and London: Associated University Presses, 2002).

3. Alan Charles Kors and Harvey A. Silverglate, *The Shadow University: The Betrayal
of Liberty on America's Campuses* (New York: Free Press, 1998).

4. Margaret A. Crouch, *Thinking About Sexual Harassment: A Guide for the Perplexed*
(New York: Oxford University Press, 2001).

5. Crouch, *Thinking About Sexual Harassment* [emphasis hers].

6. Leslie Pickering Francis, ed., *Sexual Harassment as an Ethical Issue in Academic
Life* (Lanham, Md.: Rowman & Littlefield, 2001).

7. Francis, *Sexual Harassment;* [Superson's italics].

18

MacKinnon as Bully

Catharine MacKinnon was not happy. And when Catharine MacKinnon is not happy, she makes her displeasure known. So it was that on May 2, 2003, Noretta Koertge and I were surprised to hear from the publisher of our book *Professing Feminism* that a letter had arrived from one Paul Kleven, Esquire, accusing us of misrepresenting MacKinnon's views on heterosexual relations in an effort to dissuade the public from reading her work. Kleven further charged us with harming MacKinnon's "professional standing as a respected expert and scholar." His demands were perfectly clear: That we "correct and retract the false and defamatory statements, implications, and innuendos, . . . immediately withdraw the book from circulation, and . . . remove the falsehoods from any future editions." Failure to do so, Kleven threatened, would lead to a defamation lawsuit.

The offending passage had first appeared in 1994, with the publication of our book *Professing Feminism: Cautionary Tales from the Strange World of Women's Studies.* Thereafter, the passage appeared in identical form in the newly published and much expanded second edition of our book which had appeared in February 2003. In a chapter called "Semantic Sorcery: Rhetoric Overtakes Reality," we included a subsection titled "Accordion Concepts," an image meant to suggest that much "music" could be made by stretching concepts into unrecognizable forms.

Our case in point was the term "rape." We began with Robin Morgan's suggestion that the legal definition of rape be extended to cover cases where women, though not actually forced to have sex, would rather be doing something else, such as playing Scrabble (an image Morgan took from

Margaret Atwood's dystopian novel *The Handmaid's Tale*). We then commented:

> And Andrea Dworkin and Catharine MacKinnon have long argued that in a patriarchal society all heterosexual intercourse is rape because women, as a group, are not in a strong enough social position to give meaningful consent—an assault on individual female autonomy uncannily reminiscent of old arguments for why women should not have political rights.[8]

The accompanying note 8 read as follows:

> See, for example, Andrea Dworkin, *Intercourse* (New York: Free Press, 1987) and Catharine A. MacKinnon, *Feminism Unmodified: Discourses on Life and Law* (Cambridge: Harvard University Press, 1986).

We assumed these statements would be clear to anyone familiar with MacKinnon's and Dworkin's work, for we had based our general characterization of their position on extensive acquaintance with their writings and considered our summation both reasonable and accurate. Yet here was Catharine MacKinnon's lawyer, claiming that this brief comment in our book was false and defamatory, and demanding that we make amends or face draconian consequences. Neither Noretta nor I had ever before been threatened with a lawsuit, and, though we felt confident in what we had written, it was hard to avoid visions of losing our houses and being reduced to penury by a vengeful MacKinnon. Our contract with our publishers, like most such contracts, indemnified them from any legal claims. We, therefore, would have to deal with the problem posed by Kleven's threats on our own.

Fortunately, by then I had for some years been acquainted with Harvey Silverglate, a criminal defense and civil liberties attorney based in Boston. Silverglate had first contacted me in the mid-nineties, when he was working on a book with Alan Charles Kors, a history professor at the University of Pennsylvania. The two men had been friends since their undergraduate days at Princeton, and out of their collaboration came not only their book, *The Shadow University: The Betrayal of Liberty on America's Campuses*, published in 1998, but also a new organization. In response to the hundreds of accounts of gross abuses of individual rights on campus and pleas for help, Kors and Silverglate had decided to start an outfit they called FIRE: The Foundation for Individual Rights in Education, which opened its doors in 1999. FIRE is a nonpartisan, nonprofit organization whose mission is to defend students' and faculty members' civil rights: "freedom of speech, legal equality, due process, religious liberty, and sanctity of conscience, the essential qualities of individual liberty and dignity"—as FIRE's mission statement puts it—against the assault on these rights that have become commonplace in American colleges and universities. I was delighted to be asked, early in the planning stages of FIRE, to serve on its advisory board, made up of a few dozen individuals of differing political persuasions but united in their passionate defense of individual rights on campus. A few years later, I was invited to serve on FIRE's board of directors, a position I am proud to occupy to this day.

Given that, over the years, I had come to know and respect Silverglate, it was inevitable that I should turn first of all to him for advice about the threatening letter Noretta and I had received. And indeed, once Silverglate became acquainted with the facts of the case, he offered to represent us *pro bono* in negotiating with MacKinnon's attorney.

I had first taught MacKinnon's work in the mid-eighties, in a graduate seminar on Marxist and feminist theory, and I had never forgotten the shock expressed by a young, newly married woman in the course upon reading MacKinnon's analysis of heterosexual relations. Having read, over the years, many texts by and about MacKinnon, I was confident that Noretta and I had in no way misrepresented her work. As a result, from the moment we heard from MacKinnon's lawyer, we tended to see her threatened action as primarily an intimidation tactic, designed to frighten us (and other critics of her work, who would of course eventually hear about her charges against us) into silence. We were well aware of MacKinnon's scorn for the First Amendment and her notorious efforts, along with Andrea Dworkin, to impose their anti-pornography sentiments on North America.

We had heard, as well, that MacKinnon not only refused to debate her critics but was vicious in her characterization of them. Even well-known civil rights activists whose views on First Amendment rights didn't match her own tended to be dismissed as shills for pornographers. When, for example, Nadine Strossen, president of the American Civil Liberties Union, in 1995 published a book called *Defending Pornography: Free Speech, Sex and the Fight for Women's Rights*, the MacDworkenite camp had rallied its forces. John Stoltenberg, Andrea Dworkin's gay roommate and eventual husband, evidently saw nothing wrong in publishing an article entitled "Nadine Strossen: The Pornography Industry's Wet Dream" in the summer 1995 issue of *On The Issues* (a feminist magazine he then edited). Compared to this sort of assault, Noretta and I felt like very small fish indeed.

Reassured by Silverglate's support that we had a strong champion in our corner, I began compiling evidence of the accuracy of Noretta's and my representation of MacKinnon's views. And by the end of the month, Silverglate responded to Kleven's opening salvo with a long and carefully documented rejoinder, to which I contributed page upon page of citations, complete with chapter and verse, from MacKinnon's own quite well-known writings and from those of other scholars who, regardless of whether they supported or rejected her views, had understood her writings precisely as Noretta and I had.

Here, then, is Silverglate's first letter (composed together with FIRE attorney Greg Lukianoff, who is now FIRE's president), responding to Kleven's demands and threats. Given its incisive statement of the key issues, I am reproducing it in full, including its footnotes:

May 29, 2003
Re: **Professors MacKinnon, Patai, and Koertge—and the First Amendment**

Dear Mr. Kleven:

I am writing on behalf of my clients Daphne Patai and Noretta Koertge, in response to your letter of April 28, 2003, in which you accuse them of "falsely represent[ing] Professor MacKinnon as too deranged to distinguish between wanted and forced sexual activity, presumably to dissuade readers of your book from reading her work." This claim is frivolous, and I would submit that going forward with efforts to enforce this claim, either by seeking the withdrawal of the book or filing a defamation or other such lawsuit, would harm Professor MacKinnon's "professional standing as a respected expert and scholar" far more than any conceivable damage caused by Profs. Patai and Koertge continuing to disseminate their quite reasonable summary and assessment of Professor MacKinnon's long-standing views.

Before I commence my explanation for why this effort by Professor MacKinnon, with your professional assistance, is such a doomed undertaking, I want to express my view as to why it is such an *inappropriate* one.

I am aware of the fact that Professor MacKinnon has undertaken a campaign to dissuade her critics (she might call them "enemies," but in fairness they are for the most part critics) from keeping up their criticism of Professor MacKinnon's rather harsh views of much that characterizes the role of women, and of men, in our society. Your letter to Profs. Patai and Koertge is just the latest (and by now it may not even be the latest) in a long-standing effort by Professor MacKinnon to use the law of defamation as a weapon in order to win the political debate into which she launched herself quite a number of years ago. The controversies engendered by Professor MacKinnon have in some instances attracted support within certain communities, and in other communities have produced derision. In the "free marketplace of ideas," Professor MacKinnon has been a vigorous warrior with some successes, and some failures. In the legal marketplace, however, the courts have been clear that if Professor MacKinnon is to convince American society of the rightness of her cause and the reasonableness of her proposed remedies for what is wrong in the relations between the genders and in the manner in which the society treats women, she is going to have to succeed by *persuasion* and not by an unfair use of the coercive powers of the state.

Thus, in the landmark case of *American Booksellers Association Inc. v. Hudnut*, 771 F.2d 323 (7th Cir. 1985), the Court of Appeals for the 7th Circuit dealt with Professor MacKinnon's effort to impose her views on the rest of society via the law—in that case, municipal legislation. As is explained in Alan Charles Kors and my book, *The Shadow University*[1]:

> The city of Indianapolis had enacted and enforced an antipornography ordinance that claimed to protect women from "subordination." [Judge Frank] Easterbrook saw through the ordinance's veneer of a "civil rights" law and described it as an effort to coerce a change in attitudes. Noting that supporters of the ordinance "say that it will play an important role in reducing the tendency of men to view women as sexual objects," he concluded that it faced an insurmountable constitutional obstacle: It not only sought to alter attitudes, but it did so in a manner that discriminated by viewpoint, that is, favoring only "speech treating women in the approved way—in sexual encounters 'premised on equality.'" The First Amendment, he ruled, prohibits the state both from establishing a "preferred viewpoint" for or about a group, and from taking steps to change private attitudes to suit that ideological preference.
>
> . . . [T]he court concluded that a free society lets individuals freely choose, for themselves, those things that affect "how people see the world, their fellows, and social relations." Responding to the city's argument that pornography poisoned the atmosphere for women, the judge rejected any "answer [that] leaves the government in control of all of the institutions of culture, the great censor and director of which thoughts are good for us." The First Amendment, Judge Easterbrook and his colleagues ruled, permitted neither "thought control" nor an officially "approved view of women, of how they may react to sexual encounters [and] of how the sexes may relate to each other." Further, notions of "low value speech" and "fighting words" did not affect this case. The city did not consider the speech of low value, because it "believes this speech influences social relations and politics on a grand scale," and it had not banned all fighting words, but only those of a particular ideology and viewpoint, a selectivity that itself violated the First Amendment.
>
> The city of Indianapolis applied to the U.S. Supreme Court, which, after accepting the case for review, found the issues so clear that it affirmed Judge Easterbrook's judgments summarily—that is, without even calling for briefs and oral arguments.[2] The Court of Appeals's holding now has the imprimatur of the U.S. Supreme Court. Under the First Amendment, clearly, there can be no "approved view of women" and of "how the sexes may relate to each other." There can be no imposition of regimes aimed at changing the attitudes of free citizens by censorship and coercion.

Having thus failed to achieve the imposition of her views on the citizens of this nation—or at least on the citizens of Indianapolis as a start to a national campaign—by means of an inappropriate use of municipal law, Professor MacKinnon turned to an oftentimes improper use of the law of defamation in order to silence her most persuasive critics. This use of a threat to bring a defamation action unless one's critics cease being one's critics (or at least being one's *effective* critics) has become an all-too-common fixture in modern American life. The irony is that it has been adopted by some people who have been favored with an extraordinarily broad access to the communications media. It is a weapon that has been adopted by Professor MacKinnon in particular,[3] despite her easy access to the print and electronic media, including the ability to publish numerous books with prestigious publishers. Further, Professor MacKinnon has been rewarded with tenure at a very fine law school, in part on the basis of her writings. (In the jargon that describes a professor's position in higher academia today, Professor MacKinnon has "published rather than perished.")

Apparently, the fact that Professor MacKinnon has life tenure in the world of higher academia, plus ready access to the media of communications, is not deemed satisfactory as a platform with which to promulgate her views and arguments. Having been unsuccessful in imposing her views on the citizens of this country by legislation, she appears intent on being able both to serve her views to the public and yet to attain a certain amount of protection from criticism by using the law of defamation as an *in terrorem* weapon to silence her critics, including (perhaps *especially*) those critics who, like Professors Patai and Koertge, are well respected and whose views are taken seriously.

It is quite inappropriate for a person in Professor MacKinnon's position to act as a "legal terrorist," using the law of defamation to silence her legitimate critics for doing nothing more than focusing entirely appropriate criticism on her writings. But I hope that you and your client, after reading this letter and thinking more about it, will conclude not only that it would be legally and ethically unwise for Professor MacKinnon to bring a lawsuit for this improper purpose, but that it would be professionally inappropriate as well. If Professor MacKinnon wants to win the hearts and minds of her fellow citizens, she is going to have to stick to the marketplace of ideas and not go running to the courts. A defamation suit in this case might well be legally and professionally disastrous for Professor MacKinnon (and might indeed reflect poor legal and ethical judgment on your part as well, I should add), and she should take a hint from the fact that the Supreme Court of the United States was **unanimous** in the *Hudnut v. American Booksellers Association* case when it adopted Judge Easterbrook's and the Seventh Circuit's view that an ideological campaign such as that of Professor MacKinnon is going to have to rely on persuasive, not legally coercive means.

* * * *

1. My clients' summary of MacKinnon's views has a reasonable basis because it is clearly drawn from MacKinnon's own writings

I will not bother here to attempt to give you an extended lecture on the law of defamation, since I assume that you are well acquainted with this area of the law. Otherwise, I assume that Professor MacKinnon, a law professor at a great law school, would not have selected you to write her threat letter. However, I will quickly address a few aspects of the law.

In your letter, you cite *New York Times v. Sullivan*, 376 U.S. 254 (1964). From this, I infer that you agree that "actual malice" is the standard of fault required to find someone liable for defamation in this case. This standard requires a plaintiff to show that the alleged defamer either knew that what they were publishing was false or published it with reckless disregard for the truth. What Professors Patai and Koertge published was not only a reasonable interpretation of Professor MacKinnon's writings but also essentially true. Therefore, this claim would not only clearly fail the actual malice test (and even the negligence test in place for private speech about private persons), but also has an absolute defense against any libel claim. Furthermore, judges are not in the habit of drawing fine lines about academic interpretations of sociological works and would be loathe to find Professors Patai and Koertge's interpretation of Professor MacKinnon's work "false" let alone "knowingly false."

I will now delve directly into the factual issue of why my clients' reference, in their book, to Professor MacKinnon's views and writings, is accurate or at least sufficiently reasonable (and thereby substantially true) so as to pose absolutely no issue of defamation.

Professor MacKinnon's writings often express the sentiment that normal heterosexual sex is similar to, if not indistinguishable from, rape. For example, in the opening line of chapter 9, entitled "Rape: On Coercion and Consent," in her book *Toward a Feminist Theory of the State*, she writes:

> If sexuality is central to women's definition and forced sex is central to sexuality, rape is indigenous, not exceptional, to women's social condition.[4]

In *Toward a Feminist Theory of the State,* Professor MacKinnon describes rape and normal heterosexual intercourse as indistinguishable:

> This is a culture in which women are socially expected—and themselves necessarily expect and want—to be able to distinguish the socially, epistemologically, indistinguishable. Rape and intercourse are not authoritatively separated by any difference between the physical acts or amount of force involved but only legally, by a standard that centers on the man's interpretation of the encounter. Thus, although raped women, that is, most women, are supposed to be able to feel every day and every night that they have some meaningful determining part in having their sex life—their life, period—not be a series of rapes, the most they provide is the raw data for the man to see as he sees it. And he has been seeing pornography. Similarly, "consent" is supposed to be the crucial line between rape and intercourse, but the legal standard for it is so passive, so acquiescent, that a woman can be dead and have consented under it.[5]

Note, too, this similar passage from elsewhere in *Toward a Feminist Theory of the State*:

> Compare victims' reports of rape with women's reports of sex. They look a lot alike. Compare victims' reports of rape with what pornography says is sex. They look a lot alike. In this light, the major distinction between intercourse (normal) and rape (abnormal) is that the normal happens so often that one cannot get anyone to see anything wrong with it. Which also means that anything sexual that happens often and one cannot get anyone to consider wrong is intercourse, not rape, no matter what was done. The distinctions that purport to divide this territory look more like the ideological supports for normalizing the male use and abuse of women as "sexuality" through authoritatively pretending that whatever is exposed of it is deviant.[6]

In *Feminism Unmodified: Discourses on Life and Law*, which my clients cited in the endnote to p. 129 of *Professing Feminism*, two of Professor MacKinnon's major arguments independently support their characterization of her views. The first argument is that intercourse can never be truly consensual if it takes place within the inequality of patriarchy, because sex under patriarchy is inseparable from the system of "abuse and objectification" that it supports:

> Because the inequality of the sexes is socially defined as the enjoyment of sexuality itself, gender inequality appears consensual. This helps explain the peculiar durability of male supremacy as a system of hegemony as well as its imperviousness to change once it exists. It also helps explain some of the otherwise more bewildering modes of female collaboration. The belief that whatever is sexually arousing is, ipso facto, empowering for women is revealed as a strategy in male rule. It may be worth considering that heterosexuality, the predominant social arrangement that fuses this sexuality of abuse and objectification with gender in intercourse, with attendant trauma, torture, and dehumanization, organizes women's pleasure so as to give us a stake in our own subordination. It may even be that to be "anti-sex," to be against this sex that is sex, is to refuse to affirm loyalty to this political system of inequality whose dynamic is male control and use and access to women—which would account for the stigma of the epithet.[7]

If consent is meaningless under patriarchy, then the distinction between rape and normal sex, which rests on consent, necessarily becomes meaningless as well. This argument of Professor MacKinnon therefore supports my clients' characterization of her views.

The second relevant argument begins with the assertion that pornography makes sex indistinguishable from violence and violation, *i.e.*, rape:

> Under male dominance, whatever sexually arouses a man is sex. In pornography the violence *is* the sex. The inequality is the sex. Pornography does not work sexually without hierarchy. If there is no inequality, no violation, no dominance, no force, there is no sexual arousal.[8]

MacKinnon then asserts that the violence/sexuality of pornography is the same as the violence/sexuality of female life in general under patriarchy:

> If pornography is a practice of the ideology of gender inequality, and gender *is an ideology*, if pornography is sex and gender is sexual, the question of the relation between pornography and life is nothing less than the question of the dynamic of the subordination of women to men.[9]

The resulting syllogism provides a second reasonable basis for my clients' interpretation of Professor MacKinnon: If violence and violation (*i.e.* rape) is the sex in pornography, and the sex in pornography is the same as real-life sex under patriarchy, then the logical conclusion is that under patriarchy, violation and rape are inseparable from sex.

From the above examples, it is clear that Professor MacKinnon's past writings, including those in *Feminism Unmodified*, form a reasonable basis for Professors Patai and Koertge's assertion that Professor MacKinnon believes sex under patriarchy is inherently rape. These arguments appear repeatedly in many of Catharine MacKinnon's writings over the past twenty years; I would be happy to provide additional examples, but the references above are more than enough to establish a reasonable basis for my clients' statements.

Of course, Professors Patai and Koertge's one-sentence summary is much shorter and blunter than Professor MacKinnon's extensive body of writings. I can see why Professor MacKinnon might be upset that, by boiling her argument down to its essential elements, they have stripped it of much of its nuance. But such are the limitations of one-sentence summaries, and it is unreasonable to demand that Professors Patai and Koertge rewrite their entire book to reproduce Professor MacKinnon's arguments in longer form. Besides, as I have noted in the opening portions of my letter, Professor MacKinnon has excellent access to the print media—probably considerably better that that of Professors Patai and Koertge—and it is utterly unreasonable for your client to insist on a longer summary.

After all, the disputed sentence comes from a single paragraph out of the entire book, in a 6-page subsection where Professor MacKinnon's views are only one example among many used to prove a broader point. If Professors Patai and Koertge were to make the "correction" you demand, then their own thesis would be lost in a flood of Professor MacKinnon's views on patriarchal sex, pornography, and violation.

Excising the disputed sentence would also be unreasonable. Regardless of how one chooses to word it, Catharine MacKinnon and Andrea Dworkin view "[t]he normal fuck by a normal man" to be "an act of invasion and ownership undertaken in a mode of predation: colonializing, forceful (manly) or nearly violent."[10] That perspective on rape, consent, and intercourse is a significant example of what my clients describe as a "stretched concept" in their book, and it would detract from their argument if they were forced to excise it.

2. My clients' summary of Professor MacKinnon's views has a reasonable basis because it corresponds to the interpretations of other academics.

Professors Patai and Koertge's interpretation of Professor MacKinnon is not unusual. Indeed, similar formulations are easy to find among the writings of other academics who have tried to briefly summarize Professor MacKinnon's views.

Stephen Schulhofer, my law school classmate and now a professor at the University of Chicago Law School, described Professor MacKinnon's views as follows in his book *Unwanted Sex*: "In effect, MacKinnon suggests, the search for a line separating permissible from abusive encounters is naïve [. . .] In this leading strand of feminist thought, consent can seem coerced even when a woman *initiates* a sexual encounter."[11]

Zillah R. Eisenstein, former chair of the Politics Department at Ithaca College, cited Professor MacKinnon's famous essay, "Feminism, Marxism, Method and the State: An Agenda for Theory" (*Signs* 7:3 Spring 1982), to arrive at this conclusion: "MacKinnon regards sexual harassment, rape, and ordinary heterosexual intercourse as not all that different."[12]

Sara M. Evans, a history professor at the University of Minnesota and widely recognized as one of the leading members of the Women's Studies movement, wrote that MacKinnon and Dworkin "did indeed emphasize victimization over agency. For them, most if not all heterosexual sex was comparable to rape."[13]

Manhattan Institute fellow Heather Mac Donald wrote in a *City Journal* essay: "(MacKinnon has also implied that *all* sexual intercourse is rape, which of course would make consent irrelevant.) In the United States, pressure from feminist theorists has forced changes in rape law. Some of the pressure has been salutary, but some of it aims, MacKinnon-style, to make sexual intercourse per se suspect."[14]

This interpretation is not just restricted to academics who disagree with Professor MacKinnon's views. Georgetown law professor Robin West, who has argued against what she calls the "harms of consensual sex," writes in her book *Caring for Justice* that Professor MacKinnon shares her view that female consent is of doubtful significance under patriarchy:

> First, as Catharine MacKinnon insists in many different contexts, and as I have argued elsewhere, it may be the case that a deep and thoroughly justified fear of acquisitive, violent male sexuality mars a woman's self-possession early in her development, rendering her what I have called a "giving self," ready to give, and to identify herself as one who gives, rather than endure the pain and fear of being one from whom her self is taken. If so, consensuality—the lodestar of value for the liberal legalist—is a very different experience for men than it is for women.[15]

In addition, Dee L. R. Graham, in advancing her theory of a Societal Stockholm Syndrome, cites Professor MacKinnon approvingly and concludes, "These examples suggest that sado-masochism is the model for normal heterosexual sex in our culture." Later in her book, Graham provides a summary of Professor MacKinnon's views strikingly similar to that of my clients: "Like Catherine [sic] MacKinnon (1979), [Adrienne] Rich rejects [Susan] Brownmiller's distinction between rape as violence and intercourse as sexuality, since this distinction obscures similarities between the two in male-dominated cultures. MacKinnon contends that, under conditions of male domination, female consent is not a meaningful concept."[16] (This, of course, raises the ancillary question of whether Professor MacKinnon has also threatened Robin West and Dee Graham with lawsuits for misrepresenting her views. Or do such allegedly incorrect summaries of Professor MacKinnon's views only harm Professor MacKinnon's reputation when they are published by her critics?)

In at least one private conversation, too, the other participant came away with the impression that Professor MacKinnon had confirmed that she believed "all intercourse is rape." As retold by Warren Farrell in his book *Women Can't Hear What Men Don't Say*, Farrell asked MacKinnon point blank (when he and MacKinnon were on a break while doing a special with Peter Jennings on rape, on ABC's evening news) if her perspective was correctly represented by the belief that "all intercourse is rape." He writes: "She not only confirmed, but reiterated it voluntarily and emphatically."[17]

3. Cal Thomas' retraction did not place my clients on notice of any alleged "falsehoods" in their book.

In your letter, you say that my clients were on notice that their book "falsely represented Professor MacKinnon's position" because the *Los Angeles Times* wire service issued a retraction of certain portions of Cal Thomas' March 1, 1999 column. This assertion is contradicted by the facts surrounding the retraction, not to mention the text of the retraction itself.

The retracted portion of Thomas' column reads as follows: "Catherine [sic] MacKinnon wrote in 'Professing Feminism': 'In a patriarchal society all heterosexual intercourse is rape because women, as a group, are not strong enough to give meaningful consent.'"[18] The error is simple and obvious. Catharine MacKinnon was not one of the authors of *Professing Feminism*, and the statement on page 129 is not a direct quote. The statement therefore can only be accurately described as a paraphrasing of her views, not as her views themselves.

To my knowledge, two newspapers—the *Orlando Sentinel* and the *Tampa Tribune*—published retractions of the column. Notwithstanding your tortured attempts at selective quotation of the *Tribune* retraction, the obvious interpretation is that these retractions simply correct Thomas' gross misattribution of authorship, but do not comment on the accuracy of *Professing Feminism* itself.

4. My clients did not "maliciously equate" Professor MacKinnon's views with misogynistic arguments from past generations.

When Professors Patai and Koertge described Professor MacKinnon's views on rape as being "uncannily reminiscent" of old misogynistic arguments, the context makes it clear that they are expressing their personal misgivings about potential unintended consequences of Professor MacKinnon's views, not claiming that either Dworkin or MacKinnon intentionally set out to discredit or weaken women in any way. The next paragraph—and, indeed, most of the next two pages of the book!—are focused on this problem of unintended consequences. As they write: "Most feminists [. . .] want to have it both ways. They would like to retain the charge that rape is a terrible violation of human rights and, at the same time, stretch the legal definition of the crime beyond all reason. But even the rhetorical gains won by this sort of concept stretching can backfire."[19]

Moreover, Professors Patai and Koertge are not alone in believing that Professor MacKinnon's ideas dismiss the agency of women in a manner "uncannily reminiscent" of old misogynistic ideas. In an essay published in the book *Feminists Theorize the Political*, Ruth Leys, a well-known specialist in trauma studies at Johns Hopkins University, critiqued the way in which MacKinnon's view "inevitably reinforces a politically retrograde stereotype of the female as purely passive victim." She elaborated on that critique in this footnote:

3 When MacKinnon treats women as "raped, battered, pornographed, defined by force, by a world that begins, at least, entirely outside us" (*Feminism Unmodified: Discourses on Life and Law* (Cambridge: Harvard University Press, 1987), p. 57) [sic], she implicitly subscribes to the notion of the female subject defined as external to the very power that in Foucaultian terms produces them as such. She thus fails to recognize the political violence of her own discourse, a discourse which in effect denies the female subject all possibility of agency.[20]

Similarly, political science professor Judith Grant wrote in her book *Fundamental Feminism*: "It is startling when one finally realizes that MacKinnon's argument is quite literally that male sexuality defines all that a woman is: [. . .]"[21]

5. Conclusion

If one lives long enough (I am 61 years old), one sees just about everything and anything, and one sees, too, various circles close. Professor MacKinnon's threat to sue Profs. Patai and Koertge strikes me as not only inappropriate and unworthy of your client, but as somewhat ironic for me in a personal and professional sense. Earlier in my career, I had the privilege of representing a group of Professor MacKinnon's ideological allies, including her sometime co-author Andrea Dworkin. I am able to reveal this professional engagement because the details that I am about to discuss are matters of public record and not confidential. The case was a defamation action brought by the infamous pornographer Al Goldstein. He sued the feminist writers/activists because, in their discussion of his pornographic publishing activities (including *Screw* magazine), they expressed their well-known view that pornography equals the murder of women. Such rhetoric, Goldstein alleged in his outrageous and frivolous lawsuit, was the equivalent of the activists' calling him a murderer. Needless to say, the women won their case, on summary judgment. But I was always struck by the raw nerve and blatant hypocrisy of Al Goldstein—who was for his whole career protected by the First Amendment from both civil and criminal penalties for his outrageous, inflammatory and misogynistic speeches and writings— attacking the First Amendment rights of this group of feminist writers and activists who were using *their* free speech rights to attack *his* views and words. Nat Hentoff put it succinctly in the title of one of his best books, *Free Speech for Me, but Not for Thee*.

Professor MacKinnon's and your threatened lawsuit is equally frivolous, and bringing such a lawsuit would, in my view (and I would guess in the views of many other reasonable people) be equally outrageous and hypocritical. Furthermore, I don't see how any such lawsuit could survive not only summary judgment, but an attack, under Rule 11 of the Federal Rules, as a frivolous and unprofessional tactic. I hope that cooler heads will prevail here.

In fact, I have a suggestion for an unorthodox resolution to this matter. Professor MacKinnon obviously feels that many people, not just Professors Patai and Koertge, mischaracterize her views on rape, intercourse, and consent. She is also a busy person who, according to the *Chicago Tribune*, has little spare time to launch multiple libel lawsuits against all of those whom she believes mischaracterize her views.[22] On behalf of my clients, I am therefore extending an invitation for Professor MacKinnon to join them in exploring this perceived mischaracterization in the only reasonable manner available under the First Amendment and applicable case law—by a public debate, free of spurious threats of legal action. The topic would be whether or not Professor MacKinnon's writings support the proposition that in a patriarchal society, all heterosexual intercourse is rape. If Professor MacKinnon accepts the invitation, then she and my clients can agree on a venue and format for the debate.

I know that this is a very unusual suggestion in a threatened libel matter, but your threat is such that I feel free to suggest unusual solutions. Our respective clients would probably be no closer to agreeing after such a debate, but I think that perhaps their being able to confront one another directly rather than through the medium of lawyers would have a salutary effect. Moreover, it would help bring publicity to a question which Professor MacKinnon clearly believes to be of great importance.

If, however, you insist on proceeding with this meritless lawsuit, I can assure you that my clients will step up to the plate to defend themselves as well as free speech and intellectual freedom. They are willing to marshal the necessary will and resources to defend against this unreasonable and unwarranted attack on their work as well as on the very protections that have sheltered Professor MacKinnon's career of saying and writing things unpopular in the eyes of many in the power structure. We will call upon all of the civil liberties organizations to help defend the First Amendment from this kind of cynical attack. (I wonder whether Professor MacKinnon has ever had occasion to send a threat letter to Nadine Strossen, the President of the ACLU, because of some of the highly critical things that Professor Strossen has said and written about Professor MacKinnon's views and writings.)

I look forward to hearing your response. If you have any questions, please do not hesitate to contact me by phone, letter, or e-mail.

Sincerely,
Harvey A. Silverglate

Following the departure of this magnificent missive, Noretta and I waited anxiously for a response from MacKinnon's attorney. Phone calls between our lawyer and MacKinnon's went back and forth, as the demands MacKinnon was making were slowly whittled down. Throughout this process, our position was one of caution—we didn't want to make things worse and invite her lawyer to carry out her threat, since even a nuisance suit is still a serious legal action and must be dealt with. But at each stage of the negotiations we kept coming back to the same core position: What we had written was, we believed, accurate, in fact demonstrably so, and thus we were faced with the problem of how to avoid fanning the flames of MacKinnon's wrath while also avoiding implying that she was in any way justified in her charges against us.

When Paul Kleven did respond to Harvey Silverglate's letter, among other things he chose to emphasize that we should have known MacKinnon disputed our view of her writings because she had repeatedly fought against these very interpretations. What we found intriguing about this line of argument was that it seemed unintentionally to concede that other people, independently of us, had understood her work precisely as we did—and that she was well aware of that.

At one point, I made the following argument to Silverglate: It is theoretically possible that we and the other people who have a particular view of

MacKinnon's writing were acting in unison, colluding, and intentionally maligning her. In practice, however, that happens not to be the case. But by making these accusations, MacKinnon can divert attention (or at least try to) from the evident fact that various people of quite different political persuasions have come to the same conclusion about the meaning of her arguments. It seemed to us that this inconvenient fact should have concerned her, but evidently it did not. Nor, furthermore, did we in fact know of any statements in which she had repudiated her earlier writings or even explained why they were so widely misunderstood. Instead, MacKinnon routinely attributed malice and anti-feminist impulses to those who criticized her. To us, this was simply a way to muddy the waters and keep the focus from falling where it should: on what she had indeed written.

We recalled a striking example of MacKinnon's way of responding to her critics. Some ten years earlier, Carlin Romano had written a negative review of MacKinnon's book *Only Words*.[23] Romano had opened the review with an intentionally provocative hypothetical: "Suppose I decided to rape Catharine MacKinnon before reviewing her book . . . ." Romano then proceeded to imagine that he would desist from this plan, but that another reviewer might make the same decision and, indeed, carry it out. Would both reviewers be equally guilty of rape, Romano asked? But Romano's point—that there is a crucial distinction between an act and the description of that act—evidently couldn't be grasped by MacKinnon. Her reaction was consistent with her writings: Words and actions are to be treated as interchangeable. MacKinnon's response was typical of her rhetoric and the entire episode drew national attention. As quoted in *Time* magazine,[24] she charged: "He [Romano] had me where he wanted me. He wants me as a violated woman with her legs spread. He needed me there before he could address my work." These are not the utterances of a writer who uses words carefully. She also told the *Washington Post* that Romano "should be held accountable for what he did" and ominously hinted: "There are a lot of people out there, and a lot of ways that can be done." Meanwhile, MacKinnon's then-fiancé Jeffrey Masson wrote to Romano declaring "I am not threatening you" but then went on to say: "I want you to know, if there is ever anything I can do to hurt your career, I will do it."

Uncowed, Romano tartly responded that he did something "worse" than "humiliate" and "debase" MacKinnon, as her defenders charged. "I took her seriously," he wrote. "The worst thing that can happen to a flamboyant claim is to be tested by a good example."[25]

It was in part this long history of controversy that made it hard for Noretta and me to take entirely seriously MacKinnon's threats against our little book. But upon reflection, we were convinced that the real offense we had committed was to have expressed in plain language what MacKinnon had expressed many times in far more convoluted terms. And by threatening us with a charge of defamation, MacKinnon was attempting to reverse the truth, which was that the positions she claimed not to hold when they were stated plainly were perfectly reasonable ones to draw from her best-known and most cited writings, as we had shown in great detail. Furthermore, these views were baldly expressed by people very close to MacKinnon (collaborators such as Andrea Dworkin, Dworkin's roommate and penis-hating partner, John Stoltenberg, and by others whom these three had influenced). We noted that MacKinnon's complaints against us were being made in her name and on behalf of Andrea Dworkin. And indeed, we did see the two of them as presenting a united front on certain issues that were the subject of heated debate among feminists. The main difference we discerned was that Dworkin played street fighter bad cop to MacKinnon's more patrician good cop routine.

The more time passed, the more we felt inclined to stick to our conviction that the truth is the ultimate defense. We knew there was no malicious intent or consciousness of falsehood in the innocuous and general comment we had made about MacKinnon's and Dworkin's views, and without these, we knew there was no libel either. Nothing I read in the months that I spent tracking down more and more examples of MacKinnon's views led me to modify my sense that she did indeed think of intercourse as rape—not (or at least not yet), admittedly, in the legal sense, but certainly in the political and existential sense. Equally important, her efforts to effect changes in rape law have all seemed to aim at expanding the range of actions that could be construed as rape, and her analysis of "consent" has played a crucial part in that endeavor. This is why her discussions of rape, consent, and sexuality are intertwined and mutually dependent.

Since MacKinnon had shown no interest in taking us up on the invitation to publicly debate these issues, we were not too inclined to give in to what looked like a campaign aiming to wear us down. Furthermore, knowing we were not the source of MacKinnon's "problem" of being misunderstood (if one were to call it that), we suspected that our real offense was indeed to have drawn an appropriate and plainly expressed conclusion from her often complicated-sounding arguments. True, our book was apparently read by some anti-MacKinnonites (such as Cal Thomas) who cited it and made errors in doing so. But, equally true, there were many feminist scholars who obviously had arrived at the same impression of MacKinnon's views that we had. Another detail we noted was that we've never known MacKinnon to dispute the interpretation we had made of her words when that same interpretation was being put forth by her supporters. And because we recognized that MacKinnon's writings were far better known than our book, it seemed likely that most readers had formed their impression of her views from her writings, not ours.

I compiled still further examples of both MacKinnon's views and scholars' responses to them while Silverglate and Kleven negotiated about what sort of statement we might be willing to include in acknowledgment of her complaint. Eventually, armed with all this material but above all with his confidence that a suit by MacKinnon would find it hard to pass the "giggle" test, Silverglate (again with Greg Lukianoff's help) produced a second long letter, dated January 9, 2004. Silverglate began this letter to MacKinnon's attorney with the statement:

> Thank you for your reply letter of October 1, 2003. However, my clients and I remain convinced that your threatened libel lawsuit will not succeed if pursued, and that in any event it would be an imprudent course for an academic to follow. As stated previously, Professors Patai and Koertge have a reasonable basis for their characterization of Professor MacKinnon's views, supported both by Professor MacKinnon's writings and by the writings of other academics who have interpreted those writings. We are confident this would be a successful defense in the threatened libel suit. We are equally convinced that many of the writers and scholars who have understood Professor MacKinnon's views much as Professors Patai and Koertge have, would testify as to the basis of their shared and very reasonable conclusions. The very fact that Professor MacKinnon has had to devote a substantial portion of her waking hours to correcting the record indicates that the widespread interpretation of her views, as expressed by Professors Patai and Koertge, is largely of her own making, particularly earlier in her career.

Silverglate went on to assert that we "therefore choose to make no more concessions to Professor MacKinnon beyond what they feel would fall into the category of a professional courtesy."

> Professor MacKinnon's frustration at seeing her complex ideas boiled down into a single sentence is, of course, understandable. Such summaries—especially those penned by one's critics—rarely, if ever, fully convey the subtlety and force of the original argument. As an author myself, I know what it feels like to have one's writings treated this way. Nevertheless, as long as such interpretations are derived from the original work rather than spun from whole cloth, participation in the marketplace of ideas is the only valid way to deal with this phenomenon.

As with the previous letter, Silverglate again quoted at length from other scholars whose work I had documented and who had independently interpreted MacKinnon's writings in much the same way Noretta and I had:

> Eileen Bresnahan wrote in 1999 of Professor MacKinnon that her "conviction, even single-mindedness; her propensity to engage in passionate rhetoric that arguably generates heat more effectively than light; and her designs on changing laws in ways that must fundamentally alter American society combine to leave few observers neutral on her ideas or on herself [. . .]"[26] This observation is quite accurate, and particularly so in discussions of Professor MacKinnon's

views on the relevance and legitimacy of female consent in a patriarchal society in which, as Professor MacKinnon argues, "The substantive principle governing the authentic politics of women's personal lives is pervasive powerlessness to men, expressed and reconstituted daily as sexuality"[27] and "the major distinction between intercourse (normal) and rape (abnormal) is that the normal happens so often that one cannot get anyone to see anything wrong with it."[28]

The fact that so many respected scholars—including, as you note yourself, Susan Estrich—read Professor MacKinnon's works as implying that "all heterosexual sex is rape"[29] suggests that this interpretation is not, as Professor MacKinnon claims, a mere "political libel" or an example of "visceral misogyny"[30] but a conclusion that one can legitimately and reasonably infer from Professor MacKinnon's published works. Words are inevitably subject to interpretation, and when one interpretation is supported by an interlocking series of well-known statements in major publications, as in Professor MacKinnon's case, then the author cannot credibly accuse her readers of "libel" merely for reading those words in a way she finds unsympathetic. A writer may reasonably be judged by what she writes most often and most persuasively, not by later clarifications, modifications, explanations, interpretations, and emendations that are unaccompanied by major, public withdrawal of the various works that led to what she claims is an erroneous view in the first place.

Even if one accepts Professor MacKinnon's debatable contention that the "all sex is rape" interpretation of her works originated from the likes of *Playboy* and Rush Limbaugh, the fact that subsequent scholarly works directly cite Professor MacKinnon's writings for support for similar characterizations suggests that Professor MacKinnon's writing does not rebut the "lie," but rather provides ample justification for such an interpretation. Indeed, even some women's studies course syllabi agree more with my clients' reading of Professor MacKinnon's works than with her own. (See, for example, **Exhibit B** to this letter: Excerpt from course syllabus "WSGS 101: Introduction to Women's Studies/ Gender Studies," taught by Jeffrey Tobin, assistant professor of Anthropology and Women's Studies/Gender Studies at Occidental College.)

Silverglate took issue, as well, with Kleven's response to our citation of Warren Farrell's exchange with MacKinnon (quoted above). Kleven had merely dismissed Farrell's account by saying in his letter that "Mr. Farrell can hear at least some things that women don't say." But, as Silverglate stated:

Nevertheless, Mr. Farrell has assured my clients that if this libel threat continues to escalate, he is willing to state under oath that the anecdote is true. This may be a case in which Mr. Farrell heard at least some things that Professor MacKinnon *wishes* she had not said. That particular credibility contest should not be worked out in a defamation action between Professor MacKinnon and Professors Patai and Koertge.

In this second long missive, Silverglate used further evidence that I had gathered of other scholars' understanding of MacKinnon's views. These included the following:

(1) Citing Professor MacKinnon's book *Toward a Feminist Theory of the State*, the entry for "establishment of consent" in the *Encyclopedia of Feminist Theories*, edited by Lorraine Code, even more closely tracks Professors Patai and Koertge in its interpretation of Catharine MacKinnon's writings:

> Radical feminists, such as Catharine MacKinnon and Carol Pateman, reject the liberal focus on legal reform, arguing that even if legal standards of sexual consent were changed so as to reflect women's understandings of what it is to give or withhold consent, women's consent to certain institutions, however it is given, cannot be genuine under conditions of patriarchy. What appears to be women's genuine consent to heterosexual sex and relationships is spurious since the beliefs and desires that give rise to such consent have been shaped by a male dominated and heterosexist society. Ironically, radical feminists have been criticised for reinscribing a problem identified in earlier feminist critiques: the claim that women's consent to heterosexual sex and relationships cannot be genuine implies that women cannot be taken at their word. Whereas earlier feminists criticise legal standards of consent for suggesting that women cannot say "no", the radical feminist critique implies that women can never say 'yes'.[31]

(2) Citing Professor MacKinnon's 1983 *Signs* article "Feminism, Marxism, Method, and the State: Toward Feminist Jurisprudence," Kathryn Abrams writes that: "MacKinnon's claims arise in the context of her central argument: that coercion is paradigmatic of heterosexual relations and constitutive of the social meaning of gender under gender inequality."[32] Though more cautiously worded, this interpretation is also similar to what Professors Patai and Koertge wrote. Characterizing coercion as "paradigmatic" of heterosexual relations, after all, is just another way of saying that coerced, *i.e.* unwanted, sex is the norm for heterosexual relations.

(3) Toronto journalist and author Donna LaFramboise, who holds a degree in Women's Studies from the University of Toronto and serves on the board of the Canadian Civil Liberties Association, minces no words:

> MacKinnon has become famous for her insistence that, in a society where the sexes aren't equal, women are afraid of men or depend on them for economic survival and so aren't in a position to genuinely refuse to participate in sexual intercourse. This means, then, that women can never be viewed as having given consent of our own free will. In other words: all sex is rape. Anyone who thinks this is a distortion of MacKinnon's views is invited to turn to her 1989 book *Toward a Feminist Theory of the State*[. . .]"[33]

(4) National ACLU officials are equally blunt. Citing passages from Professor MacKinnon's book *Feminism Unmodified*, pp. 130, 154, 171–72, Marjorie Heins, then-director of the ACLU Arts Censorship Project and author of *Sex, Sin, and Blasphemy: A Guide to America's Censorship Wars*, has said plainly: "Yet

MacKinnon does not distinguish between rape and intercourse; she sees them as expressing 'the same power relation,' sees sexuality itself as 'violating,' and pornography as bad because it shows that women (or some of us at least) 'desire to be fucked.'"[34]

(5) A final and particularly noteworthy example comes from Professor Nadine Strossen, President of the ACLU, whom I mentioned in passing in my previous letter. In her book *Defending Pornography*, Professor Strossen characterizes Professor MacKinnon's views in a very similar fashion to Professors Patai and Koertge:

> Both Dworkin and MacKinnon, for example, have argued that, in light of society's pervasive sexism, women cannot freely consent to sexual relations with men. Accordingly, as Cardozo Law School professor Jeanne Schroeder has observed, their analysis of pornography "functions as a critique of sexuality as such, not of violence, violent sex or sexualized violence."[35]

Professor Strossen goes on to say:

> Another unifying theme among Dworkin, Gans, and MacKinnon is that they all invoke the powerful, negative concept of rape to describe what they see as an inevitably involuntary act on the woman's part: Dworkin and MacKinnon analogize all heterosexual intercourse to rape; [. . .][36]

If Professors Patai and Koertge are guilty of libel for their characterization of Professor MacKinnon's views, then Professor Strossen and Marjorie Heins are equally guilty. And if Professor MacKinnon has issued libel threat letters to Professors Patai and Koertge but not to the President of the ACLU and the (now former) director of its Art Censorship Project, whose writings Professor MacKinnon likely finds just as objectionable as my clients', then it is difficult to escape the conclusion that she views my clients as being more likely to "roll over" because they do not have the advantage of being national officers in the country's largest civil liberties organization. In case there is any lack of clarity on this point, however, I want to emphasize that my clients will be just as resistant in the face of this libel threat as Professor Strossen would be in the same situation. My clients are not trying to be intransigent nor uncaring for Professor MacKinnon's concerns. They are not trying to be provocative. However, they firmly believe this is a dispute that should be handled by the "marketplace of ideas," not the courts, and will continue to respond according to that belief.

Despite the overwhelming evidence of the accuracy of our interpretation of MacKinnon's views, we did offer one concession, and Silverglate explained this to Kleven in his conclusion:

> My clients do promise that, as a matter of professional courtesy, they will state in any future editions of *Professing Feminism* that Professor MacKinnon has disputed their interpretation of her works. They also apologize for printing an incorrect publication date for *Feminism Unmodified* in the endnote, an error

which they will correct in any future editions. However, they respectfully refuse both your request to withdraw the current edition of *Professing Feminism* from circulation and your request to adopt the rewritten passage you propose in your October 1 letter. Their original offer to publicly debate Professor MacKinnon on this topic remains open, should Professor MacKinnon choose to accept the invitation. This debate can be in writing or in live oral format.

But the saga was not yet over. First, Attorney Kleven requested an extension of the statute of limitations, so that he and his client could consider an appropriate response. On Silverglate's advice, we agreed. Then, the two lawyers went back and forth about possible language that might be satisfactory to all parties.

On February 11, 2004, Silverglate wrote to us suggesting language that he and Kleven had agreed on, which could be inserted as a note to each copy of the second edition of *Professing Feminism* that the publisher had not yet sent out:

The proposed settlement language:

Professor Catharine MacKinnon has taken exception to our characterization of her work as arguing that all heterosexual intercourse is rape in a patriarchal society (on page 129 of the second edition). While we believe this phrase accurately characterizes her past writings on the subject, she does not agree and says that it is not her position. Hence, the relevant sentence should read: "And we interpret Andrea Dworkin and Catharine MacKinnon as arguing, or at least implying that in a patriarchal society all heterosexual intercourse is rape because women, as a group, are not in a strong enough social position to give meaningful consent—an assault on individual female autonomy uncannily reminiscent of old arguments for why women should not have political rights. Some critics of Dworkin and MacKinnon agree with us, while Dworkin and MacKinnon dispute this interpretation."

But it seemed to Noretta and me that this language and its form of delivery (an errata sheet) conceded too much. Thus, on February 25, 2004, Silverglate communicated our view to Kleven, explaining, "When I put the settlement text into writing and presented it as something that would have to be inserted into copies of books, it appeared to the authors to be too much of an admission of error rather than a mere acceptance of the fact that different people might have different opinions on the matter at issue."

On March 12 Attorney Kleven complained to Silverglate that we seemed to be moving backwards, and then made an apparently conciliatory gesture. "If the problem currently is with the concept of the errata sheet," he wrote to Silverglate, "we could make an announcement using the above language, and change the text as indicated in any new printings of the second edition, as well as in any future editions. We need some way of communicating this to the readers."

Unfortunately, Kleven's suggestion of "making an announcement" brought into sharp focus what we took to be the underlying aim of this entire process: to allow MacKinnon to publicly proclaim a victory. We foresaw that the real value of such an announcement would be to chill the speech of any future and potential critics of MacKinnon's work. And once that result of any accommodating gesture on our part became transparent, we could not agree to it.

The more we thought about it, the more it seemed we had every reason to be extremely cautious about any concession made to MacKinnon. So, after further discussion with us, Silverglate responded to Kleven on March 14, 2004, expressing our *unwillingness* to do anything other than add an endnote in any *future* edition of our book, acknowledging MacKinnon's stated point of view. Anything else, we had concluded, would suggest that we in some measure accepted her view that we had misrepresented her work, which we emphatically felt was not the case. What we were prepared to agree to, finally, was merely to place the following phrase in any future editions of *Professing Feminism*:

> Professor Catharine MacKinnon has taken exception to our characterization of her work as arguing that all heterosexual intercourse is rape in a patriarchal society (on page 129 of the second edition). While we believe this phrase accurately characterizes her past writings on the subject, she does not agree and says that it is not her position.

As Silverglate summed up for Attorney Kleven:

> Prof. MacKinnon would have in her hands the settlement agreement indicating that the authors made this concession. That would be her proof, if such is needed, that the authors have recognized the existence of a controversy between them and Prof. MacKinnon as to the meaning of Prof. MacKinnon's writings, and the nature of Prof. MacKinnon's position, on the matter. The authors feel that their doing anything more than this would appear to concede an error where none exists. They are willing to concede a difference of opinion between them and Prof. MacKinnon, but not the existence of an error in their book.

Now, with hindsight, and after rereading my extensive notes on MacKinnon's work, as well as the lengthy correspondence that took place on this matter between Noretta and me and our attorneys, Silverglate and Lukianoff, throughout 2003 and 2004, I am once again impressed by the accuracy of our brief characterization of Catharine MacKinnon's writings. Still, we do all recognize that individuals may change their minds or have second thoughts about their own past writing. In MacKinnon's case, since she has such wide access to the press, it would seem that rather than having threatened to sue us, she could easily have availed herself of her prominence to declare in a very public fashion that she did not equate heterosexual intercourse with rape, did not find them indistinguishable, did not believe that women lacked the power to give meaningful consent to heterosexual relations, and wished to advise her many feminist fans in academe to cease using in their courses those writings of hers that so readily lend themselves to such "misunderstanding." I am not aware that she has done any such thing.

As for the threatened lawsuit: After Silverglate's mid-March message to Kleven, we once again waited for a response. And waited. The statute of limitations, which we had agreed to extend, ran out.

We never heard from either MacKinnon or Kleven again.

July 2007

NOTES

1. Alan Charles Kors and Harvey A. Silverglate, *The Shadow University: The Betrayal of Liberty on America's Campuses* (New York: The Free Press, 1998; paperback from Harper/Perennial, 1999), 191.

2. *Hudnut v. American Booksellers Association, Inc.*, 475 U.S. 1001 (1986).

3. See, for example, "Fighting a Lie That Just Won't Die," by Cindy Richards, *Chicago Tribune*, May 30, 1999.

4. Catharine A. MacKinnon, *Toward a Feminist Theory of the State* (Cambridge, Mass.: Harvard University Press, 1989), p. 172.

5. MacKinnon, *Feminism Unmodified: Discourses on Life and Law* (Cambridge, Mass.: Harvard University Press, 1987), 150.

6. MacKinnon, *Feminism Unmodified*, 146.

7. MacKinnon, *Feminism Unmodified*, 6–7.

8. MacKinnon, *Feminism Unmodified*, 160.

9. MacKinnon, *Feminism Unmodified*, 161.

10. Andrea Dworkin, *Intercourse* (New York: The Free Press, 1987), 63.

11. Stephen J. Schulhofer, *Unwanted Sex: the Culture of Intimidation and the Failure of Law* (Cambridge, Mass.: Harvard University Press, 1998), 53–54. Italics in original.

12. Zillah R. Eisenstein, *Feminism and Sexual Equality: Crisis in Liberal America* (New York: Monthly Review Press, 1984), 250.

13. Sara M. Evans, *Tidal Wave: How Women Have Changed America at Century's End* (New York: The Free Press, 2003), 222.

14. Heather Mac Donald, "Law School Humbug." *City Journal* 5:4 (Autumn 1995). Online: www.city-journal.org/html/5_4_a2.html. Italics in original.

15. Robin West, *Caring for Justice* (New York: New York University Press, 1997), 281–282.

16. Dee L. R. Graham, *Loving to Survive: Sexual Terror, Men's Violence, and Women's Lives* (New York: New York University Press, 1994), 113, 214.

17. Warren Farrell, *Women Can't Hear What Men Don't Say* (New York: Tarcher/Putnam, 1999), 276.

18. Cal Thomas, "The Feminist Raping of America." *Jewish World Review*, March 1, 1999.

19. Daphne Patai and Noretta Koertge, *Professing Feminism: Education and Indoctrination in Women's Studies*, revised edition (Lanham, Md.: Lexington Books, 2003), 129.

20. Ruth Leys, "The Real Miss Beauchamp: Gender and the Subject of Imitation," in *Feminists Theorize the Political*, Judith Butler and Joan W. Scott, eds. (New York: Routledge, 1992), 168.

21. Judith Grant, *Fundamental Feminism: Contesting the Core Concepts of Feminist Theory* (New York: Routledge, 1993), 77.

22. Cindy Richards, "Fighting a Lie That Just Won't Die," *Chicago Tribune*, May 30, 1999.

23. See Carlin Romano, "Between the Motion and the Act," *The Nation*, November 15, 1993.

24. Richard Lacayo, "Assault by Paragraph," *Time*, January 17, 1994, 62.

25. David Gates, "Free Speech or a Hostile Act?," *Newsweek*, January 17, 1994, 53.

26. Eileen Bresnahan, "Catharine MacKinnon," in *Significant Contemporary American Feminists: A Biographical Sourcebook*, Jennifer Scanlon, ed. (Westport Conn.: Greenwood Press, 1999), 171.

27. Catharine MacKinnon, *Toward a Feminist Theory of the State* (Cambridge, Mass.: Harvard University Press, 1989), 120.

28. Catharine MacKinnon, "Sexuality, Pornography, and Method: Pleasure under Patriarchy," *Ethics* 99 (January 1989), 337.

29. Susan Estrich, "Teaching Rape Law," *Yale Law Journal* 509: 1992, 512.

30. Catharine A. MacKinnon, "Pornography Left and Right," *Harvard Civil Rights-Civil Liberties Law Review* 30: 1995, 143.

31. Shelley Wilcox, "Consent, Establishment of," in *Encyclopedia of Feminist Theories*, Lorraine Code, ed., (London & New York: Routledge, 2000), 104–105. British spelling in original.

32. Kathryn Abrams, "Ideology and Women's Choices," *Georgia Law Review*, 24, 761–801; reprinted in Frances E. Olsen, ed., *Feminist Legal Theory*, (New York: New York University Press, 1995), Vol. 1, 379–419.

33. Donna LaFramboise, *The Princess at the Window: A New Gender Morality* (New York: Penguin Books, 1996), 26.

34. Marjorie Heins, "Masculinity, Censorship, and Sexism Law," in *Constructing Masculinity*, Maurice Berger, Brian Wallis, and Simon Watson, eds. (New York: Routledge, 1995), 257.

35. Nadine Strossen, *Defending Pornography* (New York: New York University Press, 2000; originally published 1995), 109.

36. Strossen, *Pornography*, 197.

IV

ACADEMIC AFFAIRS

19

Why Not a Feminist Overhaul of Higher Education?

An attempted coup has hit New England universities. A remarkable document has surfaced, the handiwork of the New England Council of Land-Grant University Women (a group formed several years ago to develop an "agenda for women" in the six New England land-grant universities). "Vision 2000" proposes a number of "goals" designed to "promote equity for women" in the next century. What Neanderthal would challenge such a worthy aim? Answer: one who questions dubious premises; one who worries about means as well as ends; one who fears for the harm done to academic liberties when self-appointed agents of a supposedly oppressed group are allowed to direct a corrective program.

At the six universities, representatives of campus women's centers, women's studies programs, and commissions and councils on the status of women developed their proposals over a three-year period. Inspired by a 1993 report produced by a panel of the faculty senate at the University of Massachusetts at Amherst, the group came up with nine long-term recommendations, accompanied by the following short-term strategy: First, ask each university to endorse the document "in principle," and then work out specific measures according to each campus's needs.

This reasonable-sounding approach has already met with some success. The presidents of the Universities of Maine, New Hampshire, and Vermont have given the document their personal endorsement, and the authors of "Vision 2000" are hoping to win approval by the presidents' council of the six land-grant universities at its February meeting—and then to persuade university presidents nationwide to endorse the report.

At the University of Massachusetts at Amherst, however, misgivings among some faculty members have prompted the faculty senate to refer the document to committee for further study. For, when examined critically, "Vision 2000" reveals itself to be a stunningly imperialistic move to put in place a questionable feminist agenda, thinly disguised as a plea for equal opportunity and fairness.

"Vision 2000" makes recommendations covering virtually all aspects of university life, from salaries to course content, from research to teaching styles and campus life.

It begins by invoking the purportedly sorry state of women in higher education. Few reasonable observers would accept this claim today, given increases in female graduation rates, and women's entry into professional schools and faculty ranks, but relentless feminist propaganda has confused the evidence. At the University of Massachusetts, for example, female students interviewed in December by a local newspaper readily asserted that they had not personally encountered bias in the classroom; nonetheless, they assumed that it exists. Is the assumption correct? It is worth asking that question before endorsing calls for "women-friendly" classrooms and obligatory sensitivity training for professors and others who do not share the goals of "Vision 2000."

Most of the charges made in "Vision 2000" presuppose their own validity. The authors of the document rest their case on inflammatory rhetoric that tends, for example, to assume that sexual violence is widespread ("Women face sexual violence and sexual harassment in the classroom and in the workplace, and are too often silenced by a system that protects the perpetrators of these crimes"). Are rape and sexual assault indeed routine occurrences at universities? Is harassment really widespread?

Concerning areas in which women are underrepresented, the report assumes that such "disproportions" are a sign of discrimination. But might women not be underrepresented in engineering, for instance, because of their own preferences? The solutions proposed by "Vision 2000" are as sweeping as its charges. "Training" in how to avoid sexual harassment is prescribed for everyone in the university. Disciplinary action (unspecified) taken against offending supervisors must satisfy the injured "supervisee." "Groups" (again unspecified—fraternities? football teams?) shown to be implicated in violence against women at a higher rate than the average for other campus groups "are to be deprived of recognition and support." Campus women's centers will be established where they do not already exist, and campus leaders should "rely upon" them for guidance "in their efforts to encourage, support, and maintain new roles for women."

The curriculum should be transformed into one that is "women-friendly and culturally diverse." That process too will be "best conducted with guidance from an autonomous Women's Studies site and active Women's Studies scholars." Graduate work in women's studies must be made available at each institution, and "equitable recognition" (whatever that might mean) is to be given to the "substance and methodologies" of work in women's studies.

In these and similar ways, "Vision 2000" aims at nothing less than a feminist overhaul of the entire academic enterprise, for, the report notes, "women's status within American higher education reflects an intellectual bias that is deeply rooted in the disciplinary methods and social assumptions of university communities." Student evaluations will include questions on the inclusiveness of the curriculum and the "appropriateness of teaching methods to different kinds of students." By 2000, faculty members "whose students identify their courses, teaching styles, and mentoring as failing to be inclusive [will] not receive teaching prizes, satisfactory teaching evaluations, or merit raises." Presidents and chancellors are to hold "department heads accountable for improvement in achieving gender equity," and to "reward" departments that demonstrate measurable progress and "intervene" in those that do not.

One would hardly guess from all this that "Vision 2000" refers to universities in late-twentieth-century America. Of course, the authors had to paint a dismal picture to justify the extraordinary measures that their report proposes. But it is the distance between the actual and the putative condition of women, and between the positive-sounding goals and the sanctions threatened against resisters and nonconformists, that exposes the power game being played. If put into effect, the measures outlined above would establish women's studies and its allies in campus women's centers as the arbiters of university policy—with rights of supervision over administrators, faculty members, and programs.

It is not possible to understand fully the impulses behind "Vision 2000" without taking a long-range view of how feminism has developed within academe over the past three decades. The early seventies witnessed much debate about which of two strategies feminists should follow: Should they aim at establishing separate women's studies programs or work through existing departments? The women's studies route won out, and now about 650 women's studies programs exist in American universities, offering undergraduate concentrations, majors, and, increasingly, graduate programs as well.

Initially, separate programs were an important asset for women. They helped feminist scholars achieve tenure and promotion that they might well have been denied in other departments. But, as was foreseen in the early debate, that success has had a certain "ghettoizing" effect. Although many institutions now have adopted "diversity" requirements that students can meet by taking women's studies courses, some areas of the university do remain untouched by feminism. The hard sciences, in particular, have tended to reject the overt politicization imposed by feminist perspectives. When women's studies attacks science as "masculinist"—a routine charge in much feminist writing—few faculty members in physics or chemistry seem to care. To a feminism that rests on a totalizing epistemology, such indifference cannot be countenanced.

"Vision 2000" is designed to complete the great transformation. Above all, it is a plan for policing the struggle for gender equity, based on the anachronistic insistence that inequality characterizes women's status in every aspect of university life. The report depicts faculty members, department chairs, and deans as incapable of doing the right thing without feminist supervision. Although the word "mandatory" does not appear in the document, the spirit that animates it has little of the voluntary in it.

As "Vision 2000" makes abundantly clear, women's studies wants to be the central player in the restructuring of university life. In our 1994 book, *Professing Feminism: Cautionary Tales from the Strange World of Women's Studies*, Noretta Koertge, a professor of the history and philosophy of science at Indiana University at Bloomington, and I described the ways in which many women's studies programs have allowed the political mission of training feminist cadres to override educational concerns.[1] The strategies of faculty members in these programs have included policing insensitive language, championing research methods deemed congenial to women (such as qualitative over quantitative methods), and conducting classes as if they were therapy sessions.

At my own university, faculty members in women's studies have supported a radical speech code that would have seriously impeded free expression. They have also supported the decision to make faculty members document, on official annual report forms used in promotion, tenure, and salary reviews, their "significant contributions to multiculturalism."

Should administrators, department heads, and faculty members really surrender the university to ideologues? Women's studies got its first foothold in academe by invoking the liberal values of tolerance and intellectual openness. Once entrenched, however, and in defiance of both the historical record and common sense, women's studies has turned on those very values, rejecting them as helping to sustain the hated status quo. If the future represented in "Vision 2000" were to come to pass, 2000 would look remarkably like Orwell's 1984. Will it be any comfort that Big Brother will have turned into Big Sister?

NOTE

This piece was first published in *The Chronicle of Higher Education*, January 23, 1998, A56.

1. For an update on feminist plans for the academy, see *Professing Feminism: Education and Indoctrination in Women's Studies*, revised edition (Lanham, Md.: Lexington Books, 2003).

20

Speak Freely, Professor— Within the Speech Code

For some years now, I have been troubled by an odd shift that has taken place in academic circles. The battle cry of "academic freedom" is still aimed at assaults from outside the academy—no longer McCarthyism, but now corporatization and privatization. Yet encroachments on academic freedom from inside—speech codes and anti-harassment policies, for example—are tolerated, indeed welcomed. Opposing the former makes one progressive. Protesting the latter gets one labeled conservative at best, racist (or even fascist) at worst.

A recent conference on academic freedom held at the State University of New York at Albany, sponsored by the faculty senate of the SUNY system and attended by administrators from many SUNY campuses, brought this development home to me in a personal way.

When I agreed to participate, I did not at first realize that I was being invited to represent a "conservative" point of view. I was astonished when, still in the planning stage, one conference organizer asked me to suggest a "conservative" substitute for a speaker who had dropped out. Perhaps that should have forewarned me.

On a two-person panel on academic freedom and the culture wars, my fellow panelist was to have been Cary Nelson, a professor of English at the University of Illinois at Urbana-Champaign.[1] The week before the conference, Nelson was replaced by his coauthor on several books, Stephen Watt, a professor of English at Indiana University at Bloomington. In preparing for our session, I checked out their recent *Academic Keywords: A Devil's Dictionary for Higher Education* and was struck by the fact that, while covering pretty much the entire academic scene, it contained no entry on speech codes.

The book did, however, include an unpleasant and highly idiosyncratic article by Nelson on the National Association of Scholars (NAS), described in grossly unfair terms as an organization made up largely of academic failures dedicated to destroying academic freedom. Another article on the subject of academic freedom, also by Nelson, devoted some pages to a scathing denunciation of the NAS, but gave only the briefest attention to speech codes as a threat to academic freedom. More interesting still, the book included no discussion at all of the strange political turnabout by which former radicals are now calling for various kinds of restrictions on speech.

All that deepened my unease at being put in the position of presumptively speaking for the "conservative" side—but, after all, Stephen Watt could not be held responsible for Nelson's essays. In fact, he read a genial paper on the nefarious effects of money on university life.

But, as I listened to other speakers and members of the audience, it became clear to me that, even at a conference devoted to academic freedom and seemingly celebrating the American Association of University Professors (AAUP), a decidedly skewed view of the subject predominated. It was the defenders of a broad and nonpartisan understanding of academic freedom who were seen as conservatives, while the only attacks that I heard on academic freedom—never, of course, made explicitly—came from those who had no problem whatsoever with curtailment of speech in the service of such things as harassment policies.

This new alignment became apparent when I attended the keynote address given by Walter P. Metzger, a lifelong AAUP activist and author (with Richard Hofstadter) of the famous 1955 work, *The Development of Academic Freedom in the United States.* Metzger's talk reviewed the history of struggles over academic freedom, from the founding of the American Association of University Professors in 1915 to its famous 1940 "Statement of Principles on Academic Freedom and Tenure" and beyond. At one time, Metzger noted, most complaints of violations of academic freedom came from faculty members, typically at lesser-ranked schools, who claimed that their freedom in the classroom had been infringed. Metzger commented that such charges were often a good measure of the ranking of an institution.

Academic freedom was never an absolute, he said. It was always assumed that one's scholarship had to be competent, one's decorum professional. True, the definitions of competence and professionalism were set by white males, but the values they extolled were universal ones. And those values were mostly offered as admonition and advice, rather than rules.

For most in the audience, all of that was familiar history. Only when Metzger approached today's culture wars did he begin to tread on contested territory. After initially capitulating to "political correctness," the AAUP's Committee A issued a statement in 1992 declaring that any attempt to codify punishable speech was a threat to academic freedom, Metzger said. But although the association came out with a report on academic freedom and sexual harassment in 1994, it has been lax in defending professors against the charge that they are creating a hostile environment.

As a result, Metzger said, threats to academic freedom today come not from outside the academy, but from those seeking to enforce speech codes and policies outlawing sexual and racial harassment in the name of protecting various identity groups. Although such codes plainly infringe on academic freedom, he said, protests from the professoriate have been few. Only one academic group has clearly spoken up, Metzger noted—the National Association of Scholars.

Metzger went on to criticize that association for sometimes putting its own political agenda ahead of academic freedom. More generally, he said, the way that law has become a senior partner guiding decisions on academic procedure has been extremely dangerous—but here too there has been little discussion.

Metzger's comments also included the admission that he himself had long been silent. He too had been unwilling to make "enemies on the left." Psychological intimidation of faculty members has, indeed, worked its way into the academic scene, he concluded.

Metzger's stature is such that his views encountered no audible opposition from the audience. But no endorsement, either.

Later that day, when I spoke, similarly condemning sexual harassment policies and other feminist-inspired efforts to regulate academic discourse, I was vigorously attacked from the floor. And when Harvey Silverglate spoke the next morning, audience reactions fully revealed just how debased the notion of academic freedom has become in today's academy.

Silverglate is a Boston lawyer and civil libertarian who, together with the University of Pennsylvania historian Alan Kors, wrote the 1998 book *The Shadow University: The Betrayal of Liberty on America's Campuses*. I find the book an exemplary compilation and analysis of attacks on academic freedom and freedom of speech that occur within the university. Silverglate's focus at the Albany conference was on the surreptitious ways in which academic speech codes, struck down wherever they have been legally challenged, have been put into effect on campuses in the guise of harassment policies.

Such policies typically list ``verbal or physical acts'' that are to be proscribed, he noted. But verbal acts are, of course, speech; hence harassment policies are, in fact, speech codes and do, indeed, curtail free expression.

Silverglate further rejected the arguments of critical race theorists that offensive speech uttered by historically oppressed minorities should be protected, while comparable speech by their supposed oppressors can be suppressed. Academic freedom, he warned, cannot continue to exist with such a double standard. Equality before the law depends on a single standard. Every attempt to undermine the First Amendment by oblique attack has failed in unanimous Supreme Court decisions.

Silverglate's observations didn't go over well. When the floor was opened to responses, several people dismissed his point with comments that speech codes are a thing of the past. One man then went on to say that equality is a dangerous concept, since it leaves inequality untouched. His statement was greeted with applause from the audience.

That was the image I carried away with me: an academic conference devoted to the defense of academic freedom in which professors, administrators, and AAUP stalwarts attacked corporatization and privatization but applauded an attack on equality and the equal protection of free speech.[2]

It seemed to me that the prevailing view was that curtailing free speech is acceptable if the objective is to make women and members of minority groups "comfortable" in the university. As Silverglate wrote to me after the conference: "All in all, my impression when I left was the same as it was when I arrived—the control of speech and thought is well-advanced in the one place where it should be absent."

Forty-five years ago, Metzger and Hofstadter argued that academic freedom hangs by a slender thread. Today, instead of heeding their warning and giving serious thought to a tradition in danger of dissolution, throughout the university people convinced of their political righteousness challenge the very concepts of academic freedom and free speech, and they back that challenge up with the coercive power of rules, codes, and disciplinary tribunals.

In feminist circles in particular, academic freedom is under attack by those who advocate and put into effect coercive sexual harassment policies that are so broad, vague, and all inclusive that their application routinely violates the due process rights of the accused. In these feminists' view, harassment is an ever-expanding concept, the depths of which have yet to be plumbed.

A 1996 collection of essays with the title *Antifeminism in the Academy*, for example, begins by asserting that "intellectual harassment is the most recent version of antifeminist behavior erupting methodically in the academy and in U.S. society generally." Extending an already bad, absurdly elastic idea—that harassment consists of creating a hostile environment for various groups— some feminists have come up with the new category of "antifeminist intellectual harassment." The category is typically defined in such sweeping terms that this opinion piece would constitute an example—as, indeed, would any criticism of feminist ideas or of the women who espouse them.

That such an inflation of the powerful concept of harassment does not immediately evoke dismissal is due to the sometimes tacit acceptance of the notion—expressed explicitly in a 1997 essay by Susan J. Scollay and Carolyn S. Bratt in the book *Sexual Harassment on Campus*—that "the academy remains an essentially single sex institution." The myth of what the authors call "systemic sexism" in the university is used to justify ever greater inroads on academic freedom.

As such ideas spread throughout colleges and universities—and are not resisted by those afraid of antagonizing their far-from-helpless feminist colleagues—extraordinary revisions in the notion of academic freedom take place. In the name of a feminist-friendly academy, not only can some things not be said, but other things must be said. Thus some feminists encroach on the teaching autonomy of other faculty members when they insist that feminist methodologies and perspectives—whatever those are—be incorporated into all parts of the university curriculum.

At my own university, where such a plan was partially successful in 1997, Ann Ferguson, director of the women's studies program, proclaimed at a meeting of the faculty senate: "We can't lose track of the wider goal in order to defend some narrow definition of academic freedom, which might amount to a right not to have to respond to new knowledges that are relevant to someone's own field of expertise."

Meanwhile, attacks on unpopular views persist. The very week of the Albany conference, Robert Swope, a student writing a biweekly column for Georgetown University's campus newspaper, had his column, which was critical of the university's production of Eve Ensler's *The Vagina Monologues*, rejected. When he protested, he was removed as a columnist by the paper's editor. Although the editors denied it, Swope claimed that it was his views that were being censored. Ward Connerly, a well-known opponent of affirmative action, recounts in his recent autobiography that he was shouted down by students when he attempted to speak at Emory University.

Such events expose the frivolity of Stanley Fish's recent ruminations in *The Chronicle of Higher Education* (November 26, 1999) on the vacuousness of the liberal commitment to academic freedom. Excluding some points of view from discussion is inevitable, Fish affirmed, though liberals pretend otherwise. "All that is possible—all you can work for—is to arrange things so that the exclusions that inevitably occur are favorable to your interests and hostile to the interests of your adversaries." So specious an argument would never have been made by anyone who has actually been on the receiving end of forced academic conformity—say, an East German professor, first obliged to endorse Marxism-Leninism, later fired for having done so. Such raw power risks self-destruction when the political winds shift against reigning orthodoxies, as they inevitably do.

The modern university itself stands as a refutation of all justifications for curtailing academic freedom. It was the existence of academic freedom that helped feminists establish a foothold in the academy. It was academic freedom that contributed to scholars being able to pursue their interests in African-American, ethnic, and queer studies.

Academic freedom protects those whose thinking challenges orthodoxy. The question now is: Which ideas have acquired the status of orthodoxy in today's academy, and where are the challenges coming from? It seems to me that the recent conference in Albany provided a clear answer: The current attacks on academic freedom are launched by what used to be called the left.

NOTE

First published in *The Chronicle of Higher Education*, June 9, 2000, B7–9.

1. In April 2006, Nelson was elected president of American Association of University Professors (AAUP) for a two-year term.

2. In September 2007, the AAUP released a report entitled "Freedom in the Classroom," which had been approved by its Committee A on Academic Freedom and Tenure. The report is available at: ww.aaup.org/AAUP/comm/rep/A/class.htm. For a detailed critique of the report, see the response by the National Association of Scholars (NAS), available at: ww.nas.org.nas-initiatives/aaup_acfree_initiative/answer_aaup_01.htm.

21

The Great Tattling Scare on Campus

Fabulous—and it's about time! Academics are coming out in defense of the freedom of expression of their colleagues. Really? Let's see. They're not emerging at the many institutions that still have (or, like Harvard Law School, have recently considered adopting) speech codes. So just where are the campus defenders of free speech and untrammeled communication to be found these days? It turns out they're busy agitating against some recently created Web sites that allow academic heretics to engage in a kind of free speech that has grown unpopular inside the academy: criticism of faculty members who politicize their classrooms.

Marvelous irony here: The very same people who have been eager to promote tattling on faculty members who don't conform to the party line on race and gender are now worried that someone is tattling on them. This, they claim, "chills" free speech. It's akin to McCarthyism. And in what forum is this chilling occurring? On that harbinger of free and easy communication that is unimpeded by geographic boundaries and personal prestige: the Internet.

The advent of the Internet was hailed by many as an enormous step forward in the democratization of information and communication, and that promise has certainly been realized in many respects. Consider the unprecedented level of instant conversation, serious and casual, that we've come to take for granted. I first used e-mail in early 1992, for the purpose of collaborating on a book with a colleague a thousand miles away. Today, I'm involved in another collaboration, with a colleague three thousand miles away.

True, I have had (thus far) to put up with spam and junk mail, crank schemes from across the world, and my own sudden accessibility to people I don't know and maybe don't want to know. But those annoyances hardly seem to outweigh the positives. So it is interesting to see academic Webniks suddenly protest the ease and anonymity of communication when they don't like the political direction of the messages. And it's especially intriguing to see their protests utilizing the language of academic freedom, something not always stalwartly defended in academe in recent years.

When Websites are formed to offer an alternative space for airing complaints about professors who foist their political views on students, the sites are accused of impeding academic freedom and stifling free speech on campus—the very same kind of speech that campus activists are happy to curtail in the service of their pet ideologies.

That is the lesson to be learned from the controversy surrounding two sites inaugurated last autumn: NoIndoctrination.org (www.noindoctrination .org) and Campus Watch (www.campus-watch.org). The first identifies itself as "a nonprofit organization promoting open inquiry in academia," while the second, run by the Middle East Forum, "monitors and critiques Middle East studies in North America" and is concerned with five main problems: "analytical failures, the mixing of politics with scholarship, intolerance of alternative views, apologetics, and the abuse of power over students."

Judging by reactions to the two sites, some free speech is considered more worthy of protection than other free speech. In the case of Daniel Pipes's Campus Watch, approximately two hundred new defenders of free speech have emulated the legend of King Christian X of Denmark, who supposedly wore a yellow star during the Nazi occupation of his country in response to the edict that all Jews had to do so. In a similar spirit, faculty members have written in to the Campus Watch site proclaiming their adherence to the anti-Israeli sentiments criticized there and have insisted on their right to be honorary members of the targeted group. Once again, irony abounds. And, as usual, it is not a principle that is being defended but a particular political position. For his efforts, incidentally, Daniel Pipes was recently disinvited from two campus speaking engagements.

As for NoIndoctrination.org, its site invites students (and not, as erroneously reported in the press, parents as well) to report instances of political bias—of any sort—in the classroom. When I checked earlier this month, I saw little reason for all the outrage—there were a total of forty-three complaints relating to thirty colleges—and professors were invited to send in rebuttals, although almost none had chosen to do so. Of the forty-three complaints registered between September 30, 2002, and January 15, 2003, several involved freshmen orientation and diversity training, in which—as with required courses (which also drew complaints)—students are a captive audience. (What was surprising was the breadth of courses in which professors allegedly felt free to indulge in personal proselytizing, ranging from public budgeting to principles of literary study.)

The list-owner tells me that she investigates claims and only posts those that pass muster (approximately one-third of those received, she says). And the stories students told in the posted claims were entirely convincing and consistent with my personal knowledge of dozens of other such incidents. Contrast that with the 164 responses (mostly negative) logged on *The Chronicle of Higher Education's* colloquy about the websites just from early December through mid-January.

The controversy caused by the two offending Web sites is, in my view, welcome, for it has forced professors not otherwise known for their rousing defense of free speech to sound the alarm. Too bad they can't be bothered to express that same concern when speech that they themselves deplore is targeted for curtailment. Where are these colleagues when professors face accusations of sexual or racial harassment resulting from words uttered in class that offend some students? The selective approach to free speech suggests that today's critics are just hoping to extend their control to independent websites of which they disapprove.

In my own corner of the woods, a similar apparent about-face on the First Amendment first became noticeable after the September 11th attacks, when a local professor attracted criticism and threats for ill-timed anti-American statements she had made on September 10th. Suddenly, some of the same people who had embraced a proposed speech code a few years earlier circulated a petition supporting faculty members' rights to express their opinions free of censure or impediments. Of course, what those opinions were was a foregone conclusion. Similarly, on the women's studies e-mail list, a lengthy discussion took place immediately after September 11th about the opportunity that now existed to explain to students in class how the United States deserved the attacks (with only a few cooler heads writing in to suggest doing so was an abuse of a professor's position, not to mention offensive timing).

By contrast, in the face of successful legal challenges to speech codes, for some years now universities have been putting into effect harassment policies that restrict speech and can actually cost professors their jobs for saying something in class that someone considered sexist or racist. A score of universities have even shamefully revealed, by designating special "speech zones" on their campuses, that the college as a whole is, as the civil-liberties attorney Harvey A. Silverglate has called it, a "censorship zone."

But, like harassment policies (which invariably include "verbal acts" of certain types among proscribed conduct), such restrictions have not aroused vigorous protest, least of all from feminists and other campus activists who have seen the codes and policies as a means of enforcing their own agenda. Again, where were the newfound defenders of free speech when politically incorrect speakers were shouted down at universities around the country? When campus papers of a conservative cast were seized or stolen, with no protest from campus administrators? (Check *The Shadow University*, by Alan Charles Kors and Silverglate, for details.) Evidently, some ideas deserve not only a chill but the deep freeze.

What, precisely, does "chilling" of free speech mean? According to Greg C. Lukianoff—the director of legal and public advocacy at the Foundation for Individual Rights in Education, an organization formed for the defense of the civil rights of professors and students of all political persuasions— the concept of "chilling effect" generally refers to the likelihood that vaguely defined and overly broad rules governing acceptable speech will cause people to censor themselves, since they cannot be sure whether their speech is illegal or not. But the term is often invoked to "chill" other people's use of free speech.

"The First Amendment requires a certain minimal toughness of citizens," Lukianoff explains. "It is understandable that speech would be 'chilled' if people felt they risked arrest every time they opened their mouths. However, when people claim they have been 'chilled' by the speech of others, simply because it conflicts with their views or casts them in a bad light, they are only saying they are cowards and would like to live in a world where everyone agrees with them."

That is why mere websites outside the university cannot be equated with speech codes and harassment policies. Nobody and nothing is being "chilled" when people write in their complaints of professorial excesses. That is in striking contrast to the sorts of episodes described by NoIndoctrination.org and Campus Watch.

Consider the incident that led Luann Wright, the mother of a student at the University of California at San Diego, to start NoIndoctrination.org: the heavy-handed focus on racism in a required course ostensibly devoted to improving writing skills.

That is hardly an unusual occurrence. I, too, have long observed it in certain courses. More than ten years ago, a student in an all-white women's studies writing class (fulfilling the university's junior-year writing requirement) complained to me that her teacher, on the first day of class, had declared that the class was "an antiracist classroom" and announced that the students' initial writing assignment would be to describe their first encounter with a person of color. When this student voiced some discomfort with the approach, the teacher accused her of being in "denial" about her own racism. Limiting speech and hampering the free exchange of ideas seems to be acceptable to many people on campuses—as long as the larger purpose of promoting politically fashionable ideas is served.

At my own university, in the mid-nineties even the chancellor's office openly defended (on National Public Radio) a double standard of speech, according to which individuals from historically oppressed groups would have unrestricted speech while those from historically dominant groups would be held to restrictive standards, so as to protect the sensitivities of the formerly oppressed. Simply for protesting the speech code proposed at that time, a small group of us were labeled "racist" by the secretary of the faculty senate (in response, I defended his right to call us names).

Why shouldn't students have an outlet on the Web for their complaints? It is unfortunate that many complainants are willing to make criticisms only on condition of anonymity—but there's nothing new about that either. What do people think has been going on for years with teaching evaluations? Aren't those institutionally sanctioned anonymous statements? They, however, can be devastating to professors and have very real consequences in a world where teaching ability is all too often gauged by student evaluations alone.

In other words, the institutional backing given to critics on one side (via harassment policies that are, in effect, speech codes) is in no way matched by websites outside the university that have no campus offices or officers to enforce their views. These websites are hardly like the continuing attempts in academe to make personal comfort and current orthodoxies the order of the day. Here at the University of Massachusetts, the latest version of the sexual-harassment policy boasts "two significant modifications": "the expansion of locations where one could go to report allegations of sexual harassment and the identification of campus contacts who can provide assistance to those using the process." Nothing about expanding the rights of the accused, which continue to be given short shrift, or about the "chilled" effect on professors who never know when charges against them may surface—charges that will automatically be treated with great respect by campus political overseers.

Indeed, these days those who believe education is not and should not be "inherently political" are usually seen as conservatives retrogressively wedded to obsolete notions of objectivity and impartiality as appropriate ideals (even if imperfectly achieved) in the classroom. Thus, those who promote the politicizing of education excuse their own position and charge everyone else with identical behavior. However, consider this: As Mark Bauerlein, a professor of English at Emory University, recently commented to me, now that my generation is in charge of the university, the rules have changed. As students, they were members of free-speech movements; now that they've earned tenure, they have become advocates of speech codes. Radicals when they were on the bottom, they've become censors when they're on top. And they see no discrepancy in their actions.

What seems to be occurring at the moment, then, is an opportunistic recourse to traditional American values—the very values excoriated by campus politicos most of the time. No matter; I'm happy that some of my colleagues have come around to appreciating those values, however belatedly, and hope that the next time they find themselves promoting curtailments of other people's speech, their words will stick slightly in their craws. But I won't hold my breath.

NOTE

First published in *The Chronicle of Higher Education (The Chronicle Review)* January 31, 2003, B11.

22

Academic Affairs

I

While academic bureaucrats busied themselves in the nineties with a quixotic but persistent attempt to regulate both speech and personal interactions on their campuses, a group of creative writers struck blows against such a narrowing of our lives by providing us with delicate and nuanced, or satirical and scathing, imaginings of the complexities of actual relationships between real (though fictional) persons who find themselves caught up in the new vigilantism. Their novels demonstrate that the politically correct script of male/professorial power and female/student powerlessness is a pathetically thin distortion that negates the texture of human life and produces little but propaganda tracts ranting against a purported patriarchy and its hapless victims. In the hands of a spirited and talented writer, the resources of fictional narrative—its potential for shifting points of view, for negotiating huge jumps in time and sudden reversals, for interior monologues and musings, startling imagery and evocative turns of phrase—can at least attempt to do justice to the dense inner life and complex events that define human existence, in the academy and out of it.

The novels under discussion here take for granted a reality so simple and obvious that it has somehow escaped the notice of many social critics. People meet each other, and that is how relationships begin. Many of these encounters take place in schools and workplaces, where people spend most of their waking hours. Given these circumstances, it is likely that many of the ensuing interactions will be tainted by one or another kind of "asymmetry," since no two humans are exactly alike or occupy precisely the same positions.

What makes the concept of asymmetrical relationships resonate so negatively in the minds of those who would govern personal interactions is, of course, the obsession with power. Asymmetrical relations are bad—so this line of thinking goes—because no romantic or sexual intimacy should exist where one person has power over another. Such power imbalances are inherently evil to those for whom a simplistic conception of "equality" has become the standard of justifiable social relations. This phenomenally narrow viewpoint ignores the obvious fact that the "power" people act out in their relationships is of many and varied types, and that one person's predominance in one sphere is often matched by the other's in another sphere. Who has more brains? More charm? More beauty? More vigor? Greater emotional resources? Better health? Better taste? Not to mention more wealth, status, and all the other material aspects of life? Might a professor's ability to give a bad grade not be countered by his student's opportunity to write him a damaging evaluation? And is not virtually all professorial omnipotence these days trumped by the threat that the "weaker" party (ostensibly the student) might initiate a complaint against some supposedly offensive word or gesture that may or may not have actually occurred? A mere moment's reflection reveals that the usual critique of asymmetrical relations relies on a stunted and feeble definition that is stacked—and of course is meant to be—against men.

Sex is power, yes; but so are brains, charm, wealth, status, and, as Philip Roth teaches us over and over again, health and youth. But since it's patently absurd to try to outlaw relationships defined by all or any of these inequalities, the new academic vigilantes go for the broadest possible category and thus simply target all personal interactions. For who is there on campus who is not hierarchically differentiated from some other individual one way or another? The overly broad definitions of "sexual harassment" that have ensued, which invariably include "verbal acts" that may make someone uncomfortable, allow all other imbalances to be covered, by implication. And the stigma resulting from a charge of sexual or verbal harassment is so great (and the financial stakes of potential lawsuits so high) that, these days, a charge of harassment—a mere accusation, however flimsy, however transparently fabricated—may well cost the accused his (for men are the primary target) job.

Unable to do away with "power" altogether (and without even considering seriously whether it would be desirable, let alone remotely possible, to do so), we scurry to regulate relationships. For the church fathers' view of women as representing sexual danger, capable of luring men from their higher concerns, we have substituted an opposing view that now dominates our secular society: of men as a threat to women, compromising, impeding, and exploiting them at every turn. And since the pattern of young women seeking out older and more accomplished men does not seem to be retreating in the face of feminist critiques, what can we hope to do but discourage those relationships as best we can by stigmatizing flirtation, invitations, stares, touches, jokes (all of these explicitly addressed by the latest sexual harassment policy of my own university)—even when they have nothing to do with sexual extortion or coercion but are merely incidents of ordinary human interaction?

Fortunately, the current preeminence of sexual harassment specialists and other micromanagers of collegiate life is not without challenge, as the novels under discussion here demonstrate. True, these literary works (and others of similar tenor) are small in number—nothing to compare to the thousands of sexual harassment codes the vigilantes have composed and are attempting to enforce, egged on by the federal government and fortified by some rulings signed into law by, ironically, Bill Clinton. But long after sexual harassment codes are gone, these novels will be read both as reflections of American life in the late twentieth century and as examples of the unique abilities of fiction to reveal the human condition in all its subtle intricacies and embroilments.

II

Philip Roth is quite possibly the most assiduous and brilliant of contemporary chroniclers of American life, possessed of a seemingly boundless literary imagination. Stylistically, he has gone about as far as any author could do in cultivating the novel as dramatic monologue. In his most recent two novels, Roth takes up two personae or alter-egos that he has used repeatedly over the past few decades.

The Human Stain, Roth's twenty-fourth book, is a compelling work of art that is also a scathing depiction of America at the end of the twentieth century. It begins with the reflections of Nathan Zuckerman, a figure brought back from Roth's earlier novels and now a mature narrative voice turning into fiction the wreck of another person's life. Zuckerman recollects what happened two years earlier, in 1998, during what he calls "the summer of Bill." That was a time when the whole country thought of little else but the president's penis, while rampant hypocrisy—"an enormous piety binge, a purity binge, . . . an ecstasy of sanctimony"[1]—spread its poison throughout the land. To say, as, for example, Judith Shulevitz does, that the novel "can be read as an allegory of the Clinton presidency,"[2] is, however, to do it a profound injustice. There's an enormous difference between the president's use of the Oval Office for fellatio sessions and then lying about it and what happens to the novel's main character, Coleman Silk, who is driven out of an academic job for imaginary verbal offenses. But Roth's tolerant take on this distinction is expressed in a dream Zuckerman has, of a

mammoth banner wrapping the White House, bearing the legend "A human being lives here."[3]

In *The Human Stain*, Zuckerman, himself seventy years old, is a friend of
Coleman Silk, a classics professor and highly effective and enterprising
dean who, in his late sixties, finds himself on the wrong side of current sensitivities. Wondering aloud in class about two students who have never
showed up, he uses the word "spooks" (in its literal sense) to refer to them.
The missing students, it turns out, are black, and are quick to charge him
with racism. The ensuing inquisition leads to the death of Coleman's wife,
and to Coleman's affair with a thirty-four-year-old cleaning woman who
works at the college, a relationship that, in turn, becomes another misdeed
counted against him.

Overcome by rage at the way his career and life are unraveling—Coleman
even receives an "anonymous" letter (written by a female colleague) that
says: "Everyone knows you're sexually exploiting an abused, illiterate
woman half your age"[4]—Coleman appeals to his writer-friend Zuckerman
to write the story of his persecution at the college. But only after Coleman
has given up his obsession with the outrages he was made to suffer in the
stiflingly politically correct college does Zuckerman in fact get interested
enough to investigate Coleman's life. The novel we read is thus presented
both as the story of Zuckerman's friendship with Coleman and investigation of his life, and as the resulting fictional recreation of that life and of
those who played an important part in it. It is a brilliantly written piece of
work, fascinating in its laying bare of Coleman's youth and hidden life, its
subtle and moving delineation of secondary characters, and its relentless-
ness in exposing the mean-spiritedness, opportunism, self-righteousness,
and sheer resentment that lead an academic community to persecute one of
its own.

But nothing is quite as it seems in this novel—neither Coleman's own
identity and secret past (mercilessly revealed to the unsuspecting reader by
Michiko Kakutani in her review of the novel when it first appeared in the
spring of 2000), nor that of his lover, a woman with a tragic past who claims,
for reasons of her own, to be illiterate. Roth surprises us in this novel, as he
explores with considerable tenderness the stories and consciousness of each
of his principal and secondary characters—even that of the janitor's ex-
husband, Les Farley, a troubled Vietnam vet, who first appears to be the
novel's villain but, by the book's end, turns out to be something rather different. The same is true of another of the novel's potential culprits, Delphine
Roux, a Yale-educated professor who is the author of the poison-pen letter
Coleman receives and whose own secret is revealed later in the novel.

The one certainty the novel postulates is Roth's impatience with orthodoxies and his indignation at our society's turn toward hypocritical moral-
izing and the posture of holier-than-thouness that accompany today's pu-

rity crusades—all of them powerful weapons in the effort to bring down one's opponents. But a positive message complements Zuckerman-Roth's intemperate indictments of the small-mindedness and petty motivations found everywhere. For the novel also celebrates the poignancy, density, and fragility of individual lives, the real substance of which, we come to understand, is far removed from what we first thought them to be.

Roth's prose is glorious: intelligent, evocative, and subtle, as when his narrator contemplates what Coleman Silk's persecution has unleashed:

> There is something fascinating about what moral suffering can do to someone who is in no obvious way a weak or feeble person. It's more insidious even than what physical illness can do, because there is no morphine drip or spinal block or radical surgery to alleviate it. Once you're in its grip, it's as though it will have to kill you for you to be free of it. Its raw realism is like nothing else.[5]

Coleman's lover, the cleaning woman Faunia Farley, who wants only uncomplicated sex with a mature man, is a memorable fictional creation—a woman of subtlety and depth, an utterly unsentimental observer of what she calls the "human stain":

> We leave a stain, we leave a trail, we leave our imprint. Impurity, cruelty, abuse, error, excrement, semen—there's no other way to be here. Nothing to do with disobedience. Nothing to do with grace or salvation or redemption. It's in everyone. Indwelling. Inherent. Defining. . . . The stain so intrinsic it doesn't require a mark. That stain that *precedes* disobedience, that *encompasses* disobedience and perplexes all explanation and understanding. . . . All she was saying about the stain was that it's inescapable.[6]

The Human Stain is the third novel in what Roth described[7] as a "thematic trilogy, dealing with the historical moments in postwar American life that have had the greatest impact on my generation"—the McCarthy era, the Vietnam War, and the impeachment of Bill Clinton—each story told through the mediating perspective of Nathan Zuckerman, whom Roth has referred to as his "alter brain." The first work in the trilogy was *American Pastoral,* winner of the Pulitzer Prize in 1997, followed a year later by *I Married a Communist. The Human Stain,* in turn, was succeeded by *The Dying Animal* a short novel once again taking up a character-narrator we have met before. Roth's most recent novel resurrects David Kepesh, first introduced in 1972 in a Kafkaesque novel *The Breast* and narrator as well of Roth's controversial 1977 novel *The Professor of Desire.* Now seventy years of age, Kepesh, in *The Dying Animal,* relates the story of his affair, eight years earlier, with Consuela Castillo, a twenty-four-year-old Cuban-American student of his, possessed of enormous "erotic power" that is both "elemental and elegant."[8] Roth does not directly address the issue of current attempts to regulate professor-student relations except to ironically note Kepesh's habit of avoiding involvement with his students till the semester is over and grades are turned in, at which time he typically invites them all for a party at his house and notes which ones stay late. Who is pursuing whom in his various relationships is never entirely clear. But some of these student-teacher liaisons persist in the form of lasting friendships, as we learn near the novel's end.

Kepesh speaks in a monologue to an unidentified interlocutor whose questions and comments are implicit in Kepesh's answers, but who only on the novel's very last page (just as in *Portnoy's Complaint*) responds and, indeed, is given the last word. No longer a professor in *The Dying Animal*, Kepesh is now a well-known culture critic and media personality. In laborious detail, on an occasion that is revealed only at the novel's end, he tells the story of his obsession with Consuela, whose voluptuous beauty—and especially her gorgeous breasts—enraptured him. A year and a half into their affair, she breaks it off in anger over his failure to put in an appearance at her graduation party. Recalling this episode, Kepesh says:

> The smartest thing I did was not to show up there. Because I had been yielding and yielding in ways that I didn't understand. The longing never disappeared even while I had her. The primary emotion, as I've said, was longing. It's still longing. There's no relief from the longing and my sense of myself as a supplicant. There it is: you have it when you're with her and you have it when you're without her.[9]

But Kepesh by his own account then spent three more years longing for her, and a few years beyond that she suddenly reenters his life, bringing not joy but tragedy as she tells him she has breast cancer and not great odds for survival. Kepesh is not particularly admirable (nor does Roth attempt to make him so) as he confesses his dismay at the thought of her soon-to-be "mutilated" body, which undoes his sexual desire even as his heart breaks with tenderness for her plight.[10] Why has she come back? Apparently to ask Kepesh to photograph, before her surgery, the breasts he so adored.

In recounting his affair, Kepesh delineates his indefatigable efforts to avoid emotional entanglement and to hang on to physical lust as the wellspring of manly energy, always contrasted to the death-in-life that he considers marriage to be. Roth even subjects Kepesh to some scathing analyses by a disgruntled middle-aged son (from a failed early marriage that he'd walked out of), telling it as he sees it, and often quite on target about his father's many faults and shortcomings:

> Seducing defenseless students, pursuing one's sexual interests at the expense of everyone else—that's so very necessary, is it? No, necessity is staying in a difficult marriage and raising a little child and meeting the responsibilities of an adult.[11]

But none of this sensible criticism detracts from the compelling narrative Kepesh weaves, with its topsy-turvy version of who's really in control in this affair between an older man, who sees the end in sight, and an exuberantly beautiful much younger woman who shouldn't have to face her mortality but does, out of season. Time, Kepesh says, for the young is always made up of what is past; but for Consuela, sick with breast cancer,

> time is now how much future she has left, . . . Now she measures time counting forward, counting time by the closeness of death. . . . her sense of time is now the same as mine, speeded up and more forlorn even than mine. She, in fact, has overtaken me.[12]

It is Kepesh's intimate friend, George O'Hearn, who, in analyzing Kepesh's predicament after the affair with Consuela ended, evokes the earlier novel's image of Kepesh as "the professor of desire."[13] Recognizing that Kepesh will "always be powerless with this girl,"[14] O'Hearn urges him to avoid all contact with her. Lust and life are one thing; love quite another, and O'Hearn worries that Kepesh is "falling in love." Far from restoring a Platonic unity to the lovers, O'Hearn argues, love is a danger, because, "love fractures you. You're whole, and then you're cracked open."[15]

But if it is Consuela's "erotic power" that has kept Kepesh in thrall to her, the only power he, by contrast, held over her, Kepesh believes, was his pedagogy, his ability to instruct her in music and literature.[16] Most importantly, orgasm, for Kepesh, meant a momentary end to the sickness that is desire. It is in this context that he cites Yeats's "Sailing to Byzantium," from which the novel takes its melancholy title, alluding to the process of aging:

> Consume my heart away; sick with desire
> And fastened to a dying animal
> It knows not what it is.[17]

Even a dying animal, however, can retain some sense of propriety. "Ridiculousness," to Kepesh, is relinquishing one's freedom voluntarily.[18] While fully recognizing this, he had not been able in his relationship with Consuela to avoid it and had experienced emotions unbearable to him: jealousy and attachment: "No, not even fucking can stay totally pure and protected," Kepesh says,[19] in lines similar to those spoken by Faunia Farley in *The Human Stain*. What makes his suffering touch the reader is that Kepesh doesn't even know just what he's longing for: "Her tits? Her soul? Her youth? Her simple mind? Maybe it's worse than that—maybe now that I'm nearing death, I also long secretly not to be free."[20]

In a nasty review of *The Dying Animal* feebly entitled "Tedium of the Gropes of Roth,"[21] Elaine Showalter dismisses the novel as "cowardly, sterile, and intellectually shallow." She can muster no sympathy for Kepesh's insistence on his "freedom" as being the fulfillment of American individualism. Showalter considers the novel's ending to be its protagonist's one shot at being a "mensch," a shot we're not sure he'll take. But the novel's focus on a man who uses sex as a weapon against his mortality is no reason to despise it, unless we are prepared to judge all works of art on the basis of whether their civic message is one we wish to endorse. Showalter quotes with disdain Roth's line about the "astonishing fellators" found in this generation of young women (à la Lewinsky). Another reviewer, Anthony Quinn, refers to Kepesh's obsession with Consuela's gorgeous breasts as "just a bit creepy and objectifying."[22] It appears that critics are not very eager to hear what Roth is really saying. We seem to want our aging men to be heroes, mature and wise. We don't like seeing them as vulnerable individuals not yet finished with sexual desire, as Roth insists on representing them.

To immerse oneself in Roth's bold and erotic prose is to confront, however unwillingly, the habitual denigration of eroticism in American society, which celebrates the marriage-and-commitment narrative despite its notorious failures in our time. Roth's Kepesh wants never to pay any price for his sexual indulgences and egocentric behavior. But his protest against age and infirmity, his insistence that desire continues, that sex can be an affirmation of life against the inevitability of decay and loss—all these are worth hearing, even coming from a character as complicatedly unsympathetic as David Kepesh.

As noted above, before *The Dying Animal*, Kepesh was last encountered in Roth's 1977 novel *The Professor of Desire*, whose plot focused on Kepesh's youth (his parents ran a resort in the Borsht Belt and provided a model of marriage that both haunts and repels him) and early adulthood. Early in that novel, Kepesh had noted the fundamental conflict that characterized his life:

> In order to achieve anything lasting, I am going to have to restrain a side of myself strongly susceptible to the most bewildering and debilitating sort of temptations, temptations that . . . long ago . . . I already recognized as inimical to my overall interests.[23]

In graduate school, Kepesh meets Helen Baird, a femme fatale who hates books and schooling and what they turn life into. They marry, despite Kepesh's belief that she is still attached to her former lover in Hong Kong. Within a few years, each is locked into the other's worst image. They divorce, and Kepesh takes a job at the State University of New York on Long Island, and continues his psychoanalysis on the east coast. He bemoans his aloneness: "No woman alive thinks of me, certainly not with love."[24] But he makes friends with Ralph Baumgarten, the school's resident poet and notorious womanizer—soon to lose his job—who believes propriety and respectability are the means by which women disarm and domesticate men.

Suffering from impotence, lonely and disgruntled, Kepesh then meets Claire Ovington, who is as "physically alluring" to him as Helen had been, but, at twenty-four, devotes her energy to creating for herself a stable and ordinary life as a school teacher.[25] She has had a disorderly and difficult childhood and has consciously crafted a life for herself in opposition to that experience. Claire cures him of his impotence, his loneliness, and even his writer's block. Kepesh tries to tell himself that this sweet and stable new life, this health and happiness, are worth the loss of his feelings of lust. He tries, in short, to convince himself that "Claire is enough."[26] In one marvelous scene, set in Prague, Kepesh meets a Czech professor, to whom, in describing his earlier subjection to his sexual urges, he says:

> Of course you are the one on intimate terms with totalitarianism—but if you'll permit me, I can only compare the body's utter single-mindedness, its cold indifference and absolute contempt for the well-being of the spirit, to some unyielding, authoritarian regime. And you can petition it all you like, offer up the most heartfelt and dignified and logical sort of appeal—and get no response at all.[27]

Kepesh decides to teach a course on erotic desire in literature, and a fascinating part of the book contains an imaginary first lecture to his class, to whom he explains why he does not share the popular view that literature is "fundamentally non-referential,"[28] and to whom he wishes to disclose the story of the professor's desire. This lecture ends with the confession: "I am devoted to fiction, and I assure you that in time I will tell you whatever I may know about it, but in truth nothing lives in me like my life."[29]

Marveling at his contentment with Claire, at the regular life they lead and the clear future that it portends, Kepesh argues with himself that the diminution of their passion is a small price to pay:

> Can I think otherwise—can I possibly believe that, rather than coming to rest on some warm plateau of sweet coziness and intimacy, I am being eased down a precipitous incline and as yet am nowhere near the cold and lonely cavern where I finally will touch down?[30]

So perfect a partner is Claire that, without consulting Kepesh, she decides to have an abortion, so that he might remain free to choose whatever future he desires. She "never wanted to be anyone's prison,"[31] she tells him. Now, at the age of thirty-four, growing more suspicious of "this gentle, tender adoration " that he shares with Claire, Kepesh worries about when "the lovely blandness of a life with Claire begins to cloy, to pall, and I am out there once again, mourning what I've lost and looking for my way!"[32] He is certain his suppressed self, his lustful self, will return.

What makes the novel moving and important is Roth's evocative and compelling prose, which critics who dislike his "message" seem to be overlooking. Thus, near the novel's end, after a beautifully depicted visit from

Kepesh's father and a Holocaust-survivor friend, both representing the
world with which he has been in lifelong conflict, Kepesh mourns the loss
he knows inevitably lies before him:

> Oh, innocent beloved, you fail to understand and I can't tell you. I can't say it, not
> tonight, but within a year my passion will be dead. Already it is dying and I am
> afraid that there is nothing I can do to save it. And nothing that you can do. Inti-
> mately bound—bound to you as to no one else!—and I will not be able to raise
> a hand to so much as touch you . . . unless first I remind myself that I must. To-
> ward the flesh upon which I have been grafted and nurtured back toward some-
> thing like mastery over my life, I will be without desire. Oh, it's stupid! Idiotic!
> Unfair! To be robbed like this of you. And of this life I love and have hardly got-
> ten to know! And robbed by whom? It always comes down to myself![33]

Starting with his first novel, *Goodbye, Columbus*, and ending with *The Dying Animal*, his latest one, Philip Roth has, over a forty-year period, lavished
an unflagging energy on the effort to dissect the sexual and emotional lives
of male protagonists who often resemble himself (Jewish author/professors
with little talent for marriage and a great taste for self-analysis). What is at
times referred to by critics as his "misogyny" is, it seems to me, rather a willingness to probe the heart of the egocentricity and lust that drive his male
characters. It takes courage to do this in Roth's unabashed way, to celebrate—
as he does in *The Dying Animal*—"the charm of the surreptitious" and to
make such provocative statements as : "Marriage at its best is a sure-fire stim-
ulant to the thrills of licentious subterfuge."[34] Roth does not allow us to see
his narrators and protagonists as unproblematic or admirable exemplars.
Nor does he—like critics such as Bell Hooks and Jane Gallop—defend
"asymmetrical" relationships on the self-congratulatory grounds that brilliant professors and their best students are naturally attracted to one another
and that these associations are crucial to the intellectual and creative development of both. He insists that such relationships need no academic defense. He makes no pretense that there is a cerebral or pedagogic value to
them. Life and lust are their own justification. Nor does he, on the other
hand, idealize the ensuing relationships. Far from it, he exposes their seami-
ness and comic aspects, but also the passion and vulnerabilities from which
they spring—above all the vulnerability of older men confronting their fear
of aging and death, susceptible to female sexual power in a manner that is
presented poignantly and, I suspect, realistically.

III

Readers impatient with Roth's reluctance (not to say willful refusal) to make
the transition from lust to love can turn to Nicholas Delbanco's 1997 novel

Old Scores, a beautifully written and often lyrical work that describes in great detail the life-long relationship of two people who originally met as professor and student. To see this work merely as an exploration of an "asymmetrical" relationship would be to turn it into a sociologically oriented propaganda piece and deprive it of its heart and soul.

Narrated in the third person, the novel follows the lives of its two protagonists, separately and together. In the first four pages, Delbanco traces Paul Ballard from infancy through childhood, education, and first marriage, to the point when, in 1969, at the age of thirty-five and employed as a philosophy professor at Catamount College in Vermont, he meets Elizabeth Sieverdsen, a junior in his logic class who is young, beautiful, and rich (when she voices radical views, her parents suggest that if she really wanted to contribute to social change, she might give away her trust fund).[35] Delbanco interweaves the story of their love, told chronologically, with their perceptions and (sent and unsent) letters to one another in later years, thus layering his narrative with a sense of the passage of time and the changing perspectives and mounting problems it inevitably brings.

Paul's practicality is much in evidence: "Lovers, they were secretive; he made it clear from the beginning that his colleagues should not know." But he is also idealistic: "'I want this,'" he says, "'to be something we do without damage. With no *harm* to anyone, ever . . .'"[36] These turn out to be naïve hopes, however, as Delbanco's major theme, the cost of love, unfolds:

> Years later, [Paul] would marvel at the ease of it, the ignorance, the blithe assumption on his part that there need be no damage. Years later he would ask himself how he could ever have imagined there would be no price to pay.[37]

The damage and the price Delbanco has in mind here have nothing to do with "asymmetry" or "power imbalances"—those banal and belabored concepts—but are inflicted by life itself, which invariably links love with the pain of loss. Delbanco's unwillingness to endorse current academic orthodoxies is evident early on when he writes of Elizabeth: "She did not like to see herself as a Catamount girl with a faculty trophy, a student who slept with a teacher"; and: "Paul was her secret, as she was his secret, and the hayloft protected them both."[38] All around them, professors are marrying their students, some sequentially, but Paul and Elizabeth maintain the secrecy of their relationship. Only after a summer apart does he take her to his home: "The room was shabby and endearing and Beth understood, for the first time, her own power over her teacher. . . . They met, if not as equals now, as more of a matched pair."[39] Thinking back over their relationship later in the year, Paul wonders: "had he been the seducer or seduced?"[40]

This tender and idyllic romance, which causes Paul some measure of guilt, is brought to a sudden end when, in 1970, at the age of thirty-six—less than one-fifth of the way through the novel, and at a moment when he has realized the affair must either advance or retreat—Paul is run down by a car and nearly dies. Later he will describe this as an act taken by an "unforgiving judge," which he knows some would call "divine intervention."[41] Pregnant by then, Elizabeth, without ever telling him, has the child and gives the little girl up for adoption. "Years passed"[42]—all within the same chapter—and we follow Beth's separate life. She marries a young man in advertising, moves to Italy, and has a son and daughter. But Paul Ballard is often in her thoughts, especially when her husband Michael ends their marriage to take up life with his friend Giovanni.

The central part of the novel is punctuated by unsent letters between the two lovers. In an early one, a few years after his accident, Paul writes to Beth of what has happened to him: "it's an old, old story: when at last they throw the book at us, it's the Book of Job."[43] He quotes Flaubert's line: "Language is a kettledrum on which we beat out tunes for bears to dance to, while all the time we dream we move the stars to pity."[44] Remembering a lecture given by a dean in his early years at the college, warning new arrivals "in effect, that we should only fuck those boys and girls we respected and therefore—as a possible prelude to marriage—would choose to fuck again," Paul sees himself in retrospect as having been "prideful and primed for a fall,"[45] and Elizabeth as a tender lamb entrusted to a ravening wolf.[46]

> In my youth, I thought it lust, yet now I understand how, lost, it may transmute to love, and how much greater finally is the conjunction of the two: part fitting the ragged-edged part. And how astonishing that there should be, whether preordained or earned or found by accident, a second self, a partner in desire.[47]

All this, he knows, was choice, not chance: "The point is we both said Yes, yes."[48] But that was before the accident changed his Yes to a No.

Intermittent pain makes it impossible for Paul to teach, and he lives on a small legacy plus his disability insurance. More years pass, and suddenly it's 1995—a quarter of a century has elapsed since the lovers' last meeting. Paul has never remarried; he has been celibate for all those years. Elizabeth comes to see him, telling him they had a daughter, now twenty-five, who lives not far from him. With new information about his child and her adoptive parents, Paul finds that "the pattern of his past was rearranged."[49] In a long letter to him, after they have visited their daughter together, Elizabeth reflects upon their past, and the myths of her youth, including her own belief that "sex entailed no harm."[50] She realizes that, with her children grown, and her life in Italy not really her own, there is only Paul to return to.

When they at last embrace, Delbanco stresses the years that have passed: "He put his old man's mouth upon her fallen breast."[51] With their passion rekindled, Paul now finds that sex redeems him. It is the autumn of 1996; she is forty-eight years old; he is sixty-two, and amazed at the turn his life has taken: "His one true love restored."[52] Elizabeth, too, in a luminous passage, later contemplates what their sexual encounter had meant to her:

> In their shared syntax all was apposite, subordinate, the conjunction of his arms with hers and interrogatory of his eyebrows, the antithetical construction of his shadow on the lamplit wall and the fierce imperative of his upright cock. In her memory it all came together, all jumbled, not only object and subject but also noun and verb: despair, to despair, love, to love.[53]

At the novel's end, as Elizabeth grows old, once again alone, she comes to realize she is one of the lucky few who have had what can be called "a great passion":

> She had shared her youth and middle age with someone she adored and who adored her equally. She had been, she told herself, blessed. The love had transfigured them each and both; the record of their devotion was hers to remember and keep.[54]

IV

Quite a different emphasis governs Francine Prose's latest novel, *Blue Angel*, a darkly comic story of a besotted forty-seven-year-old writing professor and the talented and ambitious nineteen-year-old student who causes his downfall. In a witty and biting third person narrative confined strictly to the point of view of her protagonist, Ted Swenson, Prose exposes the smelly little orthodoxies (as Orwell put it, in quite another context) of the contemporary academic scene. Because this novel of a professor ruined by sexual harassment charges is of particular relevance to the travesties of justice actually being played out on many university campuses today, it is worth considering it in some detail.

Ted Swenson, a writer-in-residence at Euston College in northern Vermont, has been married for twenty-one years and is still in love with his wife, Sherrie, and capable of, as she puts it, "leering" at her. As a professor in contemporary America, however, he knows the rules, and the narrative gives us his thoughts about them:

> Such are the pleasures of intimacy: he can look [at Sherrie] as long as he wants. Given the current political climate, you'd better be having consensual matrimonial sex with a woman before you risk this stare.[55]

At his college's obligatory meeting to review the sexual harassment policy, Swenson thinks heretical thoughts:

> What if someone rose to say what so many of them are thinking, that there's something erotic about the *act* of teaching, all that information streaming back and forth like some . . . bodily fluid. Doesn't Genesis trace sex to that first bite of apple, not the fruit from just any tree, but the Tree of Knowledge?[56]

Devoted to his wife and daughter, Swenson acknowledges that "teacher-student attraction is an occupational hazard" and has therefore avoided entanglements with his students, though over the years several have made overtures to him. And he's well aware too of a case at the state university (where his daughter Ruby studies), involving a professor who, while showing a classical Greek sculpture of a female nude, had commented "Yum." Accusing him of "leering," his students charged that he'd made them uncomfortable. Suspended without pay, the professor had taken his case to court. Swenson is wary of a similar climate at his own college, and of the increasing power of the "Faculty-Student Women's Alliance" waiting to pounce on any male word or gesture. And he is suspicious of a colleague who is head of the alliance and is also the English Department's "expert in the feminist misreading of literature." For reasons he can't fathom (but guesses it's a "testosterone allergy"), she seems to want him dead.

How, then, after so many years of sound judgment, does it happen that he falls into the role of Professor Rath to his student's Lola Lola (as in the classic film *The Blue Angel*, from which the novel takes its title)? Prose's autopsy of Swenson's fall is a bracing work, funny and sly and politically incorrect at every turn, right up until the end when Swenson realizes that the movie he should have been watching was not *The Blue Angel* but *All About Eve*.

Can a talent for writing be a seducer? In the case of Ted Swenson, decades of teaching "creative writing" to mediocre students (whose stories, often involving bestiality, we get to sample), along with ten frustrating years of never quite getting around to working on his long-awaited third novel, have left him fatally vulnerable to talent, no matter how unlikely its source.

Angela Argo is far from the best-looking young woman in Swenson's class at Euston College. In fact, she has sat for weeks squirming and sighing instead of speaking, calling attention to herself primarily by means of her abundant face piercing, the orange and green streaks in her hair, and the black leather motorcycle jacket with theme-related accouterments that covers her skinny body.

But poor Swenson has few defenses against the spark of talent that Angela reveals to him after seeking a meeting in his office. And his first reaction to her work is the very thing that today gets professors in trouble: differential treatment. Wanting to protect her talent from the ritual hazing that his class has turned into as students savage one another's writing week after week, he agrees to read and comment on Angela's work in private. Thus begins the special relationship—initiated by Angela at each successive stage—that will eventually cost him his reputation, his job, and his marriage.

Interwoven into this realistic tale of a contemporary campus liaison is a sympathetic portrait of the plight of writing teachers and of writers, especially those stuck in a dry season that can last a decade. The novel captures perfectly Swenson's enraptured response to the discovery of Angela's talent. It is a generous, tender response. Swenson is alert to the students' ambiguous attitude toward him: "He's the teacher, they're the students: a distinction they like to blur, then make again, as needed."[57] But this sensibility and foreknowledge won't save him from enthusiastically gravitating toward the genuinely talented. And as Angela feeds him chapter after chapter of her novel, Swenson falls into the very mistake he constantly warns his students against: taking the story as autobiography. Thus, he begins to imagine that he himself is the teacher Angela's protagonist is enamored of, and that her first-person narrative is really a confession, made to him privately, of her troubled life.

It doesn't help matters much when a colleague who teaches poetry tells him about the graphic sexual poems Angela had written for that class. Soon the sexual content of Angela's writing and her intense anticipation of Swenson's reactions week by week lead him to sexual fantasies about her. When she says that she thinks all the time about his reactions to her writing, what he hears is that "she thinks about him all the time."[58] So they lurch from one encounter to the next, each less clear than the last. Everything in their relationship initially revolves around her writing—her eagerness for his reaction; her computer's collapse, which leads her to ask him to take her shopping for a new one, and in turn leads to his presence in her dorm room whose door (he finds out later) she'd locked as soon as they had entered.

Francine Prose explores with great subtlety Swenson's seduction and betrayal. She does not present him as a total innocent. As a man in mid-life, he is aware of his mortality and the appeal of glowing youth all around him. "Age and death—the unfairness of it, the daily humiliation of watching your power vanish just when you figure out how to use it."[59] But Angela's rapid transformation after their brief escapade is no joke; she begins demanding more of his attention to her writing, berating him when he doesn't provide it quickly enough. "What happened to the worshipful student who hung on his every word," Swenson wonders. "Now that's she's let Swenson sleep with her she doesn't respect him anymore."[60] Prose shows the reversal of all the traditional rules and values, as Angela quickly moves in for what turns out to be her real goal: getting him to show her novel to his agent. But still Swenson argues with himself about her motives:

> Does Angela—did she ever—have a crush on him, or is she just using him for his professional connections? Is Angela blackmailing him, or simply asking a favor? What does a favor mean when you have the power to wreck someone's life?[61]

By coincidence, a woman colleague also wants the same favor: "This is really too much. Two women in twenty minutes cozying up to Swenson as a way of getting next to his editor."[62] And to make matters worse, he must face the open resentment of his other students when he, with complete sincerity, praises Angela's writing in class.

Angela's fury when she learns that Swenson hadn't fought for her book with his agent finally makes her clarify her behavior: "The only reason I let you fuck me was so you would help me get this novel to someone who could do something. . ."[63] And next thing he knows, she's charged him with sexual harassment, taken a tape of this last conversation to the dean, and is threatening to sue the college. The dean immediately urges Swenson to resign.

Reviewing his own responsibility, Swenson thinks:

> He knew about the power differential between teacher and student. But this wasn't about power. This was about desire. Mutual seduction, let's say that at least. He's too embarrassed to let himself think, This was about love. [64]

Barred from his classroom, dangerously indifferent to his school's sexual harassment proceedings (not a "court of law"), Swenson insists on a hearing instead of resigning quietly.

When he tells his wife, in a restaurant, about the trouble he's in, she blames him entirely and informs him that Angela spent half her time at the school's medical clinic (where Sherrie is a nurse), ostensibly because she's suicidal—but actually, Swenson realizes, because Angela was pumping the staff for details about his life to work into her novel.

> The couple sitting beside them seems to have gotten up and left. At some point when he and Sherrie were at once so engrossed and distracted, the lovers must have retreated into their cocoon of protection and light and grace, of chosenness, of being singled out and granted the singular blessing of being allowed to live in a world in which what's happening to Sherrie and Swenson will never happen to them.[65]

As the Faculty-Student Women's Alliance demonstrates against him and Swenson rents the film of *The Blue Angel* (a film he knows Angela too has seen), he realizes at last that "there's no chance of winning, of proving his innocence."[66]

The night before the hearing,

> he lies in bed composing and revising speeches about what he thought he was doing, about his respect for Angela's novel, about the erotics of teaching, and the dangers of starting to see one's student as a real person. [67]

But he is totally unprepared for the actual hearing process, in effect a trial at which he faces six colleagues, one of them the head of the Faculty-Student Women's Alliance. "Agreed" upon (but not by him) witnesses are called, but no cross-examination of them is permitted, since this "is not, after all, a trial."[68] So much for due process.

When Angela appears, parents in tow, at the hearing, Swenson notes her changed appearance. Her hair is now a

> shiny, authentic-looking auburn. . . . And how bizarrely she's dressed—bizarre, that is, for Angela. Neat khakis, a red velour sweater, ordinary college-girl "good" clothes. For all he knows, the piercing and the black leather were always the costume, and this is the real Angela, restored to her true self. For all he knows. He doesn't know. All right. He gets that now.[69]

In a particularly subtle scene, Swenson, having deluded himself for so long, having somehow managed to avoid noting that Angela's real interest was in promoting her writing, not in him, finds at his "trial" that he would rather play the "sullen guilty lecher" that his colleagues think he is, would rather confirm their "image of him as the predatory harasser" than admit "to the truer story of obsession and degradation, the humiliating real-life update of *The Blue Angel*."[70]

Colleagues and students come forth to testify. A brave student from Swenson's writing class, initially showing far more discernment than his elders, tries to argue: "I can't see what the big deal is. Shit happens. People get attracted to other people. It's not that big a deal."[71] But Swenson watches the change that comes over the student as he realizes that what Swenson is charged with is having extorted sex from Angela in return for showing her work to his editor in New York. The student's face shows his perception of unfairness warring with his sense of loyalty to his teacher: "Swenson wants to tell him that the real unfairness involves the distribution of talent and has nothing to do with whatever happened between him and Angela Argo."[72] Bravely, the student tries to stick to his principles:

> But nothing has prepared him to resist the seduction of having the dean of his college calling him a writer and a half-dozen faculty members hanging on his every word. How can he disappoint them? How can he not offer up any scrap of information he can recall.[73]

Francine Prose gets the details of all this just right: the banality and venality of academic vindictiveness and piety; the stereotypical assumptions about professorial misconduct; the eagerness to find sexual wrongdoing; the unavoidable small-minded *Schadenfreude* as colleagues and students get to revisit old grievances and slights, and the sheer cynicism of faculty and administrators claiming to be concerned with students' welfare. When Claris, the class beauty, testifies that he took no inappropriate actions toward her, Swenson can see that no one believes her. Or they think Swenson is insane.

> How pathetic. What *is* wrong with him? He never even entertained a sexual thought about Claris and spent months mooning over Angela Argo? How abject, how ridiculous. He isn't a normal male.[74]

Another student testifies that they all knew something was going on because all their work was criticized, while Angela's was not. No one is interested in discussing the other possible reasons for admiring a student's work. "Swenson's learned his lesson. He'll never criticize another student. Not that he'll get a chance."[75]

Finally, Angela gets to speak—if she feels "strong enough to address the committee. . . . As she moves [toward the table], Swenson thinks he can still see sharp angles of sullen punkhood poking through the fuzzy eiderdown of that Jane College getup."[76] Following the familiar ritual, Angela is praised for her courage in coming forward and spared the ordeal of listening to the tape she had orchestrated to make it sound as if Swenson had indeed persuaded her to trade sex for showing her book to his agent.

> On her face is that combustive chemistry of wild irritation and boredom so familiar from those early classes, but now it's become a martyr's transfixed gaze of piety and damage, lit by the flames of the holy war she's waging against the evils of male oppression and sexual harassment.[77]

Throughout Angela's distortions and deceptions, Swenson tries to keep "his grip on the truth—on his version of the story. A grip on recent history. On reality."[78] The committee, he sees, is ready to believe the worst because he asked to see more of a student's writing. Yet, he admits to himself, her testimony isn't all made up:

> Well, there is something sexy about reading someone's work: an intimate communication takes place. Still, you can read . . . Gertrude Stein, and it doesn't mean you find her attractive . . . . Once more, the committee's version of him— the scheming dirty old man—seems less degrading than the truth.[79]

Prose avoids turning her story into a postmodern narrative in which we can never hope to learn the truth. Earlier episodes have shown us what took place, and we recognize Angela's lies in her testimony before the committee, her insistence that the sexual initiatives were his. But the narrative gives us a different perspective on where the harm really resides:

How pornographic and perverted this is, a grown woman—a professor—torturing a female student into describing a sexual experience to a faculty committee, not to mention her parents. Swenson could have slept with Angela on the Founders Chapel altar, and it would have seemed healthy and respectable compared to this orgy of filth. Meanwhile he has to keep it in mind that Angela started all this. Angela chose to be here.[80]

Only at her father's urging that she share her "good news" does Angela admit to the assembled group that Swenson's editor in fact wants to publish her novel. Swenson thinks:

Len Currie is publishing Angela's novel. So what is this hearing about? Angela should be kissing Swenson's feet instead of ruining his life. As she must have decided to do when she still believed that Swenson, her white knight, had failed to get her manuscript published. If that's when she decided. Who knows what she did, and why?[81]

On cue, Angela describes the lingering effects of the whole wretched experience, her nightmares, her distress. As Angela's testimony draws to a close, the women's studies professor once more congratulates Angela and commiserates with her:

"Angela, let me say again that we know how tough it was for you to come in and say what you did. But if women are ever going to receive an equal education, these problems have to be addressed and dealt with, so that we can protect and empower ourselves."

"Sure," Angela says. "You're welcome. Whatever."[82]

When it is finally Swenson's turn to speak, he knows what he should do is apologize—but of the many things he is sorry for, breaking the college's rules about professor-student relationships is not one of them:

He is extremely sorry for having spent twenty years of his one and only life, twenty years he will never get back, among people he can't talk to, men and women to whom he can't even tell the simple truth.[83]

And then, in an entirely predictable almost last-straw moment, Swenson's daughter's boyfriend tells the committee that Ruby told him her father had sexually abused her when she was a child. Swenson watches his colleagues' reactions:

they have taken off their masks. Jonathan Edwards, Cotton Mather, Torquemado. Swenson's crime involves sex, so the death penalty can be invoked. No evidence is inadmissible. They're hauling out the entire arsenal for this mortal combat with the forces of evil and sin.[84]

Thus, at novel's end, Angela's career is starting and Swenson's career—along with his marriage—is ending. Sounding somewhat like one of Philip Roth's heroes, Swenson finally recognizes the mystery of femaleness, acknowledges that he can never fathom Angela's motives. Only she will ever know the truth. As he hears the campus bells tolling, he wonders why they're ringing now, at 5:25 p.m.

> Then, gradually, it dawns on him. It's the Women's Alliance, announcing their triumph over another male oppressor, one small step along the path toward a glorious future. He's glad to be out of that future and headed into his own.[85]

V

If Francine Prose's novel is written in a sardonic style (lying somewhere between tragedy and farce), Eric Tarloff's novel, *The Man Who Wrote the Book*, is squarely in the light-comic mode, though touching on much the same academic reality. It is not as impressive or intriguing a book as his first novel, *Face-Time*, which dealt with a young couple working in the White House. In that novel, Tarloff gave a subtle depiction of the lure of power—not, as some reviewers had it, merely women's attraction to powerful men, but rather the human tendency to be awed by others' star quality and the ensuing desire to stay in their orbit. Ben, the male narrator of *Face-Time*, reflects on this attraction very effectively and observes it at work in his own reactions to the president. Tarloff suggests that this phenomenon is not strictly a sexual attraction, but rather a response to power. The sex is, if anything, a tool, an advantage women have, given that thus far it's mostly heterosexual men who occupy the most powerful political positions. Tarloff's female protagonist, Gretchen, says as much: that the possibility of an affair with the president was a unique opportunity, one she simply could not pass up.

More recently, as mature a writer as Benjamin R. Barber, in his memoir *The Truth of Power: Intellectual Affairs in the Clinton White House*,[86] has confirmed Tarloff's perspective. It's no accident that, in his subtitle, Barber uses the phrase "intellectual affairs." Having been invited for intellectual exchanges with Clinton about a dozen times during Clinton's presidency, Barber writes unabashedly: "I have the feeling I've had a kind of affair with him,"[87] and continues to cultivate this metaphor throughout his book. So smitten is Barber still with his brush with power that he even includes in his book facsimiles of letters of thanks he received from Clinton.

From the seductiveness of presidential political power to the relatively trivial power held by professors is but a short step for those with a vigilante mentality. Tarloff's second novel, *The Man Who Wrote the Book*, is, appropriately, a thoroughly comic story. Veering from the pattern of the novels discussed above, all of them set in small New England colleges, Tarloff's narrative follows the fortunes of Ezra Gordon, a thirty-five-year-old professor at a "Baptist cow college, very uptight,"[88] in northern California. Divorced, with nagging pains in his chest and a doctor who tells him that, since he has already had one child, Nature is through with him and he should just face that unpleasant fact, Ezra contemplates his unsatisfactory life. He is blocked in his writing and therefore knows tenure is unlikely; and he is involved in an insipid romance with Carol, the college's lawyer who is also the daughter of the forbidding Reverend Mr. Dimsdale, chaplain of the college and member of its Board of Overseers and hence with a vote on Ezra's tenure. Furthermore, Carol, a thirty-year-old divorcee who lives in her father's house and seems beset by prohibitions, is no longer returning Ezra's phone calls.

Tarloff's satire of academic life at the turn of the millennium is all too accurate, even if few places today seem to be as far outside of current trends as Beuhler College. Early in the novel, for example, a colleague criticizes Ezra's scholarship for being both scant and traditional, while revealing the backwater status of the college's faculty:

> ". . . that's why we hired you. You and Susan. To provide some modernity. Susan covers the, the, what is it, the *multicultural* end of things, literature as colonialism, and, and, you know, the feminist stuff, the canon as an expression of patriarchal fascism—I believe I've got that right—and we were led to believe you did this other nonsense, this French sort of business, what's it called? Decomposition?"[89]

Adding to Ezra's problems is "that unpleasant business last year"[90]— namely, an accusation of sexual harassment brought against Ezra by one of his students. The third person narrative describes what had actually happened: A young woman, whom Ezra considered a bit unstable, had unceremoniously bared her breasts to him one afternoon in his office. Though not unstirred, Ezra had "good-naturedly" suggested she ought to cover herself up. She complied promptly, seemed of good cheer as she left his office, but thereafter decided that she'd been scorned and, one week later, filed a complaint against him. The fact that the charges were dismissed—for lack of proof in a he-said she-said situation—hardly counts as exoneration, and Ezra finds himself "forever a suspected sex offender." Carol, the lawyer, worried about the college's potential liability, had pursued the investigation in an "unremittingly hostile" way, giving no sign that there had ever existed any trust between them and, though she'd recommended dismissal of the charges, their relationship had never quite recovered. Carol continued to be suspicious of him—even more so when the student insisted on not dropping his class and had earned an A in the course. Disillusioned with teaching, Ezra has also been chosen as mentor by a budding young gay student whose parents want him to go into engineering, not to write fiction.

In this depressing situation of apparent dead-ends, feeling like a has-been, "bowed down by failure," Ezra contacts and then goes to visit his former best friend, Isaac Schwimmer. They had been graduate students together at Michigan (where Ezra had won a poetry prize), but Isaac had taken off on his Harley one day and never returned to finish his dissertation. Instead, he had gone into publishing and is now in Southern California, running the Isaac Schwimmer Press. This outfit, Ezra soon learns, specializes in "d.b." (dirty books), as the license plate on Isaac's car announces. Drawn into Isaac's free-wheeling, hedonistic life, Ezra meets Tessa, the most beautiful woman he has ever seen, who is an aspiring model-actress and Isaac's next door neighbor.

To Ezra's initial shock at realizing Isaac isn't publishing "literature," Isaac replies: "Wake up, pal. It's a new millennium. The good books have all been published."[91] Ezra attempts to explain his negative reaction to pornography:

> "You've been away from university politics for a long time, you may not realize feminism's a whole area of scholarship now, an important niche market. Of course, these different types disagree about a lot of stuff, it's a volatile mix on campus these days, but they do seem to concur that pornography's bad news. So maybe some of that's rubbed off."[92]

To which Isaac responds: "You should be ashamed of yourself. . . . Letting yourself get bullied like that. Never apologize for having a cock." And as for social responsibility, Isaac states: "If I wanted to make a social contribution, I'd join the Peace Corps. I'm doing this 'cause it's fun and I'm making a pot of money."[93]

Unexpectedly in need of a replacement writer, Isaac offers Ezra $10,000 to write a dirty book for him. Meanwhile, Tessa seduces Ezra and, to his surprise, seems genuinely attached to him. "Being with you," she says, "it's like, it's like you're Keats and I'm an urn."[94] This second part of the novel is called "Deut."—explained by Isaac's reference to Deuteronomy: "I have set before you life and death. Therefore choose life."[95] And, surprising himself, Ezra does precisely that. He agrees to write the novel—but only under a pseudonym, in order to protect his job at Beuhler.

Thus, having chosen the pseudonymn E. A. Peau, Ezra sets to work. The novel's long third chapter (covering over one-third of the book) is titled "Every Inch a Lady"—the name Ezra/Peau gives to his novel. Rejuvenated by his affair with Tessa and by the secret of his "double life" as E.A. Peau, Ezra confronts the question of what he should write about. He realizes that what is exciting would be the contemplation of someone like Carol gradually becoming Tessa, "obsessed with her own pleasure and fearlessly aggressive about achieving it"[96] It is this character's "growing embrace of her own sensuality" that will be his subject. And to relieve his writer's cramp, he decides to use the university's computer system. Which, as it happens, has just been the object of some sabotage that leads to an investigation. As Carol makes overtures suggesting she wants to resume their relationship, Tessa decides to come to visit Ezra, whose status at the college rises instantly once students and colleagues get a look at her.

Ezra's luck continues to change: He becomes a local hero after saving the Reverend Dimsdale, who has collapsed in a grocery store, by giving him mouth-to-mouth resuscitation. "Not a bad afternoon. Saved a life and had a pleasant conversation with Carol"[97]—who is still impressed by Tessa: "Tessa . . . He sighed. It had no future, that relationship, but what a present. Which was now all in the past." Immersed in his book, he thinks:

> Strange how much pleasure he'd found in writing a stupid little dirty book; it had actually reawakened his joy in literature, reminded him why he'd gone to graduate school in the first place.[98]

In the academic world of Tarloff's imagination—as in the real one—women too make sexual advances. Thus, like the student who had raised her shirt in his office, Carol, when she pays Ezra a late-night visit after he has saved her father's life, strips to her panties while he's in the kitchen getting her a Diet Coke. Something has definitely changed; never before had he seen her "frankly and entirely exposed."[99] He's even more surprised when she suggests: "'Let's fuck'"[100]—and thus begins a new stage in their relationship.

With his novel nearly finished and a new pride in his status as a novelist, Ezra finds life imitating art: Carol has undergone a "transmogrification in bed." Isaac is enthusiastic about Ezra's novel: "It has a sort of *sweetness*, somehow, a tenderness."[101] And this has managed to arouse the thoroughly jaded Isaac, for whom porno novels are mostly nothing but technical manuals.

The novel's last part is an amusing, if predictable, unfolding of the pseudonymous novel's runaway success and the ensuing hunt for E. A. Peau, set against the backdrop of Ezra's unforeseen passionate affair with Carol. When Ezra first sees his novel in the hands of the very student who'd accused him of sexual harassment, he thinks it's a new ploy to gain control of him. But no, his novel is indeed, as Isaac says, "'a break out d.b., maybe the first since *Story of O* or one of those dopey books from the sixties. You hit a home run, pal.'"[102] Things continue to go Ezra's way: He has a scholarly article (incomprehensible to his chair) accepted in the journal *Representations*, and all around him people he knows are reading his novel, unaware that he is its author.

When at last his pseudonym is traced to the college, Ezra (his identity still undisclosed) finds himself targeted by the local mayor, up for reelection but with poor prospects. "This viper must be snatched from Beuhler's bosom!" the mayor intones at a press conference. "This wolf must be separated from these lambs immediately, and by force if necessary!" As the mayor continues to characterize E. A. Peau as "scum" and "filth," Ezra thinks about the rise of demagogues: "Here it is, happening before my eyes, a sure loser catching a wave of public anger in order to hold onto power. And possibly succeeding."[103]

As sanctimony takes over the college and the hunt for Peau tightens, Ezra and Carol join forces and take on the opposition. Unlike Prose's novel, Tarloff's ends on a positive note. Not every departure from an academic job is a catastrophe.

VI

Does it take a woman writer, a Francine Prose, to unabashedly demonstrate the stupidity of the current shibboleths regarding male professors' "power" and female students' "powerlessness?" To protest the prurient attitude that lies behind the apparent obsession with sexual relations on campus? To delineate so scathingly a young woman's methodical and self-serving manipulation of her professor? When men writers do this (e.g., David Mamet in his play *Oleanna*), their work is often dismissed with the presumptively devastating charge of "misogyny." Francine Prose's novel is an effective rejoinder to this canard. It is both touching and true: written in a melancholy, self-deprecating style befitting her protagonist's essential decency and ironic awareness, and at the same time profoundly insightful into the mechanisms of academic life at the present time.

Philip Roth presents us with a scathing portrait of the harm unleashed by the stupidity of vigilantism of language and personal relations in today's America. In novel after novel, he offers a celebration (sardonic and pathetic though it often is) of the erotic power of young women and the deep conflicts of the men who love and fear them. Nicholas Delbanco portrays a costly and enduring love, which comes in guises and moments that defy academic proprieties, and he leaves no doubt that the price is worth paying. Francine Prose details the seductiveness of talent and the egocentric drives that motivate women as much as men, despite all the lies currently circulating on this subject. Eric Tarloff, writing in a far lighter vein than these three, opts for happy endings as the essential sanity of his protagonists somehow prevails. Perhaps, indeed, he is the most idealistic of the group. But all four are writers of great skill, opening our eyes to the hidden dimensions and potentialities of those "asymmetrical" relationships conventionally viewed today as merely sordid or exploitative on the professor's part, devoid of life, forced into caricatured tableaux in which all roles are set out in advance according to the position—in terms of race, sex, and status—of the protagonists.

One turns from these works of fiction, these portraits of academic life at the end of the twentieth century, back to the everyday reality of sexual harassment officers, codes, committees, threats, and public displays of virtue with a profound sense of wonder. How can it be that rules and guidelines that should be an embarrassment to any sensible society now govern every school and workplace? How have the supposedly powerless so successfully altered the terms of everyday interactions that the supposedly powerful—who, we are constantly told, prey on them—are now so vulnerable, so much at their mercy? Is this some demented revenge from which we'll soon all wake up? Not, I fear, in the short run. But the commitment of writers such as these four to the craft of the novelist rather than to the cant of current ideologies gives us reason—however fragile—for hope.

NOTES

This essay was first published in *Academic Questions* 16:2 (spring 2003): 10–82. Reprinted with permission of Springer Science and Business Media.

1. Philip Roth, *The Human Stain* (Boston and New York: Houghton Mifflin, 2000), 2.
2. In the *New York Times*, September 23, 2001.
3. Roth, *The Human Stain*, 3.
4. Roth, *The Human Stain*, 38.
5. Roth, *The Human Stain*, 12.
6. Roth, *The Human Stain*, 242; italics in original.
7. In a *New York Times* interview conducted with Charles McGrath, May 7, 2000.
8. Philip Roth, *The Dying Animal* (Boston and New York: Houghton Mifflin, 2001), 98.
9. Roth, *The Dying Animal*, 94–95.
10. Roth, *The Dying Animal*, 138.
11. Roth, *The Dying Animal*, 90.
12. Roth, *The Dying Animal*, 149
13. Roth, *The Dying Animal*, 99.
14. Roth, *The Dying Animal*, 98.
15. Roth, *The Dying Animal*, 101.
16. Roth, *The Dying Animal*, 101.
17. Roth, *The Dying Animal*, 103.
18. Roth, *The Dying Animal*, 104.
19. Roth, *The Dying Animal*, 105.
20. Roth, *The Dying Animal*, 106.
21. In *The Times* (London), June 27, 2001.

22. "An Old Man's Fancy," *The Times* [London], June 24, 2001.

23. Philip Roth, *The Professor of Desire* (New York: Farrar, Straus and Giroux, 1977), 34.

24. Roth, *The Professor of Desire*, 81.

25. Roth, *The Professor of Desire*, 103.

26. Roth, *The Professor of Desire*, 113.

27. Roth, *The Professor of Desire*, 117.

28. Roth, *The Professor of Desire*, 125.

29. Roth, *The Professor of Desire*, 127.

30. Roth, *The Professor of Desire*, 136–137.

31. Roth, *The Professor of Desire*, 153.

32. Roth, *The Professor of Desire*, 173.

33. Roth, *The Professor of Desire*, 179–180.

34. Roth, *The Dying Animal*, 110

35. Nicholas Delbanco, *Old Scores* (New York: Warner Books, 1997), 12.

36. Delbanco, *Old Scores*, 25; italics in original.

37. Delbanco, *Old Scores*, 31.

38. Delbanco, *Old Scores*, 26–27.

39. Delbanco, *Old Scores*, 37.

40. Delbanco, *Old Scores*, 42.

41. Delbanco, *Old Scores*, 97.

42. Delbanco, *Old Scores*, 63.

43. Delbanco, *Old Scores*, 83.

44. Delbanco, *Old Scores*, 87.

45. Delbanco, *Old Scores*, 89.

46. Delbanco, *Old Scores*, 92.

47. Delbanco, *Old Scores*, 92.

48. Delbanco, *Old Scores*, 92.

49. Delbanco, *Old Scores*, 140.

50. Delbanco, *Old Scores*, 183.

51. Delbanco, *Old Scores*, 225.

52. Delbanco, *Old Scores*, 237.

53. Delbanco, *Old Scores*, 265.

54. Delbanco, *Old Scores*, 271.

55. Francine Prose, *Blue Angel* (New York: HarperCollins, 2000), 16.

56. Prose, *Blue Angel*, 22; italics in original

57. Prose, *Blue Angel*, 10.

58. Prose, *Blue Angel*, 158.

59. Prose, *Blue Angel*, 145.

60. Prose, *Blue Angel*, 187.

61. Prose, *Blue Angel*, 190.

62. Prose, *Blue Angel*, 191.

63. Prose, *Blue Angel*, 236.

64. Prose, *Blue Angel*, 245.

65. Prose, *Blue Angel*, 256.

66. Prose, *Blue Angel*, 266.

67. Prose, *Blue Angel*, 267.

68. Prose, *Blue Angel*, 273.

69. Prose, *Blue Angel*, 272.

70. Prose, *Blue Angel*, 273.

71. Prose, *Blue Angel*, 284.

72. Prose, *Blue Angel*, 285.

73. Prose, *Blue Angel*, 286.

74. Prose, *Blue Angel*, 288; italics in original.

75. Prose, *Blue Angel*, 291.

76. Prose, *Blue Angel*, 296.

77. Prose, *Blue Angel*, 297.

78. Prose, *Blue Angel*, 298–299.

79. Prose, *Blue Angel*, 301.

80. Prose, *Blue Angel*, 303.

81. Prose, *Blue Angel*, 305.

82. Prose, *Blue Angel*, 307.

83. Prose, *Blue Angel*, 308.

84. Prose, *Blue Angel*, 310.

85. Prose, *Blue Angel*, 314.

86. Benjamin R. Barber, *The Truth of Power: Intellectual Affairs in the Clinton White House* (New York: W. W. Norton, 2001).

87. Barber, *The Truth of Power*, 11.

88. Eric Tarloff, *The Man Who Wrote the Book* (New York: Crown, 2000), 47–48.

89. Tarloff, *The Man Who*, 12; italics in original.

90. Tarloff, *The Man Who*, 12.

91. Tarloff, *The Man Who*, 47.

92. Tarloff, *The Man Who*, 48.

93. Tarloff, *The Man Who*, 48.

94. Tarloff, *The Man Who*, 87.

95. Tarloff, *The Man Who*, 65.

96. Tarloff, *The Man Who*, 99.

97. Tarloff, *The Man Who*, 174.

98. Tarloff, *The Man Who*, 174.

99. Tarloff, *The Man Who*, 177.

100. Tarloff, *The Man Who*, 178.

101. Tarloff, *The Man Who*, 204; italics in original.

102. Tarloff, *The Man Who*, 218.

103. Tarloff, *The Man Who*, 251.

23

You Say Social Justice, I Say Political Censorship

Nothing is as destructive to higher education as threats from within—threats that derive from the abject failure of faculty to defend the ideals of intellectual autonomy and the pursuit of knowledge not subservient to political fashion and notions of "social justice."

"The ideal university is an autonomous institution where knowledge is pursued for its own sake, ideas contested and arguments developed, where received wisdom is questioned and students stretched intellectually." So reads the quaint but admirable opening statement of a panel I'm participating in at the "Battle of Ideas" event in London this weekend [October 29–30, 2005].

It is one thing to recognize, as the statement goes on to do, that universities have always had to function in a real world of competing interests and constraints and that their autonomy has always been imperiled by economic and political pressures. But it is quite another for faculty members who ought to know better to sign on to the hackneyed and highly distorted notions that "education is always political" and that the university has little integrity to lose—only past biases to be replaced by better (read: current) ones.

My experience is that academics spring quickly to the defense of the autonomy of higher education only when they sense an attack coming from the outside. Remove any external threats, and academics will happily insist that universities never have been, or indeed could be, anything other than mouthpieces for ideology.

I saw just such a turnabout some years ago at a seminar on higher education held at a leading research center in the United States. All the standard postmodernist clichés debunking the merits of a liberal education were voiced, and when at one point an anthropologist who specialized in Southeast Asia expressed a belief in the persistence of some universals underlying

251

human societies, the response was disdainful dismissal. Ideas of disinterested knowledge and the pursuit of truth were sneered at as mystifications long since exploded, replaced by the identity politics that goes under the name of multiculturalism.

But, toward the end of the second day, something odd happened. A local philanthropist, also attending the seminar, asked, "In view of what you've all been saying, why should anyone support higher education?" Instantly the group reconfigured its allegiances and, to my astonishment, a parade of entirely traditional justifications of the importance of the university as a site for impartial research and teaching was trotted out, replete with affirmations of commitment to precisely those liberal values that for the preceding two days had been roundly denounced.

In the decade since, the state of the university has steadily deteriorated as blatant political commitments—overwhelmingly from the left—have continued to spread throughout the academy. Speech codes and anti-harassment policies have been promoted by campus activists unable, apparently, to tolerate open debate about contentious issues and eager to avoid hurt feelings, even if this means curtailing free speech.

And yet, whenever these professors see their favored positions endangered (after 9/11, for example), they rush to uphold the very notions of "academic freedom" that they previously labeled disingenuous protection of traditional privilege.

And there is more. Identity programs such as women's studies—committed to promoting particular group interests—have tried to impose their agendas ever more sweepingly on the entire university, resting their case on increasingly fantastic claims about their group's supposedly marginalized status.

Thus, "feminist activism" is now an indispensable part of women's studies. Job postings in the field reveal just how undisguised this agenda is. One Texas university is seeking someone with specializations in "transnational or global feminisms, women's health, feminist/womanist community activism and/or feminist disability studies," while a California university is in need of a specialist in "Feminist Activism, Policy, and Social Justice." Other schools seek evidence of progressive "dispositions" or "cultural competency"—code words for political agendas.

Having thrown a belief in liberal values in education to the wind, how will campus politicos defend their programs from the next onslaught to arise from within? Or are they foolishly assuming that their brand of politics will dominate the academy forever?

NOTE

This piece first appeared in the *Times Higher Education Supplement* (London), October 29, 2005.

24

Feminist Pedagogy Reconsidered

What happens when feminism pervades academic research and teaching? Does feminist-inspired pedagogy create problems that differ fundamentally from those attending conventional teaching and research? I want to approach these questions by reflecting on the consequences of placing the qualifier "feminist" before the nouns "teaching" and "research."

As innumerable women's studies course descriptions, mission statements, and Web sites attest,[1] the adjective "feminist" adds—and is intended to add—something highly programmatic to whatever nouns it modifies, namely: a deliberate purpose, a project of political advocacy. The activist design underlying women's studies has been present since its earliest days, when the new field was defined as "the academic arm of the women's movement," but its expression has grown ever more blatant over the years, as current women's studies self-descriptions make plain. In the classroom, feminist politics expresses itself, at the least, as a commitment to fundamental feminist positions and teaching practices, and, at the most, as an unyielding ideological drive. Does such an orientation prove problematic to conscientious teaching and research? Not inevitably, perhaps, but very likely. And that is so because the political engagement underlying feminism in the academy is bound to set up a highly tendentious model for research and teaching, a paradigm most feminists would hardly accept were its objectives contrary to their own. But rather than attack this dilemma directly, women's studies prefers to measure itself against the past. And this backward-looking gauge, in turn, rests on a sweeping (and self-promoting) claim about all non- and pre-feminist teaching and research.

In order to justify and defend the introduction of "feminist" as a legitimate modifier of their "teaching" and "research," feminists have had to

253

greatly exaggerate the flaws affecting the pre- or non-feminist model they are contesting. They insist that in the routine practices of the old dispensation, teaching and research have always been, and still are, biased, exclusionary, and inimical to the interests of women. In short, they are "masculinist." To many feminists, this is a decisive claim. For only when academic procedures can be portrayed in such starkly negative terms is the feminist agenda seen as a corrective: legitimate, appropriate, fair, salutary, and urgently necessary.

Thus, what the term "feminist" introduces into the classroom is a patently political project driving its sense of the aims of education and the pursuit of knowledge. This project has a broad range of objectives—from the basic pedagogical goals of "liberal feminism" or "equality for women" that are often derided and dismissed in more radical feminist circles, to the extreme views associated with such writers as Catharine MacKinnon, who disdainfully treats the concept "liberal" as a disguise for the exercise of patriarchal privilege. MacKinnon entitled one of her books *Feminism Unmodified* precisely because her position is that her own brand of feminism alone is the genuine article and therefore tolerates no qualifier.

If we start, however, with a different set of assumptions—namely the suppositions that teaching and research are not, and ought not to be, either feminist or masculinist, and that despite the historical exclusion of women, the substance of a liberal education and the ideas on which it rests have not been entirely and always flawed—the adjective "feminist" begins to look less like a salutary corrective and more like the calamitous imposition of a political point of view. Why calamitous? Because the great thing about the university is that it provides that rare space in which emphasis can be on *how* to think, not *what* to think, on acquiring intellectual tools, not accepting hand-me-down political doctrines. To assert that indoctrination is what men have in fact traditionally perpetrated in all fields, and that it is now the turn of women to do the same, is a weak defense, even if this assertion were accurate, since it would turn the feminist program into a replica of a practice considered flawed and even malevolent. Surely the appropriate response to whatever are deemed to be the shortcomings of traditional teaching is not simply to reverse the biases of the past but rather to surpass them.

But this imperative presents a major conundrum for the feminist project, and it is precisely to avert the consequences of this conundrum that feminists have resorted to the proposition that "all teaching is political,"[2] which allows them to represent their own academic activism as no less legitimate than earlier academic procedures. For if all activities are inherently political, and they have been so in a way that has oppressed women, then the feminist-inspired activist classroom is a corrective required by both justice and fairness. This is the argument that anchors and justifies the feminist position on education.[3]

Is it, then, true that all education and research are "political" and at best (or worst) manage to conceal their biases? Though in particular cases a political slant may be demonstrated, it seems to me absurd to insist that this distortion is omnipresent and feminists alone face up to it (and embrace it). Only by turning itself into mere triviality can the "all education is political" claim survive scrutiny. To be sure, in some general sense most everything can be shown to have a political aspect. But only by means of gross extrapolation from the subject at hand can one paint all past knowledge with such a broad brush. To offer one instance of such strained extrapolation: When I made this very point on an online "chat" sponsored by *The Chronicle of Higher Education*, the example I used in my counterargument to "everything is political" was of the periodic table.[4] Where, exactly, I wondered, is the "unacknowledged political agenda" (mentioned by one of the discussants) inherent in the periodic table? I quickly got my answer from one women's studies professor:

> Doesn't the teaching of the Periodic Table imply that "man's" appropriate relationship with "nature" is one of dominance? And that we should search for the meaning of existence through science? Since when are such humanist assertions free from political implications?

Here, in a few sentences, is laid out the confusion routinely warned against by philosophers of science, namely the confounding of the *content* of science with the *context* in which scientific work is done and disseminated. It is hardly reassuring to think that college students are being encouraged to repeat such a wrong-headed argument without recognizing its inherent logical fallacy. But this attitude toward science—indeed toward knowledge generally—seems actually to be a requisite of women's studies. The philosopher of science Noretta Koertge has explained why taking on science has been a particular goal of feminists:

> Scientific inquiry embodied all of the so-called masculine virtues that feminism most wanted to challenge—objectivity (vs. subjectivity), the power of reason (instead of intuition), problem solving through logical analysis and the weighing of evidence (vs. conflict resolution through empathy and plumbing the depths of oppression).[5]

If feminists could demonstrate that even science—supposedly the most rational human pursuit—is at its core political and that claims to objectivity are always fraudulent, they could then justify similar critiques of other domains of knowledge *a fortiori*, thus undergirding their own legitimacy and warding off suspicions that they are engaged in special pleading.[6] And for that very reason, hostility to science, as this emerges from a host of feminist writings and teaching materials, is in my view an important criterion for judging the intellectual integrity that feminists bring to the classroom.

But isn't the charge that feminism is hostile to science a mere caricature? Or a part of the "backlash"? Let us see. Leaving aside such well-known critiques as that by Alan Sokal and Jean Bricmont of renowned French feminists' garbled and ignorant claims about physics,[7] I turn to the evidence of discussions taking place in women's studies classes everywhere, discussions about sex. Women's studies programs and the books on their reading lists treat as a matter of orthodoxy the view that gender differences are always socially constructed. However, unlike earlier second-wave feminist work that attempted to distinguish between gender (social) and sex (biological), many women's studies teachers these days have extended social constructionism to the point where it engulfs biology altogether.[8]

A few years ago, on the women's studies e-mail list (WMST-L), I questioned the utility of spending much class time on Anne Fausto-Sterling's work (extremely popular in women's studies courses then and now), which argues that there are more than two sexes.[9] The existence of a very small percentage of infants born with sexual anomalies, I stated, in no way challenges the reality of sexual dimorphism as a biological fact. Angry denunciations of my comment poured into the list, one of which even accused me of attacking the civil rights of minorities. But more than the tone, what startled me about these responses was the categorical insistence that Fausto-Sterling demonstrates that our very bodies are "socially constructed" as binary, the apparent underlying assumption being that "biology" itself was somehow inimical to feminist interests and had to be reconceived. This conviction led to some astonishing messages accusing me of reiterating *with no evidence* that sexual dimorphism is indeed a biological fact.[10]

At last a biologist who was also directing a women's studies program wrote in to say that she was appalled at the lack of basic knowledge of biology demonstrated in the discussion. Offering to explain the reality of sexual dimorphism, she asked: "So where would you like to start—dimorphism in utero, chromosomes and chromosomal diversity, differentiation and development? I will try to be succinct but I will also provide some facts that many of you (based on your comments) aren't going to like." Few people took her up on the offer. Instead, she was denounced in short order for claiming to have expertise and soon decided, sensibly, to stop wasting her time on the list.[11]

I recount this episode to convey the mood and characteristic reactions among faculty members most involved in teaching women's studies—those who regularly participate on the women's studies e-mail list (which at that time had about 4,500 subscribers and in 2005 is up to about 5,000) and thereby provide a fascinating portrait of the attitudes and postures prevalent in that field. But it's important to add here that even while being denounced on the list, I often get a few "behind the scenes" messages of support from women's studies faculty members and graduate students, who tell me privately that they share my concerns, are made uneasy by the dogma of social constructionism or other favored tenets of women's studies, but feel unable to say so openly for fear of jeopardizing their careers. As I argued long ago, little tolerance inhabits women's studies, and the fears expressed by young or future faculty members demonstrate that this has not changed.

The result is that, while progress occurs in many other fields, consequent on the extraordinary scientific and sociopolitical advances of our time, many teachers of women's studies, like other ideologues, prefer simply to dismiss whatever ideas seem to threaten their closed worldview. The science writer Deborah Rudacille is one who demonstrates the oddness of the feminist rejection of biology. In her recent book *The Riddle of Gender: Science, Activism, and Transgender Rights*, Rudacille argues against the social constructionist orthodoxy so prevalent in the past few decades: "Today," she writes, "the pendulum in gender research is slowly swinging back to biology. Hormones acting under the influence of genes are now thought to be the primary architects of gender identity," although the exact developmental mechanisms are not yet clear.[12]

Many feminist academics, however, evidently have great difficulty leaving their core ideas behind, no matter how anachronistic they have become. This is readily apparent when one turns to publications on science in the field of women's studies. In Mary F. Rogers and C. D. Garrett's 2002 book *Who's Afraid of Women's Studies?: Feminisms in Everyday Life*, for example, it is stated flatly that "sexual identities have been culturally constructed."[13] Another book, *Feminist Science Studies: A New Generation*, similarly reveals the feminist desire to dismiss science and put in its place politically agreeable notions. In the latter book (published in 2001), which purports to present the latest thinking in the burgeoning field of science studies, the three editors describe feminist science studies as committed to exploring "situated knowledges," in which the relationship between feminism and science and "the intersections between race, class, gender, and science and technology" are examined and which aims at a "disruption of the dichotomy between scientific inquiry and policy."[14] As the introduction explains, *Feminist Science Studies* aims at nothing less than to provide "progressive, positive readings of science, and of reconstructions of science consistent with feminist theories, ideals, and visions."[15] The extraordinary nature of this objective seems not to trouble the field of feminist science studies, nor has it hindered the uncritical adoption of articles in this field in the "multidisciplinary" women's studies courses typically taught by nonscientists.

Martha Whitaker, in her essay in *Feminist Science Studies*, affirms that Anne Fausto-Sterling's work has been of special importance "in helping me to understand that scientists' analyses and quantification of earth and natural processes *are* social and political processes"[16]—a perfect expression, this, of the reigning approach to science among feminists. Still another contributor aims to go beyond feminist science studies' penchant for "taking apart the visible workings of science to highlight the invisible factors that shaped the interconnections between nature and culture, science and society." Her project is "one of reconstruction—to use [the] insights of deconstruction to rebuild a practice that was scientifically rigorous but also informed by the rigors of feminist politics and scholarship"—as if the problem were not precisely that the "rigors" of these different endeavors are hardly to be compared.[17]

Particularly revealing is an article by Rebecca M. Herzig describing her Introduction to Women's Studies course at Bates College. Aiming to dispel students' notion that biology exists "outside the effects of culture and history," Herzig provides her class with "modules" complete with guided readings designed to help students "query received knowledge about 'the female body.'" While this appears to be an unobjectionable aim, Herzig's true goals are apparent in her tendentious module on "Sexual Dimorphism," which relies heavily on readings by Fausto-Sterling and a few others who emphasize the existence of intersexed humans. Here is how the module presents the problem:

> Lurking in most contemporary discussions about gender and sexuality in the United States [but not elsewhere?] is a presumption of the universal, timeless dimorphism between human males and females. How empirically sound are these dualistic categories? What evidence has been presented for and against universal human sexual dimorphism? How might cross-cultural ethnographic evidence challenge biomedical assumptions of a strict two-sex model? How does the presumption of sexual dimorphism inform our understandings of human sexuality?[18]

The last question of course gives the agenda away: It is important to attack the notion of biological dimorphism because the fact of dimorphism is essential to our history of sexual reproduction. And sexual reproduction, from a biological point of view, confirms the normalcy, indeed the ordinariness, of heterosexuality, which is the very thing that academic feminists routinely identify as the "institution" at the root of women's "oppression." Biology thus presents a particularly intractable problem for feminist analysis, and it is not surprising that many feminists spend considerable energy arguing that biology is merely one more ingredient in the formidable ideology sustaining patriarchy. Readers who note the contradictions in the feminist attack on biology should be reassured: These dodges seem not to be a problem for feminists who denounce the existence of biological "facts" while, at the same time, having constant recourse to essentialist—and always negative—characterizations of "males" and their intrinsic nature.[19]

There is, then, a deep and—for many feminists—vital link between attacking the biology of sex differences and undermining the "institution" of heterosexuality, seen as the linchpin to male dominance. I have documented elsewhere this salient tendency within much contemporary feminism.[20] But lest readers think that arguments against biology come only from a few doctrinaire radical feminists now perhaps out of fashion, I turn to a standard reference work, the Houghton Mifflin *Reader's Companion to U.S. Women's History* (1998), whose entry on "Heterosexuality" reveals that statements perhaps once thought to be controversial within feminism can these days be affirmed without qualification:

> Sexuality is not private, but is political and related to power. "Compulsory heterosexuality" is part of a power structure benefiting heterosexual males at the expense of women and homosexuals. This inequity is justified by an ideology that sees heterosexuality as natural, universal, and biologically necessary, and homosexuality as the opposite. The system also is reinforced by legal sanctions and violence against women (rape, battering, incest, and murder) and against lesbians, gays, and transgendered persons (verbal harassment, physical assault, and murder).

The author spells out why it is important for feminists to press such an argument: "If our sexuality is socially constructed it can also be de- and reconstructed"[21]—a clear indication, this, of feminism's urgent need to reconstitute everything about men and women's lives that it sees as hindering its own project of social transformation.

If even in relation to biology feminist educators don't shrink from their tendentious and often ill-supported arguments, we can expect comparable procedures to drive other feminist endeavors to reshape education. It should be—but isn't—needless to say that the integrity of education is always in danger when politics or ideology supersede rational inquiry and the careful consideration of evidence. Twentieth-century history has demonstrated this peril in abundance, and it is distressing that academic feminists have not taken these cautionary instances to heart.

Still, one may ask: Does it really matter that virtually all feminist teachers believe teaching to be invariably political? That they hold fairness and claims of objectivity in research to be mere illusions, if not outright frauds? I answer: Yes, definitely it matters, because teachers who hold these beliefs are left incapable of even attempting to recognize their own biases, let alone transcend them. Worse, they are programmatically committed to propagating their biases, which is exactly what they do in the "feminist classroom." Thus women's studies teachers openly declare their objective to make students confront their "privilege" or recognize the "institutional" causes of their unprivileged status.[22] And, in the name of multi- or interdisciplinarity, they pass on to their students all manner of research the merits of which they are not able to evaluate but which is accepted or rejected on political grounds. In such classes, students rarely encounter criticisms of feminist-inspired work, nor are they encouraged to develop the capacity of independent judgment and appraisal that might challenge the feminist presuppositions on which their courses rest.[23] Women's studies prides itself on constantly challenging Western society—but the one thing it shrinks from challenging is its own pet ideas.

Having written about these issues for more than a decade, I am well aware that the usual response to criticisms of this type—and often merely to raising these issues—is that the writer is an enemy of feminism, a "conservative," or a reactionary trying to force women back to the kitchen, and so on—all of which are feeble rejoinders designed to avoid engaging with the very real problems caused by the intentional politicizing of research and teaching. Not surprisingly, whole books have been devoted to attempting to prove that criticisms such as the ones I and others have made are merely examples of "backlash."[24] Indeed, the very word "backlash" has acquired a sacramental aura in feminist circles, obviating even the expectation of a reasoned response to the specific criticisms that have been voiced. And as scholars who formerly devoted years to the advancement of feminism in the academy express their dissatisfaction with where politicized teaching has taken us, they too can expect to be vilified by the feminist academics still defending their turf. Though what such scholars really want is to see research and teaching liberated from feminism's (and other identity groups') political advocacy, deviation from the feminist educational agenda is enough to have one's writing dismissed out of hand and one's character impugned.

Despite this predictable response, some well-known senior scholars closely associated with feminism in the academy have in recent years felt moved to object to the politicizing of education. In the Summer 2000 issue of *Signs*, which was devoted to dozens of essays on feminism and the academy, Elaine Marks, a widely recognized lesbian critic who until her death in late 2001 was Germaine Brée Professor of French and Women's Studies at the University of Wisconsin, Madison, complained that she was beginning to feel "isolated in Women's Studies," where she had come to be perceived as "a closet conservative." Why? Because she deplored the prevalence of identity politics in literature courses, and now agreed with Harold Bloom that "to read in the service of any ideology is not, in my judgment, to read at all." Marks confessed that she herself used to have politically correct responses, the kind that seek, in any work of literature, traces of the dreaded isms (sexism, racism, etc.). But she was no longer satisfied with such approaches. Hence her decision to air in public some of what she considered to be "feminism's perverse effects" in the academy.

"It is no simple matter," Marks concluded, "in this millennial fin de siècle, to criticize certain tendencies in cultural studies or Women's Studies or ethnic studies without being accused of participating in a conservative political agenda."[25] And she is right. In the topsy-turvy world of academe, to call for an education not bound to a political agenda *is* tantamount to being "conservative." Moreover, the fact that "conservative" has become a label of instant dismissal in academe exemplifies the ideological rigidity that now disfigures the one arena that was supposed to fearlessly and openly explore ideas and knowledge claims on their *own* merits.[26]

The philosopher Susan Haack is one critic whose work should be indispensable reading for every feminist who aspires to scholarly integrity. Her 1998 book *Manifesto of a Passionate Moderate: Unfashionable Essays* is filled with challenges to the notion that a "feminist" perspective strengthens intellectual work, the sorts of challenges routinely ignored in women's studies classrooms. To Haack, "the politicization of inquiry, . . . whether in the interests of good political values or bad, is always epistemologically unsound."[27] Haack considers that "the rubric 'feminist epistemology' is incongruous on its face, in somewhat the way of, say, 'Republican epistemology.'"[28] She explains:

> The profusion of incompatible themes proposed as "feminist epistemology" itself speaks against the ideas of a distinctively female cognitive style. But even if there were such a thing, the case for feminist epistemology would require further argument to show that women's "ways of knowing" . . . represent better procedures of inquiry or subtler standards of justification than the male. And, sure enough, we are told that insights into the theory of knowledge are available to women which are not available, or not easily available, to men.[29]

Dismissing "the egregious assumption that one thinks with one's skin or one's sex organs," Haack in another essay stresses that

> this form of argument, when applied to the concepts of evidence, truth, etc., is not only fallacious; it is also pragmatically self-undermining. . . . For if there were no genuine inquiry, no objective evidence, we couldn't know what theories are such that their being accepted would conduce to women's interests, nor what women's interests are.[30]

Haack denounces the "ambition of the new, imperialist feminism to colonize epistemology," and then makes the telling comment: "There would be a genuinely feminist epistemology if the idea could be legitimated *that feminist values should determine what theories are accepted.*"[31] And, indeed, precisely such a destructive idea is regularly embraced in women's studies circles, where few seem to note that it will undermine the ground of their own pedagogy.

In recent years, I have not seen any evidence that women's studies teachers have modified their antagonism toward claims to positive knowledge in particular, and scientific reasoning in general.[32] And, not surprisingly, they are now finding themselves in some company they may not choose to keep. As "creation science," recast these days as "intelligent design," extends its reach and threatens the teaching of basic science (reduced to a competing ideology) in the United States, its defenders make comments about the status of evolution—that it is "just a theory," for example, though one that claims for itself a privileged status—that are remarkably similar to the feminist depreciation of science.[33] Like creationists, many feminists have shown contempt for evidence—when it did not support their preconceptions. They may misunderstand science (perhaps intentionally), denounce its procedures, and ignore its commitment to self-correction—all in order to be able to characterize it as ideology, and not as honest a one as their own feminist ideology, which acknowledges its political interests.

But the rejection of the ideals of objective knowledge (however imperfectly attainable) and the deployment of the admitted limitations of knowledge into a weapon against past knowledge, to be dismissed as the product of patriarchal dead white men, along with the disdain for standards of evidence and logic, gain feminists only an illusory victory. It may leave them free to defend and promote their agenda, but it also renders them vulnerable to ignorant or politically motivated calumnies directed against them. For how will feminists respond when, with the next cultural turn, we are once again told that the blood of menstruating women causes milk to curdle? Aren't standards of evidence and objective investigation crucial to all women (to all people) as they attempt to combat prejudice and ignorance?

Because I have often observed feminists readily veering from one line of argument to another (resorting to biological determinism when denouncing men, for example, while insisting on social constructionism—the official feminist orthodoxy—most of the time), I have concluded that caring more about achieving "feminist" goals than about meeting the obligations of scrupulous teaching and research leads to an opportunistic intellectual stance in the academy and—most harmfully—in the classroom. One example of this is the reality that these days, feminist advocacy must increasingly depend upon a gross misrepresentation of the status of women in North American society generally and in the university in particular. An egregious example of this distortion is the claim made—presumably with a straight face—by some feminist scholars in the United States that "the academy remains an essentially single sex institution. It is male-dominated, and that domination exerts itself in both numbers and power."[34] Such misrepresentations of the real-life situation of women should not be seen as a pathological inability to recognize the profound changes and improvements that have occurred over the past few decades but merely as a tactical necessity for women's studies.

But as feminist pedagogues continue to rely on scare statistics regarding rape while ignoring, say, research on woman-initiated domestic violence,[35] and as women's studies courses claim multidisciplinary expertise while often resting on multidisciplinary ignorance, the result of feminist teaching is a pedagogy ever more at odds with observable reality, steeped in ever less authentic-sounding pronouncements. Never mind the massive evidence—statistical, judicial, and legislative, as well as anecdotal—of enormous and on-going improvement in women's status in the United States (and many other parts of the world). Society has changed, but feminist activists seem determined either not to notice or not to admit it.[36] Instead, self-serving stereotypes about male violence and female victimization and oppression are repeated as though they were startling insights.[37]

Oddly enough, women's studies seems to have learned little from its own criticisms of what happens when education is governed by political agendas. Nor do many feminist teachers appear to have grasped the implications of such illuminating twentieth-century cases as Lysenkoism in the USSR, a stellar example of science "reconstructed" so as to be "consistent with" a reigning political ideology—the overt goal, as we saw earlier, of the volume *Feminist Science Studies.* Embracing, as feminism in the academy does, the principle that all education is political (and declining to explore just how this might be true, to what extent, in what circumstances, and at what costs) makes it impossible for women's studies and other politically inspired programs to respond convincingly to political pressures from the other side. David Horowitz's Academic Bill of Rights (ABOR), for example, with its demand for political diversity in the name of academic freedom, has led some state legislators to attempt to ensure space in the classroom for conservative political ideas.

And why not? After all, those who claim that all education is political hardly have grounds for objecting to the inclusion of some mainstream political views not currently fashionable in the academic world. If feminists really believe their characterization of non-feminist education, why are they (like many academic organizations) in a panic over the ABOR? Horowitz is merely playing their own game, but with a different political content.[38] And at worst, if feminists and other politically committed teachers are worried about being sued by disgruntled students (as a bill introduced in Florida would have allowed), why haven't they objected to the widespread adoption of harassment policies and speech codes in academe, under which scores of professors have already been subjected to censure, job-loss, and legal action because a woman was offended by, say, a professor's non-feminist discussion of abortion or rape? I have not seen women's studies teachers rush to protect academic freedom and uninhibited class discussion for those whose views contradict their own. Quite the contrary, as I have documented at length.[39]

Where, one might well ask, will feminists be able to go in this struggle over which ideas should be protected in the academy? Presumably feminists would respond that *their* ideas are true or better. But to sustain this claim, they would be forced to resort to high standards of evidence, to rigorous logic, and to fair evaluation not in thrall to political predispositions. Yet these are the very procedures feminist academics have so often attacked. In combating other ideologues and their claims, the feminist promotion of subjectivity, value-laden theory, or "standpoint epistemology" will not serve them well. For their own practice has helped create a conflict with no rules, only with competing political passions and varieties of belief.

As many commentators have observed, feminism itself could not even have got started without embracing claims resting on objective conditions and drawing on supposedly unbiased research said to accurately assess the situation of women vis-à-vis men. In light of feminism's path, therefore, the present assertions of feminist pedagogy seem not only tendentious, but disingenuous. The feminist promotion of subjectivity, of "standpoint epistemology," and of the paradigm that "everything is political," is, thus, at best situational. It hardly justifies the pedagogy that has grown up around it. Of course women's studies is not alone in promoting these habits. Postmodernist fashions have made a variety of vulnerable intellectual and pedagogical approaches acceptable and widely used. And this is the case even among feminist critics of postmodernism, who while decrying its alienating and pretentious vocabulary and its distance from everyday political struggles, nonetheless adopt its practices whenever they prove convenient. Postmodernism's indiscriminate rejection of significant distinctions, its obsession with power, and its habit of dogmatic assertion (the very thing, ironically, that postmodernism claims to "interrogate") have influenced feminist academics' own critiques, though of course this at times contravenes their activist agenda, which would be meaningless without some firm convictions about the real world and our ability to obtain communicable knowledge of it.

To sum up: feminists pedagogues by their own accounts indulge in a series of wide-ranging, self-destructive habits. They dismiss logic as so much phallocentric baggage. They celebrate emotion and intuition, as if there were no pertinent historical examples of what actually happens when a society obeys its passions and its "gut" feelings. They (though not only they) assume that identity politics tells us most of what we need to know for adjudicating among competing views and knowledge claims. (How this assumption can be made within the context of postmodernism, which has challenged the very notion of a stable identity, is not clear, but an illogical assumption isn't much of a problem once logic and coherence are rejected as "masculinist.") They appeal to cultural relativism when that serves some immediate purpose, and deny it when it doesn't. They welcome "local knowledges" in relation to third world Others, but rigidly resist them when they come from disapproved groups within Western societies.[40] Distinctions fall by the wayside: Ear piercing and breast implants are equivalent to clitoridectomy; high-heeled shoes hardly differ from Chinese footbinding.

Double standards abound. The "authority of experience," so praised by feminists in their struggle to have women's voices heard (logocentrism notwithstanding), is subjected to cynical deconstruction when the proclaimed experience is not one that suits the feminist causes of the moment.

What all this means in practice is that there prevails an opportunism at the heart of feminist pedagogy today. To me, the evidence for this conclusion is utterly convincing. I also believe, however, that the many failures of this state of affairs are becoming more and more evident. Thus, feminist pedagogy, if it wants to have any credibility outside its own clique-like circles, will have to begin to hold itself to a higher standard. Only professors dedicated more to their teaching than to their politics—and able to tell the difference—provide us with reason for hope.

Teaching and the research upon which it rests are noble pursuits. To commit oneself to fostering the intellectual development of one's students is no small or unworthy task. And, contrary to what many feminists believe, this task requires something other than political advocacy. Though women's studies programs typically refuse to recognize the fact, there are vital distinctions to be drawn between informed and conscientious teaching and attempting to persuade students to sign on to a particular political vision. The important role of educators is precisely not to deny but to embrace these distinctions, to observe them, indeed to cherish them.

NOTES

This essay was written for the volume *Handbook of Feminist Research: Theory and Praxis*, edited by Sharlene Nagy Hesse-Biber (Thousand Oaks, Calif.: Sage Publications, 2006), 689–704.

1. Women's studies mission statements these days typically embrace the word "feminism," and proudly declare their programs' political commitments. See, for numerous examples, chapters 10 and 11 in Daphne Patai and Noretta Koertge, *Professing Feminism: Education and Indoctrination in Women's Studies* (Lanham, Md.: Lexington Books, 2003), a much-expanded edition of our 1994 book. The present essay draws on this work, which may be consulted for a more detailed discussion of the issues raised here. Feminist scholars usually retort that there are many feminisms, not one, that it is an unstable and constantly developing field. All of this may be true, and new debates may evolve (e.g., conflicts among different or newly emerging identity groups), but that does not alter the fact that there are underlying and characteristic views, positions, and beliefs—especially in relation to the non-feminist and pre-feminist world—that represent the prevailing orthodoxy.

2. This notion (resting on a vast feminist literature) underlies numerous books and is regularly repeated by feminists in academe. For recent examples of this position, from various English-speaking countries, see the WMST-L@LISTSERV.UMD

.EDU, August 22–25, 2005. The posting by J. L. Tallentire (a graduate student in history), August 24, 2005, is a particularly clear exposition of the feminist claim as it is absorbed by students. After announcing that all education is political, she summarizes: "Anyone who complains about the 'proselytizing' in some classrooms but not others is simply mistaken about the nature of teaching. Feminists have seen fit to face it & embrace it, because we recognize that politics has *always* been in the classrooms we attended—a politics that left women and marginalized peoples out, usually—and we needed to get our own in there too." Does she believe this is true of all subjects, always? Evidently: "So can we please stop pretending there's a neutral and nonpolitical (and thus more ethical) set of ideas, theories, teaching styles, and classroom activities? Because there isn't. Not in social sciences, humanities, fine arts, sciences, whatever."

3. See, for example, Gayle Letherby's assertion: "Feminist work highlights the fact that the researchers' choice of methods, of research topic and of study group population are always political acts," in *Feminist Research in Theory and Practice* (Buckingham, UK: Open University Press, 2003), 4. The adversarial stance celebrated by feminist teachers can be seen in the women's studies e-mail list (WMST-L) discussion of "poverty activities" in the classroom. One professor supported such exercises because they "force privileged students to step outside their privilege for a few minutes" (J. Musial to WMST-L@LISTSERV.UMD.EDU, August 23, 2005). Another wrote: "I have a responsibility to encourage my students (and the wider public where I can) to think outside the dominant views (lies) about 'reality'" (B. Winter to WMST-L, August 23, 2005). This last professor also wrote: "I think challenging the bullshit that our culture—'high' and 'low'—produces to prop up the abuse of women, including through education, is the most important and useful thing a feminist academic can do" (WMST-L@LISTSERV.UMD.EDU, August 25, 2005).

4. See chronicle.com/colloquylive/transcripts/2000/10/20001004patai.htm. and research.umbc.edu/~korenman/wmst/patai1.html. For a clear analysis of the issue, see Paul A. Boghossian, "What Is Social Construction?: Flaws and Contradictions in the Claim that Scientific Beliefs Are 'Merely Locally Accepted,'" *Times Literary Supplement*, February 23, 2001, 6–8.

5. Noretta Koertge, "Feminists Take on Science," in Patai and Koertge, *Professing Feminism* (Lanham: Lexington, revised edition, 2003), 321. Koertge goes on to analyze three books (including Anne Fausto-Sterling's, discussed below) that represent some of the most widely known feminist works on science, demonstrating the faulty research strategies each engages in. In an earlier chapter (chapter 7), Koertge and I analyze the very popular book *Women's Ways of Knowing* and its profound impact on feminist teaching. Cassandra L. Pinnick takes on the claim made by feminists that feminist science is better than ordinary science in her review essay "Feminist Philosophy of Science: High Hopes," *Metascience* 9:2 (July 2000), 257–266.

6. Though some feminists attempt to deny this problematic feminist "contribution," many textbooks demonstrate how mainstream the feminist critique has by now become. See, for example, Amy Koerber and Mary M. Lay, "Understanding Women's Concerns in the International Setting Through the Lens of Science and Technology," in *Encompassing Gender: Integrating International Studies and Women's Studies*, ed. Mary M. Lay, Janice Monk, and Deborah S. Rosenfelt (New York: The Feminist Press, 2002), 82, in which the view that "science and technology seek to

control and dominate nature and by extension the so-called feminine aspects of societies" is repeated without criticism and with the usual references to Sandra Harding and Evelyn Fox Keller. Or consider the simple assertion made by Philip Rice and Patricia Waugh, editors of *Modern Literary Theory: A Reader*, 4th ed. (London: Arnold, 2001), 449, that "scientific knowledge can be no more 'objective' than aesthetic knowledge." They go on to assert that "science constructs the shape of nature."

7. See Alan Sokal and Jean Bricmont, *Fashionable Nonsense: Postmodern Intellectuals' Abuse of Science* (New York: Picador, 1998), who include devastating analyses of claims such as Luce Irigaray's that $E = mc^2$ is a "sexed equation."

8. For an intriguing and amusing critique of the zealous embrace of social constructionism, see Ian Craib, "Social Constructionism as a Social Psychosis," *Sociology* 31:1 (February 1997), 1–15. Craib asks what anxieties might give rise to comforting collective beliefs not open to rational debate and suggests that extreme social constructionism (which he calls a "manic psychosis") allows us to fantasize control over change that we do not, in fact, possess (10, 11).

9. Anne Fausto-Sterling, *Sexing the Body: Gender Politics and the Construction of Sexuality* (New York: Basic Books, 2000), 20. In various of her publications, Fausto-Sterling has provided different figures for the prevalence of sexual anomalies among neonates, ranging from one or two in 2,000 to four per hundred. To make the case against sexual dimorphism as the natural condition of humans, women's studies courses are likely to select the higher figures, though even these hardly challenge the reality of sexual dimorphism.

10. See, for example, Susan Kane to WMST-L, February 24, 2001. I have discussed this episode in detail in the revised edition of *Professing Feminism*, chapter 11, "Policing the Academy." See also Koertge, chapter 12 of *Professing Feminism*, "Feminists Take on Science." Meanwhile, denunciations of others' defective feminism continue unabated on the WMST-L, with the same sorts of arguments, name-calling, and feminist grandstanding made again and again. See, for example, the exchanges in early August 2005 under the subject "Transgender discussion."

11. Ruthann Masaracchia to WMST-L, March 1, 2001. To make crystal-clear my own position, I append one of my messages, labeled "biology and silence," posted on the WMST-L, August 5, 2001:

> I would like once again to state that in no sense have I suggested it's not interesting or valuable to study anomalies. Nor have I attacked "free inquiry" or intellectual curiosity. And, of course, I have never suggested that transgendered or homosexual or any other minority should be persecuted or treated badly.

> What I have written, consistently for quite some time, has constituted a criticism of the *pretense*—for it seems clearly to be that—that the anomalies are more important and more central in women's studies than the norms, and that the anomalies are to be stressed and insisted upon in feminist classrooms.

> I got this sense from the discussions on this very list, from people's enthusiasm for Anne Fausto-Sterling's work, from their own comments about how terrific it was to teach this work in their courses because it upset their students' ideas of sex and gender. But my point was a simple one: students who believe that the vast majority of humans are biologically male and female are correct in their beliefs and do not need re-educating. When

those beliefs are assailed, as this list shows they often are in women's studies, the agenda is a political, not an educational one. That is what I am criticizing.

It has been fascinating for me to see how Ruthann Masaracchia's knowledgeable postings (the latest one on August 2nd) usually end the discussion. No one asks how these biological facts can be incorporated into introductory women's studies classes, how they might be integrated into more complicated visions that don't misrepresent the facts to students. Instead, after days of debate, there is silence—as if this information were irrelevant to women's studies—until the next round of a similar discussion in which the same dynamics arise again, the same challenges to the biological facts, again erroneously presented as social constructions, and on and on.

Let me note that last winter, when I wrote something similar, a listmember wrote back that I kept asserting the fact of sexual dimorphism without providing evidence. I refer readers to 1) our reality, notwithstanding postmodernist debates, and 2) the thousands of books, articles, and studies in the field of biology.

As to Fausto-Sterling's writing—on which many women's studies people seem to be resting their beliefs—I note her habit of verbal slippage: from a discussion of truly constructed, i.e., imposed through surgery, sexual identity on infants born with anomalies, she generalizes (often in the same paragraph) to the constructed nature of male/female, period. I see the interest in learning about these intersexed or otherwise "different" people, and I also understand and sympathize with the desire to call the treatment they've received into question—but I continue to *not* understand how this can be used to challenge the "normalcy" of male/female.

Fausto-Sterling, in her book, various times criticizes scholars (e.g., Diamond) for falling into the language of "normal" in their writing—as if "normal" were always a moral judgment and not also a statistical one. I've at times wondered if the whole point of the feminist attack on science is to clear the field for any and every claim without any standard of evidence, since all can be dismissed as masculinist or patriarchal.

I read Fausto-Sterling's work looking for some evidence that her argument was being *mis*used by people on this list for their own purposes, but I conclude that it's not being misused, and that she does indeed in the end make the same sort of case. A close analysis of her book's rhetoric shows a constant slippage from the anomalies to the norm—thus inviting women's studies professors to make the very moves they are repeatedly making on this list, which is to take the anomalies as somehow casting doubt on the biological reality of the norms.

This is not a useful debate. The only reason I bother about it is because I am concerned about what is being taught to students and what is passing as feminist education—which I believe dishonors both feminism and any notion of intellectual integrity.

A pithy rejoinder to Fausto-Sterling's views is David Barash's letter to the editor of the *New York Times* (January 9, 2002). Responding to an interview with Fausto-Sterling (January 2, 2001), Barash, the author of several dozen books on biology, psychology, and peace studies, acknowledged the interest of examining intermediate cases of all natural phenomena and then commented:

Nonetheless, scientists and laypeople alike would be seriously misled if they were to respond to the existence of rare in-between cases by questioning the legitimacy, or even the
existence, of the baseline situations from which these cases depart. Imagine a meteorol-
ogist who was so intrigued with dawn and dusk that she insisted that we abandon the categories day and night, or that we consider them to be "socially constructed."

12. Deborah Rudacille, *The Riddle of Gender: Science, Activism, and Transgender
Rights* (New York: Pantheon, 2005), 138–139. Rudacille's work aims at gaining tolerance for transgendered individuals. As she puts it: "Nature may provide the archi-
tecture of gender, but culture does the decorating." Still, she has no trouble asserting that, "as seems increasingly certain, [gender identity] is hardwired into the brain
at birth" (292).

13. Mary F. Rogers and C. D. Garrett, *Who's Afraid of Women's Studies?: Feminisms
in Everyday Life* (Walnut Creek, Calif.: AltaMira Press, 2002), 49.

14. Maralee Mayberry, Banu Subramaniam, and Lisa H. Weasel, "Adventures
across Natures and Cultures: An Introduction," in *Feminist Science Studies: A New
Generation*, ed. Maralee Mayberry, Banu Subramaniam, and Lisa H. Weasel (New
York: Routledge, 2001), 5–6.

15. Mayberry, Subramaniam, and Weasel, "Adventures," 10. Throughout the
book, the same few feminist science scholars (Barad, Bleier, Fausto-Sterling, Fox
Keller, Haraway, Harding) are cited again and again.

16. Martha P. L. Whitaker, "Oases in a Desert: Why a Hydrologist Meanders
between Science and Women's Studies," in Mayberry et al., *Feminist Science Studies*, 49.

17. Banu Subramaniam, "And the Mirror Cracked! Reflections of Natures and
Cultures," in Mayberry et al., *Feminist Science Studies*, 57. See Raymond Tallis, "Evidence-based and Evidence-free Generalisations," in *The Raymond Tallis Reader*, ed.
Michael Grant (Hampshire: Palgrave, 2000), 309–329, for a brief but telling description of the crucial distinction between these two modes of inquiry.

18. Rebecca M. Herzig, "What About Biology? Building Sciences into Introductory Women's Studies Curricula," in Mayberry et al., *Feminist Science Studies*,
183–192. While often claiming to have superseded a simple distinction between the
biological and the social, such feminist teachers' real agenda clearly emerges in their
own discussions of the subject. For simplistic core feminist beliefs about the natural sciences, intended for consumption by undergraduates, see *Transforming the Disciplines: A Women's Studies Primer*, ed. Elizabeth L. MacNabb et al. (New York: The
Haworth Press, 2001), 159ff.

19. On feminist stereotypes of men, see Alice Echols, *Daring to Be Bad: Radical
Feminism in America, 1967–1975* (Minneapolis: University of Minnesota Press,
1989), 362–363, who notes the confusion between essentialism and social constructionism in the work of radical feminists such as Andrea Dworkin and
Catharine MacKinnon. Although they indignantly proclaim that they are not es-
sentialists, these writers see male dominance as "eternal and unchanging." Echols
comments that if the social structure is "as impervious to change as [they] suggest,
it might as well be biologically fixed." Today, positions that used to be identified
with radical feminism often appear institutionalized within women's studies programs.

20. See Daphne Patai, *Heterophobia: Sexual Harassment and the Future of Feminism* (Lanham, Md.: Rowman & Littlefield, 1998), from which some passages in the present essay are adapted.

21. E. Kay Trimberger, "Heterosexuality," in Wilma Mankiller et al., eds., *The Reader's Companion to U.S. Women's History* (Boston: Houghton Mifflin, 1998), 255. Amazon.com's current listing for this book includes a review in the *School Library Journal* by Mary H. Cole, of the Polytechnic Preparatory Country Day School, recommending the volume for grades 7 and up.

22. These examples can be found on the WMST-L's discussion of "poverty activities" in the classroom. As one professor put it (J. Hatten to WMST-L, August 24, 2005):

> The beauty of the "Life Happens" exercise is that privileged students can see how they've benefited from their privilege and those who have struggled with these issues can get beyond the self-blame/self-doubt instilled in them by the individualistic notion of the "American Dream." When students are shown how institutional forces control more of their life circumstances than often their own efforts, it is very freeing for them—I've also seen this exercise promote a lot of social activism from students.

23. For an interesting example of a women's studies reader that does register a bit of criticism of the field, see Sheila Ruth, ed., *Issues in Feminism: An Introduction to Women's Studies*, 4th ed. (London: Mayfield, 1998). Ruth includes my essay "What's Wrong with Women's Studies?," and positions it between one by Susan Faludi about "pod feminists" and "pseudofeminists" and one by Suzanne L. Cataldi dismissing charges of "male bashing" in women's studies. Even so, she does not trust students to draw their own conclusions: Her introductory comments to my essay alert students that my critiques "fit within the genre delineated in the previous selection by Susan Faludi." By contrast, her agreement with Faludi and Cataldi is evident in the phrasing of her introductions to their essays.

24. See, for example, Rogers and Garrett, note 13 above.

25. Elaine Marks, "Feminism's Perverse Effects," *Signs: Journal of Women in Culture and Society* 25:4 (Summer 2001), 1163.

26. See, for example, the reactions to David Horowitz's Academic Bill of Rights, discussed below.

27. Susan Haack, "Science as Social?—Yes and No," in *Manifesto of a Passionate Moderate: Unfashionable Essays* (Chicago: University of Chicago Press, 1998), 119. For an example of work that incorporates critiques of science without falling prey to what she calls the "New Cynicism," see Haack's recent book *Defending Science—Within Reason: Between Scientism and Cynicism* (Amherst, N.Y.: Prometheus Books, 2003).

28. Haack, "Knowledge and Propaganda: Reflections of an Old Feminist," in *Manifesto*, 124. See also Noretta Koertge's essay, "Critical Perspectives on Feminist Epistemology," in *Handbook of Feminist Research: Theory and Praxis*, ed. Sharlene Nagy Hesse-Biber (Thousand Oaks, Calif: Sage Publications, 2006), 553–66.

29. Haack, "Knowledge and Propaganda," 126.

30. Haack, "Science as Social?" 118.

31. Haack, "Knowledge and Propaganda," 128; [italics in original].

32. In July 2005, in response to negative comments made on the WMST-L to a query of mine regarding "Darwinian feminism," I received an interesting private

message from a student of bioinformatics in Oregon, who had encountered hostility in women's studies students to any discussion of evolution.

> As a biologist/computer scientist-in-training I am deeply concerned by the near total absence of women in my classes. In fact, the more rigor required the fewer women are interested in the courses. To wit, in some of the more "woodsy" biology courses I've taken there was, what seemed to me, a reasonable representation of women. In my calculus, programming and the more mathematical of my biology courses (like population genetics) there are far fewer women. The issue concerns me because I believe that, without realizing it, some feminists are actively discouraging women from studying scientific subjects and then encouraging young women (I am nearly forty, returning to school) to hold forth on subjects that they know nothing about—or in many cases would be better off if they didn't know anything about the subject [rather] than the wild inaccuracies they hold now.

33. See, for example, PBS's *NewsHour* with Jim Lehrer, "Evolution Debate," March 28, 2005. For a thorough analysis of the flaws of the controversy surrounding the teaching of "intelligent design," which has implications for the feminist attack on "positive" knowledge generally, see Jerry Coyne, "The Faith That Dare Not Speak Its Name," *The New Republic*, August 22, 2005.

34. Susan J. Scollay and Carolyn S. Bratt, "Untying the Gordian Knot of Academic Sexual Harassment," in *Sexual Harassment on Campus: A Guide for Administrators, Faculty, and Students*, ed. Bernice R. Sandler and Robert J. Shoops (Boston: Allyn & Bacon, 1997), 274.

35. The literature on violence initiated by women is extensive. See, for example, Martin S. Fiebert, "References Examining Assaults by Women on their Spouses or Male Partners: An Annotated Bibliography," *Sexuality and Culture* 1 (1997), 273–286; Martin S. Fiebert and D. M. Gonzalez, "Women Who Initiate Assaults: The Reasons Offered for Such Behavior," *Psychological Reports* 80 (1997), 583–590; and Philip W. Cook, *Abused Men: The Hidden Side of Domestic Violence* (Westport, Conn.: Praeger, 1997). On lesbian violence, see, for example, Janice L. Ristock, *No More Secrets: Violence in Lesbian Relationships* (New York: Routledge, 2002). Women's studies scholars, however, typically reject this work—judging by the hostility to it evinced on the WMST-L and in feminist publications.

36. See, for example, U.S. Department of Education, *Projections of Education Statistics to 2013* (Washington, D.C.: National Center for Education Statistics, 2003), available at: nces.ed.gov/programs/projections/ch_4.asp#2: "Between 1987-88 and 2000-01, the number and proportion of degrees awarded to women rose at all levels. In 2000-01, women earned the majority of associate's, bachelor's, and master's degrees, 45 percent of doctor's degrees, and 46 percent of first professional degrees. Between 2000-01 and 2012-13, continued increases are expected in the number of degrees awarded to women at all levels." For employment trends in academe, see the *NEA Higher Education Advocate*, Summer 2005, 13, which shows that the number of women faculty continues to increase. At public institutions, full-time women faculty have increased 49 percent in the past fifteen years while the number of men has decreased by 3 percent. Women are at parity with men at community colleges but are underrepresented elsewhere, with the greatest gender disparity appearing in doctoral universities. (By contrast, minority faculty continue to be very much underrepresented).

At private and public four-year colleges, women now constitute about 40 percent of the faculty (higher than 50 percent at junior colleges) and only about 35 percent at doctoral-granting schools. As for salaries, women as a whole continue to earn less than men in almost all sectors—particularly at doctoral universities where their salaries are 78–79 percent of men's (2003–2004), while lower level schools show smaller discrepancies. These data are not sorted by field, however.

Parity is not being reached in specific academic fields, and there is considerable feminist resistance to plain talk about the possible reasons for this. Because the prevailing contention of feminists is that disparity necessarily equals discrimination, even as notable a figure as Lawrence H. Summers, president of Harvard University, can be cowed by feminist critics into abject apologies merely for wondering, at a conference on diversifying the science and engineering workforce, if innate differences might explain why fewer women than men pursue careers in science and math. See Claudia Goldin and Lawrence F. Katz, "Summers Is Right," *Boston Globe,* January 23, 2005. Summers' comments were apparently intolerable to a feminist scientist so sensitive that, according to her own account, she had to flee the room before vomiting or blacking out. What is most telling about the episode, however, is the power of feminists—who continue to cry that universities are unwelcoming places for them—to extract not only an apology from Summers but a pledge of $50 million to make the Harvard faculty more "diverse." For a chronology of the Summers' controversy, see www.anitaborg.org/pressroom/pressreleases_05/responsesall .htm. [Summers was subsequently forced to resign.]

37. See, for example, Jane Pilcher and Imelda Whelehan, *Fifty Key Concepts in Gender Studies* (London: Sage, 2004), 175, in which the authors assert the "close links between masculinities and violence."

38. Despite his careful delineation of his Academic Bill of Rights, which in many respects follows the American Association of University Professors' own famous 1940 "Statement of Principles on Academic Freedom and Tenure," Horowitz is constantly—and quite hypocritically—depicted as undermining academic freedom and attempting to impose his own politics on that hitherto pristine bastion of unfettered intellectual exploration, the university. And who leads the attack? The very same activist feminist and leftist professors who usually insist that all education is political. [See also chapter 20 in this volume.] For the text of and debates on Horowitz's Academic Bill of Rights, see www.studentsforacademicfreedom.org and www.FrontPagemag.com. For an example of how a college professor defends her teaching against Horowitz's efforts, see www.commondreams.org/views05/ 0328-30.htm.

39. See Patai, *Heterophobia: Sexual Harassment and the Future of Feminism.*

40. For analysis of the retrograde effects on less-developed countries of anti-Western, anti-science, and postmodernist fashions (including feminist critiques of science), see the important work of Meera Nanda, for example: "The Epistemic Charity of the Social Constructivist Critics of Science and Why the Third World Should Refuse the Offer," in *A House Built on Sand: Exposing Postmodernist Myths About Science,* ed. Noretta Koertge (New York: Oxford University Press, 1998), 286–311, and Nanda's recent book *Prophets Facing Backward: Postmodern Critiques of Science and Hindu Nationalism in India* (New Brunswick, N.J.: Rutgers University Press, 2003).

BIBLIOGRAPHY

ABI Staff. "News Chronicle of a Controversy." Anita Borg Institute for Women and Technology Web Site, January 16, 2005. Available at www.anitaborg.org/pressroom/pressreleases_05/responsesall.htm.

Barash, D. Letter to the editor, *New York Times*, January 9, 2002.

Boghossian, P. A. "What Is Social Construction: Flaws and Contradictions in the Claim that Scientific Beliefs Are 'Merely Locally Accepted.'" *Times Literary Supplement*, February, 23, 2001, 6–8.

Cook, P. W. *Abused Men: The Hidden Side of Domestic Violence*. Westport, Conn.: Praeger, 1997.

Coyne, J. "The Faith That Dare Not Speak Its Name." *The New Republic*, August 22, 2005.

Craib, I. "Social Constructionism as a Social Psychosis." *Sociology* 31:1 (1997): 1–15.

Echols, E. *Daring to Be Bad: Radical Feminism in America, 1967–1975*. Minneapolis: University of Minnesota Press, 1989.

Fausto-Sterling, A. *Sexing the Body: Gender Politics and the Construction of Sexuality*. New York: Basic Books, 2000.

Fiebert, M. S. "References Examining Assaults by Women on Their Spouses or Male Partners: An Annotated Bibliography." *Sexuality and Culture*, 1997, 1:273–286.

Fiebert, M. S., and D. M. Gonzalez. "Women Who Initiate Assaults: The Reasons Offered for Such Behavior." *Psychological Reports*, 1997, 80:583–590.

Goldin, C., and L. F. Katz. "Summers Is Right." *Boston Globe*, January 23, 2005.

Haack, S. *Defending Science—Within Reason: Between Scientism and Cynicism*. Amherst, N.Y.: Prometheus Books, 2003.

Haack, S. "Knowledge and Propaganda: Reflections of an Old Feminist." In *Manifesto of a Passionate Moderate: Unfashionable Essays*. Chicago: University of Chicago Press, 1998.

Haack, S. "Science as Social?—Yes and No." In *Manifesto of a Passionate Moderate: Unfashionable Essays*. Chicago: University of Chicago Press, 1998.

Hatten, J. E-mail to WMST-L@LISTSERV.UMD.EDU, August 24, 2005.

Herzig, R. M. "What about Biology? Building Sciences into Introductory Women's Studies Curricula." In *Feminist Science Studies: A New Generation*, edited by M. Mayberry, B. Subramaniam, and L. H. Weasel, 183–192. New York: Routledge, 2001.

Horowitz, D. Academic Bill of Rights. Available at www.studentsforacademicfreedom.org and www.FrontPagemag.com.

Kane, S. E-mail to WMST-L@LISTSERV.UMD.EDU, February 24, 2001.

Koerber, A., and M. M. Lay. "Understanding Women's Concerns in the International Setting Through the Lens of Science and Technology." In *Encompassing Gender: Integrating International Studies and Women's Studies*, edited by M. M. Lay, J. Monk, and D. S. Rosenfelt, 81–100. New York: The Feminist Press, 2002.

Koertge, N. "Critical Perspectives on Feminist Epistemology." In *Handbook of Feminist Research: Theory and Praxis*, edited by Sharlene Nagy Hesse-Biber, 553–66. Thousand Oaks, Calif.: Sage Publications, 2006.

Letherby, G. *Feminist Research in Theory and Practice*. Buckingham, UK: Open University Press, 2003.

MacKinnon, C. A. *Feminism Unmodified: Discourses on Life and Law.* Cambridge, Mass.: Harvard University Press, 1987.

MacNabb, E. L., et al. *Transforming the Disciplines: A Women's Studies Primer.* New York: The Haworth Press, 2001.

Marks, E. "Feminism's Perverse Effects." *Signs: Journal of Women in Culture and Society* 25:4 (2000): 1162–66.

Masaracchia, R. E-mail to WMST-L@LISTSERV.UMD.EDU, March 1, 2001.

Mayberry, M., B. Subramaniam, and L. H. Weasel. "Adventures Across Natures and Cultures: An Introduction." In *Feminist Science Studies: A New Generation,* edited by M. Mayberry, B. Subramaniam, and L. H. Weasel, 1–12. New York: Routledge, 2001.

Musial, J. E-mail to WMST-L@LISTSERV.UMD.EDU, August 23, 2005.

Nanda, M. "The Epistemic Charity of the Social Constructivist Critics of Science and Why the Third World Should Refuse the Offer." In *A House Built on Sand: Exposing Postmodernist Myths about Science,* edited by N. Koertge, 286–311. New York: Oxford University Press, 1998.

Nanda, M. *Prophets Facing Backward: Postmodern Critiques of Science and Hindu Nationalism in India.* New Brunswick, N.J.: Rutgers University Press. 2003.

Patai, D. E-mail to WMST-L@LISTSERV.UMD.EDU, August 5, 2001.

Patai, D. *Heterophobia: Sexual Harassment and the Future of Feminism.* Lanham, Md.: Rowman & Littlefield, 1998.

Patai, D. (2000). See chronicle.com/colloquylive/ transcripts/2000/10/20001004patai .htm. Retrieved 12/9/2007.

Patai, D., and N. Koertge. *Professing Feminism: Education and Indoctrination in Women's Studies,* rev. ed. Lanham, Md.: Lexington Books, 2003.

Pilcher, J., and I. Whelehan. *Fifty Key Concepts in Gender Studies.* London: Sage, 2004.

Pinnick, C. L. "Feminist Philosophy of Science: High Hopes." *Metascience* 9:2 (July 2000): 257–266.

PBS NewsHour with Jim Lehrer. "Evolution Debate," March 28, 2005.

Rice, P., and P. Waugh, eds. *Modern Literary Theory: A Reader,* 4th ed. London: Arnold, 2001.

Ristock, J. L. *No More Secrets: Violence in Lesbian Relationships.* New York: Routledge, 2002.

Rogers, M. F., and C. D. Garrett. *Who's Afraid of Women's Studies?: Feminisms in Everyday Life.* Walnut Creek, Calif.: AltaMira Press, 2002.

Rudacille, D. *The Riddle of Gender: Science, Activism, and Transgender Rights.* New York: Pantheon, 2005.

Ruth, S., ed. *Issues in Feminism: An Introduction to Women's Studies,* 4th ed. London: Mayfield, 1998.

Scollay, S. J., and C. S. Bratt. "Untying the Gordian Knot of Academic Sexual Harassment." In *Sexual Harassment on Campus: A Guide for Administrators, Faculty, and Students,* edited by B. R. Sandler and R. J. Shoops, 261–277. Boston: Allyn & Bacon, 1997.

Sokal, A., and J. Bricmont. *Fashionable Nonsense: Postmodern Intellectuals' Abuse of Science.* New York: Picador, 1998.

Subramaniam, B. "And the Mirror Cracked! Reflections of Natures and Cultures." In *Feminist Science Studies: A New Generation,* edited by M. Mayberry, B. Subramaniam, and L. H. Weasel, 55–62. New York: Routledge, 2001.

Tallentire, J. L. E-mail to WMST-L@LISTSERV.UMD.EDU, August 24, 2005.

Tallis, R. "Evidence-Based and Evidence-Free Generalisations." In *The Raymond Tallis Reader,* edited by Michael Grant, 309–329. Hampshire: Palgrave, 2000.

Trimberger, E. K. "Heterosexuality." In *The Reader's Companion to U.S. Women's History,* edited by W. Mankiller et al., 255. Boston: Houghton Mifflin, 1998.

U.S. Department of Education. *Projections of Education Statistics to 2013.* Washington, D.C.: National Center for Education Statistics, 2003. Available at nces.ed.gov/programs/projections.

Whitaker, M. P. L. "Oases in a Desert: Why a Hydrologist Meanders between Science and Women's Studies." In *Feminist Science Studies: A New Generation,* edited by M. Mayberry, B. Subramaniam, and L. H. Weasel, 48–54. New York: Routledge, 2001.

Winter, B. E-mail to WMST-L@LISTSERV.UMD.EDU, August 23 and 25, 2005.

25

On Writing *Theory's Empire**

Daphne Patai and Will H. Corral

THE PROJECT AND THE PROCESS

Mark Bauerlein, in his essay with which *Framing Theory's Empire* opens, asks: why another door-stopper of a book about theory? We are pleased to let him and the other contributors to this discussion argue about the appropriate responses to that question, and wish, here, merely to assure Bauerlein and others that *Theory's Empire* could easily have been twice its size. In fact, when we initially started compiling a list of substantive early pieces that were critical of Theory and its *maîtres*, we soon found ourselves with an entirely unmanageable list of essays (or chapters in books) that we considered very useful. This led to a bicoastal e-mail dialogue (Patai is in Massachusetts, Corral in California) as we engaged in contrapuntal readings and communications about those readings.

We recognized that a large volume of essays doing something other than celebrating or further explicating and legitimizing today's Theorists would be a hard sell to most publishers and indigestible to the type of readers we suspected would be our public. So from early in our project, we had in mind the need to select very carefully and judiciously. We were aiming not

---

*When our coedited book, *Theory's Empire: An Anthology of Dissent* (New York: Columbia Univeristy Press, 2005), appeared, John Holbo contacted us and said he wanted to sponsor a "book event" online, at TheValve.org. This indeed materialized, and for several days in July 2005, scholars debated our anthology and the state of Theory today. Holbo then edited and organized these exchanges into a volume and invited us to contribute to the book. What follows is a slightly revised version of the afterword Will Corral and I wrote for Holbo's volume, *Framing Theory's Empire.*(West Lafayette, In.: Glassbead Books, Parlor Press, 2007); also available online as a free PDF download at www.parlorpress.com/framingtheory.html.

only at breadth but also at depth, variety, and above all durability. In his first blog entry, John Holbo addresses the end result of our efforts, and in "*Theory's Empire*—Wrestling the Fog Bank," Sean McCann comments that our book "has already generated more extensive, vigorous, and fair discussion in the blogosphere than it ever will in the journals and conferences of literary academia." We are of course grateful for these posts and suspect McCann is right about the journals (though we've had generally positive reviews in the few academic journals that, thus far, have taken notice of the book).

As we worked on the book between about 2001 and 2004, key criteria in our selection from the works of well-known scholars became our own reactions to all that we read and re-read: Were the essays compelling? Were they still fresh and necessary? Had their arguments been incorporated into the discourse of the field so that their inclusion would be superfluous or too familiar? Did we find those arguments and critiques acknowledged and incorporated into recent anthologies of theory? Naturally, each essay led to others, and as a result we found ourselves with an ever-expanding corpus, going back more than four decades. And so we began to try out these essays in our own classes and by recommending them to our graduate students and inviting their responses.

Certainly there had always been disagreements, even acrimonious attacks and counterattacks, between and among theorists. What concerned us, however, was the failure of these debates to have an influence on the second and third generations of scholars, whose generally uncritical use of the *maîtres'* terms and concepts are what created the orthodoxy we refer to as Theory with a capital T. We also noticed that, if one really wanted to demonstrate one's theory credentials, the standard expectation involved the obligation to adopt politically engaged rhetoric (on the left, it need hardly be said), even though until the early nineties some major theorists, such as Derrida, had little to say about radical politics. We were concerned that where arguments had taken place, they were often couched as fights over political commitment and utility (Foucault vs. Derrida) rather than over scholarly depth.

As our list of contrarian essays grew, our initial reactions were of delight at the scope and subtlety of work challenging and demystifying the theorists who, from the early sixties on, were becoming the lords of Theory. Soon, however (and partially reiterating an argument we make in our general introduction to *Theory's Empire*), we realized with profound dismay that one after another of the standard anthologies we carefully read through failed to take account of this body of work, often to the point of simply not mentioning that such critiques had ever been voiced. Similarly, as we looked at the types of secondary or complementary sources available for use in theory classrooms, we were astonished that so rarely was there any mention of critics and criticisms of Theory—other than the occasional facile dismissal typically accompanied by slurs about challengers' politics. Thus students were being exposed to one side of a conversation, which no doubt helped explain the familiar monologues constantly heard to this day in literature departments, where merely dropping the right name or phrase served as a sufficient token of membership in a club that was increasingly hermetic even as its rhetoric became more and more commonplace in the academy.

Moreover, the concept of theory had obviously undergone a tremendous conceptual shift since the end of the sixties, and there was really no way to circumvent that development. We noticed that students born in the seventies and eighties were distancing themselves from the activism of the sixties while progressing toward merely verbal stances justified by postmodernist relativism, as we outlined in our introduction. We did not want to lament the depoliticization of theory, so our quandary was how to negotiate shifting values and perceptions while recovering what we deemed to be sensible and just readings, not the typical rereading of a rereading. The actual reading of theories and theorists that our book was designed to put in perspective has been replaced by many "guides for the perplexed," just as today there are numerous introductions to introductions to theory. It was hard to avoid skepticism as we noted that at the time Empson, Trilling, and others were theorizing, there were no guides to their writing, nor was there a need to have "accessible" accounts of the interrelationships between theory and students. As Cynthia Ozick laments in the April 2007 issue of *Harper's*, we are now missing the entire infrastructure of the serious criticism of previous decades. Thus, Ozick writes:

(Academic theorists equipped with advanced degrees, who make up yet another species of limited reviewers, are worthy only of a parenthesis. Their confining ideologies, heavily politicized and rendered in a kind of multisyllabic pidgin, have for decades marinated literature in dogma. Of these inflated dons and doctors it is futile to speak, since, unlike the hardier customer reviewers, they are destined to vanish like the fog they evoke.)

When we began looking for a publisher for our book, we first contacted Norton, which had just brought out its huge theory anthology. We hoped they might be an equal-opportunity publisher, but we were not unduly surprised when William Germano quickly responded to our query with a letter saying he doubted there was a market for our sort of book. Next we contacted an editor we shall call X, at prominent academic press Y, who was cautiously interested in our project. After considering it for about two months, he declined our proposal, telling us he had elicited "more than twenty reviews," and, even after eliminating the obviously biased negative reports, he could commit to such a project only if its market were clearly defined and if it had been, "in principle, embraced by the community." We were amused by the latter phrase, since of course what is "embraced by the community" is precisely what our book was challenging, and the clearly defined market may not emerge until the work is available and publicized. Still, we understood his concerns. What we did not readily understand was that, although X had initially assured us he would "of course" send all reports to us, we were never allowed to read them—unprecedented in our experience. Our request to see at least some of them, so that we might benefit from the criticisms of our peers, was met with silence.

This tale has an interesting postscript. In 2006, a colleague forwarded to us the letter he had initially received from X. Apparently, in 2002, X had written as follows to this potential reader (and to how many others, we wondered): "I have received the proposal below and I should be very grateful to have your advice on it. You will see that it is a reactionary project, that might be timely or not, or might be a spasm in the moribund body politic of those who never liked theory. . . ." The dismissive and prejudicial tone of this request strikes us as further evidence of the institutional hold of Theory, well beyond the academy. As for X, he has gone on to greater things at still more prestigious academic press Z.

Nonetheless, though we received half a dozen other rejections of our proposal over the next year, in late 2003 we found ourselves with two offers: from Columbia University Press and from Palgrave. When we contacted Jennifer Crewe at Columbia University Press, we were well aware that Columbia had published anthologies of the kind we criticize, as well as a considerable number of translations of work by theorists based in France. But Crewe surprised us with her enthusiasm. She made it clear she thought the timing was right for a project such as ours, and after receiving several positive reports (which were sent to us), debated with us at some length about the appropriate size and range of such a book. Just before Columbia finally accepted our project we received an offer of publication from Palgrave, but its contract required us—and this was the first we'd heard about this demand—to turn an 800-page text into a 300-page book. We both knew that a 300-page book critical of Theory would be pointless. As discussed in our introduction to *Theory's Empire*, a few such works exist and have proven easy to ignore, despite the high quality of their contents. From this reality we had taken the lesson that critical mass was important, as was the breadth and depth that a large book allowed us to achieve. Still, we understood that size is always an issue and so we reached a compromise with Crewe, forced ourselves to delete a number of essays, and the new, reduced version produced a 700-page book containing forty-seven essays by fifty scholars.

REACTIONS TO *THEORY'S EMPIRE*

For the past two years, since *Theory's Empire* appeared, we have regularly received letters and e-mails from professors and graduate students (and some general readers as well), thanking us for having published our book. We are also aware of the many comments, blurbs, and reviews on Internet bookstores stressing the timeliness and utility of our work. Almost all of the e-mail messages sent to us about our book make the same point: Any criticism of Theory or preference for a different approach to literature meets with intolerance or dismissal in the writer's academic milieu. Four examples—three of them received during March 2007—well represent these responses.

A British colleague, Brigid Lowe, who is a Research Fellow at Trinity College, Cambridge, wrote to us:

> I am part of a generation who, as students, were subjected to the Theory canon as revealed truth. In my first job I had to teach a Literary Theory course, with the capital letters. It would all have been much easier to survive if your volume had existed back then. . . . Theory is becoming accepted as common sense in English departments, and hence acquiring an invisibility that makes it hard to combat. I was quite shocked to find how hard a time I had getting my book published—presses couldn't seem to find two non-Theory readers to send it to, so I kept getting one good reader's report and one scandalized one. With typical inconsistency, the hostile readers at once claimed that Theory was all over, and that I was fighting paper tigers, and at the same time said things about it being impossible to "go back" to before Theory, and were openly outraged by my "insupportably negative" approach to Theoretical critics. I was shaken by their dismissiveness—they explicitly declined to engage with my argument, one on the grounds that she found it difficult to believe I would not change my opinion if I just re-read my opponents more carefully.

In response to our request for more details about her experiences, Lowe wrote as follows:

> My education in Theory as revealed truth began in 1997. My discontent dates to a lecture in an introductory course in my first semester, in which the lecturer gave a "feminist reading" of *Adam Bede*. I was moved to put my hand up and point out that she was what I, in my naïveté, called "misreading" the novel. I remember thinking she must really not have read it, and it seemed important to point out the facts before she embarrassed herself any further—but she told me no questions were allowed in lectures, and afterwards told me I would understand that hers was not a misreading once I'd read *The Madwoman in the Attic*. I did my BA in a small but quite well-regarded and traditional department, but by the time I left they had drawn up guidelines for students telling you what you would need to do to get each grade, in which it was explicitly stated that you could not get over 70% in an essay unless you

showed awareness of the ultimate opacity of language and the decentering of human agency, etc. . . .

To me the "Theory is over" argument is so unconvincing as to seem disingenuous. If you replied "right, so we can carry on with humanist criticism where we left off?" you would not get assent. What it really meant is that the argument is supposed to stop and that we all have to live with an apparatus of slightly washed-out and mechanical Theoretical premises and moves as our starting points. If Theory was really over, I don't think people would use that as a criticism of your book; history suggests that people don't usually have any problem dancing on the graves of cultural moments when they are genuinely over. No one criticized Lytton Strachey for ridiculing the Victorians on the grounds that the queen was already dead.

In this country, almost all English departments have at least one, and generally two, compulsory theory modules on their undergraduate programmes— and these always cover Althusser, Foucault and Lacan, and very seldom cover any recent "theorists" of literature who are not also Theorists. This is even true at those supposed bastions of traditional literary scholarship, Oxford and Cambridge. . . .

Because there is a generational frustration regarding the state of theory from the mid-nineties right up to the time we published our book, as attested by the brief testimonials in the entries by Christopher Conway and Kathleen Lowrey in *Framing Theory's Empire*, it is worth continuing with Lowe's observations:

I think in this country grad students are writing fewer really silly pure Theory dissertations these days—some "serious" study of primary texts is pretty much required in the better grad schools. But Theory has left a lot of that study a bit joyless—there's usually a thin pseudo-political Theory-ish argument used to pull together a lot of research on rather dry non-literary texts, and all the work gets done in the horribly predictable areas you mention in your intro ("constructions of national identity," for example). Everyone, but especially grads, are terrified of conveying any pleasure in or admiration for "literary texts," and they certainly aren't looking to theorize or understand the workings of pleasure or greatness.

This joylessness gets passed on in teaching—I'm shocked to see so many students utterly unenthusiastic about literature, and I do think Theory is greatly to blame.

Over here some bits of literary studies are worse hit than others. The few people who study poetry have a pretty good time, because it's harder to do that without some acknowledgment of pleasure and aesthetics, albeit implicit (I think Ricks is only able to say Theory is not worth arguing about because he works mainly on poetry rather than prose). The study of texts of the past is always more irritatingly self-righteous and accusatory than study of more recent stuff. And personally, I think the work done in my area—Victorian fiction—is worst of all.

Lowe's comments exemplify the very real and practical consequences our book sought to explore, for it is also obvious from other contributions published in *Framing Theory's Empire* (such as those by Burke and McCann) that any problem surrounding theory is now institutionally based. We are thus delighted that Lowe's story has a happy ending. Her book, *Victorian Fiction and the Insights of Sympathy: An Alternative to the Hermeneutics of Suspicion*, was indeed published, in early 2007.

A second e-mail we received recently was from Charlie Wesley, a Ph.D. student in English at Binghamton University, who describes himself as having "an uneasy relationship with theory."

> For a long time I have enjoyed theory, but of late I've experienced a discomfort with it that I couldn't quite articulate (this is often a problem for many students of postmodernism). Heck, I have even used theory dogmatically from time to time, partly because my passion for it was great. But when a few friends of mine (who are MA students quite into theory themselves) saw an advertisement for *Theory's Empire*, they rolled their eyes and instantly labeled the text a "conservative" rant against "people who are trying to change the world." The dogma of their statements—a dogma I had been participating in for quite a while—stuck with me, and has caused me to become more and more critical of the almost fanatically religious overtones that many "theory heads" espouse. That was a few years ago. A few weeks ago, I finally started reading *Theory's Empire*, and I was shocked that so many of my own feelings about the uncritical, overly political, contradictory, twisted logic of the "theory folks" were articulated in this collection. . . . Thank you for helping to give me a new insight into the English literature field, a new openness, and a sense of possibility.

Yet another graduate student, Matthew Goodwin, now at the University of Massachusetts, Amherst, by chance spoke to one of us recently of how relieved he was to come across *Theory's Empire*, whose introduction confirmed many of his own observations. We then asked him if he'd be inclined to set in writing an account of his experiences. He responded that not only would he be glad to do so, but that it was something he'd been wanting and needing to do for some time. To our surprise, he then sent us a brief essay, from which we've extracted a few paragraphs. Goodwin has a B.A. and an M.A. in philosophy, had worked for some years in nonprofit organizations dealing with immigrant communities, and had returned to school out of a love of literature. What he found were courses heavy in Theory and disinclined both to wonder why some theories become fashionable and others do not and to take a critical look at the very institutionalization of Theory that such courses presupposed. "The central tenet of Theory," he wrote, "is that literature should be examined critically using some particular theorist. And this tenet shapes undergraduate composition classes up to the highest levels of graduate study." Generally, he continued,

> the particular theorist being used has written the theory in another context such as philosophy or one of the social sciences. The theory is often taken for granted and left unquestioned. For example, I studied Wittgenstein as a philosophy graduate student and when I entered the field of literature I was amazed at how just a couple of his popular sentences were used to prove some point in an argument. Those who used him in this way generally did not understand his place in the history of philosophy or that there were alternative views. This is a problem if the theorist is taken as the *only* authority in a particular field, in this case, the philosophy of language (and there are philosophers who are guilty of the same thing). When the theory is not taken for granted and is questioned, it is done so from a perspective outside of the discipline from which it arose. This is not an absolute problem. However, it makes the arguments highly limited and normally they cannot attain to the claims made by the literary theorist.
>
> When I entered a Comparative Literature department as a Masters student, I took an introduction to Comparative Literature course. In addition to discussions about the field of Comparative Literature, a large part of the content of the course was an overview of literary theory and its application. The class was engaging, and the professor was interested in debate, yet the class took various philosophical texts out of their context in terms of the debate surrounding the theorist and the philosophical history leading up to the theorist. In my eyes this was a problem for some of the students who did not have this philosophical background. Similarly I knew that my understanding of, say, Freudian Theory was limited, as it was taken out of context of the vibrant debate among psychoanalysts. I later took Literary Theory with a professor, a Marxist critic, who generally gave a fair reading of all the major literary theorists. The class consisted of lectures and discussion was not encouraged, and the students were asked to mimic this style with their own presentations. What was clearly not criticized was Theory itself and its place in the study of literature.

Nevertheless Goodwin persisted, with the following results:

> When I started the Ph.D at another university, I again took an introduction to Comparative Literature course. Similar problems arose as students struggled to debate Derrida, but here the fashionable nature of the field was stressed and current trends were valued simply as current trends. One major concern in the class, and in the anthology of comparativists used, was to search for what Comparative Literature consisted of or what it should be, a kind of theodicy of comparative literature: how to justify our ways to the academy. My perspective was that we did not need to justify our field, and to find out what we are, we would only need to look around and see what we are in fact doing. Thinking about this issue in Comparative Literature now, I think that behind this anxiety is the desire to find the next fashion first, or at least to be on the bandwagon at its start. And of course there are budget or job concerns.

The benefits of these theory classes are many, and I certainly read many texts I would not have in a basic literature class or a normal philosophy department. However, I always felt that the classes relied too heavily on the assumed authority of the theorists. And when these theorists were questioned, they were questioned clumsily and without real dialogue since not every student could have experience in every discipline.

Once again, as with Lowe, the consequences of challenging the received wisdom about Theory were not good:

> [Early in my PhD program] I said to another graduate student that I was skeptical of the arbitrary use of theory. Eventually this discussion got around the department, and I ended up being labeled as anti-theory. This result was strange to me for a variety of reasons, the biggest being that I have been, in my opinion, very theoretically-oriented my whole life. Nevertheless, it seems to be the case that in the current situation, where Theory is the status quo, to question Theory is to not do Theory at all. But it does not need to be so.

In many ways the concerns of the younger scholars we have quoted at length mirror those expressed in some of the blogs entries collected in *Framing Theory's Empire*, and together they are additional proof of the need to have similar forums widely disseminated. What these individuals experience is group-thought that reinforces the view that one has to stake out an already well-established political and rhetorical posture if one wants to succeed in literature departments today. Self-congratulatory professions of commitment from teachers of theory make it impossible to divorce theory from its purported radicalism and from its role in carving out a career for oneself, since the goal is to see oneself as a powerful agent of political advocacy all the while enjoying the considerable perks of the academic life. Nor is this merely a current defect of literature departments. As should be obvious to anyone in the academy, though with a bit of a lag, the same assumptions have found their way beyond language and literature departments. It is now no surprise to meet historians and colleagues in other fields who tell us that their kind of work is disdained by colleagues who are "into Theory."

Several years ago, before our book came out, we received an unexpected e-mail from a professor in the Midwest, recounting his own recollections of graduate school in the eighties:

> My name is Jon Erickson, I am an associate professor in the English Department at Ohio State University. I've been meaning to write to you for a while, partially because I was asked by a publisher last year to review the proposal of your book [*Theory's Empire*]. I was very enthusiastic about your project, not least because I have been teaching critical theory in our department almost since the time I was hired, in 1990, both to grads and undergrads.

I spent the 1980s in grad school at the University of Wisconsin, Milwaukee, getting one of the first degrees in "Modern Studies" there, out of the English Department, and connected with the functions of the Center for Twentieth Century Studies. My attitude toward Theory is a lot more sanguine than many of my colleagues', largely because I was so inundated with it in my time there, not simply in the forms of texts, but in encountering the famous theorists first-hand. Here are a few of those I encountered in lectures, classes, workshops, and even lunch: Lyotard, Jameson, Said, Kristeva, de Man, Hartmann, Baudrillard, Stuart Hall, Dick Hebdige, Marjorie Garber, Mary Poovey, the list goes on.

What's more, there were the people who taught there: Andreas Huyssen, Teresa de Lauretis, Jane Gallop, Tania Modleski. There was only one professor, Ihab Hassan, who, while well respected for his work in postmodernism, was resistant to the over politicizing of every aspect of literary study. He was even called a fascist by a few radical Leftist students, which was upsetting to him. I have come to respect his principled stance, his willingness to stand by litera-ture and the value of individual creativity in the face of ideological dogmatics.

In any case, I found your proposal exciting because after so many years of teaching the same material over and over, Barthes, Derrida, Foucault, Lacan, various Marxists, gender feminists, etc., etc., it was becoming clearer to me just how little sense much of it was making to me. This was abetted by the fact that I also read Anglo-American philosophy (in particular moral and political phi-losophy), stuff that is much clearer and more rigorous in its argumentation.

My interest in this philosophy was stimulated by my brother-in-law who teaches moral philosophy in a small college in Massachusetts, and who has been suggesting authors to me ever since I was in grad school. (I recall once giving him Baudrillard to read, and hearing peals of laughter coming from his office as he did so.)

What has happened in the last couple of years is that I started giving students in my "Foundations of Contemporary Critical Theory" graduate class critical essays and some bibliographies of works critical of the theory they were learn-ing. When I looked over your proposal I discovered that several of the authors in your book were authors I recommended in my lists. . . .

We then wrote back to Erickson, and received some further comments:

I was thinking about your question about why students are still so attracted to Theory. When I was in grad school, Theory was just coming in, so there were real fights with the old guard (who usually took the position of E. D. Hirsch), and so there seemed to be something real at stake. It was also the case that not everyone who was reading the new theory bought it all either; so, for instance, there were real arguments between Marxists and Foucauldians and Derrideans.

Once all the new approaches became orthodoxy in the nineties, those ten-sions seemed to have disappeared, and people picked and chose their theories without worrying about contradictions, and one could be a Marxian Fou-cauldian without blinking. Now the attraction I think is this: on the one hand the rhetoric of Theory is still operating at that guerrilla warfare kind of pitch, which will always attract post-adolescents (up until their 30s these days) who want to appear anti-authoritarian and radical. At the same time it is completely safe, because it is, in fact, the orthodoxy of the academy that completely protects you from the nature of real life, and indeed, authorizes you. (I tell my students that my response to the bumper sticker "Question Authority" is: "who says I should question authority?") "Radical" ends up taking on the same kind of meaning that it does in style for skatepunks, for instance. I remarked in the seminar where I gave a paper [on this subject] that people wear the names of Foucault and Derrida and (above all) Deleuze & Guattari in their papers and conversation like they wear Tommy Hilfiger clothes. Theory has become "designer theory" in effect. (It actually seems all of a piece with how David Brooks describes bohemian capitalism in his book *Bobos in Paradise*.)

I think the other thing is that there is some kind of mythic power attached to theory, as if it is some form of intellectual martial art: you learn the language like you would learn fighting moves. The only problem is that your opponents are all straw men, since it can't really be used in arguments with people who don't know what you're talking about. So it's basically a form of braggadocio among the cognoscenti. I think of the word "strategic" for instance, as in Gayatri Spivak's "strategic essentialism." Who among those not in the know, that one is presumably using "strategic essentialism" against, would have any idea, or care, what you are doing? (Outside of the fact that you're not being honest with them.) Replace the word "strategic" with the word "convenient" and it makes as much sense.

We have always known that some colleagues teach theory from a critical point of view, but more—whether those who came to maturity with Theory (and are now reaching retirement age) or others, perhaps newer to the profession and seeking to demonstrate their credentials—seem content to teach the "greatest theoretical hits" without inviting criticism, and often in fact discourage or disallow it. In recent years we've encountered few graduate students, and also few young colleagues, who are at all acquainted with earlier theorists or with basic texts preceding the advent of Theory. No lessening of the expectation that new Ph.D.s will always be able to "do Theory" is in the wind, and few are the departments that address this issue directly and ask whether indeed all their faculty need to have the same sort of orientation.

Theory, with the capital T we specified in our introduction to *Theory's Empire*, it would appear, though still hanging on as a now-institutionalized, hardly transgressive presence in the academy, has come to a standstill. Nevertheless, Theory's hold over humanities departments, like its status as the preferred academic discourse today, does not seem to be waning—judging by the job ads, course descriptions, and dissertation topics we repeatedly encounter. Meanwhile, it is likely that serious challenges to received theorists' status will keep appearing—challenges such as Robert Irwin's recent (2006) rereading of Said's *Orientalism*, or the revised, enlarged, and retranslated version of Foucault's *Madness and Civilization* that is raising questions about the

French master's "isolation from the world of facts and scholarship," according to a (March 21, 2007) review by Andrew Scull in the *Times Literary Supplement*. Whether or not these challenges will find their way into literature departments is a separate matter. So far, we see little sign of that at an institutional level. However, the kinds of comments we've quoted at length above suggest to us that some younger colleagues and soon-to-be colleagues are indeed approaching the entire Theory scene from a fresh perspective, and that in a piecemeal way they are helping to restore some much-needed balance and rationality to the study of literature. To assist them in such an endeavor was a primary aim of our book.

April 2007

Index

abortion, 101, 141, 159, 168, 231, 263
Abrams, Kathryn, 198
academic affairs, novels relating to,
    223–49 (passim)
Academic Bill of Rights, 263, 272n38
academic freedom: 6, 37–38, 211–16,
    216n2, 218, 252, 263, 272n38;
    conference on, 211–16; feminist
    attacks on, 49, 214–15, 263;
    feminist dependence on, 215;
    history of, 212; vs. license, 35;
    purpose of, 216; threats to, 32, 35,
    38, 49, 21, 211–16; values assumed
    by, 212
Academic Keywords (Nelson and Watt),
    211–12
academics: liberal values of, 66, 212;
    orthodoxies of, 6, 215–16, 221, 233;
    solipsism of, 79
Adam Bede (Eliot), 281
advocacy, and education, 27, 95, 110,
    125, 214, 221, 253, 260, 262, 265,
    285
Affirmative action, 111, 168, 215
Afghanistan, 163
Against All Hope (Valladares), 115
Against Our Will (Brownmiller),
    161–62

Agosin, Marjorie, 114
Ahmadinejad, 62
All About Eve (film), 236
Althusser, Louis, 282
America: attacks on, 61, 62, as "rape
    culture," 10n8; sexual repression in,
    144, 230
American Association of University
    Professors (AAUP), 212, 214, 216,
    216n1, 272n38; on academic
    freedom, 212–13, 272n38
*American Booksellers Association Inc. v.
    Hudnut*, 184, 186
American Civil Liberties Union
    (ACLU), 167, 183, 193, 198, 199
American Pastoral (Roth), 227
Anderson, Hans-Christian, 33
Animal Farm (Orwell), 60n30
anthropology: development of, 74
anti-Americanism, and free speech,
    219
Antifeminism in the Academy (Clark,
    Garner, Higgonet, and Katrak), 214
"antifeminist intellectual harassment,"
    214–15
Antioch College, 175
anti-intellectualism, of women's
    studies, 90–91, 109, 110

anti-pornography: activism, 179, 184; ordinance, 185
anti-Semitism, 65–66; in Muslim world, 65, 146; in Europe, 65
anti-utopian fiction, 25, 26, 27
anti-war movement, in U.S., 65: politics of, 65
anti-Zionist propaganda, 65
Aphra: The Feminist Literary Magazine, 157
Arab countries: and anti-Semitism, 65; inequalities in, 63; Israel and, 63–67; number of, 63; population of, 63; problems of, 63
Arabs: hostility to Israel, 63; hostility toward, in U.S., 66; and identity, 64; migration from Palestine, 63; and non-Muslims, 63; and propaganda war, 63
Archard, David, 175
argumentation, norms of, 5
Armenians, slaughter of, 1
"asymmetrical relationships:" 34, 50, 173, 223, 224, 233; defenses of, 232, 246
Atkinson, Ti-Grace, 139
Atwood, Margaret, 37, 182
"authority of experience," 117, 160, 265
autobiographical writing, 79–82, 92

backlash, charges of: 29, 85, 91, 92, 123, 135, 256, 260
Backlash (Faludi), 85
Bailey II, Charles W., 153
Barash, David, 268–69n11
Barber, Benjamin R., 242
Barthes, Roland, 82, 286
Bates College, 258
Baudrillard, Jean, 286
Bauerlein, Mark, 221, 277
de Beauvoir, Simone, 133
Bedard, Rachel, 140
Behar, Ruth, 80
Bengalis, massacre of, 2
Benz, Stephen, 122
Berkeley free speech movement, 32

Beverley, John, 115–16, 121, 123, 126n1, 127n11
Bible, Hebrew, 61
Bin Laden, Osama, 67
Binghamton University, 283
BIODENIAL, 86, 165n4
biology: feminist attacks on, 4–6, 162–63, 256–59, 269n18, 270–71n32; in patriarchal society, 258; significance of, 162–63. *See also* feminism: and science; sexual dimorphism; social constructionism.
"biophobia," 159
birth rate: and women's education, 99
blacks, 144
black studies, 3
Blasquez, Adélaïde, 119
Bloom, Harold, 260
Blue Angel (Prose), 235–42, 246
The Blue Angel (film), 236, 238, 239
Bobos in Paradise (Brooks), 287
Bockris, Victor, 139
Bok, Sissela, 120
books: burning of, 36, 41n13; censorship of, 39; as dangerous, 36
Bourne, Jenny, 18
Bradbury, Ray, 36
Bratt, Carolyn, 215
Brave New World (Huxley), 25, 27–28, 34, 48
Brawley, Tawana, 11n8, 113–114
Brazil: military rule in, ix–x, 32; research in, 71–72, 118; slum-dwellers in, 99; teaching in, 32; women in, 71, 74, 76, 79, 103, 118
Brazilian Women Speak (Patai), 71, 118
The Breast (Roth), 227
Bresnahan, Eileen, 196
Bricmont, Jean, 256
Brittain, Vera, 47
Brooks, David, 287
The Brothers Karazmaov (Dostoyevsky), 36–37
Brownmiller, Susan, 161–162, 163, 190
Bunch, Charlotte, 161
Burdekin, Katharine, 52, 145

Burgos, Elisabeth, 114, 118, 119, 120, 127n21
Burke, Timothy, 283
Bush, George W., 65, 66
Bushspeak, 52
Butler, Samuel, 110

A Cadre School Life (Jaing), 41–42n19
Caird, Mona, 133
Campus Watch (website), 218, 220
Can We Wear Our Pearls and Still Be Feminists? (Mandle), 105–107
Canadian Civil Liberties Association, 198
Cardoso, Fernando Henrique, 32
Cardozo Law School, 199
Carey-Webb, Stephen, 122
Caring for Justice (West), 190
Castro, Fidel, 115, 124
Cataldi, Suzanne, 270n23
celibacy, 161
Chamberlain, Mariam K., 108
Chicago Tribune, 192
"chilly climate," as feminist charge, 91, 108
China, lack of freedom in, 33–34, 38–39, 41n19
Christian studies program, 95
Christian X, King of Denmark, 218
Christianity, 61; Muslim attacks on, 66; reform of, 62
The Chronicle of Higher Education, 16, 26, 58, 114, 219, 255
Church, Roman Catholic, 37
Churchill, Ward, 9–10n4
City Journal, 190
civil rights: and identity politics, 1, 3; of minorities, 256
Civil Rights Act, 1964, 168
"The Classroom Climate: A Chilly One for Women?" (report), 91
Cline, Sally, 161
Cleveland, Grover, 134
Clinton, Bill, 225, 227, 242
Cockburn, Alexander, 55
Code, Lorraine, 198
Colgate University, 105–106

Collins, Catherine Ann, 122
Columbia University Press, 280
Comfort, Alex, 56, 57
Coming Up for Air (Orwell), 99
community/collective values: criticism of, 124; idealization of, 123–24, 125. *See also* individualism.
competition, feminist critique of, 90
"compulsory heterosexuality," 161, 259
Connerly, Ward, 215
"consensual relations," banning of, 173
consent, meaning of: 49, 133, 141, 154, 173, 175; MacKinnon on, 181–203 (passim)
"conservative," as slur, 27, 175, 211, 212, 221, 260–61, 283
Conway, Christopher, 282
Cooper, Edmund, 28
Corral, Will H., 277–88
Coyne, Jerry, 158, 163–64
Craib, Ian, 267n8
creation science (creationism), 6, 261, 262, 271n33
Crewe, Jennifer, 280
critical race theorists, 40n4, 50, 177, 213
Crosson, Patricia, 44
Crouch, Margaret, 171–74, 176
Cuba, 115, 124, 127
Cuban Revolution, 124
cultural feminists, 97, 100, 101
cultural relativism, 7, 264
Cultural Revolution (China), 33, 38, 41n19
Cutler III, William, 117

defamiliarization, 28
Daly, Martin, 159, 162, 163
Daly, Mary, 29, 136, 138
Daring to Be Bad (Echols), 269n19
"Darwinian feminism," 270–71n32
Darwinism, hostility to, 159, 163, 164, 270–71n32
Davison, Peter, 54, 56, 57
The Day of the Women (Kettle), 28
The Death of Nature (Merchant), 160

defamation, law of, 181, 184, 185–86, 187, 192, 195, 197; "actual malice" test in, 186
Defending Pornography (Strossen), 183, 199
Delbanco, Nicholas, 232–35, 246
Deleuze, Gilles, 287
Demolition Man (film), 27–28
Denmark: and Islam, 62; and Jews, 218
Derrida, Jacques, 5, 278, 284, 286, 287
Descartes, 111
The Development of Academic Freedom in the United States (Metzger and Hofsadter), 212
Dhimmitude, 64
Diary of a Survivor (Rodríguez), 124
Dickstein, Morris, 57
Diegues, Carlos, ix–xi
difference, sexual: as social construct, 49
dimorphism. *See* sexual dimorphism.
Domestic Tranquility (Graglia), 97–104
Dostoyevsky, Fyodor, 36
due process: decline of, 30, 50, 143, 144, 167, 170, 178, 179, 182, 239
Duke University, 11n8
Dworkin, Andrea, 29, 101, 136, 138, 141, 182, 183, 189, 191, 192, 195, 200, 269n19
The Dying Animal (Roth), 227–30, 232
dystopias and dystopian fiction, 27, 34, 36, 48, 182; "Grand Inquisitor" scene in, 36; and misogyny, 28; privacy effaced in, 50; regulation of sexuality in, 34
Dziech, Billie, 173, 175

Easterbrook, Frank. H., 185
Echols, Alice, 269n19
economic dependency, of women, 98
education: aims of, 175, American, xi; biases of, 254; and declining birth rate, 99; feminist approach to, 83–95 (passim), 207–10, 253–75 (passim); feminist policing of, 49, 207–10; of girls, 91; as harmful to women, 97; and imagination, 38,

58; vs. indoctrination, 92, 92, 110, 111, 218, 220, 222, 254, 265n1; law's role in, 213; liberal, 252, 254; as political, 58, 67, 85, 93, 221, 251–252, 254–255, 263, 265–266n2, 272n38; politicization of, 84, 88, 210, 218, 221, 259, 260, 261, 263; and rhetoric of activism, 31, 58, 253, 254; statistics on, 271–72n36; and women's studies, x, 49, 84, 91, 105–12, 208–10, 253–75 (passim)
Egypt, 64,
Eisenstein, Zillah, 189
e-mail lists, problems of, 38–39
Emory University, 215, 221
Empson, William, 279
Encyclopedia of Feminist Theories, 198
Enlightenment: bankruptcy of, 68; tradition of, 2
Ensler, Eve, 215
epistemology: feminist, 210, 261, 264; of oppressed groups, 8; politics and, 261; standpoint, 5, 261, 264
Equal Employment Opportunity Commission (EEOC), 171, 180n1
equality: attacks on, 26, 214; demand for, 25, 126, 145, 160, 172, 173, 182, 185, 224
Erickson, Jon, 285–287
Eros, defense of, 149–50
essentialism: and feminist contradictions, 258, 269n19
Estrich, Susan, 197
ethnography, feminist, 75, 119, 258
"Eurocentric"/Eurocentrism, as slur, 17, 68, 110
Evans, Sara M., 189
evolution, teaching of, 6, 261–62, 270–71n32m 271n33; and feminism, 261–62
The Evolution of Human Sexuality (Symons), 162
evolutionary biology, 158–59; feminist hostility to, 159, 161, 162, 163, 270–71n32; and social policy, 162–63, 164

evolutionary psychology, 6, 163–64, 172

Face–Time (Tarloff), 242
Fahrenheit 451 (Bradbury), 36
Faludi, Susan, 85, 270n23
Farrell, Warren, 190, 197
fascism: Islamic, 66; Orwell on, 52, 54, 56
fathers, attacks on, 137, 144
Fausto-Sterling, Anne, 161; on sexual dimorphism, 256, 257, 258, 266n5, 267n9, 267–69n11
feminism, 48: and the academy, ix, 49, 84, 93, 207–10, 214–15, 253–75 (passim); achievements of, 83, 84, 162; anti-intellectualism of, 85, 90–91; authoritarianism of, 141, 177; and "authority of experience," 265; as beleaguered, 94; biological determinism of, 262; on the body, 75, 135, 258; and celibacy, 161; and censorship, 167; and conflict resolution, 140–41; and concept stretching, 164; criticisms of, x, 83, 147–51; critics vilified by, 149–51, 260; and desire, 149; development of, 209–10; and "difference," 136, 160; and disparities, 271–72n36; distinctions disregarded in, 149–50; double standards of, 49, 85, 93, 134, 179, 264, 265; as dystopian, 144; emotion and reason in, 158; on epistemology, 5, 210, 261, 264; and essentialism, 258; ethnography and, 75, 119, 258; exaggerations of, 150, 208–10; and family life, 97–104; fragmentation of, 136; future of, 83–95 (passim); on gender vs. sex, 256; generational conflicts in, 150; and "genital myth," 161; goals of, 145, 259; and hostility to heterosexuality, 101, 133–46 (passim), 154, 15, 161. *See also* Heterophobia; ideological policing in, 15–16; illiberalism of, 94; inconsistencies of, 160, 161, 262; and indoctrination, 92, 93; and informed consent, 154; and integrated/intersectional analysis, 7, 109, 110, 257; and intersex, 258; and joy, 149; law and, 85, 155; "leveling" impulse in, 31, 91; liberal, 254; and literature, 260, 281, loss of faith in, 147; men caricatured in, 149–50; and pedagogy, 253–75 (passim); personal, vs. political in, 153–55; "perverse effects" of, 260; political activism and, 95, 107, 142, 160, 252, 255, 259; and pornography, 167, 183, 185; and postmodernism, 264; power of, 142–43, 150, 272n36; public/private distinction in, 141, 143, 144, 153–55; punitive attitude of, 148–50; and race, 81, 89, 90; radical, 29, 254; rape and, 92, 159, 164, 191; and research, 75, 80–82, 253–75 (passim), 266n5; rhetoric of, x, 93, 142, 144, 149, 191; science attacked by, 49, 87, 160, 255, 256–59, 263, 266n5, 266–67n6, 269n18, 272n40; second-wave, 256; self-criticism in, 145; and sexual dimorphism, 256–59; and sexual harassment, 154, 155, 167–80, 213; and sexuality, 149–50, 154–55; and social constructionism, 256; and standards of evidence,8, 262, 263; state censorship and, 38; strategies of, 85; successes of, 107–108, 143, 145; True Believers in, 88, 93; truth and, 92, 93, 261, 263; as utopian, ix, 84; and victim status, 93, 178; vigilantism of, 50, 56, 58, 144, 149, 150, 155, 167, 179, 223, 224, 225, 242, 246; vilification of critics of, 150; and warped judgment, 148; and white privilege, 92; women's alienation from, 135, 142, 144. *See also* women's studies.
Feminism Unmodified (MacKinnon), 173, 182, 187, 188, 191, 198, 199, 254

The Feminist Classroom (Maher and
   Tetreault), 88
feminist classrooms, 88, 90, 259, 262,
   267
feminist extremism/extremists, 29, 101,
   133–46 (passim) 162; harms of,
   144–45; on rape, 162, 198. *See also*
   MacKinnon.
feminist pedagogy, ix, 49, 253–75
   (passim); anti-intellectualism of,
   102; critics of, 109, double
   standards of, 265; examples of,
   90–92, 108, 109, 110, 111, 264;
   experience vs. knowledge in, 90,
   108; and identity, 108, 264; law
   and, 146; opportunism of, 262,
   262–65; political agenda of, 89, 90,
   92, 145–46, 253, 254, 259, 263,
   265; political conformity in, 108;
   problems of, 253, 254, 259, 260,
   261; vs. reality, 263; self-destructive
   habits of, 261, 264; weaknesses of,
   88, 100, 255, 264. *See also* women's
   studies.
The Feminist Press (publishing house),
   107
feminist purity: search for, 15–19
Feminist Science Studies (Mayberry,
   Subramaniam, and Weasel),
   257–58, 263
feminists, American: on Islamism, 66
Feminists Theorize the Political (Butler
   and Scott), 191
FEMISA (e-mail list), 38, 39, 137
Ferguson, Ann, 215
fiction, power of, 223, 225
First Amendment, 4, 26, 171; defense
   of, 9n2, 144, 182, 183, 184, 185,
   192, 193, 214, 219, 220; and public
   debate, 192
The First Stone (Garner), 147–51
Fish, Stanley, 215
Fisher, Elizabeth, 157
Fitzgerald, Edward, 25
Flaubert, Gustave, 234
Ford Foundation, and women's studies,
   108

Foucault, Michel, 73, 278, 282, 286,
   287
Foundation for Individual Rights in
   Education (FIRE), 3, 58, 60n38,
   182–83; creation of, 182; mission
   of, 182
FOX (news network), 66
Framing Theory's Empire (Holbo), 277,
   282, 283, 285
France, 138
Francis, Leslie Pickering, 174–78
free press, in Middle East, 65
free speech: and American Association
   of University Professors (AAUP),
   212–13, 214; attacks on, 49, 143,
   192, 214; "chilling" of, 217, 220,
   221; and coerced speech, 171;
   decline of, xi; 3, 62; defense of, 58;
   181–203, 217–18, 219; double
   standards for, 27, 40, 49, 214, 219,
   221; and First Amendment, 4, 26,
   171, 185, 192, 214, 219, 220; and
   Internet, 217–19; regulation of,
   25–42; and viewpoint neutrality,
   171, 185
Free Speech for Me, but Not for Thee
   (Hentoff), 192
free speech movement, 32, 221
freedom: as burden, 36–38, 39; and
   state censorship, 38; intellectuals
   and, 57
French feminists, on science, 256
Frisch, Michael, 80
Fundamental Feminism (Grant), 192
Fundamentalism/fundamentalists, 7:
   agendas of, 67; Christian, xi, 10n8,
   37, 61–62, 63, 66, 95; creationism
   and, 6; Jewish, 63; Muslim/Islamic,
   xi, 10n8, 61–68; religion and, 7
Furedi, Frank, 5, 6

Gallop, Jane, 175, 232, 276, 286
Garber, Marjorie, 286
Garner, Helen, 147–151
Garrett, C. D., 257
Gaston Lucas, serrurier (Blasquez), 119
gay rights, 142. *See also* homosexuality

Gearhart, Sally Miller, 139–40, 142
gender: and biology, 161; and sex, distinguished, 161, 256; as social construct, 107, 161, 256, 257; feminist "problematizing" of, 141
GENDERAGENDA, 87
Gender Genocide (Cooper), 28
gender identity: biology of, 256–57, 267; as hardwired, 269n12; as protected category, 3. *See also* sexual identity.
genetic fallacy, 5
Georgetown University, 190, 215
Germany, war with, 54
Gilman, Charlotte Perkins, 83, 102, 141
Gitlin, Todd, x
Gladstein, Mimi Reisel, 109
Glazer, Nona, 109, 110
The Golden Notebook (Lessing), 57, 81
Goldstein, Al, 192
Goodbye, Columbus (Roth), 232
Goodwin, Matthew, 283–285
Gornick, Vivian, 139
Graglia, F. Carolyn, 97–104; on abortion, 101, as ahistorical, 97–98; on educating women, 97; essentialism of, 97, 100; on ideal housewife, 100; on Jews, 102; on male and female natures, 98; on men, 98, 100, 101; on mothering, 97, 98, 100; 1; on separate spheres, 97, 98; on sexual intercourse, 10; on traditional roles, 97, 98, 99, 100; on women's choices, 97, 103; on "women's pact" 101
Germano, William, 279
Graham, Dee, 190
"Grand Inquisitor" scene, in fiction, 36–37
Grayling, A. C., 6
The Great Scourge (Pankhurst), 134
Guatemala, 113, 114, 123, 126n5, 127n21
Guattari, Félix, 287
Guedalla, Philip, 55, 60n30

Haack, Susan, 261, 270n27
hagiography, and history, 113

Hajdin, Mane, 168–171, 172, 173, 176, 178–79
Haldane, J. B. S., 56
Hale, Sondra, 119
Hall, Radclyffe, 39
Hall, Stuart, 286
Hamas, 63
The Handmaid's Tale (Atwood), 37
Hankiss, Agnes, 118
harassment: definitions of, 26; policies, 3, 10n5, 21–24, 26, 50, 58, 171, 211, 213, 214, 219, 220, 221, 252, 263; hostile environment, 21, 167, 174, 180, 213, 214; intellectual, 214; quid pro quo, 21, 174; third party, 21, 50, 177, 189; types of, 21–24, 29, 50, 144, 174, 214; and violence, conflated, 149. *See also* sexual harassment.
Hartman, Geoffrey, 286
Harvard Crimson, 3
Harvard Law School, 217
Harvard University, 3, 10n5, 272n36
Hassan, Ihab, 286
Hebdige, Richard, 286
Heins, Marjorie, 198, 199
Hemingway, Ernest, 110
Herland (Gilman), 141
Herzig, Rebecca, 258
Hentoff, Nat, 192
Heterophobia (Patai), 29
heterophobia, 29, 30, 133–46, 155: criticism of concept, 145; as damaging to feminism, 144–45; defined, 94, 133; double standards of, 134; heterosexual women and, 94, 101, 155; history of, 133–134; lesbians and, 94, 133; and totalitarianism, 144; Victorianism and, 144
heterosexism, 5, 31, 161
heterosexual intercourse: as coereced, 198; as corrupting, 134; and rape, 133, 136, 161–62, 181–203 (passim); and sado-masochism, 190
heterosexuality: 134, 135, 140, 142; and biology, 161, 162, 258, 259;

caricatured, 29; as compulsory, 161, 259; and consent, 49, 133; feminist views of, 28, 29, 94, 101, 133, 134, 141, 142, 143, 154, 155, 161, 162, 173, 188, 258; as institution, 258–59; as key to male dominance, 161, 162. 258–59; as natural, 162, 258; as social construct, 4, 49, 142, 161, 162, 173, 188, 257, 259
Hezbollah, 62
hierarchy, feminist opposition to, 27, 75, 90, 108
higher education: corporatization of, 211, 214; deteriorization of, 252; feminist overhaul of, 207– 10; goals of, 175; ideals of, 251, identity politics in, 252; identity programs in, 6, 252; integrity in, xi, 255, 259, 261, 267–68n11; political agenda of, 252, 255, 262, 263; political rhetoric in, 31; threats from within, 211, 251, 252; women in, 108, 209, 271n36
Hilfiger, Tommy, 287
Hillel, Rabbi, 68
Hirsch, E. D., 286
Hirsi Ali, Ayaan, 10–11n8
Hispanics, 144
Hitchens, Christopher, 53–54
Hitler, Adolf, 1, 52, 55, 159
Hofstadter, Richard, 212, 214
Holbo, John, 277
Holmes, Robert, 175
Homicide (Daly and Wilson), 159, 162
homosexuality, 134, 142; in Israel, 65; Muslims and, 66
homosexuals: Orwell on, 53, 56; rights of, 66, 142, 161, 259, 267n11, "honor" killings, and domestic violence, 10–11n8
hooks, bell, 89, 232
Horney, Karen, 98
Horowitz, David, 263, 272n38
housewife, "status degradation" of, 97
Howe, Florence, 107
human rights, xi, 8, 33, 114, 115, 121, 122, 125, 191

The Human Stain (Roth), 225–27, 229
humanism: 1–9
Hussein, Saddam, 52
Huxley, Aldous, 27, 34
Huyssen, Andreas, 286

I Married a Communist (Roth), 227
I, Rigoberta Menchú (Menchú), 113–29; authenticity of, 115–16; background of, 119; editing of, 199; as hagiography, 113; and Holocaust, 123; motives for teaching of, 123; reliability of, 116; teaching of, 113, 114, 116, 121–24; student reactions to, 122–23; writing strategies in, 115–16, 118–21. *See also* Menchú.
I Shot Andy Warhol (film), 138, 139
Ibrahim, Fatma Ahmed, 119
identity: as collective, 1; minority, 2; integrated/intersectional analysis of, 7, 109, 110, 257; Palestinian, 64; postmodernist view of, 264; as "real" feminists, 105–12; sexual: *see* sexual identity; as teaching qualification, 17
identity politics, 1–9: and education, 2, 213, 252; ; in feminism, 15–19, 81, 136; gender and, 1; humanism and, 1–9; minority identity and, 2, 16, 43–45; race and, 1, 3, 16–18; rise of, 4; standards of, 5; and subjectivity, 5; violence and, 10–11n8; in women's studies, x, 88, 93, 108, 110, 264
ideological patrols, ix
ideological policing: academy and, x; and feminism, 15–16, 87, 88
ideological purity, 106. *See also* feminist purity.
IDPOL, 87, 88, 89
illiteracy, of women worldwide, 98
imperialism, Orwell on, 54
impotence, 142
India, British rule in, 54
Indiana University (Bloomington), 210, 211

Indianapolis, antipornography ordinance in, 185–86
individual rights, on campus, 182–83
individualism/individuality, 1, 34; antagonism toward, 123–24, 143
indoctrination: vs. education, x, 92, 93, 110, 111, 218, 220, 222, 254, 265n1
inequality: economic, 31, 72; and sexuality, 188
infant mortality, 98
Inquisition, 62
intellectual autonomy, importance of, xi, 125
intellectuals: feminist attacks on, 90; Marxist, 73; privileging of, 73; self-importance of, 72–73
intelligent design, 261. *See also* creation science.
Intercourse (Dworkin), 182
intercourse (heterosexual), xi; as degrading, 101; as rape, 32, 181–203 (passim). *See also* heterophobia.
Internet: and free speech, 217–22
intersex, 257
interview, methodology of, 75–76, 79–80
Invisible Privilege (Rothenberg), 110
Iran, 62
Iraq, war in, 54, 65
Irwin, Robert, 287
Islam/islamism, 61–68; as anti-Western, 66; and caliphate, 65; and fascism, 66; forced conversion to, 63, 66; fundamentalism, 61–68; growth of, 62, 67; intolerance of, 67; on Israel, 62; on Jews, 2, 62, 63, 64, 65, 164n5; as political movement, 67; radicalism of, 62, 63; reform of, 62; and *Sharia*, 65; and terrorism, 61, 67; as threat to liberal values, 66, 67; violence of, 62; women in, 67
Israel: and anti-Semitism, 65–66; creation of, 63; democracy in, 66; dissent in, 65; divestment

campaigns against, 66; existence of, 64; freedom in, 65, hostility toward, 63, 64, 218; and Lebanon, 65; media attacks on, 66; and Nazi Germany, 66, 67; population of, 63; and radical Islam, 62–63, 146; women's rights in, 65
Issues in Feminism (Ruth), 270n23
Ithaca College, 189

Jaing, Yang, 41n19
James, Henry, 127n11
Jameson, Storm, 52
Jennings, Peter, 190
Jerome, Jerome K., 23–24
Jews, 144, 218; forced conversion of, 63; Graglia on, 102; and Hitler, 1; 2, 159; Islamist attacks on, 62, 146n5; migration from Arab countries, 63; Muslim views of, 2, 64, 65, 66, 164n5; numbers of, 63; Orwell's views of, 53, 55, 56; as Palestinian, 64; Virginia Woolf's views of, 53; and World Trade Center, 65
Jerusalem, 64; Arab riots in, 63
Johns Hopkins University, 191
Jones, Robin, 122
Judaism: reform of, 62
Johnson, Samuel, 2

Kakutani, Michiko, 226
Kennedy, Florence, 139
Kettle, Pamela, 28
Kingsborough Community College, 109
Kleven, Paul, 181–203 (passim)
Knebel, Fletcher, 153
knowledge: attacks on, 18, 87, 175, 251–52, 253–73 (passim) ; emotions and, 264; experience as, 90, 108; and higher education, 111, 175, 251, 261; ideals of, 262; and identity, 5, 261; "local," 8, 264; and politics, 8, 251, 254, 255 ; as self-interested, 7; as situated, 7, 257; standards of, 8, 261, 262. *See also* epistemology.

Koertge, Noretta: x, xi, 2, 30, 84, 155, 210, 255, 265n1, 266n5; on feminist hostility to science, 255; and MacKinnon lawsuit threat, 181–203 (passim)
Kors, Alan Charles, 60n38, 171, 182, 185, 213, 220
Kristeva, Julia, 286
Ku Klux Klan, 142
Kunstler, William, 114

Lacan, Jacques, 282, 286
Lady Chatterley's Lover (Lawrence), 39
LaFramboise, Donna, 198
language: censorship of, 27, 38, 167; feminist redefinition of, 49; of hate, 142; injuries caused by, 31; opacity of, 282; policing of, 210; postmodernism and, 47–48; reform of, 31; and social engineering, 27; and social problems, 31; women's lack of, 18
de Lauretis, Teresa, 286
The Law of Sexual Harassment (Hajdin), 168–71
Lawrence, D. H., 39
Lebanon, 65
The Lecherous Professor (Roth), 173
Lees, Sue, 163
Legal studies: critical, 4–5; feminism and, 4; and race, 5
Lejeune, Philippe, 119
Lerner, Max, 56
lesbian couples: and children, 101–102; and traditional roles, 102
lesbian feminists, 32, 94, 135, 140; as "the real thing," 134
lesbian separatism, 140
lesbians, 15, 32, 133, 135, 136, 260; rights of, 142, 259; violence among, 271n35
Lessing, Doris, 57, 81
Lewis, Anthony, 25
"Lex Sexualis," 34
Leys, Ruth, 191
Liano, Dante, 114

libel, 27; defense against, 186–187; and lawsuit threat, 181–203 (passim)
liberal education, 251, 254,
liberal values, xi; 34; feminists and, 94, 109, 210, 252, 254
The Life and Death of Andy Warhol (Bockris), 139
life history, narration of, 74, 117, 118. See also *testimonio*
Limbaugh, Rush, 197
literacy, of women worldwide, 98
literature: defense of, 286; feminist reading of, 260, 281; graduate study of, 278–79, 281–88; and Theory (with a capital T), 277–88
"local knowledge," 8, 264
Los Angeles Times, 191
Lowe, Brigid, 281–83, 285
Lowrey, Kathleen, 282
Lucas, Gaston, 119
Lukianoff, Greg, 58, 184, 196, 201, 220
lying/lies, 49, 120–22
Lyotard, Jean-François, 286
Lysenkoism, and politicization of research, 263

McCann, Sean, 278, 283
Mac Donald, Heather, 190
MacKinnon, Catharine, 29, 136, 141, 181–203, 254; on heterosexual intercourse, 162; on language, 49; lawsuit threatened by, xi, 181–203 passim); on male violence, 162; on pornography, 167, 183, 185, 187–89, 192, 199; on rape, 162, 181–203 (passim); on sexual harassment law, 167, 173, 175, 180n1; on words and deeds, 194; writing style of, 189, 195, 196
MacNabb, Elizabeth, 269n18
Madness and Civilization (Foucault), 287
The Madwoman in the Attic (Gilbert and Gubar), 281
Malcolm, Janet, 147, 150

Male-bashing, and feminism, 29,
89–90, 91, 92, 137, 270n23. *See also*
heterophobia.
Mamet, David, 246
de Man, Paul, 286
The Man Who Wrote the Book (Tarloff),
242–46
Mandle, Joan D., 105–107, 109, 111;
criticisms of feminism: 105–107
Manifesto of a Passionate Moderate
(Haack), 261
Mankiller, Wilma, 161
manners, reform of, 31
Mao Tse-Tung, 1–2, 33
Marcuse, Herbert, 68
Marks, Elaine, 260
marriage, as con game, 162
Martinez, Inez, 109
Marxism, 5, 286
Marxism-Leninism: and academic
freedom, 215
Masaracchia, Ruth, 267–268n11
"masculinist," as feminist slur, 49, 87,
140, 144, 158, 209, 254, 264, 268
masculinity: erosion of, 47; and female
dependence, 100
Masson, Jeffrey, 194
Mathieu, Nicole-Claude, 75
Mayne, Richard, 55
Melville, Herman, 110
men: and dominance, 144; economic
burdens of, 103, 138; and
education, 254; elimination of,
137–39, 140; feminist antagonism
toward, 38–39, 85, 93, 94, 136,
154–55, 164, 258; in feminist
utopias, 141; groveling, 93; and
infant mortality, 92; and
institutions, 147–48; as menace,
149, 173; nature of, 25, 262,
269n19; as potential rapists, 136,
164; power of, 149, 246; and sexual
harassment, 167–80; as supporters
of feminism, 140; as targets of
feminism, 29, 137, 138, 144, 172,
263; as threat to women, 134, 224;

as "universal scapegoat," 29, 136;
violence of, 10, 137, 148–149, 263;
white, 7, 10, 16, 49, 68, 90, 110,
111, 114, 136, 212, 262; in
women's studies classes, 17, 88,
89–90, 92
Menchú, Rigoberta, 49, 113–29;
evasions of, 118; inaccuracies of,
114, 117; defenses of, 113–16;
Latinos and, 120; lies of, 120–22;
motives of, 120, 121, 125; and
Nobel Peace Prize, 113, 122; as
saint, 113; schooling of, 118, 120,
121; self–defense of, 118, 119, 125;
and rhetoric of truth, 118; as victim,
117; as voiceless, 122
Merchant, Carolyn, 160
Metzger, Walter, 212–13, 214
Middle East, 63, 64, 65, 66; studies,
218
Middle East Forum, 218
Miller, Nancy K., 80
Min, Anchee, 33
minority students, at University of
Massachusetts, 43–45
misandry, 144
misogyny, 28, 50, 144, 197, 232, 246
Mischler, Linda Fitts, 175
Mitchison, Naomi, 52, 56
modernization: and women, 98, 99,
100; Islam and, 67
Modleski, Tania, 286
Mohammed, cartoons of, 62
More, Thomas, 103
Morgan, Robin, 181
mothers: as controlling, 99; women as,
97
Mount Vernon College, 122
multiculturalism, 44, 66, 92, 98, 110,
111, 114, 123, 210, 243, 252; and
anti-Western bias, 98
multiculturalism, 66, 92, 98, 110, 114,
123, 210, 243, 252; and academic
evaluations, 44; student ignorance
and, 92
Muslim Brotherhood, 63

Muslims: and anti-Semitism, 65; and dissent, 66; and honor killings, 8, 10–11n8; as moderate, 66; standards applied to, 65; and terrorism, 61. *See also* Islam.

Nanda, Meera, 272n40
Nasrallah, Hassan, 62, 67
National Association of Scholars (NAS), 212, 213
National Association for Women in Education (NAWE), 91
National Organization for Women (NOW), 139
National Public Radio (NPR), 162, 221
National Women's Studies Association (NWSA), 106
A Natural History of Rape (Thornton and Palmer), 157–66 (passim); criticisms of, 158–59,160
natural selection, 163; and rape: 158, 159
"naturalistic fallacy," 160
nature, human: arguments over, 163
Nazism: in Denmark, 218; in Europe, 64; in Germany, 41n13, 54, 66, 67, 123, 218
Nazis, Orwell on, 54
Nelson, Cary, 211, 212, 216n1
New England Council of Land-Grant University Women, and "agenda for women," 207
New Republic, 163
New York Times v. Sullivan, 186
The New Yorker, 147
Newspeak, 52, 57
Nineteen Eighty–Four (Orwell), 27, 48, 51, 52, 57
NoIndoctrination.org (website), 218, 220
Norton Anthology of Theory and Criticism (Leitch et al.), 58
Norton, W. W., 279
"nouveau solipsism," of scholars, 79–82

Oakley, Ann, 75
Occidental College, 197

Ohio State University, 285
Old Scores (Delbanco), 233–35
Oleanna (Mamet) 246
On Human Nature (Wilson), 164
On the Issues, 183
Oncale v. Sundowner Offshore Services, Inc., 174
Only Words (MacKinnon), 194
oppression, 31, 66, 78, 113, 164, 255, of women, 17, 81, 98, 103, 149, 176, 240, 258, 263
"oppression sweepstakes," 2, 9, 18, 136
oral history, 71; accuracy of, 117, 118; construction of self in, 117; control over, 119; methodology, 79–80, 117; problems of, 72, 74–78, 79, 119. See also *testimonio*.
Orientalism (Said), 287
Orlando Sentinel, 191
Ormond College (Australia), 147–150
Orwell, George, 27, 34, 47–60, 99, 143, 210; androcentrism of, 51; and anti-Semitism, 53; coercive discourse of, 55; *Complete Works of*, 54, 56; on "Fascifists," 54; on fascism, 52, 54;; and fear of socialism, 47, 50; feminist critique of, 47; on Joseph Conrad, 50; on language, 47–48, 57; misogyny of, 50; as moral exemplar, 47, 50; 53; and nostalgia for tradition, 99; and Notebook of Names, 55; on orthodoxies, 235; on pacifism, 54–55, 56, 57; pessimism of, 51; prejudices of, 53m 55, 56; self-presentation of, 52; on Spain, 56; on totalitarianism, 57; usefulness of, 51, 58; view of reality, 48, 50; on violence, 54–55; writing style of: 55, 60n30. See also *Animal Farm, Nineteen Eighty-Four*.
The Orwell Mystique (Patai), 47
Ozick, Cynthia, 279

pacifism: Orwell on, 54–55, 56, 57
Paglia, Camille, 163

Palestine, 64; Jewish immigration to, 64
Palestinians: academic views on, 64;
  displaced, 63; identity of, 64; Jews
  as, 64; and one-state solution
Palgrave (publisher), 280
Palmer, Craig T., 157–66
Pankhurst, Cristabel, 134
Patai, Daphne: debates with feminists,
  255, 256, 267n10, 267n11;
  education of, 159; experience in
  women's studies, 84, 139, 159, 160;
  family background of, 64; and
  feminist orthodoxies, 160; and
  MacKinnon lawsuit threat, 181–203
  (passim)
Pateman, Carole, 198
patriarchy: and biology, 258–59,
  267–68n11; and due process, 143;
  as explanation for everything
  feminists don't like: 7, 8, 18, 85, 92,
  108m, 140, 149, 164; inequality
  within, 188, 190, 191, 192, 197,
  198, 200, 267–68n11; and
  institutions, 10, 135, 258–59;
  knowledge and, 262; liberalism and,
  254; as original sin, 85; persistence
  of, 94; as pretext for bad feminist
  policy, 50; and rape, 164, 181–203
  (passim); and two sexes, 165n7;
  sexual "consent" in, 154, 181–203
  (passim); weakness of, 108; in
  universities, 10n5, 107, 111, 159,
  223; and women's powerlessness,
  133
patrulhas ideológicas, ix
Paul, Ellen Frankel, 173, 175
Pearl, Daniel, 65
Periodic Table, as political, 255
"personal is political," feminist slogan:
  50, 62, 81, 85, 93, 97, 165, 167;
  reversal of, 153–55
phallocentrism, 142
Piercy, Marge, 145
Pinnick, Cassandra, 266n5
Pipes, Daniel, 218
Playboy (magazine), 197
poetry, study of, 282

political activism: on campus: ix, x, xi;
  teaching as, 58, 88, 92, 125. 218,
  219, 254
political correctness (PC), x, 15, 77,
  123,223, 226, 260
politicizing the personal, 153–55
The Politics of Women's Studies (Howe),
  107
Pollitt, Katha, 11n8
Poovey, Mary, 286
pornography, 35, 38, 103, 158, 167,
  168; and sexuality, 183, 185, 187,
  188, 189, 192, 199, 244
Portland State University, 109
Portnoy's Complaint (Roth), 228
"positioning," of scholars, 79, 80
postmodernism: characteristics of, 264;
  equanimity of, 65; ; and feminism,
  264; language in, 47; and Orwell,
  47–48; rhetoric of, 4–5; and
  scientific objectivity, 4, 7; and
  sexuality, 141–42
power: differentials, 24, 31, 35, 118,
  154, 155, 224, 233, 238; of sex,
  224, 232, 246; types of, 150, 224; of
  the weak, 224
Pratt, Mary Louise, 123
private sphere: erasure of, 34, 48, 50,
  141, 143, 153–55; and public, 81,
  90, 102
Professing Feminism (Patai and Koertge),
  x, xi, 30, 55, 84, 86, 88, 91, 135,
  136, 210; and MacKinnon lawsuit
  threat, 181–203 (passim); writing
  of, 84
The Professor of Desire (Roth), 227,
  230–232
professor-student relationships, 26,
  34–35, 173, 175, 224–25, 232–33,
  246
professors: allegations against, 30; and
  "asymmetrical" relations, 26, 34–35,
  173, 224, 233
Prose, Francine, 235–42, 246
prostitution, 134
Protocols of the Elders of Zion, 65
Proud Man (Burdekin), 145

Pryluck Calvin, 72
Pulitzer Prize, 227
purity campaigns of feminists, 134,
227; as political platform, 155. *See
also* heterophobia.

Quinn, Anthony, 230
quotas, and minority students, 43

race, and feminism, 81
racism, charges of, 11, 16, 66, 89, 93
"radical," as academic fashion, 287
Rand, Ayn, 109
rape: analyses of, 157–66; biological
bases of, 157–66 (passim); charges
of, 11n8; concept of, 85;
evolutionary biology and, 158, 159,
164; feminist views of, 137, 159,
161, 162, 164; function of, 158,
162, 259; and heterosexual
intercourse, 32, 136, 161–162,
181–203 (passim), 259;
institutionalizing of, 37; and
language, 49; legal definitions of,
181–82, 195; MacKinnon on,
181–203 (passim); male-male, 158;
penalties for, 163; prevention of,
158, 160; reproduction and, 158; as
routine, 208; statistics, 37, 158;
violence of, 259; writing about,
157–66
*The Reader's Companion to U.S. Women's
History* (Mankiller et al.), 161, 259
reality: as a "text," 47; and everyday life,
57
reality TV, 57
reason, xi, 5, 48, 57; defense of, 58,
261–62; feminist attacks on, 48,
158; and humanism, 8–9
"recovered" memories, 143m 179
relations, personal: regulation of,
33–35, 37, 50
relationships, "asymmetrical," 34, 50,
173, 224, 232–33, 246
relationships: in the academy, 223–49
(passim): power imbalances in, 24,
31, 35, 118, 154, 155, 224, 233,

238; regulation of, 26, 34, 35, 37,
39, 142, 155, 246
reproduction: biology and, 158–59,
164, 258; control of, 28, 37, 139;
via parthenogenesis, 141; sexual: 28,
37, 139, 258
research: and advocacy, 260; cross-
cultural, 79; distance in, 75–76;
ethics of, 72; and feminism, 72, 74,
75, 253–75 (passim); and identity,
79; limits of, 76; as political, 80,
254–55, 259, 266n3; positivist
model of, 79; problems of, 72, 73,
77, 79; and self-reflexivity, 77, 79–82
reversals of privilege, 16–17, 144, 145,
254
rhetoric: of feminism, 81, 93, 144
Rich, Adrienne, 190
Ricks, Christopher, 282
The Riddle of Gender (Rudacille), 257
*Rigoberta Menchú and the Story of All
Poor Guatemalans* (Stoll), 113
Rochelson, Meri-Jane, 123
Rodden, John, 52
Rogers, Mary F., 257
Rodriguez, Ana, 124
Romano, Carlin, 194
Rose, Steven, 158
Roth, Joseph, 52
Roth, Philip, 224–32, 242, 246
Rothenberg, Paula S., 110–11
Rudicille, Deborah, 257, 269n12
rules, demand for, 25–42, 142–44
Ruse, Michael, 159
Russell, Bertrand, 125–26
Ruth, Sheila, 270n23

Said, Edward, 286, 287
Sartre, Jean-Paul, 133
"scare statistics," of feminists, 37–38,
92–93, 134, 262
Schlafly, Phyllis, 102
scholarly integrity, defense of, 261
Schroeder, Jeanne, 199
Schulhofer, Stephen, 189
science: feminist attacks on, 6, 49, 68,
87, 160, 161, 209–210, 256–59,

261–63, 266n5, 272n40; Lysenkoism and, 263; as male-dominated, 262, 271–272n36; as masculine, 209, 255; as political, 255, 257; politicization of, 257, 258, 261, 263; standards of, 262

science studies, feminist: aims of, 257–59, 263. *See also* science.

Scollay, Susan, 215

Scott, David K., 26, 40n3

Screw (magazine), 192

Scull, Andrew, 288

SCUM Manifesto (Solanas), 138–39

Searle, John, 5

self: construction of, 117; reflexivity, 75–77, 79–82, 117

"sensitivity training," 82, 171, 208

sentiment: tyranny of, 75

September 11, 2001, 6, 219, 252

Seven Days in May (Knebel and Bailey), 153–54

sex differences: and biology, 160, 161; and gender, as distinct, 161; as threat to feminism, 160

sex and power, in fiction, 223–49 (passim). *See also* sexual harassment.

Sex, Sin, and Blasphemy (Heins), 198

Sexing the Body (Fausto-Sterling), 267

sexual abuse, of children, 143

sexual dimorphism: as biological fact, 256; as social construct, 4, 49, 161, 256, 258–59, 267n9, 267–269n11. *See also* social constructionism.

sexual extortion, 167, 172, 225. *See also* sexual harassment.

sexual harassment, 167–180 (passim), 247; allegations of, 30, 43, 142, 148, 167, 171, 175, 219, 224; and behavior, 168, 169, 174; biological view of, 172; bisexual, 174; categories of, 50, 143, 149; in classroom, 208, 219; codes, 225; and "comfort," 168, 224; concept stretching and, 85; definitions of, 34, 154, 168, 170, 173, 174, 176, 224, 225; as discrimination, 167, 170, 172–73, 174, 176, 208;

distinctions in, 149; due process and, 178; education about, 177; examples of, 168, 170; false charges of, 175, 178, and free speech, 167, 171, 175, 214; gender and, 174; as harmful only to women, 173; "hostile environment," 21, 167, 174, 180n1, 213, 214; investigation of, 178, 179; lawsuits, 178, 179; male-male, 174; as done only by men, 173, 175, 177; of men, 173, 174; need for complaints about, 177–178; as "objective" harm, 176–77; penalties for, 167, 170, 171, 208; policies, 50, 143, 171, 175, 177–78, 179, 213, 214; privacy and, 175; procedures, 178; "quid pro quo," 21, 167, 172–73, 174; and rape, 170, 175; sanctions for, 170; in schools, 94, 143, 144, 208; and seduction, 176; as sex discrimination, 167, 170, 172–73, 174, 176, 208 ; vs. sexual interest, 168, 170, 174, 176; sociocultural view of, 172,176; specialists, 225; as tort, 173; training about, 169, 171, 178, 208; "verbal acts" as, 171, 213, 219, 224; and victim advocate, 178. *See also* academic affairs; sexual harassment law.

Sexual Harassment as an Ethical Issue in Academic Life (Francis), 174–175

Sexual Harassment Industry (SHI), 94, 168; goals of, 168; manuals produced by, 170

sexual harassment law, 154–55, 167–80, 225; as anti-sex, 168, 169–70; 174, bisexual, 174; categories of, 167, 172; and compelled speech, 171; competing views of, 171–72; creation of, 167, 168; criteria of, 170; defenders of, 169, 175; "demarcation problem" in, 169, 170; development of, 169; and "discrimination," 167, 170, 172–73, 174; and due process, 30, 50, 143, 144, 167, 170, 171, 178,

179, 214; employers and, 35, 170–71; feminist goals of, 167, 169, 172–73, 214, 215; free speech and, 3, 34, 40n3, 58, 70, 167, 170, 171, 175, 213–14, 219; Hajdin on, 168–71; harms of, 169–70; impact of, 168; "infinite regress" problem in, 176; injustices of, 179; and "legal moralism," 169; and liability, 170, 171, 243; limitations of, 174, 176–77; men as targets of, 167, 168, 172; as morally justified, 168, 169; as patchwork, 169; and retaliation, 178; same-sex, 167, 174; and stereotypes, 173; and "third party," 21, 50, 177, 189; as "Trojan horse," 167; two-tiered system of, 170–71; and universities, 34, 171, 178, as unjustified, 168–69; as weapon, 171, 173, 174, 246; and "welcomeness" standard, 176; and workplace, 35, 143, 168, 169–71

Sexual Harassment on Campus (Scollay and Bratt), 215

sexual identity: as socially constructed, 141–42, 257–58n11

sexual morality, and politics, 134, 153–55

sexual pleasure: MacKinnon on, 181–203 (passim); regulation of, 28; suppression of, 33. *See also* heterophobia.

sexuality: banishment of, 149; and biology, 4, 157–66 (passim), 161, 259; in dystopian fiction, 34, 143; in fiction, 223–49 (passim); MacKinnon on, 181–203 (passim); management of, 34; manipulation of, 246; as political, 161, 259; repression of, 98; as socially constructed, 4, 161, 256, 259

Shakespeare, William, 110

The Shadow University (Kors and Silverglate), 171, 182, 185, 213, 220

Sharia, 65

Showalter, Elaine, 229

Shulevitz, Judith, 223

Signs: Journal of Women in Culture and Society, 189, 198

Silvergate, Harvey, 3–4, 58, 60n38, 220; on harassment policies as speech codes, 3, 40n3, 58, 70, 171, 213–14, 219; and MacKinnon threat, 182–203

Singapore, 37

Skinner, B. F., 44

social constructionism, 6, 49; and biology, 256; bodies and, 256; defined, 4; feminist dogma of, 161, 256, 257, 262, 269n19; and gender, 107; and heterosexuality, 4, 49; motives for, 162–62, 267n8; of sexual identity, 141–42, 257–58n11; of sexual preference, 141

Societal Stockholm Syndrome, 190

Society for Cutting Up Men (SCUM), 138

sociobiology, 159

Sociologists for Women in Society, 106

Sokal, Alan, 48, 256

Solanas, Valerie, 138–39

Sommer, Doris, 123–24

South Africa, 67

speech: attacks on, 62, 14, 223; as verbal action, 3; chilling of, 200, 217, 220, 221; self-censorship of, 220

speech codes, 10n5, 26, 33, 37. 210–14, 217, 220, 252, 263; and American association of University Professors (AAUP), 212–13, 214; and "censorship zones," defined, 58; demand for, 25–42, 58; double standards in, 27; 40n4, 49, 213–14; feminist support of, 10n5, 26, 49, 210, 219–20; harassment policies as, 3, 40n3, 50, 58, 70, 153, 171, 213–14, 217, 219, 221, 232, 252, 263; legal status of, 26, 219; as norm, 10n5, 58; 219; tenured advocates of, 221

Spitzack, Carole J., 75

Spivak, Gayatri Chakravorty, 71–77, 122, 287

Stacey, Judith, 75
Stalinism, 48, 53
Stallone, Sylvester, 28
Stanford University, 123
State University of New York (SUNY): (Albany), 211; (Buffalo), 80; (New Paltz), 105
Stein, Gertude, 240
Sternhell, Carol, 88
Stojkovic, Stan, 179
Stoll, David, 49, 113–29 (passim)
Stoltenberg, John, 183, 195
Stone, Lucy, 134
Strachey, Lytton, 282
Strossen, Nadine, 167, 183, 193, 199
subaltern: as category, 71–78, 116, 125; defined, 72; as label, 76; vs. superalterns, 72; as unable to speak (voiceless), 71, 73, 74, 122
Sudan, 119
suffrage movement, 83
Summers, Lawrence H., 10n5, 272n36
Superson, Anita, 173, 176–77
Swope, Robert, 215
"surplus visibility," 16
Symons, Donald, 162
"systemic sexism," of universities, 108, 215

Taliban, 163; and restriction of women, 98
Tallis, Raymond, 6, 269n17
Tampa Tribune, 191
Tarloff, Eric, 242–246
Teaching and Testimony (Carey-Webb and Benz), 121
terrorism: and Islamism, 61–68; Basque, 67; IRA, 67
Testimonio, 114, 115, 116, 117, 123, 124, 125; definitions of, 115, 116; and oral history, 117; politics of, 114–117
theory: as resistance, 58; student hostility to, 92; teaching of, 281, 283–287
Theory (with a capital T), 278, 287; arguments over, 286; benefits of, 285; challenges to, 281, 283, 285, 286; compulsory study of, 282, 283; concept of, 279; critiques of, 278–79, 286; and dissertations, 282; enjoyment of, 282, 283; guides to, 279; and ideology, 279; institutional hold of, 280, 281–88; on language, 282; and literature departments, 279, 281–82, 283, 284, 285; as orthodoxy, 278, 281, 286; and political commitment, 278, 283; pseudo-politics of, 282, 287; rhetoric of, 286, 287; self-righteousness of, 283; spread of, 285, 286; student reactions to, 279, 281–82, 283; as truth, 281; uncritical study of, 283, 284; and Victorian fiction, 282
Theory's Empire: An Anthology of Dissent (Patai and Corral), 277–88: aims of: 277–78, 288; as conservative, 283; private correspondence about, 281–87; publishing history of, 279–80; reactions to, 278, 281–87; selection criteria for, 278; vs. standard anthologies, 278; writing of, 277–78
Thinking About Sexual Harassment (Crouch), 171–74
Thomas, Bertha, 23, 24
Thomas, Cal, 190–91, 195
Thornhill, Randy, 157–66
"thoughtcrime," 57
Tiefer, Lenore, 142
Time (magazine), 194
Times Literary Supplement, 158, 163, 288
Title VII (1976), terms of, 168
Title IX, 174
Tobin, Jeffrey, 197
TOTAL REJ, 86, 91
totalitarianism, 32, 57, 143, 144; and view of human nature, 163
Toward a Feminist Theory of the State (MacKinnon), 187, 198
Transforming the Disciplines (MacNabb et al.), 269n18
transgender rights, 257, 269n12

transgendered people, 3, 259, 267n10; rights of, 257, 267n11, 269n12
Trilling, Lionel, 279
Trimberger, E. Kay, 161
Trinity College (Cambridge), 281
Truth: as contingent, 118; as defense, 195; dismissal of, 4, 5, 49, 92, 114; feminist possession of, 95; "higher," 113; indeterminacy of, 116; irrelevancy of, 114; of oral history, 117–18, 119; politics and, 114, 116–17, 118–19, 120; Rigoberta Menchú and, 113–29 (passim); search for, xi, 4, 93, 120; western notions of, 122, 125
The Truth of Power (Barber), 242
The Twilight of Common Dreams (Gitlin), x
Tuana, Nancy, 175

United States Court of Appeals, Seventh Circuit, 184, 185, 186
United States Supreme Court, 185, 186, 214
universities: anti-Israeli sentiment in, 218; "asymmetrical" relationships in, 34, 50, 173, 223, 224, 232, 233, 246; autonomy of, 251; "comfort" in, 221; demand for regulations in, 26, 27, 30, 31; diversity training in, 218; ideals of, 251; indoctrination in, 254; liberal values of, 252, 254; and literary study, 277–88; as male-dominated, 215, 262; as meritocracies, 3; political bias in, 218; political rhetoric in, 31; as secular, 6; sensitivity training in, 82, 171, 178, 208; "social justice" in, 251–52; speech codes in, 26, 143, 144, 211–16; and subalternity, 116; "systemic sexism" of, 108, 215; teaching evaluations in, 221; vigilante atmosphere of, 32, 144
University of British Columbia, 29
University of California (San Diego), 220
University of Cambridge, 282, 282

University of Chicago, 158, 189
University of Colorado: (Boulder), 122; (Colorado Springs), 158
University of Guelph, 159
University of Illinois (Urbana-Champaign), 211
University of Maine, 207
University of Massachusetts (Amherst), 16, 27, 84, 87, 283; Graduate Employee Organization at, 26, 39; multiculturalism at, 44; pursuit of justice at, 43–45, 215; proposed harassment policy at, 39n3, 221; protests at, 44; sexual harassment policy at, 225; speech codes at, 44, 221; and "Vision 2000" proposal, 207–10
University of Melbourne, 147
University of Minnesota, 189
University of New Hampshire, and "Vision 2000" proposal, 207
University of New Mexico, 158
University of Oxford, 282
University of Pennsylvania, 182, 213
University of São Paulo (Brazil), 32
University of Texas (El Paso), 109
University of Toronto, 198
University of Vermont, and "Vision 2000" proposal, 207
University of Wisconsin: (Madison), 260; (Milwaukee), 178, 286
Unwanted Sex (Schulhofer), 189
utopias and utopian fiction: ix, 23–24, 25; and dystopias, 84, 145; feminist, 84, 135, 140–41, 142; function of, 28

The Vagina Monologues (Ensler), 215
Valladares, Armando, 115
Varas, Patricia, 122
Victorian Fiction and the Insights of Sympathy (Lowe), 283
Vietnam war, 227
violence: in China, 41–42n19; and harassment, conflated, 149; of men, 137, 159, 160, 162, 263; Orwell on, 54–55; pornography as,

188; and race, 10n8; and radical Islam, 62; and rape, 159, 161, 162, 190; and religion, 61–62; sex as, 188, 190, 191, 199, 208; against women, 148, 161, 162, 190, 191, 199, 208, 259, 263; in universities, 208; woman-initiated, 262, 271n35

"Vision 2000," as feminist agenda for education, 207–10

"visual harassment," 29, 143

Voigt, Frederick, 52

Vonnegut, Kurt, 24

Walden Two (Skinner), 44

The Wanderground (Gearhart), 142

"wandering womb," and women's education, 97

Warhol, Andy, 139

Washington Post, 194

Watt, Stephen, 211, 212

We (Rand), 34, 48

We Have Been Warned (Jameson), 56

Weiner, Linda, 173, 175

The Well of Loneliness (Hall), 39

Wellesley College, 114

Wesley, Charlie, 283

West, Robin, 190

Western culture/values, xi; academic attacks on, 62, 67–68, 122, 123–24, 161

Whitaker, Martha, 257

White privilege, 4, 68, 92, 110, 111

whites, antagonism toward, 3, 68, 81, 87, 90, 108, 110, 114, 136, 262

"whiteness studies," 3

Who Needs Men? (Cooper), 28

Who's Afraid of Women's Studies? (Rogers and Garrett), 257

Willamette University, 122

William Paterson University, 110

Williams, Raymond, 60n30

Williams v. Saxbe, 168

Wilson, E. O., 164

Wilson, Margo, 159, 162, 163

Wittgenstein, Ludwig, 284

"womb envy" (Horney), 98

women of color, 16, 17, 81, 93, 110, 117, 121, 136

women: agency of, 191; and alienation from feminism, 135; "comfort" level of, 168, 214; and conflict, 139; "discomfort" of, 143; controlling men, 154; and curriculum, 208–209; discrimination against, 208; economic dependency of, 98, 134, 198; and education, 98, 99, 134, 254; and the future, 139, 145; and gender equity in education, 208, 271n36, as givers, 190; health of, 134; Graglia on, 97–104; in higher education, 108, 207–10, 254, 271–72n36; as inferior, 173–74, 176; lack of rights of, 98, 200; literacy of, 98; as nurturing, 100; oppression of, 149, 176, 258, as Other, 73, 75, 116; as passive, 191; as political activists, 134; powerlessness of, 195, 247; rule of, 139–40; as sexual danger, 224; and sexual harassment, 167–80; sexual preferences of, 134; as sexual specialists, 83, 102; as silenced, 74, 75, 80, 208; as similar to men, 134, 145; status of, in U.S., 209, 210, 262, 263; as victims, 38, 92, 93, 107, 109, 116, 137, 149, 150, 160, 162, 175, 178, 187, 189, 191, 223, 263; violence against, 148, 161, 162, 208, 263; as violent, 137, 149, 150, 176, 178, 262, 271n35

Women Can't Hear What Men Don't Say (Farrell), 190

The Women's Review of Books, 88

women's studies: and academic achievement, 90; and academic freedom, 263; activism in, 89, 90. 92–93, 95, 106, 108, 111, 252, 253–75 (passim), 270n22; anti-intellectualism of, 90, 91, 109, 110; appraisal of, 87; author's experience in, 84, 139, 159; avoidance of, 91; on biology, 256, 257, 267–69n11, 269n18; challenges ignored by, 261;

collectivism in, 31, 108, 109; and conflict resolution, 140–41; consensus model in, 106; and control of education, 49, 208–10; as corrective, 243–254; and creation of fear, 37–38; criticism of, 83, 107, 106, 260, 270n23; cross-listing of courses in, 88; defense of, x, 83, 84, 105–12; definition of, 253; and dismantling inequality, 108, 210; dissension within, 91, 106, 108, 109; dogmas of, 17, 85, 107, 108, 109, 159, 160; double standards of, 265; "empowerment" in, 121; as endangered, 94; and epistemology, 5, 8, 210, 261, 264; feminist extremists and, 29, 254; founding mothers of, 107–10, 166n6; future of, 83–95, 111; games in, 85–88; on gender roles, 159; and gender studies, 109; as ghettoizing, 209; graduate work in, 208, heterosexuality and, 135; history of, 107–10, 209–10; hostility within, 92–93; identity issues in, 105–107, 260; on infant mortality, 159; "integrated analysis" in, 7, 109, 110; intolerance in, 68, 84–85, 93, 257; institutional response to, 107; institutionalization of, 109; isolation of, 106; isolation of critics of, 260; job ads in, 252; language of, 32, 86, 106; "leveling" in, 91; and "masculinist" education, 254; men in, 17, 88, 89–90, 107, 109, mission of, x, 106, 110; mission statements, 265n1; as multidisciplinary, 159, 257, 259, 262; objectives of, 254, 259; political agenda of, 160, 252, 253–75 (passim); politics of,

107–109, 207–10, 220; and postmodernism, 264; "poverty activities" in, 270n22; propagandizing in, x, 85, 111, 259; and race, 16, 1, 87, 89, 90, 93, 108, 109, 110, 220; and radical feminism, 29, 269n19; on rape, 159, 208; relationship to feminism, 84, 253; and research, 253–275 (passim); and "safe spaces," 105; "scare statistics" of, 38, 134, 262; scholarly standards in, 91, 93, 105, 106, 111, 121, 261, 265, 267–68n11; and science, 6, 159–60, 209–10, 255, 256–59, 261, 267–69n11; search procedures in, 91, 92; separatism of, 109, 209; on sexual dimorphism, 256–59; on social constructionism, 256–57, 269n19; and speech codes, 210, 220, 263; student ignorance in, 92; tactics of, 262; texts used in, 160, 256; underlying views in, 265n1; underrepresentation of, 208; values of, 106, 108; view of the past in, 253–54; on women's violence, 271n35; worldview of, 256, 257

women's studies e-mail list (WMST-L), 10n8, 27, 49, 88, 90, 94, 107, 145, 219, 256, 267n10, 267–68n11, 270–71n32, 271n35

Women's Ways of Knowing, 266n5

Woolf, Virginia, 47, 53

WORDMAGIC, 86

work, meanings of, 103

World Trade Center, 65

Wriggins, Jennifer, 161–62

Wright, Luann, 220

Zamiatin, Eugene [Zamyatin, Yevgeny], 34, 36, 41n13; 48, 143

About the Author

Daphne Patai was born in Jerusalem and grew up in New York City. She is a professor in the Department of Languages, Literatures, and Cultures at the University of Massachusetts Amherst, where she teaches utopian and dystopian literature, Brazilian literature and culture, and literary theory. Years in the academic world (including ten years spent in a women's studies program, where she taught feminist theory and feminist research methods) have alerted her to the dangers of politicizing education. She is the author and editor of twelve books, among them *The Orwell Mystique: A Study in Male Ideology* (1984); *Brazilian Women Speak: Contemporary Life Stories* (1988); *Women's Words: The Feminist Practice of Oral History* (1991, co-edited with Sherna Berger Gluck); *Rediscovering Forgotten Radicals: British Women Writers 1889-1939* (1993, co-edited with Angela Ingram); and *Heterophobia: Sexual Harassment and the Future of Feminism* (1998). Her 1994 critique of women's studies programs, written with Noretta Koertge, was reissued in a new and expanded edition in 2003 as *Professing Feminism: Education and Indoctrination in Women's Studies*. Patai's most recent book (co-edited with Will H. Corral) is *Theory's Empire: An Anthology of Dissent* (2005), a collection of essays by fifty scholars criticizing contemporary theory fads and their effect on literary study. She has received fellowships from the National Endowment for the Humanities, the Guggenheim Foundation, and the National Humanities Center.

Long concerned about the rise of speech codes and harassment policies on American campuses, Patai has been involved with the Foundation for Individual Rights in Education (FIRE) since its inception and currently serves on its Board of Directors.

She can be contacted at: daphne.patai@spanport.umass.edu